GRAMMAR
MASTER ③

WorldCom Edu

Grammar Master

구성과 활용법

01 복습과 예습을 한 번에!

어려운 문법 용어를 알기 쉽게 풀이
했어요.

학습할 Lesson들의 주요 내용만을
간추려 미리 예습 할 수 있으며,
또는 배운 내용들을 마지막에 한 번
더 확인할 수 있어요.

02 Note

지문의 단어를 정리한 부분이에요.

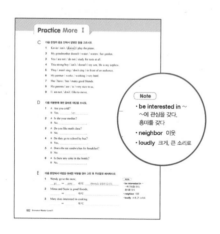

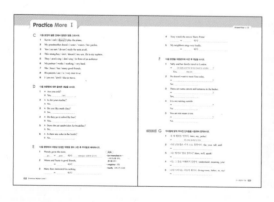

Point Check I

◆ **인칭대명사** : 사람, 동물, 사물의 이름을 대신하여 가리키는 말이다. 1, 2, 3인칭으로 구분되며, 문장에서의 역할에 따라 주격, 소유격, 목적격으로 사용된다.

◆ **be동사 (am, are, is)** : 주어의 상태를 나타내는 말이다.

◆ **일반동사** : 주어의 동작이나 상태를 나타내는 말이다.

1. 인칭대명사와 be동사

be동사는 주어의 인칭에 따라 그 형태가 'am, are, is'로 다르게 사용된다.

	단수형	be동사	복수형	be동사
1인칭	I	am	we	
2인칭	you	are	you	are
3인칭	he, she, it	is	they	

2. 인칭대명사와 일반동사

일반동사는 주어의 인칭에 따라 '동사원형' 또는 '동사원형+-s / -es'의 형태로 사용한다.

(1) 1, 2인칭 단수 / 복수, 3인칭 복수	I, you, we, they	동사원형 사용
(2) 3인칭 단수	he, she, it	동사원형+-s / -es
(3) 단수의 사람, 사물, 동물	Mary, a book, a dog	

3. Yes / No 의문문

Be동사 의문문 [Am / Are / Is+인칭대명사~?]	일반동사 의문문 [Do(es)+인칭대명사+동사원형~?]
• Are you a teacher? Yes, I am. / No, I'm not. (= No, I am not.)	• Does she teach English? Yes, she does. / No, she doesn't. (= No, she does not.)

4. There is… / There are… : ~이 있다

There is [셀 수 없는 명사, 셀 수 있는 명사 단수]	• There is an orange on the table. [셀 수 있는 명사 - 단수] • There is some salt in the bottle. [셀 수 없는 명사]
There are [셀 수 있는 명사 복수]	• There are many toys in the box. [셀 수 있는 명사 - 복수]

다양한 유형의 문제풀이!

앞서 학습한 내용들의 확실한 이해를 돕기
위한 다양한 유형과 난이도를 가진 문제
풀기 연습을 통해 문법에 대한 자신감을
높여 줄 수 있어요.

Lesson 1-1

문장의 종류

인칭대명사와 be동사

- 명사: 이름이 있는 사람, 동물, 사물을 말한다.
  ex) Susie, Tom, a cat, a book, Seoul, Korea
- 인칭대명사: 명사를 대신하여 나타내는 말을 가리킨다.

1. 인칭대명사와 be동사

	인칭대명사	be동사	줄임말		인칭대명사	be동사	줄임말
단수	I	am	I'm (= I am)	복수	we		we're (= we are)
	you	are	you're (= you are)		you		you're (= you are)
	he she it	is	he's (= he is) she's (= she is) it's (= it is)		they	are	they're (= they are)

2. be동사의 쓰임

(1) [be동사 + 명사] ~이다
  • I am Woody from *Toy Story*.
(2) [be동사 + 형용사] ~이다
  • She is kind.
(3) [be동사 + 형용사 + 명사] ~이다
  • We are good friends.
(4) [be동사 + 전치사 + 장소] ~에 있다
  • He is in Seoul, Korea.

Grammar Plus +

be동사 뒤에 오는 형용사, 명사 단어를 '보어'라고 한다. be동사 뒤에 오는 이 단어들이 주어를 보충 설명하고 있기 때문이다.
I am an engineer. (*I* = *an engineer*)
➡ "내"가 "기술자"라는 것을 보충 설명해 준다.

☆Check up!

Answer Keys p. 01

A 다음을 인칭대명사(I, you, we, they, he, she, it)로 바꾸어 쓰시오.

1	my cat	➡ It	2	Jack and me	➡
3	her brother	➡	4	our sisters	➡
5	Mary and you	➡	6	the oranges	➡
7	a short boy	➡	8	you and I	➡
9	this long ruler	➡	10	their cousins	➡

01. 문장의 기초 **011**

---

03 단계별 설명과 문제풀이!

많은 분량의 문법을 단계적으로 나누어 학습하는데 부담을 덜어 주었어요.

04 Grammar Plus +

본문에서 다루어진 핵심 문법사항보다 좀 더 심화된 내용을 살펴볼 수 있어요.

05 Check up

학습한 내용에 맞는 반복적인 문제풀이 연습을 통해 문법을 확실히 이해할 수 있도록 했어요.

내신대비를 위한 마지막 단계!

내신 최다 출제 유형

전국 중학교의 중간 / 기말고사 기출 문제들을 분석하여 가장 많이, 자주 출제되는 문제들의 유형을 파악하고 학습해요.

내신 대비 문제

해당 Chapter의 문법을 이용한 다양한 유형의 문제풀이로 내신에 완벽 대비할 수 있어요.

Grammar Master

Grammar Master Level 3

CHAPTER 10 비교 구문

CHAPTER 11 가정법

CHAPTER 12 관계사

CHAPTER 13 접속사

CHAPTER 14 전치사

01

Chapter
문장의 형식

Point Check I

◆ **부가의문문**: 앞의 문장(주절)에서 말했던 내용을 한 번 더 확인하는 의문문이다.

◆ **간접의문문**: 의문문이 문장 안으로 들어가서 의문의 내용을 간접적으로 전달한다.

◆ **문장의 형식**: 동사, 보어, 목적어의 유무와 쓰임에 따라 사용하는 문장의 형식이 나뉜다.
각 문장은 '완전/불완전 자동사', '완전/불완전 타동사'로 분류한다.

1. 부가의문문

- You aren't good at speaking Chinese, **are you**? [be동사]

- They help many sick people, **don't they**? [일반동사]

- He can dance very well, **can't he**? [조동사]

- Don't be afraid of it anymore, **will you**? [명령문]

- Let's participate in the contest, **shall we**? [Let's 명령문]

- They have been in Greece for three months, **haven't they**? [완료시제]

2. 간접의문문

- She didn't know. + What was that?
  ➡ She didn't know **what** that was. [의문사 + 주어 + 동사]

- Please let me know. + Will you call him?
  ➡ Please let me know **if (whether)** you will call him. [if (whether) + 주어 + 동사]

- Can you guess? + What happened to her?
  ➡ **What** can you guess happened to her? [의문사 + guess]

3. 문장의 형식

1형식 [완전 자동사]	[주어 + 동사] • Konggi lived happily ever after.
2형식 [불완전 자동사]	[주어 + 동사 + 보어] • Her hobby is going fishing.
3형식 [완전 타동사]	[주어 + 동사 + 목적어] • Fortunately, we liked the city.
4형식 [수여 동사]	[주어 + 동사 + 간접목적어 + 직접목적어] • She gave us some fried chicken.
5형식 [불완전 타동사]	[주어 + 동사 + 목적어 + 목적격보어] • The war made everything more expensive.

1-1 부가의문문

• **부가의문문**: 문장의 뒤에 의문문을 붙여서 앞의 내용을 한 번 더 확인하는 역할을 하는 의문문을 말한다.

◈ **부가의문문의 종류와 형태**

동사의 종류	부가의문문
be동사	• Olivia is so pretty, isn't she?
조동사	• Jack will be able to do better next time, won't he?
일반동사	• Dean likes to help his friends, doesn't he? • You don't want to be with them, do you?
명령문	• Let's not play here, shall we? • Please be careful, will you?
There is (are)~	• There is some juice in the bottle, isn't there? • There aren't any potatoes in the box, are there?
완료시제	• Harry has studied archeology since then, hasn't he?

(1) 주절이 긍정일 경우 부가의문문은 부정으로, 주절이 부정일 경우 부가의문문은 긍정으로 한다.

(2) 주절과 부가의문문의 시제는 일치시켜야 한다.

(3) 부가의문문이 부정일 경우 반드시 줄임말을 사용한다.

(4) 명령문의 부가의문문은 긍정, 부정에 상관없이 'shall we'와 'will you'를 사용한다.
  ➡ Let's (not) ~, shall we? / 명령문(부정 명령문), will you?

Grammar Plus +

• 주어가 'this'나 'that'일 경우 부가의문문의 인칭대명사는 'it'을 사용하고, 'these'나 'those'일 경우 'they'를 사용한다.
• 주어가 'I'일 경우 부가의문문은 '**aren't I**'를 쓴다.
  ➡ 'am I not'이라는 표현을 쓰기도 하지만, 'aren't I'를 더욱 많이 사용한다.

A   다음 문장의 빈칸에 알맞은 부가의문문을 쓰시오.

1   John is watching a movie, _isn't he_ ?

2   It won't snow tomorrow, _____ ?

3   Jane hasn't turned in the paper yet, _____ ?

4   The professor said there would be an English exam next week, _____ ?

5   Be quiet when you are in the library, _____ ?

6   I'm your English teacher, _____ ?

7   She can play the piano, _____ ?

8   It's my first novel, _____ ?

9   We don't have to get up early tomorrow morning, _____ ?

10   Alice has been to LA, _____ ?

11   Let's go on a picnic tomorrow, _____ ?

12   You can make a speech in English, _____ ?

13   They finished the project, _____ ?

14   There wasn't enough time to prepare for the party, _____ ?

15   She still doesn't know what the important thing in her life is, _____ ?

16   Don't put anything on the table, _____ ?

17   You are a middle school student, _____ ?

18   I'm John's best friend, _____ ?

19   You don't want to go to the concert, _____ ?

20   Let's take a taxi, _____ ?

Lesson 1-2 간접의문문

• **간접의문문**: 의문사가 이끄는 절이 그 문장의 일부로 쓰이는 경우, 의문사가 이끄는 절을 간접의문문이라고 한다.

◆ 간접의문문

간접의문문 형태	예문
의문사가 있는 경우 [의문사 + 주어 + 동사] / [의문사 + 동사]	• I don't know. + How do I get there? ➡ I don't know how I get there. [의문사 + 주어 + 동사] • Can you tell me? + Who likes you? ➡ Can you tell me who likes you? [의문사 + 동사]
의문사가 없는 경우 [if(whether) + 주어 + 동사]	• I wonder. + Will you come to my party? ➡ I wonder if (whether) you will come to my party.
의문사가 문장 앞에 위치할 경우 [의문사 + think]	• Do you think? + What is his problem? ➡ What do you think his problem is?

(1) 의문사가 있는 경우: 의문사가 주어로 쓰일 경우 직접의문문의 어순을 그대로 사용한다.

(2) 의문사가 없는 경우: 'if' 또는 'whether'를 사용하여 문장을 연결한다.

(3) 의문사가 문장 앞에 위치할 경우: 'think, believe, suppose, guess'처럼 생각이나 추측을 나타내는 동사가 올 때는 의문사가 문장의 맨 앞에 위치한다.

Answer Keys p. 01

A 다음 주어진 문장을 간접의문문으로 바꾸어 완성하시오.

1 Where is the nearest French restaurant?
➡ Could you tell me ____*where the nearest French restaurant is?*____

2 What made you so sad?
➡ Can you tell me _____

3 Does he have an appointment today?
➡ I don't know _____

4 How far is it from here to your house?
➡ Do you know _____

5 When did the car accident happen?
➡ Can you tell me _____

6 Who will look after Tom while his mother is cooking?

⇒ I wonder _____

7 Did she get married to the Korean man?

⇒ Can you tell me _____

8 Does she have any children?

⇒ I don't remember _____

9 Will your dream come true?

⇒ I'd like to know _____

10 Can you finish it by tomorrow?

⇒ I wonder _____

B 다음 주어진 두 문장을 연결하여 한 문장으로 바꾸어 쓰시오.

1 Do you think? + Why did she start exercising?

⇒ _____ *Why do you think she started exercising?* _____

2 Do you think? + Where is she from?

⇒ _____

3 I know. + Where did you go after school last Friday?

⇒ _____

4 Do you believe? + When can you buy this car?

⇒ _____

5 Please tell me. + Are you Tim's father?

⇒ _____

6 Do you think? + Why did they break up?

⇒ _____

7 Do you suppose? Who will be the team leader?

⇒ _____

문장의 형식 _1형식과 2형식

- 1형식 문장: '주어 + 동사'만으로 이루어진 문장이다. 문장을 보충하기 위해 부사(구)와 같은 수식어가 나온다.
- 2형식 문장: '주어 + 동사 + 보어'의 형태를 가진 문장이다. 동사로는 'be동사, 감각동사'가 나오며, 보어의 자리에는 '형용사' 또는 '형용사 + 명사' 등이 온다.

1. 1형식 문장 [동사_완전 자동사]

- Mary and her dog **run**.
- Mary and her dog **run** *along the river*.
  (주어)   (동사)   (부사구)
- **There is** a computer *on the table*.
  (동사)   (주어)   (부사구)

➡ 'there is / there are'의 경우 주어가 뒤에 나온다.

2. 2형식 문장 [동사_불완전 자동사]

- Nancy **is** a teacher. [be동사 + 명사]
- Linda **became** a beautiful lady. [불완전 자동사 + 형용사 + 명사]
- This coffee **tastes** great. [감각동사 + 형용사]

3. 2형식에 쓰이는 동사들

불완전 자동사	• be동사 • keep, remain, stay • get, grow, become, go, turn	+ 명사/형용사
감각동사	• sound smell taste feel • look, seem, appear	+ 형용사

Grammar Plus +

- '감각동사 + like'의 형태: 뒤에 명사가 온다.
  ex) sound like + 명사: ~처럼 들리다
  That sounds like an excuse.

A 괄호 안에서 알맞은 것을 고르시오.

1 (There are / There is) many people at the festival.

2 The world is changing so (fast / fastly).

3 My sister seems so (happy / happily).

4 Exercising alone at night is very (danger / dangerous).

5 The cat you raised looks so (love / lovely).

6 This device looks (useful / usefully)

7 The clothes feel (rough / roughly).

8 John looks (disappointing / disappointed).

9 His parents look (anger / angry). Probably because Mike was late for school.

10 This music sounds (sweetly / sweet).

11 This cake looks (delicious / deliciously). I want it.

12 It seems (good / well) to me.

13 When I feel (tired / tiring), I drink a lot of coffee.

14 Look at her. She (looks / looks like) a princess.

15 The beef stew was (tasteless / tastelessly).

B 다음 괄호 안의 단어를 이용하여 우리말에 맞게 문장을 완성한 후 문장의 형식을 쓰시오.

1 들판에는 들꽃들이 아주 많다. (a lot of, on the field)
➡ There are _____. (_____)

2 저 핫도그들은 역겨운 냄새가 난다. (disgusting)
➡ Those hot dogs _____. (_____)

3 Elly는 큰 무대에서 춤을 췄다. (on a big stage)
➡ Elly _____. (_____)

4 그녀의 월광 소나타는 황홀하게 들린다. (ecstatic)
➡ Her version of 'Moonlight Sonata' _____.
(_____)

5 그것은 거대한 괴물이 되었다. (a big monster)
➡ It _____. (_____)

> **Note**
> • **festival** 축제
> • **lovely** 사랑스러운
> • **rough** 거친
> • **tasteless** 맛없는, 무미건조한
> • **disgusting** 역겨운
> • **ecstatic** 황홀한, 설레는

1-4 문장의 형식 _ 3형식과 4형식

- **3형식 문장**: '주어 + 동사 + 목적어'의 형태를 가진 문장이다. 목적어의 자리에는 명사가 온다.
- **4형식 문장**: '주어 + 동사 + 간접목적어 + 직접목적어'의 형태를 가진 문장이다.
  목적어가 두 개 있으며, 간접목적어는 사람이, 직접목적어는 사물이 된다.

1. 3형식의 동사 [동사 _ 완전 타동사]

• say • put on • wake up	• mention • put off • turn on	• explain • turn off • take off	**+ 목적어**
• want • hope • refuse	• wish • decide • agree	• expect • plan • need	**+ to부정사**
• mind • admit • stop • quit	• enjoy • practice • deny • avoid	• dislike • finish • consider • give up	**+ 동명사**
• begin • love	• start • hate	• like • continue	**+ 동명사 + to부정사**

2. 4형식의 동사 [동사 _ 수여동사]

동사	4형식	3형식으로 전환할 때
• bring, give, lend, offer, pay, send, show, tell, teach 등	+ 간접목적어 + 직접목적어	+ 직접목적어 + to + 목적격
• make, buy, cook, get, find 등		+ 직접목적어 + for + 목적격
• ask, inquire, require		+ 직접목적어 + of + 목적격

- Jerry **drank** <u>some cold water</u>. [3형식: 주어 + 동사 + 목적어]

- Mina **gave** <u>him a present</u>. [4형식: 주어 + 동사 + 간접목적어 + 직접목적어]
  = Mina **gave** <u>a present to him</u>. [3형식으로 전환: 주어 + 동사 + 목적어 + to 목적격]

Answer Keys p. 01

A 다음 주어진 단어를 활용하여 빈칸에 알맞은 말을 쓰시오.

1 Sam wants ___to become___ a doctor. (become)

2 He doesn't mind _____ the window. (open)

3 We have to finish _____ the letter by tomorrow. (write)

4 Jieun dislikes _____ hiking during summer vacation. (go)

5 She hoped _____ an A on the math test. (get)

6 They refuse _____ the meeting. (attend)

7 She gave up _____ a new novel. (write)

8 Mr. Park continued _____ the piano everyday. (practice)

9 Please, stop _____ the medicine. You are okay now. (take)

10 I decided _____ my job on Tuesday. (quit)

B 다음 빈칸에 to, for, of 중 알맞은 것을 골라 쓰시오.

1 Jane gave a cake ____to____ him.

2 Olivia made a dress _____ her daughter.

3 I showed my old pictures _____ my boyfriend.

4 She asked difficult questions _____ her students.

5 The tutor bought a wooden desk _____ his mother.

6 Mr. Kim teaches English _____ us.

7 I required more information _____ John.

8 They got some toys _____ their children.

9 My parents gave endless love _____ us.

10 They found a new house _____ him.

Lesson 1-5 문장의 형식 _5형식

- **5형식 문장**: '주어 + 동사 + 목적어 + 목적격보어'의 형태를 가진 문장이다.
  목적어만으로는 완전한 문장이 될 수 없어서 목적격보어가 와야 한다.

◈ 5형식의 동사 [동사 _불완전타동사]

동사			목적격보어 형태
• keep • turn	• find • elect	• call • make	+ 명사/형용사
• want • allow	• tell • encourage	• ask • get	+ to부정사
[사역동사]　let, make, have, *help [지각동사]　feel　　see　　hear　　watch			+ 원형부정사 (동사원형)

*help : '준사역동사'이며, 목적격보어로 '원형부정사' 또는 'to부정사'가 올 수 있다.

- We **called** him a coward. [목적격보어: 명사]

- They **found** the movie interesting. [목적격보어: 형용사]

- He **asked** me to give him some information. [목적격보어: to부정사]

- Hyemi can **make** the baby smile. [목적격보어: 원형부정사]

- Jaeho **feels** something touch(touching) his shoulder. [목적격보어: 원형부정사(현재분사)]
  → '지각동사'의 목적격보어로 '원형부정사' 또는 '현재분사'가 올 수 있다.

 Check up!

Answer Keys p. 01

A 주어진 단어를 활용하여 빈칸에 알맞은 말을 쓰시오.

1 I asked him _to pick me up_ at the airport. (pick up)

2 Minwoo found the book _____. (interest).

3 Mom made me _____ my room. (clean)

4 They elected him _____. (class president)

5 Linda often watches Minsu _____ the piano. (play)

6 She called me _____. (baby)

7 Don't tell me _____ those shoes. That's terrible. (buy)

8 Sujin had him _____ his hair. (cut)

9 They found the drama _____. (fantasy)

10 He encouraged his daughter _____ the National Sports Festival. (take part in)

Practice More I

A 빈칸에 알맞은 말을 넣어 문장을 완성하시오.

1 He wouldn't do that, _____would he_____?

2 She has lived here for five years, _____?

3 Let's not speak ill of her, _____?

4 People wait for him, _____?

5 Don't be late for lunch, _____?

6 The media should deliver the facts, _____?

7 Don't forget your homework, _____?

8 Let's climb the mountain together, _____?

9 I'm your sister, _____?

B 밑줄 친 부분을 어법에 맞게 고치시오.

1 Jane didn't remember how old <u>is the girl</u>.　　　_____the girl is_____

2 <u>Do you who</u> suppose will win the game?　　　_____

3 Please tell me <u>can who</u> bring the table.　　　_____

4 I wonder <u>which</u> I can finish this report by five.　　　_____

5 You don't want to fail the exam, <u>you do</u>?　　　_____

6 Don't wear a hat in the house, <u>do you</u>?　　　_____

7 These books are so interesting, <u>aren't these</u>?　　　_____

8 Who <u>you do</u> believe is guilty among them?　　　_____

9 I would like to know <u>made what</u> him happy.　　　_____

C 주어진 단어를 빈칸에 들어갈 알맞은 형태로 바꾸어 쓰시오.

1 John forgot Helen's phone number, _____*didn't*_____ he? (do)

2 You look really _____. (happy)

3 I had him _____ the radio. (fix)

4 I decided _____ to America to study English. (go)

5 Andy will make a photo album _____. (his son)

6 She asked some difficult questions _____.
   (her students)

7 I found this novel _____. (bore)

8 He wants _____ his daughter smile. (make)

D 다음 우리말 해석에 맞게 주어진 단어를 알맞게 배열하여 문장을 완성하시오.

1 그들은 Amy를 영어 말하기 팀의 리더로 뽑았다.
   (they, team, leader, elected, english speaking, Amy, of)
   ➡ _____*They elected Amy leader of English speaking team.*_____

2 그 소식은 나를 더 열심히 공부하게 했다. (the news, made,
   harder, me, study)
   ➡ _____

3 할머니는 우리에게 맛있는 아침을 차려주셨다.
   (breakfast, grandmother, for, cooked, us, delicious, a)
   ➡ _____

4 그들은 그 건물에 접근했다. (they, building, approached, the)
   ➡ _____

5 Helen은 자기의 아이들이 집에서 뛰는 것을 허락하지 않았다.
   (Helen, in the house, allow, her, didn't, run, children, to)
   ➡ _____

6 나는 그가 꿈을 이뤘는지 궁금하다. (I, true, if, wonder, his
   dream, came)
   ➡ _____

7 누가 영어 시험에서 A를 받을지 제발 말해줘.
   (please, on the English test, tell, who, get, me, will, an A)
   ➡ _____

내신 최다 출제 유형

01 다음 중 밑줄 친 부분이 어법상 틀린 것을 고르시오.
[출제 예상 85%]

① This book looked boring.
② This chicken soup tastes very well.
③ The scarf feels very soft.
④ I felt very nervous at that time.
⑤ He turned pale when he went into the haunted house.

02 다음 중 어법상 옳은 문장을 고르시오. [출제 예상 80%]

① Let me knowing the answer, please.
② His song makes me to feel happy.
③ She made me to play soccer.
④ Why did she have you work on Saturday?
⑤ Mom had me cleaned my room.

03 다음 두 문장을 5형식으로 바르게 바꾼 것을 고르시오. [출제 예상 90%]

A bird sang in the morning. I heard it.

① I heard a bird sings in the morning.
② I heard a bird was singing in the morning.
③ I heard a bird sing in the morning.
④ I hear a bird sing in the morning.
⑤ I hear a bird sings in the morning.

04 다음 빈칸에 들어갈 말이 바르게 짝지어진 것을 고르시오.
[출제 예상 85%]

• We saw two boys _____ a fight at the school gate.
• My hobby is _____ brochures about sightseeing.

① start − collect
② started − to collect
③ starting − collected
④ to start − to collect
⑤ start − collecting

05 다음 4형식 문장을 3형식 문장으로 바르게 바꾼 것을 고르시오. [출제 예상 80%]

My mom made me a beautiful dress.

① She made me for a beautiful dress.
② She made a beautiful dress for me.
③ She made a beautiful dress to me.
④ She made a beautiful dress of me.
⑤ She made to me a beautiful dress.

06 다음 중 어법상 옳은 문장은 모두 몇 개인지 고르시오. [출제 예상 85%]

ⓐ The little birds look so cute.
ⓑ The milk smelled badly.
ⓒ Sally felt tired yesterday.
ⓓ The music sounds terribly.
ⓔ The broiled eels tasted so delicious.

① 1개
② 2개
③ 3개
④ 4개
⑤ 5개

[01~02] 다음 빈칸에 들어갈 전치사로 알맞은 것을 고르시오.

01

> Harry bought a pair of gloves _____ his mother.

① of   ② for   ③ on
④ at   ⑤ in

02

> She couldn't do anything when a foreigner asked a question _____ her.

① for   ② to   ③ by
④ at   ⑤ of

[03~05] 다음 주어진 문장과 형식이 같은 문장을 고르시오.

03

> Jerry will make his dreams come true in three years.

① Jay made a model airplane for his nephew.
② Sometimes problems can make people strong.
③ Make a plan like reading several books in a month.
④ I want to make a study group.
⑤ They traveled around the world for three years.

04

> All the people around him called it a miracle.

① She feels someone behind her.
② I taught her a lot of things about the history of Korea.
③ Jisu gave him a big hand on his new project.
④ He let me know the secret.
⑤ I can't save this on my USB.

05

> Emily will take a trip with her family.

① Mindy looks beautiful tonight.
② Jessy makes him a model.
③ He teaches English to us.
④ The birds are flying in the sky.
⑤ He gave me some pebbles.

[06~08] 다음 두 문장을 간접의문문으로 바르게 바꾼 것을 고르시오.

06

> Does she know? + Do the other friends like Helen better?

① Does she know the other friends like Helen better?
② Does she know if the other friends like Helen better?
③ Does she know that the other friends like Helen better?
④ Does she know who the other friends like Helen better?
⑤ Does she know what the other friends like Helen better?

07

> Do you think? + What should we do to win the game?

① Do you think what we should do to win the game?
② Do you think what should we do to win the game?
③ What do you think should we do to win the game?
④ What do you think we do to win the game?
⑤ What do you think we should do to win the game?

★★★
08

> Tell me honestly. + Who broke the window yesterday?

① Tell me honestly who broke the window yesterday?
② Tell me who broke the window yesterday?
③ Tell me honestly who did break the window yesterday?
④ Tell me honestly who broken the window yesterday?
⑤ Tell me honestly who was broken the window yesterday?

[09~10] 다음 중 어법상 어색한 것을 고르시오.

09 ① Our project helped her father recover from the disease.
② This kind of environment has made them strong.
③ We should not let the noise disturbs you.
④ He makes me practice songs a lot.
⑤ Jerry didn't make her sad.

★★★
10 ① He has many friends but he still feels lonely.
② I can get healthy through exercising.
③ We're sure that you can make it easily.
④ I think your symptom is a part of growing older.
⑤ As he became richly, he became much greedier.

[11~12] 다음 중 어법상 올바른 것을 모두 고르시오.

11 ① I used to read comic books day and night.
② A young man saw the cattle block the road.
③ He wants his friends understand him.
④ Finally, she felt the train to start to move.
⑤ She didn't want anyone see her diary.

★★★

12
① We have to get him finish his homework.
② This prize will to encourage people to work hard.
③ It will help you to conduct research to find good sources.
④ I wanted you to be happy there.
⑤ She's wrote a letter to ask me take care of her cats.

[13~15] 다음 빈칸에 들어갈 알맞은 말을 고르시오.

13
A There are so many things to know in this world, _____?
B You're right.

① isn't it   ② are there
③ are they   ④ aren't they
⑤ aren't there

14
A Let's find a best way to improve our English speaking skills, _____?
B That sounds good.

① will you   ② shall we
③ will we   ④ shall you
⑤ would us

15
Don't eat a lot of junk food, _____?

① shall we   ② will you
③ shall you   ④ will we
⑤ would you

16 다음 빈칸에 들어갈 알맞은 말을 고르시오.

She got me _____ a teaspoonful of sugar to the soup.

① add   ② adding   ③ added
④ to add   ⑤ to adding

17 주어진 우리말과 같은 뜻이 되도록 빈칸에 들어갈 알맞은 말을 고르시오.

선생님은 우리가 필요할 때 도망가는 사람은 사귀지 말라고 말씀하셨다.
➡ The teacher told us _____ friends who will run away when we need them.

① not to have   ② having not
③ not have   ④ to not have
⑤ have not to

[18~19] 다음 우리말을 영어로 바르게 옮긴 것을 고르시오.

18
Mary는 그것이 무슨 의미였는지 몰랐다.

① Mary didn't know what meant.
② Mary didn't know what mean is.
③ Mary didn't know what it means.
④ Mary doesn't know what it mean.
⑤ Mary didn't know what it meant.

19

Harry의 부모님은 그가 혼자 여행하는 것을 허락하셨다.

① Harry's parents allowed him to travel alone.
② Harry's parents allowed him travels alone.
③ Harry's parents allowed him travel alone.
④ Harry's parents allowed he travels alone.
⑤ Harry's parents allowed him traveled alone.

★★★
20 다음 중 어법상 어색한 것을 모두 고르시오.

① Everything in the ads sounds truly but is false.
② Children play all day long but never look tired.
③ His story seems very likely, but I don't believe it.
④ Sometimes Anne seems to be sillier.
⑤ When I visit this town, I feel friend for no reason.

◇◇◇◇◇◇◇◇◇ 서술형 평가 ◇◇◇◇◇◇◇◇◇

[21~23] 다음 우리말과 같은 뜻이 되도록 빈칸에 알맞은 말을 쓰시오.

21

Sara가 자기 여동생이 디자이너가 되었다고 말했을 때, 그건 매우 흥미롭게 들렸다.
➡ When Sara said that her sister became a designer, it _____ very interesting.

➡ _____

22

너는 어젯밤 여러 편의 영화를 보느라고 밤새 늦게까지 있었어, 그렇지 않니?
➡ You stayed up late to watch several movies last night, _____?

➡ _____

23

많은 종류의 과일들은 우리가 병에 걸리는 것을 막아줄 수 있다.
➡ Many kinds of fruits may _____ us _____ getting sick.

➡ _____

[24~25] 다음 문장에서 <u>틀린</u> 부분을 찾아 고쳐 쓰시오.

24
> Thank you for finding a house to me.

_____ ➡ _____

25
> Does he where suppose he comes from?

_____ ➡ _____

[26~28] 다음의 문장들을 괄호 안의 지시어대로 바꾸어 쓰시오.

★★★
26
> Did you think?
> Where did they go last weekend?

[간접의문문]

➡ _____

★★★
27
> My father cooked us some food.

[3형식]

➡ _____

28
> Robert shows something funny to us everyday.

[4형식]

➡ _____

[29~30] 다음 괄호 안의 단어를 우리말에 맞게 바르게 배열하여 문장을 완성하시오.

★★★
29
> 그것은 참가자들에게 운동을 바르게 하는 방법을 배울 기회를 제공한다.
> (it / the / with / a chance / how to / provides / participants / to learn / correctly / exercise)

➡ _____
_____

★★★
30
> 나는 쇼핑하는 것보다 도서관에서 책을 읽는 것을 더 좋아한다.
> (I / reading / in the library / to / prefer / books / going / shopping)

➡ _____
_____

Note

02

Chapter
동사의 시제

Point Check I

◆ **현재형 :** 현재의 사실, 반복적인 일상, 속담, 불변의 진리에 대해서 말할 때 사용한다.

◆ **과거형 :** 과거의 어느 시점에 일어났던 사실이나 습관을 말할 때 사용한다.

◆ **현재 진행형 :** 현재 일어나고 있는 일을 말할 때 또는 가까운 미래를 말할 때 사용한다.

◆ **과거 진행형 :** 과거의 어느 시점에서 일어나고 있었던 일에 대해서 말할 때 사용한다.

◆ **미래형 :** 미래에 예정되거나 계획된 일을 말할 때 사용한다.

1. be동사와 일반동사

		현재형	과거형
be 동사	평서문	am/are/is	was/were
	부정문	am/are/is not	was/were not
	의문문	Am/Are/Is + 주어~?	Was/Were + 주어~?
일반 동사	평서문	I/we/you/they + 동사원형 he/she/it + 동사 (-s/-es)	I/we/you/they/he/she/it + 과거동사
	부정문	I/we/you/they do not + 동사원형 he/she/it does not + 동사원형	I/we/you/they/he/she/it did not + 동사원형
	의문문	Do I/we/you/they + 동사원형~? Does he/she/it + 동사원형~?	Did I/we/you/they/he/she/it + 동사원형~?

2. 진행형

	현재진행형	과거진행형
평서문	am/are/is + 동사-ing	was/were + 동사-ing
부정문	am/are/is not + 동사-ing	was/were not + 동사-ing
의문문	Am/Are/Is + 주어 + 동사-ing~?	Was/Were + 주어 + 동사-ing~?

3. 미래형

	will	be going to
평서문	will + 동사원형	am/are/is going to + 동사원형
부정문	will not + 동사원형	am/are/is not going to + 동사원형
의문문	Will + 주어 + 동사원형~?	Am/Are/Is + 주어 + going to + 동사원형~?

2-1 be동사, 일반동사 현재형

- **be동사**: 'am, are, is'로 구분되며, 인칭의 수에 따라 사용한다. '∼이다, ∼있다'의 뜻을 가지고 있으며, 주로 2형식 문장의 동사로 많이 쓰인다.
- **일반동사**: 인칭의 수에 따라 동사원형을 쓰기도 하고, 동사 뒤에 '-s/es'를 붙여 사용한다.
- **현재형**: 현재의 습관, 사실, 진실, 속담 등을 말할 때 사용한다.

1. be동사

현재형 [주어＋am/are/is]	• I am a Korean. • She is a good student. • They are very polite.
부정문 [am/are/is＋not]	• I am not an actress. [I am not＝I'm not] • He is not at the publishing house. [is not＝isn't] • We are not studying. [are not＝aren't]
의문문 [Am/Are/Is＋주어∼?]	• Is she your sister? Yes, she is. / No, she isn't. • Are they your classmates? Yes, they are. / No, they aren't.

2. 일반동사

평서문	I, we, you, they	＋동사원형
	he, she, it	＋동사(s/es)
부정문	I, we, you, they	do not＋동사원형
	he, she, it	does not＋동사원형

의문문	Do	I, we, you, they	＋동사원형
	Does	he, she, it	

평서문	• I watch the quiz show on TV. • He reads a book about Korean history.
부정문	• She does not want to go shopping. [does not＝doesn't] • We do not study Chinese. [do not＝don't]
의문문	• Do you go to church? Yes, I do. / No, I don't. • Does she jog in the morning? Yes, she does. / No, she doesn't.

3. 3인칭 단수의 현재형 동사 변화

대부분의 경우	동사원형 + -s	• work – works • grow – grows	• say – says • leave – leaves
'-o, -x, -s, -sh, -ch'로 끝나는 경우	동사원형 + -es	• go – goes • wash – washes	• teach – teaches • relax – relaxes
'자음 + y'로 끝나는 경우	y를 i로 고치고 + -es	• cry – cries • try – tries	• fly – flies • study – studies

☆Check up!

Answer Keys p. 04

A 다음 주어진 동사를 이용하여 현재시제 문장을 완성하시오.

1 Mr . Brown ____drives____ his car to pick up his daughter.
(drive)

2 Helen _____ English because there will be a final exam
tomorrow. (study)

3 She _____ to go hiking this week. (not want)

4 Mr. Kim and I _____ best friends. (be)

5 Water _____ at one hundred degrees Celsius. (boil)

6 She _____ coffee whenever she _____ tired.
(drink / feel)

7 They _____ going to concerts every weekend. (enjoy)

8 My mother _____ a doctor. (be)

9 Her parents _____ in LA. (live)

10 Summer _____ the best season for swimming in the sea.
(be)

11 A rolling stone _____ no moss. (gather)

12 She _____ up early everyday. (get)

13 We _____ that bag. That's too expensive. (not buy)

14 She _____ all ingredients in the bowl. (mix)

15 Paul _____ because of the sad movie. (cry)

2-2 **be동사, 일반동사 과거형**

• **과거형**: 과거에 일어난 동작이나 상태, 역사적 사실처럼 과거에 이미 끝난 일을 나타낸다.

1. be동사

과거형 [주어 + was/were]	• She was <u>very rude.</u> • They were at the shopping mall.
부정문 [was/were + not]	• I was not <u>at home.</u> [was not = wasn't] • He was not <u>full.</u> [was not = wasn't] • We were not <u>scared.</u> [were not = weren't]
의문문 [Was/Were + 주어~?]	• Was I at the beach? Yes, you were. / No, you weren't. • Was she at the bus stop? Yes, she was. / No, she wasn't. • Were they your teachers? Yes, they were. / No, they weren't.

2. 일반동사

과거형 [주어 + 일반동사(d/ed)]	• I looked for my favorite shirt. • He washed the dishes. • We dropped a box.
부정문 [did not + 동사원형]	• They did not <u>have</u> any classes in the morning. [did not = didn't]
의문문 [Did + 주어 + 동사원형~?]	• Did she <u>build</u> a sand castle? Yes, she did. / No, she didn't.

3. 일반동사의 과거형_규칙변화

대부분의 경우	동사원형 + -ed	• brush – brushed	• pull – pulled
-e로 끝나는 경우	동사원형 + -d	• close – closed	• use – used
'자음 + y'로 끝나는 경우	y를 i로 고치고 -ed	• reply – replied	• deny – denied
'단모음 + 단자음'으로 끝나는 경우	자음을 한 번 더 쓰고 -ed	• drop – dropped	• stop – stopped

A   다음 동사의 과거형을 쓰시오.

1   cook   —   _____cooked_____

2   help   —   _____

3   play   —   _____

4   borrow —   _____

5   change —   _____

6   worry   —   _____

7   try   —   _____

8   hug   —   _____

9   plan   —   _____

10 love   —   _____

B   다음 빈칸에 알맞은 형태의 과거 동사를 쓰시오.

1   Harry _____was_____ sick yesterday, so he was absent from his class. (be)

2   He _____ mom to clean the house. (help)

3   I _____ to his email last night. (reply)

4   We _____ a lot of fun last weekend. We went to a rock festival. (have)

5   Mike read a book and I _____ the dishes. (wash)

6   _____ you unhappy? You looked very sad last night. (be)

7   John's family _____ to another city last week. (move)

8   The crowd _____ the president. (welcome)

9   _____ they Korean? I didn't know that. (be)

10 Tom _____ his mother to buy him chocolate cookies. (beg)

일반동사 과거동사 _ 불규칙 변화

◆ 일반동사의 과거형_불규칙변화

원형	과거형	과거분사형	원형	과거형	과거분사형
be	was / were	been	bear	bore	born
beat	beat	beaten	become	became	become
begin	began	begun	blow	blew	blown
bring	brought	brought	build	built	built
buy	bought	bought	choose	chose	chosen
come	came	come	cost	cost	cost
cut	cut	cut	do	did	done
draw	drew	drawn	dream	dreamed/ dreamt	dreamed/ dreamt
drink	drank	drunk	drive	drove	driven
eat	ate	eaten	fall	fell	fallen
feel	felt	felt	fight	fought	fought
find	found	found	fly	flew	flown
forget	forgot	forgotten	get	got	got(ten)
give	gave	given	go	went	gone
grow	grew	grown	have	had	had
hear	heard	heard	hide	hid	hidden
hit	hit	hit	hold	held	held
hurt	hurt	hurt	keep	kept	kept
know	knew	known	lay	laid	laid
lead	led	led	leave	left	left
let	let	let	lie(눕다)	lay	lain
lose	lost	lost	make	made	made
mean	meant	meant	meet	met	met
overcome	overcame	overcome	pay	paid	paid
put	put	put	read	read	read
ride	rode	ridden	ring	rang	rung
rise	rose	risen	run	ran	run
say	said	said	see	saw	seen
sell	sold	sold	send	sent	sent
set	set	set	shut	shut	shut
sing	sang	sung	sink	sank	sunk
sit	sat	sat	sleep	slept	slept

원형	과거형	과거분사형	원형	과거형	과거분사형
smell	smelled/smelt	smelled/smelt	speak	spoke	spoken
spend	spent	spent	spread	spread	spread
stand	stood	stood	steal	stole	stolen
sweep	swept	swept	swim	swam	swum
take	took	taken	teach	taught	taught
tell	told	told	think	thought	thought
throw	threw	thrown	understand	understood	understood
wake	woke	woken	wear	wore	worn
win	won	won	write	wrote	written

☆Check up!

Answer Keys p. 04

A 다음 동사의 과거형과 과거분사형을 쓰시오.

1 sweep — _swept_ — _swept_

2 throw — _____ — _____

3 get — _____ — _____

4 stand — _____ — _____

5 arise — _____ — _____

6 see — _____ — _____

7 shake — _____ — _____

8 eat — _____ — _____

9 strive — _____ — _____

10 weave — _____ — _____

11 sink — _____ — _____

12 think — _____ — _____

13 fly — _____ — _____

14 sow — _____ — _____

15 steal — _____ — _____

16 forgive — _____ — _____

17 lie — _____ — _____

18 hear — _____ — _____

Note
- **arise** 생기다, 발생하다
- **strive** 분투하다
- **weave** (옷감, 꽃 등을) 짜다, 엮다
- **sow** (씨 등을) 뿌리다, 심다

B 주어진 단어를 과거형으로 바꾸어 빈칸에 쓰시오.

1 They _____*left*_____ the party without saying a word. (leave)

2 I _____ an email to him last night. (send)

3 Do you know who _____ the car? (drive)

4 She _____ some cookies to us. (bring)

5 Helen _____ the garbage on the field. (throw)

6 While is mother cooked, John _____ in the park. (jog)

7 I think he _____ the window last night. (break)

8 All the people _____ for the survival of the lost woman. (pray)

9 She _____ me how to read. (teach)

10 They _____ three months ago. (marry)

진행형

- **진행형**: 과거 어느 시점에서 진행 중이었던 일에 대하여 표현한다.
- **현재진행형**: 'be동사 (am/are/is) + 동사-ing'의 형태로 '~하고 있는 중이다'로 해석한다.
- **과거진행형**: 'be동사 과거(was/were) + 동사-ing'의 형태로 '~하고 있었던 중이었다'로 해석한다.

1. 진행형

	현재진행형	과거진행형
평서문	[am/are/is + 동사-ing] • I am taking a shower. • She is brushing her teeth.	[was/were + 동사-ing] • He was listening to music. • They were playing soccer.
부정문	[am/are/is + not + 동사-ing] • He isn't riding a bicycle. • We aren't studying science.	[was/were + not + 동사-ing] • He wasn't writing a letter. • They weren't singing songs.
의문문	[Am/Are/Is + 주어 + 동사-ing~?] • Is Anna playing the piano? 　Yes, she is. / No, she isn't.	[Was/Were + 주어 + 동사-ing~?] • Were they buying jams? 　Yes, they were. / No, they weren't.

2. 현재형과 현재진행형

현재형	현재진행형
• 현재의 사실, 상태, 습관, 반복적인 동작, 불변의 진리, 격언 등을 표현 • Luck comes to those who look for it. • 시간과 조건의 부사절을 쓸 때 사용 • Annie plays the drums after she finishes her work. • '왕래발착 동사 + 미래를 나타내는 부사(구)'의 형태로 미래를 표현 • Jane comes here tonight.	• 현 시점에서 진행 중인 일에 대하여 표현 • Mario is dancing now. • 미래를 나타내는 부사(구)와 함께 쓰여 가까운 미래를 표현 • **A** Are they going camping tomorrow? 　**B** Yes, they are. / No, they aren't.

3. 과거형과 과거진행형

과거형	과거진행형
• 단순한 과거의 일을 표현 • Cathy saw a handsome man.	• 과거의 어느 시점에 진행 중이었던 일을 표현 • Alison was taking a nap when I came home

Grammar Plus +

- 진행형을 만들 수 없는 동사
  ⓐ 지각: know 알다, understand 이해하다, remember 기억하다, think 생각하다
  ⓑ 소유: have 가지다, own 소유하다, belong to ~에 속하다
  ⓒ 존재: be 있다, exist 존재하다
  ⓓ 감정: love 사랑하다, like 좋아하다, hate 싫어하다, prefer 더 좋아하다
  ⓔ 감각: see 보다, hear 듣다, smell 냄새 나다, taste 맛이 나다
  ⓕ 기타: want 원하다, resemble 닮다, keep 유지하다, seem ~인 것 같다
- 현재진행형과 함께 쓰이는 부사: now, right now, at the moment

 **Check up!**

Answer Keys p. 04

A 괄호 안의 말을 현재/과거진행형으로 바꾸어 쓰시오.

1 It ___is snowing___ outside. (snow)

2 He _____ ill of him. (speak)

3 Kate _____ a dress for her daughter last night. (make)

4 The woman _____ a blue coat. (wear)

5 I knew the girl who _____ in the street. (dance)

6 They _____ about the issue right now. (not, talk)

7 I _____ lunch at that time. (not, have)

8 _____ you _____ for the party now? (prepare)

B 다음 문장에서 어법상 어색한 것을 찾아 바르게 고치시오.

1 The book was belonging to John.

　　　　　　　　　　　　　was belonging ➡ ___belonged___

2 Water is freezing at zero degrees Celsius.

　　　　　　　　　　　_____ ➡ _____

3 He is having a large house.　　_____ ➡ _____

4 I am wanting to become a nurse._____ ➡ _____

5 Mario runs now.　　　　　　_____ ➡ _____

6 John made a chocolate cake when she came home.

　　　　　　　　　　　　　_____ ➡ _____

7 Kate was seeing the musical yesterday.

　　　　　　　　　　　　　_____ ➡ _____

8 The girls studied when their teacher visited them.

　　　　　　　　　　　　　_____ ➡ _____

2-5 미래형

- 미래형: 앞으로 하게 될 일이나 일어날 일에 대해 말할 때 사용한다.
  미래를 말할 때 'will'과 'be going to'를 사용하며, 둘 다 '～할 것이다'라는 뜻으로 뒤에는
  동사원형이 나온다.

◈ will과 be going to

	will ～일 것이다	be going to ～일 것이다
쓰임	• 즉석에서 결정할 때 사용 • 가까운 미래나 대략적인 미래 상황을 말할 때 사용	• 추측할 근거가 있을 만한 상황에서 사용 • 이미 계획하거나 하려고 생각했던 일을 말 할 때 사용
평서문	• The train will leave in 20minutes.	• It is windy a lot. It is going to storm soon.
부정문	• The Jackson will not take a trip this vacation. [will not = won't]	• We aren't going to go swimming this weekend.

의문문	• A Will she have a part-time job this summer?
	  B Yes, she will. / No, she won't.
		• A Are you going to visit the house of Shin Saimdang's birth on this trip?
		  B Yes, we are. / No, we aren't.

☆Check up!

Answer Keys p. 04

A 다음 괄호 안의 단어를 이용하여 빈칸을 채우시오.

1 I _____will buy_____ a ring for Sally's birthday. (will, buy)

2 They _____ a violin lesson tomorrow.
(be going to, have)

3 He _____ every night. (will, write in a diary)

4 _____ she _____ to Japan this weekend?
(be going to, go)

5 I _____ it! (will, catch)

6 They _____ hiking this month.
(be going to, not, go)

7 Our bus _____ in 30 minutes. (will, leave)

8 I _____ to see you more often. (will, not, come)

9 _____ you _____ the English class during
summer vacation? (be going to, take)

Practice More I

Answer Keys p. 05

A 다음 밑줄 친 부분을 어법에 맞게 고치시오.

1 She <u>feel</u> sad because she failed to pass the exam.

_____ *felt* _____

2 In Korea, it <u>snow</u> a lot every winter.

_____

3 He <u>buys</u> the car when he was twenty.

_____

4 How was the weather in LA when you <u>are</u> there?

_____

5 I <u>forget</u> my homework, so I was punished.

_____

6 The family <u>moves</u> to another city last year.

_____

7 Many flowers usually <u>blossomed</u> in April.

_____

8 After he reached the top of the mountain, the sun <u>rises</u>.

_____

9 Before I arrived there, the party had already <u>starts</u>.

_____

10 When I finished singing, the girl <u>gives</u> a happy smile.

_____

B 문장이 올바르면 T로, 올바르지 <u>않으면</u> F로 표시하시오.

1 The wallet belongs to my mom.   (*T*)

2 The child is looking happy.   (   )

3 He is owning the company.   (   )

4 We are thinking about the plan.   (   )

5 It will be raining when we will arrive at the town. (   )

6 My brother was taking a bath when mom came home.   (   )

7 Where were you going this evening?   (   )

8 The V sign showed a desire for victory.   (   )

9 Helen is watching a video while her mom is cooking. (   )

Practice More I

C 괄호 안에서 알맞은 것을 고르시오.

1 We (are taking / took) a basic English course this winter vacation.

2 When I (got / get) up, there was no one left at home.

3 Harry (is knowing / knows) the answer, so he can solve the problem.

4 When I studied for the exam, my father (was cooking / is going to cook) dinner.

5 The professor says that there (is going / will be) a pop quiz tomorrow.

6 We will be having lunch when Helen (finishes / is going to finish) the interview.

7 What were the girls (done / doing) during class?

8 Sam (played / was playing) soccer when the teacher called him.

9 All the students (are reading / read) the book right now.

10 I (had / am going to have) an important appointment next week.

D 주어진 단어들을 알맞게 배열하여 우리말 해석에 맞게 문장을 완성하시오.

1 그녀는 부엌에서 설거지 중이다.
   (she, kitchen, doing, the dishes, is, the, in)
   ➡ _____ *She is doing the dishes in the kitchen.* _____

2 너는 이번 주말에 무슨 일을 할 거니?
   (what, this, to, are, weekend, going, you, do)
   ➡ _____

3 내가 방에 들어왔을 때 그는 방 청소 중이었다.
   (he, I, the room, cleaning, his room, when, was, entered)
   ➡ _____

4   그는 엄마가 만든 체리 주스를 마시고 있는 중이다.
    (mom, his, the cherry juice, made, drinking, is, he, that)
    ➡ _____

5   내가 춤추는 것을 멈췄을 때 관객들은 큰 박수를 보냈다.
    (when, a big hand, stopped, the audience, I, gave, me, dancing)
    ➡ _____

6   John이 집에 돌아왔을 때 아기는 잠을 자고 있었다.
    (when, sleeping, John, was, came back, the baby)
    ➡ _____

7   나는 박 감독의 다음 영화를 보는 것을 기대하는 중이다.
    (I, watching, director, looking, am, Park's, next movie,
    forward to)
    ➡ _____

8   Tommy는 자전거를 타다가 다리가 부러졌다.
    (Tommy, a bike, broke, while, his, riding, leg, was, he)
    ➡ _____

9   숙제가 너무 어려워서 그는 그것에 대해 걱정했다.
    (because, he, was, the homework, worried, too, hard, was)
    ➡ _____

10 나는 방의 불을 끄는 것을 잊어버려서 다시 집으로 돌아가야 했다.
    (I, home, turn off, so, forgot to, had to, I, my room, go, in,
    the light, back)
    ➡ _____

Point Check II

◆ **현재완료**: 과거에 일어난 사건이 현재에 영향을 끼쳐 관계가 있음을 나타낼 때 사용한다.

◆ **과거완료**: 과거의 한 시점을 기준으로 그 이전의 시점부터 과거의 어느 시점 사이에 일어난 일을 나타내는 경우에 과거완료를 사용한다.

◆ **미래완료**: 미래의 어느 시점까지 완료될 것으로 예상되는 일을 나타낸다.

1. 완료의 형태

had + 과거분사	have/has + 과거분사	will + have + 과거분사
과거완료　　　　　　　　　과거	현재	미래

- Jennifer **had studied** English for six months before going to England. [과거완료]
- Kate **has done** exercises to lose weight since last year. [현재완료]
- Robert **will have stayed** here for a month. [미래완료]

2. 완료시제와 사용되는 말

완료	already, yet, just, now
경험	ever, never, before, often, sometimes, once, ~times
결과	go, come, leave, lose, buy
계속	for, since

3. 완료의 진행형

현재완료 진행형	have/has been + 동사-ing	• Sally has been studying since this morning.
과거완료 진행형	had been + 동사-ing	• I had been cleaning my room since last Tuseday.
미래완료 진행형	will have been + 동사-ing	• He will have been working on the project for over a year.

현재완료

• **현재완료**: 과거에 일어난 일이 현재에 영향을 미쳐 관계가 있는 것을 나타낸다.

1. 현재완료의 형태

have/has + 과거분사	

과거 　　　　　　　　　　　　　　　　현재 　　　　　　　　　　　　　　　　미래

형태	1, 2인칭 단수/복수	3인칭 단수
평서문	have + 과거분사	has + 과거분사
부정문	have not + 과거분사	has not + 과거분사
의문문	Have + 주어 + 과거분사~?	Has + 주어 + 과거분사~?

2. 현재완료의 용법

용법	예문	함께 쓰이는 말
완료	• The parcel hasn't arrived yet.	already, yet, just, now
경험	• I have never ridden a merry-go-round.	ever, never, before, often, sometimes, once, ~times
결과	• He has bought a used car.	go, come, leave, lose, buy
계속	• She has studied Anglo-American literature for seven years.	for, since

Grammar Plus +

• for / since
- **for**: '~동안'의 뜻으로 사건이 일어난 시간의 길이를 나타낸다.
- **since**: '~이후로'의 뜻으로 사건이 시작된 시점을 나타낸다.
➡ since 뒤에는 구뿐만 아니라 절도 올 수 있는데, 이때 절에 속해있는 동사의 시제는 과거형으로 한다.
   Grace has studied Latin dance **since** she was twenty years old.

Answer Keys p. 05

A 다음 괄호 안의 단어를 이용하여 문장을 완성하고, 현재완료 시제의 용법을 쓰시오.

1 She ___has___ just _finished_ her homework. (finish)

                                                                   [완료]

2 The boy _____ for a week. (sick) _____

3 _____ you ever _____ this fruit? (eat) _____

4 She _____ her room now. (clean) _____

5 I _____ to Paris twice. (be) _____

6 I _____ already _____ at the party. (arrive) _____

7 They _____ to Korea, so they aren't here. (go)

                                                                  _____

8 She _____ never _____ the car. (drive) _____

9 Tommy _____ the window. (break) _____

10 I _____ Tim since we were young. (know) _____

B 빈칸에 for, since 중 알맞은 것을 쓰시오.

1 I have studied English ___for___ a year.

2 We have visited the volunteer center _____ 2005.

3 She has been a teacher _____ 30 years.

4 I have been here _____ I was five.

5 Has she stayed in LA _____ three months?

6 He has waited for her _____ two hours.

7 The graduation exam has been going on _____ 3 p.m.

현재완료와 과거형

- **현재완료**: 과거의 사건이 현재까지 영향을 미치는 것을 표현할 때 사용한다.
- **과거형**: 과거의 사실을 표현할 때 사용한다.

◆ 현재완료와 과거형

현재완료	과거형
• 과거에 시작되어 현재까지 계속되는 일을 말한다. • I have practiced the piano every single day for five years. [= I still practice the piano.]	• 과거에 시작되어 과거에 끝난 일을 말한다. • I practiced the piano every single day for five years. [= I don't practice the piano.]
• 과거의 불특정한 시점에 일어난 사건을 말하며, 과거의 특정한 때를 가리키는 부사(구)와는 함께 사용하지 않는다. • Have you ever been to China before?	• 과거의 특정한 때를 가리키는 부사(구)와 함께 사용된다. • Did you go to China last year?

 Check up!

Answer Keys p. 05

A 괄호 안에서 알맞은 것을 고르시오.

1 My daughter (is / has been) very sick, but isn't now.

2 She (has studied / studies) Korean history for five months.

3 (Did you eat / Have you ever eaten) pasta before?

4 Long time no see! How (were you / have you been)?

5 The man (has lost / lost) his wallet. He is still looking for it.

6 We remember it (didn't snow / hasn't snowed) last weekend.

7 I (has known/ knew) her. She was my classmate.

8 Did you (go / have been) to England last month?

9 Jane (has lived / lived) in the house since she was a middle school student.

10 He (made / has made) the cake yesterday for his mom.

현재완료 진행형

• **현재완료 진행형**: 과거에 시작한 동작이 현재까지 계속되고 있는 것을 뜻한다.

1. 현재완료 진행형

형태	1, 2인칭 단수/복수	3인칭 단수
평서문	have been + 동사-ing	has been + 동사-ing
부정문	have not been + 동사-ing	has not been + 동사-ing
의문문	Have + 주어 + been + 동사-ing~?	Has + 주어 + been + 동사-ing~?

• It **has been raining** since this morning.

• My brother **has not been studying** since he came back home.

• **A** **Have** you **been watching** TV for three hours?
  B Yes, I have. / No, I haven't.

2. 진행형을 쓰지 않는 동사: 상태를 나타내는 동사는 진행형으로 쓰지 않는다.

소유	have, own, belong
감정	like, love, prefer, hate, respect, want, wish, need, admire
인식	believe, forget, know, remember, think, understand, realize, appreciate
지각	see, smell, taste, hear, feel
기타	seem, appear, consist, contain, keep, continue

• This smartphone **belongs** to me.

• Mike doesn't **know** what Jack is saying.

• This grammar book **consists** of 15 chapters.

※ 동작을 나타내는 의미로 쓰이는 경우 진행형으로 사용할 수 있다.

• Hannah and I **were having** lunch together.

• We **are thinking** about Newton's theory.

A 주어진 동사를 이용하여 현재완료 진행형 문장을 완성하시오.

1 She _____ has been making _____ a dress for three hours. (make)

2 I _____ for the graduation exam since
   12 o'clock. (study)

3 He _____ the book since yesterday. (read)

4 I _____ my lost bag. (look for)

5 We _____ soccer for 30 minutes. (play)

6 They _____ for the party since last week.
   (prepare)

7 How long _____ she _____ her homework? (do)

8 _____ Molly _____ the piano? (play)

9 Sam _____ to that music. (not, listen)

B 다음 밑줄 친 부분을 바르게 고치시오.

1 I <u>have been knowing</u> her.   ➡ _____ have known _____

2 She <u>fixes</u> this computer for an hour.   ➡ _____

3 It <u>has seeming</u> so difficult to solve.   ➡ _____

4 John <u>studies</u> math since two o'clock.   ➡ _____

5 She <u>has</u> lunch with him for 20 minutes. ➡ _____

6 They <u>have been wanting</u> to go hiking. ➡ _____

7 Kelly <u>has been not</u> finishing her work lately.
                                            ➡ _____

8 <u>Have they are</u> studying English for five months?
                                            ➡ _____

9 Mario and Johnny <u>has been</u> fishing for two hours.
                                            ➡ _____

2-9 과거완료

- **과거완료**: 과거의 한 시점을 기준으로 그 이전부터 과거 사이에 일어난 일을 나타낸다.
- **과거완료 진행형**: 과거의 한 시점을 기준으로 그 이전에 진행 중이었던 동작을 나타내기 위해 사용한다.

1. 과거완료의 형태 [had + 과거분사]

had + 과거분사	

대과거   과거   현재

평서문	had + 과거분사	• The show had <u>already</u> started when we got to the theater.
부정문	had not + 과거분사	• I had not played soccer <u>before</u> I joined the team.
의문문	Had + 주어 + 과거분사 ~?	• Had she <u>ever</u> bought cell phones before?

2. 과거완료 진행형

평서문	had been + 동사-ing	• My sister and I had been cleaning before the doorbell rang.
부정문	had not been + 동사-ing	• Sammy had not been expecting a letter from Gloria.
의문문	Had + 주어 + been + 동사-ing ~?	• Had he been waiting for her since 4 o'clock?

Grammar Plus +

- **before / after**: 시간의 앞뒤 순서를 정확하게 알 수 있는 접속사의 경우 과거형을 사용하기도 한다.
  Raemi **had** sometimes **swum** in the river **before** she hurt her legs.

  = Raemi sometimes **swam** in the river **before** she hurt her legs.

- 과거완료는 '대과거'라고도 하며, 과거 이전의 과거를 표현하며 상태나 동작의 앞뒤 시간을 나타내기도 한다.
  Jim **was** very tired because he **had stayed** up all night for two days.
  <u>과거</u>   <u>과거 이전</u>

A 괄호 안에 주어진 동사를 이용하여 과거와 과거완료 중 알맞은 것을 채우시오.

1 The train ___had___ already ___left___ when
   I arrived at the station. (leave)

2 He _____ an English teacher. (become)

3 I _____ him before I came to the party. (meet)

4 She couldn't buy the bag because she _____ to bring
   her wallet. (forget)

5 Jina _____ the ring that her boyfriend had given to
   her. (lost)

6 After he _____ his homework, he started to play the
   game. (finish)

7 The festival _____ when we arrived there. (end)

8 I _____ until I got a job. (sad)

9 Mom _____ already _____ a meal, so she
   didn't want to have more. (have)

10 When I came home, my son _____ asleep. (fall)

B 다음 주어진 동사를 과거완료 진행형으로 바꾸어 문장을 완성하시오.

1 Mary _had been thinking_ about the problem for an hour. (think)

2 I _____ math since finishing school. (not, study)

3 _____ he _____ for Helen for two hours? (wait)

4 They _____ the social issue when I came back.
   (discuss)

5 He _____ here since he graduated. (work)

6 _____ she _____ the musical 'Cats'? (enjoy)

7 Jinny _____ the bill after losing her job. (not, pay)

8 Jack _____ alone until he married. (live)

9 She _____, so her boss was angry. (not, work)

10 We _____ as a punishment for breaking the
   window. (run)

2-10 미래완료

- **미래완료**: 미래의 어느 시점까지 완료될 것으로 예상되는 일을 나타낸다.
- **미래완료 진행형**: 미래의 어느 시점까지 계속 진행 중인 것을 나타낼 때 사용한다.

1. 미래완료

평서문	will have + 과거분사	• I will have baked this cake by 7 o'clock.
부정문	will not have + 과거분사	• Romeo will not have bought a car for a while.
의문문	Will + 주어 + have + 과거분사 ~?	• Will he have arrived here before the concert starts?

2. 미래완료 진행형

평서문	will have been + 동사-ing	• She will have been reading for two hours before dinner.
부정문	will not have been + 동사-ing	• We will not have been cooking dinner by the time our big brother comes.
의문문	Will + 주어 + have been + 동사-ing?	• Will you have been waiting for him by the time I arrive?

☆Check up!

Answer Keys p. 06

A 다음 우리말과 뜻이 같도록 주어진 단어를 이용하여 문장을 알맞게 완성하시오.

1 나는 5시 전에 내 차를 수리하게 될 것이다. (fix)

➡ I ___will have fixed___ my car before five o'clock.

2 내일 저녁이 되면 아빠가 집에 돌아오실 것이다. (come back)

➡ My father _____ home by tomorrow evening.

3 그는 내일이면 6주동안 공부하게 되는거니? (study)

➡ _____ he _____ for six weeks by tomorrow?

4 이 영화를 한 번 더 보면 난 네 번 보게 되는 것이다. (watch)

➡ If I watch this movie again, I _____ it four times.

5 경기가 시작되기 전에 그들은 여기 도착하지 못하게 될 것이다. (arrive)

➡ They _____ here before the game starts.

Practice More II

Answer Keys p. 06

A 괄호 안에서 알맞은 것을 고르시오.

1 The boys have (did / done) a lot of homework.

2 Have you (talked / talking) to a foreigner on the street?

3 We have lived here (for / since) seven years.

4 I (met / have met) him twice before.

5 The men (worked / have been working) since this morning.

6 I (have seen / am seeing) the famous movie many times.

7 The boy next door has (broken / been breaking) the window.

8 Jane had already left when I (had arrived / arrived) there.

9 I (had fallen asleep / am sleeping) when my mom came back home.

10 My family has (been / gone) to the island before.

B 주어진 지시대로 문장을 바꾸어 쓰시오.

1 Alex starts to learn how to bake bread. (과거완료)

　➡ _____Alex had started to learn how to bake bread._____

2 They didn't stay in the hotel. (현재완료)

　➡ _____

3 She was weak until the age of fifteen. (과거완료)

　➡ _____

4 The boy wakes up at seven. (미래완료)

　➡ _____

5 I knew Helen when I was young. (현재완료)

　➡ _____

6 He left the house before she called him. (과거완료)

　➡ _____

7 It snowed last week. (현재완료 진행)

　➡ _____

8 He has studied for an hour before he came. (과거완료)

　➡ _____

9 We join the soccer club. (과거완료)

　➡ _____

Practice More II

C 밑줄 친 부분을 어법에 맞게 고치시오.

1 Hurry up, our bus <u>has left</u> in an hour.

     leaves

2 I have been <u>painted</u> the fence since two o'clock.

3 I <u>finished</u> my homework before the bell rang.

4 He lost the hat his mom <u>has given</u> to him.

5 Nick remembers the girl whom he <u>has met</u> yesterday.

6 I <u>will going to</u> get it now.

7 She <u>played</u> baseball since she was five.

8 Have you ever <u>reading</u> 'Romeo and Juliet'?

9 Max didn't want to see the movie because he <u>saw</u> it before.

10 I <u>have taken</u> care of Tim's dog when he was in LA.

D 우리말 해석에 맞게 주어진 단어를 바르게 배열하여 문장을 완성하시오.

1 Joy는 내가 주었던 그 시계를 잃어버렸다.

   (Joy, her, lost, I, which, given, watch, to, the, had)

   ➡   *Joy lost the watch which I had given to her.*

2 나는 한 달 전부터 스페인어를 배우기로 결심해왔다.

   (I've, learn, ago, month, decided, to, one, Spanish)

   ➡

3 나의 아버지는 내가 초등학생 때 7년간 일본에서 공부하는 중이었다.
(My father, studying, seven, had, for, been, years, in Japan)

➡ _____ when I
was in elementary school.

4 민수는 3년 전에 대전으로 이사 가서 지금까지 거기서 살고 있다.
(Minsu, lived, moved, three, ago, to, and, there, he, Daejeon, years, has, since)

➡ _____

5 내 여동생이 나간 이후로 내가 이 방을 쭉 사용하고 있다.
(I, this room, used, moved, have, since, out, my sister)

➡ _____

6 그들은 내일 기말고사를 위해 10시부터 공부를 하고 있다.
(they, ten, studying, have, final exam, been, for, since, tomorrow's, o'clock)

➡ _____

7 4시간 동안 비가 계속 내리고 있다.
(it, four, has, for, been, hours, raining)

➡ _____

8 John은 내 딸과 몇 번 전화 통화한 적이 있다.
(John, several, has, daughter, on the phone, talked, times, my, to)

➡ _____

9 나는 3시간 동안 그를 기다리고 있는 중이었다.
(I, three hours, have, for, him, for, waiting, been)

➡ _____

10 Linda는 2주 전에 산 드레스를 엄마께 전해 드렸다.
(Linda, before, her mom, two, gave, she, that, weeks, bought, a dress, had)

➡ _____

내신 최다 출제 유형

01 다음 빈칸에 알맞은 말을 고르시오. [출제 예상 80%]

> I do like being a dancer, but ever since I was a kid, I _____ drawing.

① have loved   ② loved
③ had loved   ④ love
⑤ loving

02 다음 보기 와 현재완료의 용법이 같은 것을 고르시오.

[출제 예상 90%]

보기
> Henry has always wanted to help poor people.

① Her uncle has just come back from Russia.
② We have studied English since we were 12.
③ I have never spoken Japanese before.
④ We have been to Thailand four times.
⑤ Has she ever eaten Mexican food?

03 다음 중 어법상 옳은 것을 고르시오. [출제 예상 90%]

① Mr. McFly had lived here since last year.
② She has studied for three hours yesterday.
③ Ms. Grace has been reading the storybook for two hours.
④ Elly said she have never been to Jeju Island.
⑤ I have been studying math for 4 p.m.

04 다음 빈칸에 들어갈 말이 순서대로 바르게 짝지어진 것을 고르시오. [출제 예상 80%]

> My family is on vacation in California.
> For a week, the sun has been _____.
> We have been _____ everything.

① shining − enjoying
② shining − enjoyed
③ shiny − enjoy
④ shining − to enjoy
⑤ shin − enjoy

05 다음 두 문장과 같은 뜻이 되도록 알맞은 문장을 쓰시오.

[출제 예상 85%]

> Peter started playing the drums three hours ago.
> He is still playing the drums.

➡ _____

06 다음 우리말을 조건에 따라 영어로 바르게 옮겨 쓰시오.

[출제 예상 90%]

> 우리가 공항에 도착했을 때 비행기는 이미 이륙해 버렸다.

〈조건〉 ① arrive, take off, already를
　　　　　 사용하여 만들 것
　　　② 먼저 일어난 일의 시제를 생각할 것

➡ When we _____

_____

[01~02] 다음 중 동사 변화가 <u>잘못된</u> 것을 고르시오.

01
① break – broke – broken
② sell – sold – sold
③ spend – spent – spent
④ write – wrote – wrote
⑤ buy – bought – bought

02
① teach – taught – taught
② run – ran – run
③ fall – fell – fallen
④ hide – hid – hidden
⑤ think – though – though

[03~04] 다음 밑줄 친 부분을 바르게 고친 것을 고르시오.

03

> Rob didn't want to bungee jump because he <u>already did</u> it.

① has already done
② had already done
③ already done
④ have already done
⑤ is already done

04

> When I saw her at the park, she found something. I thought she <u>lose</u> it.

① loses
② has lost
③ had lost
④ is losing
⑤ was losing

[05~06] 다음 문장의 밑줄 친 부분과 용법이 같은 것을 고르시오.

05 ★★★

> She <u>has been</u> to China twice with her family.

① He <u>has lost</u> his watch.
② They <u>have</u> never <u>tasted</u> such delicious food.
③ We <u>have</u> already <u>cleaned</u> our house.
④ I <u>have</u> just <u>called</u> him.
⑤ They <u>have lived</u> in Daegu for 3 years.

06

> I <u>have read</u> the series three times.

① I <u>have lived</u> in this town for 12 years.
② She <u>has gone</u> to Canada.
③ The actor <u>has visited</u> Korea many times.
④ They <u>have finished</u> their homework.
⑤ My friends and I <u>have lost</u> the invitation cards.

[07~08] 다음 빈칸에 들어갈 말이 알맞게 짝지어진 것을 고르시오.

07

> Yesterday I _____ a book which he _____ a month before.

① borrow – have bought
② borrow – was bought
③ borrowed – have bought
④ borrowed – had bought
⑤ have borrowed – have bought

08

> A Have you finished the report of
>   Korean history, _____?
> B Yes, I've _____ finished it.

① already – yet ② yet – already
③ already – already ④ yet – before
⑤ since– yet

[09~10] 주어진 우리말에 맞게 빈칸에 들어갈 알맞은
것을 고르시오.

09

> 그는 런던으로 떠나버렸다.
> ➡ He _____ for London.

① leaves ② left ③ is left
④ has left ⑤ have left

10

> Betty는 내가 그녀에게 주었던 시계를 잃어
> 버렸다.
> ➡ Betty lost the watch which
>   I _____ to her.

① gave ② had given
③ has given ④ given
⑤ is given

11 다음 괄호 안의 주어진 단어의 올바른 형태를 고르
시오.

> Timmy (be) sick since he went to the
> beach.

① is ② have been ③ was
④ had been ⑤ has been

12 다음 두 문장을 한 문장으로 표현한 것 중 올바른
것을 고르시오.

> I moved to Sinsa-dong two years ago.
> I live in Sinsa-dong now.

① I have lived in Sinsa-dong for two years.
② I have lived in Sinsa-dong since two
   years.
③ I had lived in Sinsa-dong for two years.
④ I have been living in Sinsa-dong since
   two years.
⑤ I have been live in Sinsa-dong for two
   years.

13 다음 두 문장의 뜻이 같도록 할 때 빈칸에 알맞은
것을 고르시오.

> She is going to go shopping for James
> tonight.
> = She _____ for James tonight.

① shop ② shopped
③ is shopping ④ has shopped
⑤ had shopped

[14~15] 다음 빈칸에 들어갈 말로 올바른 것을 고르시오.

14

> I couldn't taste the Spanish food
> because my baby _____ it.

① spilled ② spills
③ has spilled ④ had spilled
⑤ spilling

15

There was a big fire. The firefighters said that a spark _____ the fire.

① started   ② starting
③ had started   ④ have started
⑤ has started

[16~17] 다음 중 밑줄 친 부분이 어법상 맞지 <u>않는</u> 것을 고르시오.

★★★
16 ① We <u>had been reading</u> it for two hours when he came.
② They <u>will have been studying</u> Chinese characters for three months by next month.
③ I <u>had seen</u> the movie three times if I see it once again.
④ It <u>has been raining</u> since last night.
⑤ She <u>has been jogging</u> for 30 minutes.

17 ① The girls <u>will help</u> their mother.
② Robby and Jenny <u>is not going to study</u> together.
③ I <u>won't join</u> the dancing club.
④ She <u>is going to leave</u> for Chicago on Monday.
⑤ They <u>are going to visit</u> my country.

[18~20] 다음 대화의 빈칸에 알맞은 것을 고르시오.

18

A I wonder if _____ tomorrow.
B Don't worry. He will win.

① Billy win the game
② Billy won the game
③ Billy wins the game
④ Billy has won the game.
⑤ Billy will win the game.

19

A Have you ever read 'King Lear'?
B Yes, _____.

① I had read it once.
② I had never read it.
③ I haven't ever read it.
④ I have read it several times.
⑤ I read it.

20

A _____?
B We're planning to go hiking with our club.

① Where did you go last weekend?
② What are you going to do this weekend?
③ Where are you going now?
④ What do you usually do on weekends?
⑤ When did you go hiking?

[21~22] 다음 밑줄 친 부분의 쓰임이 바른 것을 <u>모두</u> 고르시오.

★★★
21
① He hasn't <u>overcome</u> the difficulties yet.
② The authority has <u>forbade</u> reading those books.
③ I <u>shook</u> hands with our school principal, Mrs. Jude.
④ She <u>lied</u> the book on the table for a while.
⑤ Oil prices have <u>rose</u> 15% since this month last year.

★★★
22
① I <u>have already finished</u> my homework an hour ago.
② We <u>have often visited</u> the orphanage last year.
③ I <u>have never been</u> to any foreign countries.
④ He <u>has stayed</u> at my house last night.
⑤ The price <u>has been</u> going up by 5%.

23 다음 중 어법상 옳지 <u>않은</u> 것을 <u>모두</u> 고르시오.
① Jen said they had passed the exam.
② They are so glad that their son's dream has come true.
③ I have been sick since last night.
④ His name tag have been stuck on the bag.
⑤ The pond has been froze for a month.

★★★
24 다음 중 어법상 옳은 것을 <u>모두</u> 고르시오.
① How have you were?
② Everybody said he had failed the test.
③ I've decided to learn Japanese.
④ I didn't know that he has asked the question.
⑤ She has never see such a cute koala.

25 다음 우리말과 뜻이 같도록 바르게 영작한 것을 고르시오.

> 그곳에 도착하면 그들이 널 기다리고 있을 거야.

① They will wait for you when you get there.
② They will be waiting you when you get there.
③ They are waiting for you when you get there.
④ They will be waiting for you when you get there.
⑤ They will be waiting for you when you'll get there.

★★★
26 다음 밑줄 친 부분의 쓰임이 나머지 넷과 <u>다른</u> 것을 고르시오.
① Sammy <u>is typing</u> his report.
② Jane and Tina <u>are cooking</u> in the kitchen.
③ We <u>are meeting</u> the singer this afternoon.
④ My parents <u>are watching</u> a movie together.
⑤ I <u>am watering</u> flowers in the garden.

27 다음 빈칸에 들어갈 말이 바르게 짝지어진 것을
고르시오.

- Dad tells me to go on a diet,
  but I _____.
- The weather reporter says it
  _____ tomorrow afternoon.
---

① won't - will windy
② won't - is windy
③ will - will be windy
④ will - windy
⑤ won't - will be windy

◇◇◇◇◇◇◇◇◇◇ 서술형 평가 ◇◇◇◇◇◇◇◇◇◇

[28~30] 다음 괄호 안에 주어진 단어를 알맞은 형태로
고쳐 쓰시오.

28

A What is she reading?
B She's reading a book about Chinese
  food. She _____ _____
  _____ it since this morning.
  (read)

➡ _____

29

Since I was eight years old, I _____
_____ _____ in playing the
piano. (be interested)

➡ _____

30

Her sons and daughters _____
_____ _____ the house very
hard for three hours. (clean)

➡ _____

[31~32] 다음 주어진 문장의 어색한 부분을 찾아
고쳐 쓰시오.

★★★
31

Amy has taken care of my cat when
I visited London for a month.

_____ ➡ _____

32

The patient has suffered from a cardiac
disorder since several years.

_____ ➡ _____

(Note) a cardiac disorder 심장 질환

[33~35] 다음의 두 문장을 한 문장으로 바르게 고쳐
쓰시오.

★★★
33

Susie ate breakfast first.
Then she took a shower.

➡ _____ after
_____

중간 기말고사 예상문제

★★★
34

> I began waiting for a taxi twenty minutes ago.
> I am still waiting for a taxi.

➡ _____

35

> Alie's father gave the glove to him.
> He lost it.

➡ _____

[36~37] 우리말을 참고하여 빈칸에 알맞은 말을 쓰시오.

36

> 나는 드디어 나의 할아버지가 나에게 특별한 선물을 주었던 것을 기억했다.

➡ I finally _____ that my grandfather _____ me a special gift.

37

> 우리가 공항에 도착했을 때 Tim은 이미 떠나버린 뒤였다.

➡ When we _____ at the airport, Tim _____ already _____.

[38~40] 다음 괄호 안의 단어를 바르게 배열하여 문장을 완성하시오.

★★★
38

> (my / the / grandmother / watering / garden / be / will)

➡ _____

★★★
39

> (Tom / homework / his / just / has / started)

➡ _____

40

> (Elly / not / when / had / started / yet)

➡ _____ Tom arrived.

03

Chapter
조동사

Point Check I

◆ **조동사 :** be동사나 일반동사 앞에서 특정한 의미를 더해 주는 보조 동사를 말한다. 조동사는 동사원형과
함께 쓰이고, 주어의 수와 인칭에 관계없이 항상 같은 형태를 가진다.

1. do

조동사 do	일반동사의 부정문과 의문문에 사용	• I do not think so. • Does she live here?
대동사 do	앞에서 언급한 내용의 반복을 피하기 위해 사용	• **A** I got a good grade on the test. 　**B** So did I. 　　　[did = got a grade on the test]
강조를 위한 do	강조를 위한 do	• We do think Mr. White is kind.

2. can / may / must / have to

can	• Could you help us a little? [요청] • That gentleman can be her father-in-law. [추측] • You can lose weight if you exercise hard. [가능성] • I can make a model warship very well. [능력]
may	• This may (might) be very expensive in this shop. [추측] • You may take a shower first. [허가]
must	• You must finish your homework before your mom comes. [의무] • You must not kick a ball in front of the window. [금지]
have to	• We have to be quiet in the library. [의무] • She doesn't have to eat some dessert. [불필요]

Lesson 3-1 do

- **do** : 'do'는 부정문이나 의문문을 만드는 데 필요한 조동사 역할을 하기도 하고, '∼하다'의 뜻을 가진 동사의 역할을 하기도 한다.

1. 조동사 do : 일반동사를 도와주는 역할을 하며 뜻은 없다.

- We **do** not believe that is true.
- **Do** they want to take a field trip to the farm?

2. 대동사 do : 앞에 있는 문장이나 절에 나온 동사(구)의 반복을 피하기 위해 사용된다.

- **A** I think Willy had to listen to his mother.
  B She <u>did</u>. So she isn't here.
  (did = listened to her mother)
- **A** I like to sing songs.
  B So **do** I. (do = like to sing songs)
- **A** She doesn't like to study math.
  B Neither **do** I. (do = like to study math)
  → 'neither'이 부정의 의미를 가지고 있기 때문에 뒤의 동사에 'do'가 온다.

3. 강조의 do : 동사의 의미를 강조하기 위해 써 준다.

- Klaud **does** <u>tell</u> you the truth.
- I **do** hope you are happy with him.

Answer Keys p. 08

A 다음 밑줄 친 부분을 바르게 고쳐 쓰시오.

1 I <u>met not</u> her yesterday.
➡ *didn't meet*

2 Jerry and Mike <u>does like</u> pizza and hamburgers.
➡ _____

3 Mr. and Mrs. Black <u>not teaches</u> English at Seoul National University.
➡ _____

4 **A** She acts politely. **B** So <u>am</u> I.
➡ _____

5 Wendy <u>do loves</u> her children.
➡ _____

6 Scarlet <u>does makes</u> dresses very well.

➡ _____

7 The little princess <u>do laughed</u> at a frog.

➡ _____

8 Liz <u>doesn't like</u> to speak in front of many people when she was young.

➡ _____

9 A Jamie couldn't climb a tree when he was young.
  B Neither <u>can</u> I.

➡ _____

10 Alice <u>did likes</u> go shopping with her mother every month.

➡ _____

B 'do'를 알맞은 형태로 바꾸어 빈칸을 채우시오. (정답이 두 개인 것은 <u>모두</u> 쓰시오.)

1 James ___does/did___ not know her name and phone number.

2 She _____ have a diamond necklace.

3 _____ they have any plans for this summer vacation?

4 My school teachers _____ encourage students to speak English well.

5 A Mary sold her shoes to buy new ones.

  B So _____ I.

6 I _____ hope this road takes me home.

7 Jessica _____ not study at all. She likes to sing and dance.

8 A He doesn't come back this month.
  B Neither _____ his brother.

3-2 can (could)

• **can**: 능력, 허락, 요청, 가능성 등의 의미를 나타낼 수 있다. '~할 수 있다'의 뜻은 'be able to'와 바꿔 쓸 수 있다.

1. can _ 능력: [can + 동사원형] ~할 수 있다

현재	• We can go to the movie theater by bus. • They cannot take a nap. • Can she have a little break?
과거	• We could finish this research in 30 minutes. • They could not take an art class. • Could she have lunch this afternoon?
미래	미래형 'will'과 'can'은 모두 조동사이기 때문에 함께 사용할 수 없다. '능력'을 의미하는 미래형 표현은 'be able to'를 사용한다. • She will be able to draw him fast. • Will you be able to catch the bus?

2. can과 could의 다른 용법

허락, 요청 ~해도 될까요?/~해 주세요	• Can I carry the box for Sally? • Could you finish this before she comes?
추측 ~일지도 모른다 / ~일 리 없다	• The tall man can be our new coach. • The woman cannot be our new teacher.
가능성 ~할 가능성이 있다	• Don't worry. This event can happen again.

➡ cannot = can't / could not = couldn't / will not = won't

➡ 'Could you~?'는 'Can you~?'보다 더 공손한 표현이다.

Answer Keys p. 08

A 다음 두 문장의 의미가 같도록 빈칸에 알맞은 말을 넣으시오.

1 Helen can dance very well.

➡ Helen _____*is able to dance*_____ very well.

2 Wendy and Mike are able to stop playing games.

➡ Wendy and Mike _____ playing games.

3 Sara couldn't catch the ball.

➡ Sara _____ the ball.

4 We didn't know we could win the game.

➡ We didn't know we _____ the game.

5 Were you able to drive a car?

➡ _____ you _____ a car?

B 다음 우리말을 괄호 안의 지시어를 사용하여 바르게 영작하시오.

1 Emily는 다음에는 시험에 통과할 수 있을 거야. (be able to)

➡ _____*Emily will be able to pass the exam next time.*_____

2 나는 어렸을 때 자전거를 탈 수 없었어. (can, when)

➡ _____

3 그가 우리 그룹의 리더일 리가 없어. (can, be)

➡ _____

4 숙제하기 전에 나를 좀 도와주겠니? (can, doing your homework)

➡ _____

5 그는 그녀에게 무슨 일이 일어났는지 설명할 수 있을까요?
(can, what happened)

➡ _____

3-3 may (might)

- **may**: '허락, 불확실한 추측'의 의미를 가지고 있다. 'may'가 허락의 의미로 사용될 때는 'can'과 바꿔 쓸 수 있다.

- **might**: 'may'의 과거형으로 쓰이기도 하지만, 실현 가능성이 'may'보다 더 희박한 불확실한 추측을 나타낼 때 쓰이기도 한다.

◆ **may / might**: [may (might) + 동사원형]

추측	~일지도 모른다 아마 ~일 것이다	• This may help you to find your bag. • They may not be in the gym. • We might not totally understand what it means.

허가	~해도 좋다	• You may go now if you want.
		• May I help you?
		  – Yes, you may.
		  – Yes, please.
		  – No, you may not.
		  – No, you must not.

➡ 'might'는 'may'보다 불확실한 추측을 나타낸다.
➡ 'must not'은 'may not'보다 더 강한 금지의 표현이다.

Answer Keys p. 08

A 다음 중 어법상 <u>어색한</u> 부분을 찾아 고쳐 쓰시오.

1 Jimmy may goes camping with his friends.

<u> goes </u> ➡ <u> go </u>

2 May we eats some cookies now? <u>   </u> ➡ <u>   </u>

3 She doesn't may go to the party. <u>   </u> ➡ <u>   </u>

4 Do may I take a test one more time?

<u>   </u> ➡ <u>   </u>

5 They are may be models. <u>   </u> ➡ <u>   </u>

6 I not might fail this exam. <u>   </u> ➡ <u>   </u>

7 He may arrives at the airport this evening.

<u>   </u> ➡ <u>   </u>

8 We might studied in the library together.

<u>   </u> ➡ <u>   </u>

3-4 must / have to

> • **must**: 강한 추측, 의무를 나타내는 말로 '~해야만 한다'의 뜻을 가지고 있다. 강한 의무를 나타낼 때는 'have to'와 바꿔 쓸 수 있다.
>
> • **have to**: 강한 의무를 나타내며 'must'와 바꿔 쓸 수 있다. 부정형의 경우 '~할 필요가 없다'는 뜻으로 쓰인다.

◈ **must / have to:** [must + 동사원형], [have to + 동사원형]

must 의무: ~해야만 한다 추측: ~임에 틀림없다 금지: ~해서는 안 된다	긍정 must + 동사원형	• Jessy has been crying for an hour. She must <u>be</u> very sad. [추측] • They must <u>wear</u> their uniforms. [의무]
	부정 must not + 동사원형	• We must not <u>cheat</u> on the test. [금지]
have to 의무: ~해야만 한다 금지: ~할 필요가 없다	긍정 have to + 동사원형	• Becky has to <u>listen</u> to her teacher. • He had to <u>make</u> his bed after waking up.
	부정 do(es) not have to + 동사원형	• You don't have to <u>work</u> this weekend. • Jessy didn't have to <u>buy</u> a new cell phone last month. • He won't have to <u>go</u> fishing next month.

➡ 'must'는 과거형이 없으므로 과거를 표현할 때는 'had to'를 사용한다.

➡ must not = mustn't

➡ 'do(es) n't have to'는 '~할 필요가 없다'는 뜻으로 'must not'과는 뜻이 전혀 다르다.
   = do(es) n't need to, need not [불필요:~할 필요가 없다]

A 다음 밑줄 친 부분을 must 또는 have to를 넣어 다시 쓰시오.

1 Most students in Korea <u>wear</u> uniforms in middle school.

➡ wear : <u>_must (have to) wear_</u>

2 Jennifer will <u>wait</u> in line to ride the roller coaster like everyone else.

➡ wait : _____

3 Mary doesn't <u>take</u> an art lesson today.

➡ take : _____

4 Many children <u>go</u> to several academies after school these days.

➡ go : _____

5 In class, students <u>are</u> quiet and listen to their teacher carefully.

➡ are : _____

B 다음 괄호 안의 단어를 바르게 배열하여 문장을 완성하시오.

1 Eddie didn't eat breakfast. (he / hungry / be / must / now)

➡ _____ _He must be hungry now._ _____

2 (some / uniforms/ don't / wear / have to / students)

➡ _____

3 (we / on / must / not / play / the / grass)

➡ _____

4 (Harry / Maria / and / a couple / be / must). They are always together.

➡ _____

5 (the / doctor / that / I / have to / says / for / health / exercise / my)

➡ _____

6 (every / go to / Sunday / church / he / has to / morning)

➡ _____

7 (he / test / have / a / not / need)

➡ _____

8 (must / she / the / every day / dogs / feed)

➡ _____

Practice More I

A 다음 밑줄 친 부분과 바꿔 쓸 수 있는 표현을 쓰시오.

1   <u>Can</u> I ask you a question about your comment?

(*May*   )

2   Everyone <u>has to</u> fasten their seatbelt in a vehicle.

(   )

3   You <u>may</u> use my electronic dictionary. (   )

4   I <u>couldn't</u> believe it when I heard the news. (   )

5   She <u>could</u> escape from the hole. (   )

6   She <u>doesn't have to</u> tell them everything. (   )

7   We <u>have to</u> cross the street when the light is green.

(   )

8   You <u>don't have to</u> hide your feelings. (   )

9   I <u>can't</u> give you the answer to the questions. (   )

B 다음 중 어법상 틀린 곳을 찾아 고쳐 쓰시오.

1   She may well being proud of her family.

_____*being*_____ ➡ _____*be*_____

2   We may not copies the book. _____ ➡ _____

3   They will must wear sunglasses to protect their eyes from the sunlight. _____ ➡ _____

4   Sammy is strong. He could lift that heavy box.

_____ ➡ _____

5   I had to read this book until I understand it perfectly.

_____ ➡ _____

6   Sara not needs retest this time.

_____ ➡ _____

7   People will must wear a mask when the yellow dust blows.

_____ ➡ _____

8   John does tells me the truth. _____ ➡ _____

9   **A** I don't like his hair style. **B** Neither did I.

_____ ➡ _____

C 다음 괄호 안의 말을 바르게 배열하여 문장을 완성하시오.

1 (does / act / love / to)

→ Elly _____*does love to act*_____ like a princess.

2 (have / in / line / to / wait)

→ People in front of the roller coaster _____.

3 (play / not / must)

→ Children _____ in the street.

4 (can / twenty / walk / miles)

→ He _____ a day.

5 (not / repair / may / radio / the)

→ You _____.

6 (did / his students / practice / encourage / to)

→ Mr. Smith _____ more.

7 (be / buy / to / able)

→ She will _____ a guitar.

8 (find / couldn't / the / difference)

→ We _____.

9 (must / not / exercise)

→ You _____ too hard.

10 (don't / buy / have to)

→ I _____ a new camera.

Practice More I

Answer Keys p. 09

D 다음 우리말과 같은 뜻이 되도록 빈칸에 알맞은 말을 쓰시오.

1 우리는 변화하는 시대에 따라야 한다.

➡ We ____*have*____ ____*to*____ keep up with the changing times.

2 그들은 그들의 결정을 바꾸어선 안 된다.

➡ They _____ _____ _____ their decisions.

3 원한다면 당신은 이곳에 머물러도 된다.

➡ You _____ _____ here if you want.

4 그렇게 긴 여행을 하고 나서 그는 피곤한 것이 틀림없다.

➡ He _____ _____ _____ after such a long journey.

5 당신의 휴대전화를 빌릴 수 있을까요?

➡ _____ I _____ your cell phone?

6 아이들 중 몇몇이 창문을 깰지도 모른다.

➡ Some of the children _____ _____ the window.

7 비가 너무 많이 왔기 때문에 나는 택시를 타야 했다.

➡ I _____ _____ _____ a taxi because it was raining a lot.

8 나는 일 년 만에 스페인어를 할 수 있게 될 것이다.

➡ I _____ _____ _____ _____ _____ Spanish in a year.

9 그게 진실일 리가 없어.

➡ It _____ _____ true.

10 James는 파티에 갈 필요가 없다.

➡ James _____ _____ _____ go to the party.

Point Check Ⅱ

◆ **조동사**: be동사나 일반동사 앞에서 특정한 의미를 더해 주는 보조 동사를 말한다. 조동사는 동사원형과 함께 쓰이고, 주어의 수와 인칭에 관계없이 항상 같은 형태를 가진다.

1. 조동사 will / would : [will(would) + 동사원형]

미래형 will ~할 것이다	• We will <u>watch</u> Shakespeare's 'King Lear'.
Will (Would) you + 동사원형~? ~해 주시겠어요?	• Will you please <u>turn</u> off the faucet?
would like + 명사 ~을 원하다	• Amy would like some chocolate cake.
would like to + 동사원형 ~을 하고 싶다	• Andy would like to <u>go</u> fishing.
would rather + 동사원형 차라리 ~하는 편이 낫다	• I would rather <u>say</u> everything honestly.

2. should / ought to / had better

should / ought to 의무: ~해야 한다 추측: ~일 것이다	• Thomas should (ought to) <u>practice</u> more for the game. [의무] • James should not (ought not to) <u>take</u> a train. [추측]
had better 충고: ~하는 게 낫다	• You had better <u>take</u> this medicine.

3. would / used to : [would / used to + 동사원형] ~하곤 했다

과거의 행위를 나타낼 때 'would'와 'used to' 모두 사용

• Tommy and Bill climbed tall trees before, but they don't anymore.
➡ [would] Tommy and Bill **would** <u>climb</u> tall trees.
➡ [used to] Tommy and Bill **used to** <u>climb</u> tall trees.

4. 조동사 + have + 과거분사

should have + 과거분사 ~했어야 했다	**may have** + 과거분사 ~했을지도 모른다
must have + 과거분사 ~였던 것이 틀림없다	**cannot have** + 과거분사 ~했을 리가 없다

3-5 will (would)

- **will**: 미래에 대한 예측, 의지 또는 요청을 나타낼 때 사용한다.
- **would**: 'will'의 과거형으로 쓰이기도 하지만, 'Would you~?'의 형태로 '~하실 수 있나요?'라고 상대방에게 정중하게 요청할 때도 사용한다.

1. will : [will + 동사원형] ~할 것이다 (미래)

평서문	• She will go to Africa to help the sick and the poor.
부정문	• They will not (=won't) have a party for him.
의문문	• **A** Will you visit Sam's farm this weekend? **B** Yes, I will. / No, I won't.

➡ 미래형 'will'은 'be going to'와 바꿔 쓸 수 있다.

2. will과 would의 용법

Will (Would) you +동사원형~? ~해 주시겠어요?	• Will you please be quiet? = Would you please be quiet?
would like + 명사 ~을 원하다	• Would you like some juice? = Do you want some juice?
would like to +동사원형 ~을 하고 싶다	• Would you like to go to the beach to see the fireworks? = Do you want to go to the beach to see the fireworks?
would rather +동사원형 차라리 ~하는 편이 낫다	• I would rather wait and eat together. ➡ 부정형: [would rather not + 동사원형] 차라리 ~하지 않는게 낫다

➡ will보다는 would가 더 정중한 표현이다. 문장의 끝, 또는 주어 뒤에 please를 붙여주면 더욱 공손한 표현이 된다.

Would you do me a favor, <u>please</u>?
= **Would you** <u>please</u> do me a favor?

A 괄호 안의 말을 참고하여 보기 에서 알맞은 말을 골라 빈칸을 채우시오.

보기
would rather   would   be able to
would like   would like to

1 We ____would rather____ look for ways to get out of this room. (차라리 ~하는 편이 낫다)

2 She _____ exchange this bag for a bigger one. (~하고 싶다)

3 Will you _____ take a trip next month? (~할 수 있다)

4 _____ you like some coffee and cookies? (~하겠습니까?)

5 Jane _____ bake cakes by herself than buy them. (차라리 ~하는 편이 낫다)

6 We _____ some hot water. It's very cold. (~을 원한다)

B 다음 괄호 안의 말을 이용해서 우리말과 같은 뜻이 되도록 문장을 만드시오.

1 나는 잠을 자느니 차라리 운동을 하겠다. (would rather)

➡ I ____would rather exercise than sleep____.

2 버튼 좀 눌러주시겠어요? (would, press)

➡ _____ the button, please?

3 그들은 이번 겨울에 러시아에 갈 것이다. (will, Russia)

➡ They _____ this winter.

4 나는 걷느니 차라리 버스를 타겠다. (would rather)

➡ I _____.

5 세상에서 제일 맛있는 음식을 먹고 싶어. (would like to)

➡ I _____ in the world.

3-6 should / ought to / had better

> · **should/ought to/had better** : 상대방에게 충고나 조언을 해줄 때 주로 사용하며, 약한 의무의 뜻을 갖기도 한다.

◈ **should/ought to/had better**

should / ought to	의무 (~해야 하다)	· This is why you should (ought to) learn Chinese characters. · You should not (ought not to) blame other people thoughtlessly.
	추측 (~일 것이다)	· He should (ought to) be safe. · They should not (ought not to) come back soon.
had better	충고, 권유 (~하는 것이 낫다)	· I think you had better go to him to apologize. · She had better go home early and get some rest.

➡ **should/ought to** : 도덕적인 책임이나 추측을 나타낸다.

➡ **should/ought to 부정형** : should not, ought not to

➡ **had better** : 'should/ought to'와 비슷하지만 더 강한 어조의 표현이다.

➡ **had better 부정형** : had better not

Answer Keys p. 09

A 보기 에서 알맞은 말을 고른 후, should (ought to)를 함께 사용하여 빈칸을 채우시오.

> 보기
> | be | tell | listen | apply |
> |---|---|---|---|
> | apologize | | give | reply |

1 Mary made the same mistake. She ___*should (ought to) listen*___ more carefully.

2 Kelly is very angry at Jim. He _____ to her right now.

3 Why don't you check out the drawers? There _____ colored pencils somewhere.

4 It's my brother's birthday. His friends _____ him many presents.

5 Professor Lee sent an email to me. I _____ to him tomorrow.

would / used to

• **used to / would**: 과거에 반복적으로 일어났던 일에 대해서 표현할 때 사용하며, '~하곤 했다'의 뜻으로 해석한다.

1. would / used to

> • Jenny and I studied English before, but we don't anymore.
>
> ➡ [would] Jenny and I **would** study English.
>
> ➡ [used to] Jenny and I **used to** study English.
>
> • Mr. Jackson played soccer with his young sons before, but he doesn't anymore.
>
> ➡ [would] Mr. Jackson **would** play soccer with his young sons.
>
> ➡ [used to] Mr. Jackson **used to** play soccer with his young sons.

2. 행위가 아닌 과거의 상태를 나타낼 때는 'used to'만을 사용한다.

• Helena was very sick when she was young, but she's healthy now.

➡ [used to] Helena **used to** be very sick when she was young.

Check up!

Answer Keys p. 09

A 다음 빈칸에 used to 또는 would를 넣어 문장을 완성하시오.

1 I _used to (would) get_ up early to read the newspaper. (get)

2 She _____ money to buy toys. (spend)

3 There _____ a stream flowing behind my house. (be)

4 My dog _____ my stuff deep in the ground. (hide)

5 I _____ looking out the window when it rained. (like)

6 Harrison _____ afraid of snakes and worms. (be)

7 My sister and I _____ care of our youngest brother. (take)

8 Jacky _____ in Beijing when he was young. (live)

9 Gina _____ long straight hair when she was a high school student. (have)

조동사 + have + 과거분사

· 조동사 + have + 과거분사: 조동사와 현재완료형을 사용한 표현이다.

◆ 조동사＋have＋과거분사

should have＋과거분사 ~했어야 했다	· They should have studied much harder. · They should not have stayed there for a long time.
must have＋과거분사 ~였던 것이 틀림없다	· She must have been famous in her country. · It must have rained a lot there.
may have＋과거분사 ~했을지도 모른다	· I may have bought the tickets with my credit cards. · He may have remembered her.
cannot have＋과거분사 ~했을 리가 없다	· He cannot have known the answer yet. · You cannot have cleaned the big house alone.

Check up!

Answer Keys p. 10

A 다음 우리말에 맞게 주어진 단어를 이용하여 문장을 완성하시오.

1 우리들은 수업 중에 휴대전화를 사용하지 말았어야 했다.
➡ We ___shouldn't have used___ cell phones in class. (use)

2 그녀가 그런 상황에서 슬펐을 리가 없다.
➡ She _____ sad in that situation. (be)

3 지난밤에 바람이 불었던 것이 틀림없다.
➡ It _____ windy last night. (be)

4 나는 그런 말을 하기 전에 두 번 생각했어야 했다.
➡ I _____ twice before I said such a thing.
(think)

5 우리는 오전에 더 서둘렀어야 했다.
➡ We _____ in the morning. (hurry up)

Practice More II

Answer Keys p. 10

A 괄호 안의 우리말을 참고하여 보기 에서 알맞은 말을 골라 빈칸을 채우시오.

> 보기
>
> used to   should   can   may   must   have to
> would rather   be able to   might   would

1 ___Can___ you carry this heavy box for me? (~해 주시겠어요)

2 She will _____ speak English perfectly soon.
   (~할 수 있다)

3 He _____ to go shopping with her. (결정할지도 모른다)

4 I thought that they _____ in the library together.
   (공부할지도 모른다)

5 We _____ rude to other people. (해서는 안 된다)

6 She _____ wait for him anymore. (~할 필요가 없다)

7 I _____ clean my room than take a nap.
   (차라리 ~하는 것이 낫다)

8 We _____ tell a lie. (~하면 안 된다)

9 Greg _____ play soccer on weekends. (~하곤 했다)

10 Sally _____ quarrel with her sister. (~하곤 했다)

B 다음 중 어법상 어색한 곳을 찾아 바르게 고치시오.

1 You will can pass through this tunnel by car.
   will can ➡ _can_

2 We must take a math lesson yesterday.
   _____ ➡ _____

3 She ought to not eat too much junk food.
   _____ ➡ _____

4 He thought that she may not come to his house.
   _____ ➡ _____

5 I had better study English than go outside to play.
   _____ ➡ _____

6 Sally should have did her best. _____ ➡ _____

Practice More Ⅱ

Answer Keys p. 10

C 다음 괄호 안의 말을 이용해서 우리말과 같은 뜻이 되도록 빈칸을 채우시오.

1 나는 너와 이야기를 하느니 차라리 밖에 나가 운동을 하겠다.
(would rather)

  ➡ I _would rather exercise_ than talk with you.

2 그들은 이번에는 경기를 이길 수 있을 것이다. (will, be able to)

  ➡ They _____ win the game this time.

3 그 농부들은 지난 여름에 홍수로 고통을 겪었던 것이 틀림없다.
(must, have, suffer)

  ➡ The farmers _____ from a flood last summer.

4 우리는 오전에 훨씬 더 일찍 도착했어야 했다. (arrive)

  ➡ We _____ much earlier in the morning.

5 거기 소금 좀 전해 주시겠어요? (would, pass)

  ➡ _____ me the salt, please?

6 그들은 그런 행동을 하기 전에 두 번 생각했어야 했다. (think)

  ➡ They _____ twice before they did such a
thing.

D 다음 괄호 안의 단어를 배열하여 우리말과 같은 뜻이 되도록 문장을 만드시오.

1 그녀는 지금 떠나는 것이 낫다. (she / leave / now / had / better)

  ➡ _____ She had better leave now. _____

2 너는 그 차를 수리할 수 없을 것이다.
(won't / be / to / able / you / repair / the / car)

  ➡ _____

3 그는 과거에 학교에서 과학을 가르쳤다.
(he / at / used to / science / school / teach)

  ➡ _____

4 가끔씩 나는 이곳에서 커피를 마시곤 했다.
(I / would / coffee / sometimes / drink / here)

  ➡ _____

5 나는 낚시를 하러 가기보다는 차라리 수영을 하겠다.
(I / than / fishing / go / would / go swimming / rather)

  ➡ _____

6 너는 그 모델을 설계할 수 있니? (can / model / design / the / you)

  ➡ _____

내신 최다 출제 유형

01 다음 밑줄 친 부분과 바꿔 쓸 수 있는 것을 고르시오.
[출제 예상 90%]

> To be a sports referee, you <u>don't have to</u> have experience as a player.

① may not
② must not
③ need not
④ ought not to
⑤ should not

02 다음 빈칸에 알맞은 말을 고르시오. [출제 예상 90%]

> She is badly damaged. She _____ an accident.

① must have
② has to have
③ should have
④ must have had
⑤ should have had

03 다음 중 연결된 두 문장의 의미가 <u>어색한</u> 것을 고르시오.
[출제 예상 85%]

① Mary can't find her book in her room. She must have left it at school.
② You cannot have seen Jack this morning. He had been in the hospital since last week.
③ Emma went to Hong Kong with her family, and it was sunny everyday in Hong Kong.
   They must have enjoyed their vacation.
④ Mira became a hair designer. She must have been interested in hair.
⑤ I got an A on the test without studying for it. The test must have been difficult.

04 다음 중 어법상 <u>어색한</u> 것을 고르시오. [출제 예상 85%]

① I should have been more careful.
② You may choose what you want.
③ I would not rather put the sticker on my car.
④ He cannot have told a lie.
⑤ You should listen to your teacher.

05 다음 중 밑줄 친 부분의 쓰임이 나머지 넷과 <u>다른</u> 것을 고르시오. [출제 예상 80%]

① I <u>must</u> not forget to take my cell phone with me.
② She <u>must</u> be hungry after exercising.
③ Jack <u>must</u> have stayed up too late last night.
④ They <u>must</u> be tired after running all day.
⑤ She <u>must</u> have fallen asleep.

06 다음 대화를 읽고 괄호 안에 주어진 단어를 이용하여 후회를 나타내는 문장을 쓰시오. [출제 예상 85%]

> A What's wrong?
> B Jamie asked me if I spoke Japanese well and I said I did.
> A Why did you do that?
> B I just wanted to look smart.
>   I _____. (tell her the truth)

➡ I _____

[01~03] 우리말과 같은 뜻이 되도록 빈칸에 들어갈 알 맞은 말을 고르시오.

01

> 우리는 같은 마을에서 함께 살아왔기 때문에 그들을 돕고 싶다.
> = We _____ them since we live together in the same village.

① would to help
② would like help
③ would like to help
④ would like helping
⑤ would help

02

> 너는 그의 조언을 따르는 것이 낫겠다.
> = You _____ follow his advice.

① better   ② had better
③ have better   ④ having better
⑤ do not better

03

> 그 당시 사람들은 비닐봉지를 들고 긴 줄을 짓기도 했다.
> = At that time, people _____ form long lines with their vinyl bags.

① had   ② could   ③ might
④ should   ⑤ would

[04~05] 다음 빈칸에 들어갈 말로 알맞은 것을 고르시오.

04

> We _____ see many foreigners here lately.

① do   ② can   ③ should
④ had better   ⑤ would

05

> We _____ forget that they are suffering from hunger.

① ought to not   ② not ought to
③ don't ought to   ④ ought not to
⑤ ought to

[06~07] 다음 밑줄 친 부분의 쓰임이 나머지 넷과 다른 것을 고르시오. ★★★

06
① I <u>must</u> do what you told me to do right now.
② The farmers <u>must</u> do their best to protect the crops.
③ Imagine how excited they <u>must</u> have been when they see the superstar!
④ They <u>must</u> look for food, clothes and a shelter by themselves.
⑤ Every student <u>must</u> learn to play musical instruments.

07
① You <u>may</u> ask a question if you don't understand.
② She <u>may</u> be able to be a leader.
③ One book <u>may</u> affect your life.
④ The subway <u>may</u> be delayed by the accident.
⑤ Some students <u>may</u> say that is difficult.

[08~09] 다음 중 어법상 어색한 문장을 고르시오.

★★★
08 ① I don't have to bring that many books.
② You should not be afraid of start something new.
③ I don't know how long I will have to stay here.
④ I'm going to make some friends through the Internet.
⑤ You must not go there more than twice a month.

★★★
09 ① You will have to go back to Canada in the near future.
② Many people will buy the new iPhone 6 next month.
③ We will can go to the concert tomorrow.
④ They will not do what they are told to do.
⑤ That will be my first experience to an unknown world.

10 다음 주어진 문장의 밑줄 친 부분과 쓰임이 같은 것을 고르시오.

> This training <u>does</u> help increase people's concentration.

① Where <u>do</u> you want to go this summer?
② She sings songs better than I <u>do</u>.
③ Never put off until tomorrow what you can <u>do</u> today.
④ <u>Do</u> your homework, before dinner.
⑤ When you go jogging, you <u>do</u> run fast.

★★★
11 다음 밑줄 친 부분 중 생략할 수 있는 것을 고르시오.

① She <u>does</u> it without any help.
② I <u>do</u> have many memories of my youth.
③ <u>Did</u> you watch the terrible accident over there?
④ She <u>does</u> not share her things with friends.
⑤ I <u>did</u> not answer his questions.

12 다음 밑줄 친 부분과 바꿔 쓸 수 있는 것을 고르시오.

> <u>May</u> I borrow your collection of stamps?

① Could   ② Do   ③ Must
④ Shall   ⑤ Would

13 다음 두 문장이 같은 뜻이 되도록 할 때 빈칸에 들어갈 알맞은 말을 고르시오.

> It is possible that Billy told her everything about the rumor.
> = Billy _____ told her everything about the rumor.

① may   ② cannot have
③ should have ④ may have
⑤ may not have

14 다음 주어진 우리말과 같은 뜻이 되도록 빈칸에 알맞은 것을 고르시오.

> 너 혼자 이 그림을 그렸을 리가 없다.
> = You _____ drawn this picture by yourself.

① need not have
② must not have
③ cannot have
④ could not have
⑤ should not have

★★★
15 다음 빈칸에 들어갈 말로 가장 알맞은 것을 고르시오.

> A A man rescued a child from the river.
> B Wow! It's not easy to do that. _____.

① He had better be a good swimmer.
② He needs to be a good swimmer.
③ He would rather be a good swimmer.
④ He should be a good swimmer.
⑤ He must be a good swimmer.

16 다음 밑줄 친 do동사의 쓰임이 나머지 넷과 다른 것을 고르시오.

① I did go to the science camp last winter.
② You would look silly if you did this to your friends.
③ You did travel from Rome to Paris this winter.
④ She did taste the same food that the soldiers eat.
⑤ I do need her right now.

17 다음 대화의 빈칸에 들어갈 말로 적절하지 않은 것을 고르시오.

> A Can I throw these old toys away over there?
> B _____.

① No, you can't.
② No, you must not.
③ No, you should not.
④ No, you will not.
⑤ No, you may not.

18 다음 빈칸에 공통으로 들어갈 알맞은 것을 고르시오.

> • _____ you tell me his phone number?
> • _____ the news be true?
> • _____ I try these shoes on?

① May   ② Can   ③ Should
④ Do   ⑤ Might

[19~20] 다음 주어진 우리말을 영어로 바르게 표현한 것을 고르시오.

19
> 뭐 마실 것 좀 드실래요?

① Would you like something drink?
② Would you like to drink?
③ Would you like something to drink?
④ Would you something to drink?
⑤ Would you like to drink something?

20 ★★★

당신은 당신이 좋아하는 인스턴트음식들을
포기해야 할 것이다.

① You have to give up junk food
  that you like.
② You will give up junk food that you like.
③ You give up junk food that you like.
④ You would have to give up junk food
  that you like.
⑤ You will have to give up junk food that
  you like.

21 다음의 빈칸에 들어갈 수 <u>없는</u> 것을 고르시오.

You _____ change your eating
habit, and exercise regularly to be
healthy.

① ought   ② should   ③ must
④ had better   ⑤ need to

22 다음 문장의 밑줄 친 부분과 바꿔 쓸 수 있는 것을
<u>모두</u> 고르시오.

She <u>doesn't need to</u> give us any
information about the test.

① should not   ② might not
③ need not   ④ doesn't have to
⑤ could not

[23~24] 주어진 우리말과 같은 뜻이 되도록 괄호 안의
단어를 바르게 배열한 것을 고르시오.

23

그들은 회의에 참석하지 않았다. 그들은
바빴던 것이 틀림없다.
= They didn't take part in the meeting.
  (they / been / have / must / busy)

① They have must been busy.
② They have been busy must.
③ They have must been busy.
④ They must have been busy.
⑤ They have been must busy.

24

전문 댄서가 되기 위해선 우선 춤을 잘 출 수
있어야 해요.
= First of all, you (be / should / well /
  to / dance / able) in order to become
  a professional dancer.

① should be to dance able well
② should be able to dance well
③ be able to should dance well
④ should dance be able to well
⑤ should well be able to dance

[25~26] 다음 빈칸에 공통으로 들어갈 알맞은 것을 고
르시오.

25

· You _____ keep your friends'
secrets.
· You _____ have collected a lot
of data.

① shall   ② must   ③ should
④ are able to   ⑤ had better not

Answer Keys p. 10~11

26

· _____ I take your order, sir?
· She _____ be young, but she believes in herself.

① should   ② may   ③ has to
④ shall   ⑤ would

◇◇◇◇◇◇◇◇ 서술형 평가 ◇◇◇◇◇◇◇◇

[27~28] 다음 두 문장을 한 문장으로 바르게 바꿔 쓰시오.

27

I wrote in my diary in English before.
But I don't anymore.

➡ _____

28

Jessy danced at a dancing club before.
But she doesn't anymore.

➡ _____

[29~30] 주어진 우리말과 같은 뜻이 되도록 빈칸에 알맞은 말을 쓰시오.

29

A I think we should save energy to protect nature.
B 나도 그렇게 생각해.

➡ _____

30

A She couldn't eat any food on the show.
B 나도 그러지 못했어.

➡ _____

[31~33] 다음 괄호 안의 주어진 단어를 사용하여 우리 말을 영어로 바르게 옮기시오.

★★★
31

그가 냉장고의 오렌지를 다 먹었던 것이 틀림없다. (refrigerator)

➡ _____

★★★
32

Nancy는 학급에서 최고의 학생이었다. (used to)

➡ _____

33

우리는 지도를 가져왔어야 했어. (bring, a map)

➡ _____

04

Chapter
명사, 관사와 대명사

Point Check I

◆ **명사:** 세상의 이름이 있는 모든 것(사람, 동물, 사물 등)을 가리킨다.

◆ **관사:** 정해지지 않은 것의 앞에는 부정관사 'a/an', 정해진 것의 앞에는 정관사 'the'가 붙는다.

1. 명사

(1) 명사의 종류

셀 수 있는 명사	**보통명사**: 일반적인 명사	**집합명사**: 사람 또는 사물의 모임
셀 수 없는 명사	**물질명사**: 정해진 형태가 없는 사물	**고유명사**: 각 명사의 고유한 이름
	추상명사: 사람의 생각으로 나타내는 감정이나 개념	

(2) 명사의 복수형

대부분의 명사	-s	자음＋y	y를 i로 고치고 -es
-s, -x, -ch, -sh, 자음＋o	-es	f(e)	f(e)를 v로 고치고 -es

(3) 셀 수 없는 명사의 양 표현

• **a piece of** 한 조각의	• **a glass of** 한 잔의	• **a loaf of** 한 덩어리의
• **a bottle of** 한 병의	• **a slice of** 한 조각의	• **a bar of** 한 개의
• **a cup of** 한 잔의	• **a bowl of** 한 그릇의	• **a pound of** 한 파운드의

(4) 명사의 소유격

's 를 붙이는 경우	-s로 끝나지 않는 단수 / 복수명사	• Teddy's bike, people's opinions
' 를 붙이는 경우	-s로 끝나는 복수명사	• ants' world
	신화에 나오는 이름, 유명한 인물	• Venus' son
of＋명사	무생물의 소유격	• legs of a table

2. 관사

부정관사 a/an	① 하나의 (one)	③ 약간 (some)	⑤ ～마다 (per)
	② 어떤 (certain)	④ 같은 (the same)	⑥ 대표단수
정관사 the	① 서수, 최상급 앞	② only, very, same 앞	③ 악기이름 앞 ④ 대표단수

명사

명사의 종류

- **명사**: 세상의 이름이 있는 모든 것(사람, 동물, 사물 등)을 말하며, 크게 셀 수 있는 명사와 셀 수 없는 명사로 나누어진다.

1. 셀 수 있는 명사

[보통명사]

사람, 동물, 사물 등을 가리키는 일반적인 명사를 말한다.
하나일 경우 단어 앞에 'a(an)'을 붙이고, 둘 이상일 경우 복수형을 사용한다.
- A rose is a beautiful flower.
- There are three dogs and two cats in the box.

[집합명사]

사람 또는 사물(동물)이 모인 집합을 나타내는 말이다.
집단을 강조할 때는 단수형으로, 구성원을 강조할 때는 복수형으로 취급한다.
- The team usually wins the game.
- My team practice a lot every day.

2. 셀 수 없는 명사

[물질명사]

일정한 형태가 없는 명사를 말한다. 'a(an)'이나 '복수형'을 함께 쓸 수 없고 'much, little, some, any'와 같은 수량 형용사와 함께 쓰인다.
- We need water and air to live.
- When you cook food, you need to use some salt.

[고유명사]

사람, 강, 산, 나라의 이름 등과 같이 고유한 이름이 있는 명사를 말한다.
- William is from America.
- My dog has a name, Walter.

[추상명사]

일정한 형태나 성질이 없이 사람의 생각으로만 그려낼 수 있는 감정과 개념을 나타내는 명사이다.
- Eddie wants some advice.
- Peace is what everyone wants.

Answer Keys p. 12

A 괄호 안에서 알맞은 것을 고르시오.

1 (Dogs / Dog) are clever animals.

2 (The family / Families) consists of two parents and three children.

3 Last month, several (families / family) moved to this city.

4 That (houses / house) that burned is Jim's.

5 There are forty (students / student) in the class.

6 I want to get some (informations / information).

7 The cattle (eats / eat) grass in the field.

8 She was satisfied with her (lives / life).

9 Flowers are helped by (bee / bees).

10 Please, can you call the (police / polices) right now?

11 She recommended the music (equipment / equipments).

12 They said that they need more (water / waters) and (food / foods).

13 I put some (salt / salts) and (oil / oils) in the bowl.

14 The (ceremonies / ceremony) was really exciting.

15 (Worker / A worker) tried to find out the fastest way to solve the problem.

4-2 셀 수 있는 명사의 복수형

- **명사의 복수형**: 셀 수 있는 명사가 하나일 경우 앞에 'a/an'이 붙고, 여러 개를 나타낼 때는 뒤에 '-s/-es'가 붙는다.

1. 규칙 변화 복수형

대부분의 경우	-s	• ribbon – ribbons • table – tables	• pen – pens • bird – birds
-s, -x, -ch, -sh로 끝나는 경우	-es	• bush – bushes • ax – axes	• march – marches • dish – dishes
'자음+y'로 끝나는 경우	y를 i로 고치고 -es	• family – families • city – cities	• lady – ladies • fly – flies
'모음+y'로 끝나는 경우	-s	• ray – rays • boy – boys	• lay – lays • key – keys
f(e)로 끝나는 경우	f를 v로 고치고 -es	• thief – thieves • leaf – leaves 〈예외〉 • roof – roofs • belief – beliefs	• knife – knives • wife – wives • safe – safes • chief – chiefs
-o로 끝나는 경우	-es	• potato – potatoes • hero – heroes 〈예외〉 • radio – radios • kangaroo – kangaroos	• tomato – tomatoes • mosquito – mosquitoes • zoo – zoos • piano – pianos

2. 불규칙 변화 복수형

- **goose – geese**
- **man – men**
- **sheep – sheep**
- **foot – feet**
- **woman – women**
- **deer – deer**
- **tooth – teeth**
- **fish – fish/fishes**
- **child – children**
- **ox – oxen**
- **mouse – mice**

 **Check up!**

Answer Keys p. 12

A 다음 명사의 복수형을 쓰시오.

1 goose – _geese_   2 house – _____

3 river – _____   4 thief – _____

5 mouse – _____   6 belief – _____

7 aisle – _____   8 child – _____

9 leaf – _____   10 deer – _____

11 knife – _____   12 knee – _____

13 tooth – _____   14 giraffe – _____

15 superhero – _____   16 bus – _____

17 hairbrush – _____   18 ax – _____

19 volcano – _____   20 challenge – _____

21 diary – _____   22 jewel – _____

23 church – _____   24 eyelash – _____

B 주어진 단어를 이용하여 빈칸에 알맞게 바꾸어 쓰시오.

1 There are many interesting _parties_ in the city. (party)

2 They have seen some _____ in the field. (wolf)

3 I want to have many _____. (baby)

4 There are a few interesting _____ in Seoul. (exhibition)

5 She has lost several _____ since May. (hat)

6 A lot of application _____ have already arrived before the deadline. (form)

7 Do you think that _____ are safe to use? (ax)

8 Please, get me some _____ on your way home. (potato)

9 There are some _____ in the zoo. I like them. (giraffe)

10 I'm so worried about his broken _____. (ankle)

4-3 셀 수 없는 명사의 복수형

- **명사의 복수형**: 셀 수 없는 명사의 수는 하나, 둘, 셋 등으로 표현할 수 없다.
  '양'을 나타내기 위해서는 그릇이나 단위 등을 사용하거나 수량 형용사를 사용해서 대략적인 양을 표현한다.

1. 셀 수 없는 명사 + 수량 형용사

much 많은 (= a lot of, lots of)	• There is much <u>water</u> in the bottle.
some/any 조금	• Jenny needs to put some <u>gas</u> in her car. • I don't want to drink any <u>juice</u>.
a little 조금	• Willy has a little <u>money</u> to buy it with.
little 거의 ~없는	• We have little <u>salt</u> and <u>pepper</u>.

➡ 셀 수 없는 명사는 양에 상관없이 항상 단수 취급을 한다.

➡ 'some'은 긍정문과 제안을 하는 의문문에, 'any'는 부정문과 의문문에 사용되며, 둘 모두 셀 수 있는 명사와도 함께 사용할 수 있다.

2. 셀 수 없는 명사의 양 표현하기

단수		복수		명사
• a piece of	한 개의	• two pieces of	두 개의	bread, cake, cheese, cloth, furniture
• a bottle of	한 병의	• two bottles of	두 병의	beer, ink, juice, water
• a cup of	한 잔의	• two cups of	두 잔의	coffee, tea
• a glass of	한 잔의	• two glasses of	두 잔의	water, milk, juice
• a slice of	한 조각의	• two slices of	두 조각의	cheese, pizza, meat
• a pound of	한 파운드의	• two pounds of	두 파운드의	sugar, meat, beef, pork
• a bar of	한 개의	• two bars of	두 개의	soap, chocolate, gold
• a bowl of	한 그릇의	• two bowls of	두 그릇의	soup, rice
• a sheet of	한 장의	• two sheets of	두 장의	paper, blanket, plastic
• a loaf of	한 덩어리의	• two loaves of	두 덩어리의	bread, meat
• a spoonful of	한 스푼의	• two spoonfuls of	두 스푼의	sugar, salt, yogurt
• a bunch of	한 다발의	• two bunches of	두 다발의	cattle, flower, grapes

Answer Keys p. 12

A   주어진 단어를 단위를 이용하여 알맞은 형태로 바꾸시오.

1   She ate three ___*loaves of bread*___ for breakfast. (bread)

2   There's only one _____ on the plate. (pizza)

3   I'd like to order two _____. (coffee)

4   Harry bought four _____ in the market. (milk)

5   Would you please help me move this _____? (furniture)

6   There are five _____ in the basket. (bananas)

7   My brother drank three _____ at once and he has a stomachache now. (cold water)

8   He bought a _____ to make bread. (flour)

9   The boy begged his mother to buy a _____. (snacks)

10 Let me give her a _____. (advice)

11 I had two _____ for lunch. (chocolate cake)

12 Jane buys a _____, two _____, and three _____. (soup/juice/meat)

13 I ordered a _____ rice, a _____ ice cream. (rice/ice cream)

14 Every student has to bring two pens and five _____. (paper)

15 She wants to put three _____ in the bowl. (salt)

4-4 추상명사의 관용적 표현

- '전치사 + 추상명사'는 문장 안에서 부사 또는 형용사의 역할을 한다.

1. [of + 추상명사] = 형용사

• of use = useful 유용한	• of no use = useless 쓸모없는
• of importance = important 중요한	• of courage = courageous 용기 있는
• of value = valuable 가치 있는	• of wisdom = wise 현명한

- Jamie is a woman **of wisdom**. = Jamie is a **wise** woman.
- This brand is **of value** in the world market. = This brand is **valuable** in the world market.

2. [전치사 + 추상명사] = 부사

• with ease = easily 쉽게	• in haste = hastily 서둘러서
• on purpose = purposely 고의로	• with care = carefully 조심스럽게

- I get tired **with ease** because of overwork these days.
  = I get tired **easily** because of overwork these days.
- Sammy asked her to have a date **with care**.
  = Sammy asked her to have a date **carefully**.

☆Check up!

Answer Keys p. 12

A 다음 두 문장이 같은 뜻이 되도록 빈칸에 알맞은 말을 쓰시오.

1 You seemed to break the promise on purpose.
   ➡ You seemed to break the promise ___*purposely*___.

2 I think Max is a man of courage.
   ➡ I think Max is a _____ man.

3 She said the information was of no use to our project.
   ➡ She said the information was _____ to our project.

4 Tommy always does his work to perfection.
   ➡ Tommy always does his work _____.

5 It is important for us to pass the final exam.

  ➡ It is _____ for us to pass the final exam.

6 His novel will be useful for my movie script.

  ➡ His novel will be _____ for my movie script.

7 They ended their performance in haste.

  ➡ They ended their performance _____.

8 Sam broke the window by mistake.

  ➡ Sam broke the window _____.

9 On occasion, people make the same mistakes.

  ➡ _____, people make the same mistakes.

10 It was of value for him to buy the car.

  ➡It was _____ for him to buy the car.

11 My grandfather says like a man of wisdom.

  ➡My grandfather says like a _____ man.

12 Tobby is good at math. He can solve the math problems easily.

  ➡Tobby is good at math. He can solve the math problems

  _____.

13 Mary always treats others kindly.

  ➡Mary always treats others _____.

14 Mr. McFee ignores others on purpose.

  ➡Mr. McFee ignores others _____.

15 Dean gave me the information of no use.

  ➡Dean gave me the _____ information.

Lesson

4-5 명사의 소유격

• **명사의 소유격**: 일반 명사의 소유를 표현한다.

'~의' 뜻을 나타낼 수 있도록 명사 뒤에 ['-s]를 붙이거나 'of + 명사'로 나타낸다.

1. 명사의 소유격: ['s], [']

['s]를 붙이는 경우 ⇒ 대부분의 명사	• deer's horn	• Jackie's telephone
	• women's closet	• a crocodile's tear
[']를 붙이는 경우 ⇒ -s 로 끝나는 명사	• my babies' toy	• the boys' middle school

➡ 일반적인 사람의 이름이 '-s'로 끝나는 경우에도 ['s]가 붙는다.

• Jones**'s** goal   • Chris**'s** clothes

2. 무생물의 소유격: [of + 명사]

• a new door **of my house**
• Jack found another size **of this shirt**.
• '시간, 가격, 거리, 중량, 행성명' 등을 나타내는 명사는 ['s], [']를 사용한다.
  • today**'s** news   • ten mile**s'** distance
  • Jupiter**'s** size (= the size **of** Jupiter)

3. 소유격 뒤 명사의 생략

(1) 집, 상점, 교회 등을 나타내는 명사가 소유격 뒤에 오면 생략 가능
  • Lucy and I will eat out at **McFly's** (restaurant).

(2) 소유대명사의 역할을 할 때 생략 가능
  • Look at the red car over there. That's my **sister's**. [sister's 여동생의 것(= sister's car)

4. 이중소유격 : 소유격 (my, your, her, his, our, their, its)은 관사, 지시대명사, 부정대명사와 나란히 쓰일 수 없다. 이때는 'of + 소유대명사' 또는 'of + 's'의 형태로 사용한다.

a an the		
this that	**+**	명사 + of + 소유대명사/'s
some any no		

• **Some of my friends** are over there.
• We knew **this camera of Larry's** was expensive.

 **Check up!**

Answer Keys p. 12~13

A 괄호 안에서 알맞은 것을 고르시오.

1 (Helen's leg / Leg of Helen) was broken in the accident.

2 The (boy's / boy) house has a large garden.

3 (His jackets' color / The color of his jacket) is blue.

4 My (parents's car / parents' car) was fixed yesterday.

5 She wants to enter a (university of women / women's university).

6 Father bought (today's newspaper / newspaper of today).

7 Her (aunt's dress / aunt' dress) was made by her.

8 That's no (your business / business of yours).

9 Here's a new suit. It's my (father's / fathers').

B 주어진 말을 사용하여 우리말의 뜻과 같도록 빈칸에 쓰시오.

1 Tomas의 취미는 강가에서 연 날리기이다. (hobby)
   ➡ ___Tomas's hobby___ is flying kites along the river.

2 나의 딸은 여고에 입학할 예정이다. (high school)
   ➡ My daughter is going to enter _____

3 나의 한 친구는 등산하는 것을 좋아한다. (friend)
   ➡ _____ likes climbing mountains.

4 저 아름다운 여자는 Helen의 엄마이다. (mother)
   ➡ That beautiful woman is _____

5 그 아이들의 옷은 자선단체에 기부되었다. (clothes)
   ➡ _____ were donated to charity.

6 탁자의 다리는 파란색이었다. (leg)
   ➡ _____ were blue.

7 나는 그녀에게 내 남동생의 사진을 보여 주었다. (photo)
   ➡ I showed her _____.

8 장모님의 파스타는 언제나 맛있다. (mother-in-law)
   ➡ _____ is always delicious.

9 베토벤의 그 음악은 인상적이었다. (music)
   ➡ _____ was impressive.

10 그의 옷이라면 내 옷과도 마찬가지이다. (any, his, mine)
   ➡ _____ clothes _____ are clothes _____.

관사

부정관사 a / an

> • 부정관사 a(an): 주로 '하나의'라는 뜻을 가지고 사용되며, 종족을 대표할 때나 '어떤'의 의미로 사용되기도 한다.

◈ a / an의 의미

one	하나의	• We'll stay in this guest house for a day or two.
a certain	어떤	• In a way, strict rules are needed for students.
some	약간, 어느 정도	• He couldn't say a word at that time.
the same	같은, 동일한	• Thomas and I are all of an age.
per	~당, ~마다	• Some people eat two meals a day.
종족/집단을 대표		• An ant is a diligent insect.

Check up!

Answer Keys p. 13

A 다음 문장의 빈칸에 a, an 중 알맞은 것을 쓰시오.

1 My father eats ____*a*____ fresh apple every morning.

2 What _____ fantastic day! I want to go there.

3 The man bought _____ MP3 player to study English.

4 I think it might be _____ hour's work.

5 Park is so hungry, so he'd like to have _____ hamburger.

6 There was _____ big tree around the corner.

7 Our family went to _____ natural history museum.

8 He has worked at _____ cookie store since 2004.

9 In _____ way, exercising regularly is really fun.

10 Mom said I should take vitamin C three times _____ day.

11 It took half _____ hour to get there.

12 I think John is _____ honest boy. He never lies.

4-7 정관사 the

• 정관사 the : 정관사 'the'는 앞의 명사를 반복하거나 세상에 하나뿐인 것을 가리킬 때 사용한다.

1. the의 쓰임

앞에 나온 명사가 반복될 때	• There is an apple tree in the backyard. The apple tree was planted the day I was born.
문맥, 상황으로 보아 무엇을 가리키는지 모두가 알 수 있을 때	• Can you pass me the book next to you?
유일한 것을 말할 때	• The earth goes around the Sun.
서수, 최상급, only, very, same 앞	• John is the second son of his parents.
종족/집단을 대표할 때	• The elephant is a huge animal.
악기명을 나타낼 때	• Johnny plays the piano and the guitar well.
특정한 고유명사 앞	• I want to visit the White House in America.
the + 형용사/분사	• They want to help the poor in Africa.
구나 절이 뒤에서 명사를 꾸며줄 때	• This is the robot that my son and daughter want to have.
동작의 대상이 되는 신체의 일부를 나타낼 때	• Sam couldn't look me in the eye.

2. 관사를 쓰지 않는 경우

식사를 나타내는 명사 앞	breakfast, lunch, dinner
운동 경기를 나타내는 명사 앞	tennis, baseball, soccer, badminton
'by + 교통수단'	by bus, by bike, by subway
장소를 나타내는 명사가 본래의 목적으로 쓰일 경우	bed, work, church
가족 구성원을 나타내는 명사	father, mother, sister, brother
관직, 신분, 호칭을 나타내는 명사	president, professor
과목을 나타내는 명사 앞	English, social studies, science

Answer Keys p. 13

A 괄호 안에서 알맞은 말을 고르시오.

1 This is one of (a / (the)) biggest palaces in Korea.

2 Jane has (a / the) big bag. (A / The) bag was given to her by her mom.

3 It was (a / the) fourth time I've watched this exhibition.

4 I go hiking twice (a / the) month.

5 (The / A) sun rises in the east and sets in the west.

6 Would you mind if I open (a / the) window?

7 I wonder what (a / the) weather is like in LA.

8 There is (a / the) beautiful picture of flowers in (the / a) middle of the hall.

9 My hobby is playing (the / a) violin.

10 My best friend and I lived in (the / a) same village.

B 다음 밑줄 친 부분을 바르게 고치시오.

1 I already ate a dinner. _____X_____

2 He took her by a arm. _____

3 My mother likes to listen to a radio while she is cooking.

_____

4 The angry girl stared at me in a face.

_____

5 It was the clear night, so I can see a few stars.

_____

6 A disabled should be protected by the government.

_____

7 They usually go to school by the bus.

_____

8 Let's do it step by a step. _____

9 I will send this package by the express.

_____

10 You should go to the bed early.

_____

Practice More I

A 괄호 안에서 알맞은 것을 고르시오.

1 There are two (knifes / (knives)) on the table.

2 I read all (kind / kinds) of detective novels.

3 She received a few text (messages / message) from her daughter.

4 Harry's speech usually draws a big (crowd / people).

5 People (says / say) it's possible, but he failed to move the statue.

6 The (cow / cattle) are running in the field.

7 He caught a lot of (fishes / fish) in the river.

8 The police (was / were) not able to catch the thief last night.

9 I will save enough (moneys / money) to buy the red car.

10 There are twelve (candle / candles) in the box.

B 괄호 안에 주어진 말을 이용해 밑줄 친 표현을 바꾸어 문장을 완성하시오.

1 There is a boy on the sofa. (four)
   ➡ *There are four boys on the sofa.*

2 We have a special holiday this year. (a few)
   ➡ _____

3 I have an exciting hobby. (many)
   ➡ _____

4 There is an old table in my grandmother's room. (some)
   ➡ _____

5 There is a woman dancing in the park. (two)
   ➡ _____

6 He has an important piece of evidence related to this accident. (three)
   ➡ _____

Note
- **detective novel** 탐정소설
- **receive** 받다, 얻다
- **speech** 연설
- **draw** 인기를 끌다, 남을 끌어들이다
- **crowd** 군중, 대중
- **cattle** 소 무리, 소 떼
- **evidence** 증거, 증명
- **related to** ~와 관련 되다, ~과 관계가 있다
- **accident** 사고

7 I ate a piece of pizza for lunch. (two)

   ➡ _____

8 He bought a bottle of juice. (four)

   ➡ _____

9 The English teacher used a piece of chalk. (many)

   ➡ _____

10 I bought an apple. (two box)

   ➡ _____

C 다음 문장에서 어법상 어색한 것을 찾아 바르게 고치시오.

1 She thinks John answers are right.

   _____John_____ ➡ _____John's_____

2 Our club meets three times the week.

   _____ ➡ _____

3 There are some sheet of paper on the desk.

   _____ ➡ _____

4 The mom said that I should eat breakfast for my health.

   _____ ➡ _____

5 Here is a report. You should review a report by five.

   _____ ➡ _____

6 A young respect the old in Korea.

   _____ ➡ _____

7 It was a last night I was in LA.

   _____ ➡ _____

8 He likes to travel by the air.

   _____ ➡ _____

9 I like to play the soccer with my friends.

   _____ ➡ _____

10 The Mr. Kim has taught math for three years.

   _____ ➡ _____

Practice More Ⅰ

Answer Keys p. 13

D 다음 우리말 해석에 맞게 주어진 단어를 이용하여 문장을 완성하시오.

1 책상에는 깨진 유리 조각이 몇 개 있었다.
(there, on the desk, broken, some, were, pieces, glass, of)
➡ *There were some pieces of broken glass on the desk.*

2 Helen은 배로 여행해 본 적 있니? (has, sea, ever, by, Helen, traveled)
➡ _____

3 그 학생들은 두 시간째 선생님을 기다리고 있었다. (the students, for, two, have, their teacher, for, waiting, hours, been)
➡ _____

4 이것은 세계에서 두 번째로 긴 강이다.
(this, in the world, the, is, river, longest, second)
➡ _____

5 그 소년의 성적은 내 딸의 것보다 더 우수했다.
(the boy's, my daughter's, was, grade, than, higher)
➡ _____

6 나는 세 조각의 피자와 두 팩의 우유를 샀다. (I, three, of, bought, milk, pieces, of, two, and, cartons, pizza)
➡ _____

7 그녀의 삼촌 집은 좋은 야경을 가지고 있다.
(her, view, has, uncle's, a, night, house, good, at)
➡ _____

8 내 딸은 하루 이틀 안에 괜찮아 질 것이다.
(two, will, my daughter, better, in, or, be, a day)
➡ _____

9 얼마나 멋진 날이야! 얼른 소풍을 가자. (what, picnic, a, day, let's, wonderful, go to the)
➡ _____

10 그들은 위험에 처했을 때 불을 피웠다.
(they, in, a fire, they, made, danger, when, were)
➡ _____

Point Check II

◆ **대명사:** 사람이나 사물을 대신해서 가리키는 것을 말한다.

◆ **재귀대명사:** '~자신(oneself)'을 표현하는 말을 가리킨다.

◆ **부정대명사:** 정해지지 않은 사람이나 사물을 가리키는 대명사를 말한다.

1. 재귀대명사 용법

재귀용법	• Maria hurt herself when she fell. [Maria = herself]
강조용법	• Veronica herself enjoys doing arts & crafts . (Veronica = herself)

2. 가주어와 가목적어

가주어 **it**	• It is fun to play chess.
가목적어 **it**	• Jenny thought it very exciting to draw and paint pictures on the wall.

3. 부정대명사

one ~ the other...	(둘 중) 하나는 ~, 다른 하나는...
one ~ the others...	(셋 이상) 하나는 ~, 나머지는...
one ~ another...	(셋 이상) 하나는 ~, 다른 하나는...
some ~ others...	(불특정한 다수의 사람/사물) 몇몇은 ~, 다른 사람(것)들은...
some ~ the others...	(특정한 수의 사람/사물) 몇몇은 ~, 나머지는...
one ~ another... the other ~	(셋 중에) 하나는 ~, 다른 하나는 ... 나머지 하나는 ~

4. 전체부정과 부분부정

전체부정에 사용	no, none, nothing, nobody, neither
부분부정에 사용	• 부정어 + all, every, both • 부정어 + always, necessarily, entirely, completely, absolutely

4-8 대명사

재귀대명사

> • 재귀대명사: '~자신'을 표현하는 말로서 주어와 목적어가 같을 때 '자기 자신'의 의미로 목적어 자리에 쓰이거나, 주어, 보어, 목적어를 강조할 때 '직접'의 뜻으로 쓰인다.

1. 재귀대명사 형태

단수	• I – myself	• you – yourself	• he – himself	• she – herself	• it – itself
복수	• we – ourselves	• you – yourselves	• they – themselves		

2. 재귀대명사 용법

재귀용법	주어와 목적어의 대상이 같을 때 사용 ➡ 목적어 자리에 위치 • First of all, we should know ourselves. [we = ourselves] • Van Gogh drew himself. [Gogh = himself]
강조용법	명사나 대명사를 강조하기 위해 사용 ➡ 강조하고자 하는 (대)명사 바로 뒤, 문장의 끝에 위치하거나 생략 가능 • Iris herself cooked a lot of food for the poor. [Iris = herself] • Thelma herself made a toy robot that moves automatically. [Thelma = herself]

3. 재귀대명사 숙어

- enjoy oneself 즐기다
- by oneself 홀로
- help oneself 마음껏 먹다
- of itself 저절로
- say(talk) to oneself 혼잣말하다
- for oneself 혼자 힘으로
- make oneself at home 편히 쉬다
- in itself 본질적으로, 원래

☆Check up!

Answer Keys p. 14

A 다음 밑줄 친 부분을 어법에 맞게 고치시오.

1 I can't fix my broken watch <u>in</u> myself. _____*by*_____

2 Help <u>yours</u> to the food. _____

3 She'll take care of <u>her</u> from now on. _____

Answer Keys p. 14

4 I drew <u>me</u>. _____

5 Bob is not going to tell this to <u>themselves</u>. _____

6 They think Helen needs space to be <u>her</u>. _____

7 I'll lend my car to <u>yourself</u>. _____

8 My motto is "Know <u>you</u>." _____

9 I can go to hospital by <u>mine</u>. _____

10 I keep saying to <u>me</u>, "I'll do my best." _____

B 다음 우리말 해석에 맞게 문장을 완성하시오.

1 그녀는 혼자 그 파티를 준비했다.

➡ She prepared for the party _____*by herself*_____ .

2 주말 내내 집에서 편히 쉬세요.

➡ _____ all weekend.

3 마음껏 드세요! 파티에 와주셔서 감사합니다.

➡ _____! Thank you for coming to our party.

4 그녀는 당황할 때마다 혼잣말을 한다.

➡ Whenever she is nervous, she _____

5 Harry는 스스로 그 프로젝트를 끝냈다.

➡ Harry _____ the project himself.

4-9 'it'의 용법

- **'it'의 용법**: 사물을 가리키는 지시대명사로도 사용되고, 진짜 주어를 대신하는 가주어, 진짜 목적어를 대신하는 가목적어로도 사용되며, 시간, 날씨, 날짜 등을 나타낼 때는 뜻이 없는 비인칭 주어로 사용된다.

1. 가주어 it

to부정사(구)를 진주어로 하는 경우	• It is very difficult **to swim across the sea**.
동명사(구)를 진주어로 하는 경우	• It is dangerous **crossing the street when the light is red**.
명사절을 진주어로 하는 경우	• It is so silly **that you act like a fool**.

2. 가목적어 it

to부정사(구)를 진목적어로 하는 경우	• I found it very interesting **to deliver the news as a reporter at school**.
동명사(구)를 진목적어로 하는 경우	• We thought it exciting **climbing the mountain**.
명사절을 진목적어로 하는 경우	• She knew it that **I tried to leave alone**.

3. 비인칭 주어 it: 특별한 뜻을 가지지 않기 때문에 해석하지 않는다.

날씨	• It will be a little chilly tomorrow.	날짜	• It is December 4th.
거리	• It is five blocks to the art gallery.	온도	• It is 34 degrees Celsius outside.
시간	• It is three o'clock now.	계절	• It is always cold in the Arctic.
요일	• It is Thursday today.	명암	• It is so bright outside of the cave.

4. It의 다른 용법

It seems (appears / happens) that...	• It seems that you are very pleased with something.
It is ~ that... 강조하는 말을 it is와 that 사이에 쓴다. (동사는 쓸 수 없음)	• It is a digital camera that we need now.
상황을 나타내는 it	• How's it going? (=How are you?)

Answer Keys p. 14

A 보기와 같은 it의 용법을 골라 그 번호를 쓰시오.

> 보기
> ① It is still raining outside.
> ② How is it going?
> ③ It is I that prepared for Helen's present.
> ④ It was important to study hard.
> ⑤ I knew it that I didn't write the answers on the paper.

1 Maria thinks **it** interesting learning foreign languages.

⑤

2 **It**'s not necessary to buy the bag now. _____

3 **It** will soon be winter. I'm looking forward to going skiing.

_____

4 **It** was on the table that I found my lost key. _____

5 Stop **it**. You and Helen talk too much. _____

6 **It** was six o'clock, and the party started at that time. _____

7 I found **it** difficult to complete the puzzle alone. _____

8 **It**'s important for you to follow the rules. _____

9 **It** is the bag that he gave me for my birthday present.

_____

10 He thought **it** boring to read books. _____

B 'It'용법을 사용하여 두 문장의 의미가 같도록 빈칸에 알맞은 말을 쓰시오.

1 To work hard is important if you want a promotion.

➡ ___*It is important*___ to work hard if you want a promotion.

2 To persuade my mom was very difficult.

➡ _____ to persuade my mom.

3 I found that it was impossible for you finish the work by five.

➡ I found _____ for you to finish the work by five.

4 I think that to ask for others' opinions is a good idea.

➡ I think _____ for others' opinions.

Answer Keys p. 14

5   My husband moved the heavy box.

➡ _____ that moved the heavy box.

6   Participating in the debate is necessary.

➡ _____ to participate in the debate.

7   He found the book under the sofa.

➡ _____ under the sofa.

8   Talking to you again was nice.

➡ _____ to you again.

9   My dog caught the thief last night.

➡ _____ that my dog caught last night.

10 Staying up all night makes people exhausted.

➡ _____ makes people exhausted to _____ all night.

4-10 부정대명사 _ one / another / other (1)

- **부정대명사**: 정해지지 않은 사람이나 사물을 가리키는 대명사를 말한다.
- **one**: 'one'은 정해지지 않은 '하나'를 가리키거나 앞의 명사의 중복을 피하기 위하여 사용한다.
- **another**: 정해지지 않는 사람이나 사물을 가리키며 '또 다른 하나'로 해석한다.
- **other**: 'one'이나 'some'과 짝을 이루어 'one ~, the other(s)', 'some ~, (the) others'로 사용한다.

1. one

앞에 나온 명사와 종류는 같지만 대상이 다른 경우 명사의 반복을 피하기 위해 사용	• I have lost my sleeping bag, so I have to buy a new one. [my sleeping bag ≠ one] → 잃어버린 침낭과 똑같은 것이 아닌 그러한 종류를 의미
복수일 때는 'ones'를 사용	• I want to buy jeans. Would you please show me blue ones? [jeans = ones]
일반적인 사람들을 나타낸다.	• One must follow the rules. [one = 일반적인 사람들]

2. another

또 다른 하나(것), 또 다른 사람	• Andy ate three pieces of pizza, but he wants to eat another (piece).
one another 서로 (셋 이상)	• Kate, Jimmy and Paul usually help one another. • Kate and Jimmy seem to like one another.
one thing, ~another ~와 ...는 별개이다	• Designing it is one thing, but making it is another.

* 원칙적으로 'one another'은 '셋 이상', 'each other'은 '둘'일 경우에 사용하나 요즘엔 구별없이 사용하기도 한다. 하지만 둘의 차이는 확실히 알아두자.

3. other

the other 나머지 하나	• I found five of the jades, but I couldn't find the other (one).
others 다른 사람(것)들	• They are always kind to others.
the others 나머지 모두들	• I only made one flower. Can you please make the others for me?

Check up!

Answer Keys p. 14

A 괄호 안에서 알맞은 것을 고르시오.

1   They don't have a laptop, so they decided to buy (one / ones).

2   I can't find my car. Where is (it / one)?

3   This coat is too long. Can you show me (another / other)?

4   (Other / One) should help the poor.

5   Some students study harder than (another / others).

6   The cats seem to like (one another / another cat).

7   The picture is the oldest (one / ones) that he owns.

8   You should not talk like that to (others / another).

9   Semi is kind to (others / another).

10 I've had a loaf of bread, but I'll have (another / one).

B   밑줄 친 부분을 바르게 고치시오.

1   I have a cup, but I have left <u>one</u> in the classroom.

                                                    _____it_____

2   They fell in love each <u>another</u>.   _____

3   My sister doesn't have a Smartphone, so she'll buy <u>it</u>.

                                                    _____

4   This skirt is too short. Show me <u>others</u>.   _____

5   She only ate a piece of cake. Her son ate up all <u>another</u>.

                                                    _____

6   This shirt is large. Can you show me <u>other</u> one?

                                                    _____

7   I can see Minhyuk, but where are all <u>other</u>?

                                                    _____

8   Sometimes helping <u>the other</u> does not pay.

                                                    _____

9   I need to take a taxi. Please call <u>it</u> for me.

                                                    _____

10 Do you think there's <u>other</u> meeting this week?

                                                    _____

4-11 부정대명사 _ one / another / other (2)

◆ one / another / other 관용표현

one~ the other...	(둘 중) 하나는~, 다른 하나는...

• I have two mangoes. One is an apple mango, the other is a yellow mango.

one~ the others...	(셋 이상) 하나는~, 나머지는...

• Kelly bought four dresses. One fitted her very well, the others didn't fit her.
➡ 네 개 중 한 개와 나머지 세 개를 의미

one~ another...	(셋 이상) 하나는~, 다른 하나는...

• There were many kinds of kites at the shop. Jude bought one for his nephew.
And he bought another for his girlfriend's niece.
➡ 여러 개 중에서 하나와 다른 하나를 의미 (★ ★★ ● ● ● ◆ ◆ ◆ ■ ■ ■)

some~ others...	(불특정한 다수의 사람/사물) 몇몇은~, 다른 사람(것)들은...

• There are many flowers. Some are lilies and others are tulips.
➡ 많은 것들 중에서 몇 개와 다른 몇 개를 의미 (★ ★★ ★ ★ ★ ● ● ● ● ◆ ◆ ◆ ■ ■ ■)

some~ the others...	(특정한 수의 사람/사물) 몇몇은~, 나머지는...

• Juliet has ten crowns. Some are made of silver, the others are made of gold.
➡ 열 개 중 에서 몇 개와 나머지 남은 것들을 의미 (★ ★ ★ ★ ★ ◆ ◆ ◆ ◆ ◆)

one~ another... the other...	(셋 중에) 하나는~, 다른 하나는..., 나머지 하나는...

• Jane has three kittens. One is white, another is brown and the other is white with black dots.

Answer Keys p. 14

A 다음 보기 에서 알맞은 말을 골라 빈칸에 쓰시오.

보기

another one   the other   some   others   the others

1 I have two pets. One is a dog and _____the other_____ is a cat.

2 _____ people enjoy swimming, but others prefer climbing mountains.

Answer Keys p. 14

3 One of the boys likes playing soccer, while all _____ like playing baseball.

4 There are three caps. One is blue, _____ is green, and _____ is gray.

5 There are two flowers. One is a cosmos and _____ is a lily.

6 Do you have _____ blankets to share with us?

7 In Tim's class, some students go to America and _____ go to France over summer vacation.

8 Some students buy the blue hat, _____ buy the red hat.

9 I have five sisters. Some has long hair and _____ have short hair.

B 다음 우리말 해석에 맞게 빈칸에 알맞은 말을 쓰시오.

1 나에게 두 켤레의 운동화가 있다. 하나는 검정색이고 하나는 회색이다.
➡ I have two pairs of sneakers. _____One_____ is black and _____the other_____ is gray.

2 그녀는 3개 국어를 말할 수 있다. 하나는 한국어이고 다른 하나는 영어, 나머지는 일어이다.
➡ She can speak three languages. One is Korean, _____ is English, and _____ is Japanese.

3 공원에 많은 사람들이 있다. 몇몇은 줄넘기를 하고 있고 어떤 사람들은 테니스를 하고 있다.
➡ There are many people in the park. Some are jumping rope, _____ are playing tennis.

4 어떤 사람들은 록 음악을 좋아하고 어떤 사람들은 발라드를 좋아한다.
➡ _____ people like rock music, and _____ like ballads.

5 바구니 안에 사과는 몇 개는 시지만 나머지는 달다.
➡ _____ of the apples in the basket are sour, but _____ are sweet.

4-12 부정대명사 _ all / both

- all: '모든, 모두'의 뜻을 가진다. 'of'가 함께 올 경우 뒤에 관사나 소유격이 온다.
- both: '양쪽, 둘 다'의 뜻을 가진다. 'of'가 함께 올 경우 뒤에 관사나 소유격이 온다.

1. **all**: 모든, 모두

   (1) [all + 복수명사 + 복수동사]
- **All** the students are enjoying the school festival.

   (2) [all (of) + 관사/소유격 + 복수명사 + 복수동사]
- **All (of)** the computers are used by students.

   (3) [all (of) + 관사/소유격 + 셀 수 없는 명사 + 단수동사]
- **All (of)** my coffee was spilled.

   (4) [동격: 대명사 + all]
- **They all** want to go home before they finish their work.

2. **both**: 양쪽, 둘 다

   (1) [both + 복수명사 + 복수동사]
- **Both** parents were angry with their children.

   (2) [both (of) + 관사/소유격 + 복수명사 + 복수동사]
- **Both (of)** his daughters want to be famous artists.

   (3) [both A and B] A와 B 둘 다
- **Both** Sara and Claire are tall and pretty.

   (4) [동격: 대명사 + both]
- **They both** always help their mother clean the house.

☆Check up!

Answer Keys p. 14

A 괄호 안에서 알맞은 것을 고르시오.

1 They found that all their money (was / were) stolen.

2 Both of the girls (have / has) the same doll.

3 (All they / They all) should wait for their teacher.

4 All of the furniture there (was / were) bought by my mom.

5 (Both they / They both) are going to go hiking this weekend.

6 All the members of the community (are / is) under the age of twenty.

7 Tom planned to buy both of the (shirts / shirt) in the store.

8 All the claims (have / has) been made by the same customer.

4-13 부정대명사 _ each / every

- **each**: '각자, 각기, 각각의'의 뜻으로 명사를 수식하며 단수 취급을 한다.
- **every**: '모든'의 뜻으로 해석하지만 단수 취급을 한다.

1. each : 각자, 각기, 각각의

(1) [each + 단수명사 + 단수동사]
- **Each** <u>person has</u> a different way to relieve stress.

(2) [each of + 관사/소유격 + 복수명사 + 단수동사]
- **Each of** <u>the animals survives</u> in winter in a different way.

(3) 부사적 용법
- Some of the guests paid 10 dollars **each** for the extra charge.

2. every : 모든

(1) [every + 단수명사 + 단수동사]
- **Every** <u>season has</u> its own beauty in Korea.

(2) ~마다, 매~
- Phillip and his family go to Japan **every** winter.

(3) [every + 기수사 + 복수명사] = [every + 서수사 + 단수명사] ~간격으로, ~마다
- Jim has to go on a business trip **every three months**. [every + 기수 + 복수명사]
- = Jim has to go on a business trip **every third month**. [every + 서수 + 단수명사]

✪Check up!

Answer Keys p. 15

A 주어진 단어를 알맞은 형태로 바꾸어 빈칸에 써 넣으시오.

1 Each of the ____students____ should choose what to do in summer. (student)

2 Every _____ is blocked because of the national event. (road)

3 I listened carefully to every _____ John said. (word)

4 Every person in the subway station _____ watching the soccer game. (be)

5 I buy a cake for dessert every two _____. (week)

6 They are planning to invite every _____ to their picnic. (child)

Lesson 4-14 부정대명사 _ some / any / no

- **each**: 'some'은 긍정문에, 'any'는 부정문, 의문문에 주로 쓰인다.
- **no**: 'no'는 부정문에 사용하며, 'no〜'는 'not〜 any'와 바꿔 쓸 수 있다.

◈ some / any / no 의 사용

somebody(someone), something	
긍정문에 사용	• Jenny would like to show us someone who is very handsome.
권유나 요구의 의문문에 사용	• Would you like some coffee?
긍정의 대답을 예상하는 의문문에 사용	• Does Bill have a date with someone tonight?

anybody (anyone), anything	
부정문에 사용	• Lynn didn't get anything on her birthday.
의문문에 사용	• Do you have any vegetables left?
'어떠한 〜라도'의 뜻으로 긍정문에 사용	• Anybody can come to the aquarium to experience marine life.
조건을 나타내는 'if'절에 사용	• If there is anyone else who needs to leave, just let me know.

nobody(no one) = not anybody(anyone)
nothing = not anything

- He told nobody that it was my fault.
    = He did not tell anybody that it was my fault.
- There is nothing to eat.
    = There is not anything to eat.

Answer Keys p. 15

A 다음 빈칸에 들어갈 말을 보기 에서 골라 쓰시오.

보기

something anybody somebody anything

1 ___*Somebody*___ threw away a lot of garbage in the park.

2　She is eager to learn ＿＿＿＿＿＿＿＿ interesting from the exhibition.

3　＿＿＿＿＿＿＿＿ can enter the conference hall after passing the security check.

4　If ＿＿＿＿＿＿＿＿ goes wrong, just call me.

5　Isn't there ＿＿＿＿＿＿＿＿ who can swim in the sea?

6　Did ＿＿＿＿＿＿＿＿ call while Helen was cooking? She is wondering.

7　Can I say ＿＿＿＿＿＿＿＿ about what you said?

8　Don't let ＿＿＿＿＿＿＿＿ speak loudly in the library.

9　Would you like to have ＿＿＿＿＿＿＿＿ to drink?

10　If you have ＿＿＿＿＿＿＿＿ to ask, contact Jane.

B　다음 주어진 우리말에 맞게 빈칸에 알맞은 말을 쓰시오.

1　그녀는 약간의 설탕을 수프에 넣었다.
➡ She put ___some sugar___ in the soup.

2　너는 최근에 좋은 책들을 좀 읽었니?
➡ Have you read ＿＿＿＿＿ lately?

3　그 부유한 남자는 어떤 돈도 기부하지 않았다.
➡ The rich man didn't donate ＿＿＿＿＿.

4　그들에게는 먹을 것이 아무것도 없었다.
➡ They have ＿＿＿＿ to eat.

5　우리에게 조금의 물을 주실 수 있으세요?
➡ Could you give us ＿＿＿＿＿?

6　나는 입을 수 있는 드레스가 전혀 없다.
➡ I ＿＿＿＿ have ＿＿＿＿ dresses that I can wear.

부정대명사 _ either / neither

- either : '둘 중 어느 하나, 각각'의 의미로 단수 취급을 한다.
- neither : '둘 중 어느 것도 ～이 아니다'의 뜻을 가지며, 부정을 의미하고 단수 취급을 한다.

1. either

(1) [either+단수명사] 둘 중 어느 쪽도

- **Either these caps** is nice. [단수 취급] (= **Both these caps** are nice.)
- Elly and Tommy don't want to drink **either of** them. [둘 다]

  (= Elly and Tommy want to drink **neither of** them.)

  ➡ 'neither'는 단어 자체가 부정을 의미하며, 'not either'와 바꿔 쓸 수 있다.

  ※ [either+of+명사구]가 나란히 올 경우 단수와 복수 모두 사용할 수 있다.

  Either of pencils is (are) yours. [단수/복수 가능]

(2) [either A or B] A나 B 둘 중 하나

- **Either** Larry **or** Natasha has to go there instead of me.

  ➡ 'either A or B'의 동사는 두 번째 주어에 맞춘다.

2. neither

(1) [neither+단수명사] 둘 중 어느 쪽도 ～아닌

- **Neither** the singer was wonderful. [단수 취급] (= **Both the singers** weren't wonderful.)

  ※ [neither+of+명사구]가 나란히 올 경우 단수와 복수 모두 사용할 수 있다.

  Neither of them has (have) any stationery. [단수/복수 가능]

(2) [neither A nor B] A도 B 도 ～아니다

- **Neither** Jennifer **nor** I want to eat cake.

  ➡ 'neither A nor B'의 동사는 두 번째 주어에 맞춘다.

Check up!

Answer Keys p. 15

A 다음 우리말 해석에 알맞게 문장을 완성하시오.

1 너희 중에 아무나 저 박스를 옮겨 줄 수 있니?

➡ Could _____either_____ of _____you_____ move the box?

2 어느 바지도 다 잘 어울리네. 하나만 선택하기 어려워.

➡ _____ of the pants are a good choice, so choosing

one is difficult.

3 그 시계 두 개는 다 비싸서 난 어느 것도 사지 않았다.

➡ The two watches were expensive, so I bought

_____ of _____.

4 그녀는 이 책을 Tom이나 Sam 둘 중 한 명에게 줄 것이다.

→ She will give this book to _____ Tom _____ Sam.

5 어느 쪽도 정답이 아니다.

→ _____ answer is correct.

6 Mike나 Marry 둘 중 하나는 오늘 나를 도와줘야 한다.

→ _____ Mike _____ Marry should help me today.

7 내 남자친구는 놀이공원을 싫어하고 나 역시 그러하다.

→ My boyfriend doesn't like going to amusement parks, and I don't like, _____.

8 우리 엄마나 나 둘 다 토마토 파스타를 좋아하지 않는다.

→ _____ my mom _____ I like tomato pasta.

9 나는 Harry에게 두 벌의 셔츠를 보여줬지만 그는 아무것도 원하지 않았다.

→ I showed Harry two shirts, but he wanted _____.

10 Mina는 더 이상 슬프지 않았다. Andrew 역시 그렇지 않았다.

→ Mina wasn't sad any more. _____ was Andrew.

4-16 전체부정과 부분부정

- **전체부정**: 문장에 'not'이나 'never'가 와서 문장 전체를 부정하는 것을 말한다.
- **부분부정**: 'not'이 'all, every, both, always' 등과 함께 쓰이면 문장의 일부만을 부정하게 된다.

1. 전체부정

(1) no, none, nothing, nobody, neither 사용
- **No one** likes him in this company.
- **None** of the members of the group want to go fishing.

(2) not (never)~any 사용
- She did **not** want to meet **any**body tonight.

2. 부분부정

(1) [부정어 + all, every, both] 사용
- **Not all** friends are good to you.
- **Not every** person's dream came true.

(2) [부정어 + always, completely, absolutely, necessarily, entirely] 사용
- She does **not always** depend on you.
- The diamond ring is **not completely** necessary for a wedding.

Answer Keys p. 15

A   다음 우리말을 참고하여 빈칸에 알맞은 말을 쓰시오.

1   내 친구 중 누구도 영어 공부를 좋아하지 않는다.

➡ ____*None*____ of my friends ____*like*____ to study English.

2   모든 학생이 미국을 갈 수 있는 것은 아니다.

➡ _____ students can go to America.

3   친구들이 항상 내 편인 것은 아니다.

➡ Friends are _____ on my side.

4   그 당시에 그는 누구도 만나고 싶지 않았다.

➡ At that time, he did _____ want to meet

_____.

5   그는 두 학생을 다 아는 것은 아니었다.

➡ He did _____ know _____ of the students.

Practice More II

A 빈칸에 들어갈 알맞은 대명사를 쓰시오.

1 Tina, _____this_____ is my sister Jane. Both of you are the same age.

2 _____ doughnuts are John's, and those cookies are mine.

3 Can you see _____ boy in front of the bank?

4 This is my laptop and _____ is his.

5 Would you take a look at _____, please?

6 Our pants are much cheaper than _____ of other brands.

7 _____ will soon be winter. We should find a warmer house.

8 Is _____ your brother over there?

9 His cats are bigger than _____ of other owners.

10 Linda didn't expect the ring to cost _____ much.

B 빈칸에 알맞은 부정대명사를 쓰시오.

1 Presents : books and cups

➡ _____Some_____ of the presents were books and
_____the others_____ were cups.

2 Colors : gray, yellow, black

➡ I like three colors. _____ is gray, _____ is yellow, and _____ is black.

3 Twin daughters : actress, nurse

➡ Helen has twin daughters. _____ is an actress and _____ is a nurse.

4 Club members : Americans, Koreans, Chinese

➡ _____ members of the club are Americans, and _____ are Koreans and Chinese.

5 Pets : a dog, a bird, an iguana

➡ Sam has three pets. _____ is a dog, _____ is a bird, and _____ is an iguana.

C 다음 밑줄 친 부분을 어법에 맞게 고치시오.

1 He asked for help, but <u>somebody</u> tried to help him.

　➡ ___*nobody*___

2 Each student <u>have</u> to hand in the report by today.

　➡ _____

3 Jane and Tom worked hard and helped them each <u>one</u>.

　➡ _____

4 Neither he nor she <u>like</u> this musical.

　➡ _____

5 The man worked on the novel <u>every</u> his life.

　➡ _____

6 I couldn't answer <u>none</u> of these questions.

　➡ _____

7 Ted is <u>always not</u> on my side when I make mistakes.

　➡ _____

8 Neither my uncle <u>or</u> my aunt can attend my wedding.

　➡ _____

9 Every <u>students</u> should attend tomorrow's event.

　➡ _____

10 The tickets cost five dollars <u>one</u>.

　➡ _____

11 All the <u>boy</u> have a guitar.

　➡ _____

12 Almost <u>every</u> the food was prepared for by the chef.

　➡ _____

13 I don't have a raincoat. So, I'll buy <u>it</u>.

　➡ _____

14 We don't agree with <u>nothing</u> you say.

　➡ _____

15 Each of the boys <u>want</u> to play soccer.

　➡ _____

Practice More Ⅱ

Answer Keys p. 15

D 다음 우리말 해석에 맞게 주어진 단어를 알맞게 배열하여 문장을 완성하시오.

1 엄마와 아빠 모두 영어를 유창하게 말하신다.

(both, fluently, mom, speak, dad, English, my, and)

➡ _____ *Both my mom and dad speak English fluently.* _____

2 나는 생일에 오빠로부터 아무것도 받지 못했다.

(I, on my birthday, from, didn't, anything, receive, my brother)

➡ _____

3 10명의 사람 중 한 명만이 그 제안을 받아들였고 나머지는 거절했다.

(Only, refused, it, the proposal, ten people, of, the others, accepted, one, and)

➡ _____

4 그 학생들 중 누구라도 시험에 떨어질 수 있다.

(any, the exam, of, fail, students, could, the)

➡ _____

5 나는 몹시 바빠서 거의 아무것도 사갈 수 없다.

(Because, I, busy, can, anything, hardly, buy, very, I'm)

➡ _____

6 슬프게도 우리 안에는 어떤 새도 남아 있지 않았다.

(sadly, of, the cage, none, in, were left, the birds)

➡ _____

7 매일 운동하는 것은 중요하다.

(it, everyday, is, exercise, important, to)

➡ _____

8 가방 안에는 아무 책도 없었다.

(there, the bag, were, any, in, books, not)

➡ _____

9 Jake는 세 개의 취미가 있다. 하나는 등산, 다른 하나는 영화감상, 나머지 하나는 독서이다.

(the other, and, books, reading, is)

➡ Jake has three hobbies. One is climbing mountains, another is watching movies, _____

내신 최다 출제 유형

01 다음 중 어법상 옳은 것을 고르시오. [출제 예상 85%]

① All the windows were broke.
② Both of her sisters like their mother.
③ Both sons hate eat beans.
④ All of her music makes me sadness.
⑤ All of the flowers is beautiful.

02 It의 쓰임이 나머지 넷과 다른 하나를 고르시오. [출제 예상 90%]

① It takes thirty minutes.
② It was snowing last night.
③ It is hot and humid in summer.
④ It is bright outside.
⑤ It is hard to speak foreign languages fluently.

03 다음 밑줄 친 부분이 어법상 옳지 않은 것을 고르시오. [출제 예상 85%]

① He cut himself when he was cooking.
② One of them enjoyed themselves.
③ We are washing ourselves in the river.
④ Tom hurt himself while driving.
⑤ Miran hid herself behind the sofa.

04 다음 중 어법상 어색한 문장을 고르시오. [출제 예상 85%]

① Plastic is a useful material.
② James is a man of wise.
③ The diamond is of value to the world.
④ I asked the question with care.
⑤ We think Sam is a man of courage.

05 다음 밑줄 친 부분이 어법상 어색한 것을 고르시오. [출제 예상 90%]

① Mia hurt herself while swimming in the river.
② I cut myself when I was cooking.
③ Teddy hid himself under the bed.
④ They are washing the cars himself.
⑤ One of them enjoyed himself.

06 다음 빈칸에 들어갈 말이 바르게 짝지어진 것을 고르시오. [출제 예상 80%]

> • Jane has two dolls. One has blond hair and _____ has red hair.
> • I have five marbles. One is for you, another is for your sister, and _____ are for me.

① the other − the other
② another − the others
③ the other − the others
④ another − the other
⑤ the other − other

07 다음 밑줄 친 it과 쓰임이 같은 것을 고르시오. [출제 예상 95%]

> It is good for your children to grow pets.

① It is in front of the post office.
② It is exciting to watch a soccer game.
③ It is much better than your car.
④ It is getting dark. Let's hurry up.
⑤ It is a nice sunny day.

[01~02] 다음 중 명사의 단수형과 복수형이 바르게
연결된 것을 고르시오.

01
① sheep – sheeps   ② ox – oxes
③ mouse – mice   ④ branch – branchs
⑤ woman – woman

02
① Chinese – Chinese
② deer – deers
③ souvenir – souvenires
④ fly – flys
⑤ goose – gooses

[03~04] 다음 중 명사의 단수형과 복수형이 바르게 연
결되지 <u>않는</u> 것을 고르시오.

03
① monkey – monkeys
② diary – diaries
③ bush – bushs
④ tooth – teeth
⑤ man – men

04
① basis – bases   ② cliff – cliffs
③ thief – thieves   ④ leaf – leaves
⑤ belief – believes

[05~06] 다음 빈칸에 들어갈 알맞은 단어를 고르시오.

05
| The other people gave up crossing the desert, so I had to walk on all _____ myself. |

① of   ② to   ③ in
④ by   ⑤ for

06
| There are two official languages in Canada. One is English and _____ is French. |

① another   ② the other
③ other   ④ others
⑤ the others

07 ★★★
다음 글의 빈칸에 들어갈 말이 바르게 짝지어진 것
을 고르시오.

| Three women wanted something to drink. _____ woman ordered a glass of juice, _____ a cup of coffee, _____ a glass of iced tea. |

① One – other – the others
② One – another – others
③ One – another – the other
④ One – another – other
⑤ One – other – the other

08 다음 중 어법상 옳은 것을 <u>모두</u> 고르시오.

① I saved enough money to buy a car.
② The matches is on your right hand.
③ Blue was chosen for the ocean and the sky.
④ We can save water by using a cup when we brush our tooth.
⑤ I can cook this meat in a different ways.

09 다음 중 밑줄 친 대명사가 생략 가능한 문장을 고르시오.

① She thinks to <u>herself</u>, "Everything is okay."
② I have a dream <u>myself</u>.
③ Please help <u>yourself</u>.
④ Her cat is not <u>herself</u> today.
⑤ He devoted <u>himself</u> to the project.

10 다음 중 밑줄 친 <u>it</u>이 가주어로 쓰인 것을 고르시오.

① <u>It</u> is hot and humid in summer.
② <u>It</u> seems that she is the leader.
③ <u>It</u> was I that bought some fruit yesterday.
④ <u>It</u> is not my computer but my brother's.
⑤ <u>It</u> is hard to speak Korean like a native.

11 다음 중 <u>itself</u>가 강조용법으로 쓰이지 <u>않은</u> 것을 고르시오.

① Mary is nice <u>itself</u>.
② She will be impressed with the building <u>itself</u>.
③ Nothing is evil in <u>itself</u>.
④ Even the well <u>itself</u> was dried up.
⑤ The mountain is a green forest <u>itself</u>.

[12~13] 다음 중 어법상 옳은 것을 고르시오.

12 ① He still practices for a hour a day.
② Busan is Korean's most beautiful seaport.
③ One day a old lady asked me for directions.
④ Many people loved her because she was honest.
⑤ I studied at an university to become a doctor.

13 ① This will help us work for clean waters.
② If teachers give more homework, will students do better?
③ I need a few knowledge about art in order to enjoy the paintings.
④ We found that it had many information.
⑤ People who aren't physically health get tired easily.

14 다음 밑줄 친 <u>a(an)</u>의 의미가 나머지 넷과 <u>다른</u> 것을 고르시오.

① Can you give me <u>an</u> example, please?
② <u>A</u> month later, she invited her friends to dinner.
③ They allowed me to play outside for an hour <u>a</u> day.
④ At the end of the sentence, write <u>a</u> period.
⑤ Do you have <u>a</u> question about this?

15 ★★★ 다음 중 빈칸에 the가 들어가야 하는 것을 고르시오.

① If you don't eat _____ breakfast, your health will be suffer.
② He wants to watch _____ TV now.
③ Actually, I don't have much interest in _____ baseball.
④ She always listens to _____ music when she works.
⑤ I think he is _____ first man to win the competition.

16 다음 밑줄 친 someone의 쓰임이 잘못된 것을 고르시오.

① Harry wants to meet someone who can have a date.
② I'm sure that she's not going to invite someone.
③ This sign shows that someone likes you.
④ I saw someone in the classroom.
⑤ she is waiting for someone now.

17 다음 빈칸에 it이 들어갈 수 없는 것을 고르시오.

① _____ was by accident that he met his old friend.
② How long does _____ take for you to go to work?
③ I thought _____ Jim had a great idea.
④ I make _____ a rule to work out every night.
⑤ _____ seems to be somebody else who knows the truth.

18 ★★★ 다음 문장의 밑줄 친 one과 같은 용법으로 쓰인 것을 고르시오.

> People say that one should never judge a person by his or her appearance.

① This machine is the first one to be called a car.
② One cannot fly in the sky.
③ As an old thing dies, a new one is born again in its place.
④ I saw one of your classmates in the cafe over there.
⑤ Try to concentrate on your work in one sitting.

19 다음 중 어법상 어색한 것을 고르시오.

① Every student in this room studies very hard.
② Each of the girls are interested in plastic surgery.
③ All of the trains were delayed due to the traffic jam.
④ I don't like this dress. Show me another.
⑤ Both of the sisters agree to quit the struggle.

Note plastic surgery 성형수술

20 다음 밑줄 친 anyone의 쓰임이 잘못된 것을 고르시오.

① Anyone took my purse that I bought yesterday.

② He will offer a great reward to anyone who cures his eyes.

③ Don't forget that anyone can guess who you are.

④ I didn't want anyone to teach me English.

⑤ She doesn't want anyone else to succeed in this.

[21~22] 다음 문장의 밑줄 친 it과 같은 용법으로 쓰인 것을 고르시오.

21

It was her that both of us wanted to be with.

① It is disappointing that she cheated on the exam.

② It is believed that human beings are born equal.

③ I thought it exciting to swim in the river.

④ It was in the closet that I found my lost wallet.

⑤ He knew it that she didn't like him.

22

It is not difficult to swim.

① It takes two hours to get from here to Namyangju City.

② It is snowing. All kids are making snowmen.

③ It is often foggy and rainy in London.

④ It is dangerous to ride a motorcycle without a helmet.

⑤ It will soon be Christmas.

23 다음 중 부분부정 문장이 아닌 것을 고르시오.

① Not everyone can catch fish well.

② We don't always follow her advice.

③ Both of them don't think he is guilty.

④ She likes to invite everyone.

⑤ He didn't understand any of them.

24 다음 중 어법상 어색한 것을 고르시오.

① Both of the dresses are too pretty to choose one.

② All we had to run away from the fierce dog.

③ They both wanted to take part in the plan.

④ All the furniture in that house is now for sale.

⑤ All of them are studying at school.

★★★
25 다음 글의 빈칸에 들어갈 말이 바르게 짝지어진 것을 고르시오.

> Jinsu has five kittens. This is his favorite _____. _____ calls _____ Eddie and it was named after the respected inventor, Edison. It is much cuter than his _____ kittens.

① one − Other − it − other
② one − He − one − other
③ one − He − it − other
④ one − The other − it − other
⑤ one − He − it − the other

26 다음 주어진 우리말과 같은 뜻이 되도록 빈칸에 알맞은 말을 고르시오.

> 우리 둘 다 네 말이 진실이라고 생각해.
> = _____ of us think your words are true.

① Most   ② Both   ③ Almost
④ All   ⑤ Rest

[27~28] 다음 중 어법상 옳은 것을 고르시오.

★★★
27 ① She loved to play piano.
② He pointed to third man and asked a question.
③ She had the dinner with her boyfriend's parents.
④ Would you teach me how to play the basketball?
⑤ The first chapter is my favorite part in this book.

28 ① She doesn't understand why I spend so many money on CDs.
② I'm going study science, history and English.
③ They said that they felt guilty for the poor.
④ The woman who is carrying two boxes have brown eyes.
⑤ I had to cross the field in order to going to church.

[29~30] 다음 중 어법상 어색한 것을 고르시오.

29 ① The police is chasing after a bank robber.
② The audience is crazy about the music.
③ My family members are all diligent.
④ Sheep are grazing in the pasture.
⑤ Her family is large.

30 ① He has a lot of interest in politics.
② Could I try a little of your wine?
③ The theory is difficult, and few students understand them.
④ We had few snow this year.
⑤ A few of us can say that we always tell the truth.

31 다음 중 명사의 단수형과 복수형이 바르게 연결된 것을 모두 고르시오.

① thief − thiefs   ② cliff − cliffs
③ bush − bushes   ④ cry − crys
⑤ children − childrens

★★★
32 다음 문장을 'It was ～that' 구문으로 바꿀 때 어법상 틀린 것을 고르시오.

> She won the gold medal for the first time in figure skating.

① It was for the first time that she won thegold medal in figure skating.

② It was in figure skating that she won the gold medal for the first time.

③ It was the gold medal that she won for the first time in figure skating.

④ It was she that won the gold medal for the first time in figure skating.

⑤ It was won that she did the gold medal for the first time in figure skating.

33 다음 중 어색한 표현을 고르시오.

① a cup of black tea　② a slice of cheese
③ a loaf of milk　　　④ a piece of advice
⑤ a pound of gold

34 다음 중 어법상 옳은 것을 모두 고르시오.

① Only thing that I could do was to tell some advice.

② She appeared in the stadium in an cheerleadering uniform.

③ Sally had the same feeling as me.

④ I want to be a lawyer, but my parents want me to be an artist.

⑤ A man saved a old lady in danger.

35 다음 중 어법상 어색한 것을 모두 고르시오.

① We should remember that we can't live without others's help.

② Are you sending the same message back?

③ The book is the oldest record of European history.

④ I will never forget the week's journey.

⑤ A proverb says that Rome was not built in the day.

◇◇◇◇◇◇◇◇ 서술형 평가 ◇◇◇◇◇◇◇◇

[36~38] 다음 중 틀린 부분을 찾아 바르게 고쳐 쓰시오.
★★★
36

> A Can I borrow your brother's a notebook?
> B Let me ask him first.

_____ ➡ _____

37

> If you have any difficulty in opening these applications forms, please download this program.

_____ ➡ _____

Answer Keys p. 16~17

38

> If one part of an ecosystem is damaged, it affects others parts of the ecosystem.

_____ ➡ _____

[39~41] 다음 두 문장이 같은 뜻이 되도록 할 때 빈칸에 알맞은 단어를 쓰시오.

39

> When you travel on a train, just think of what you have read.
> = When you travel _____ train, just think of what you have read.

➡ _____

40

> Wild animals are hard to tame.
> = _____ _____ hard to tame wild animals.

➡ _____

41

> Phillip and Grace seem to be interested in a musical film.
> = _____ _____ that Phillip and Grace are interested in a musical film.

➡ _____

[42~43] 주어진 우리말과 같은 뜻이 되도록 빈칸에 알맞은 말을 쓰시오.

42

> 옛 물건들 중 일부는 현대에서도 유용하다.
> = Some the old things are _____ _____ in modern times.

➡ _____

43

> 그녀는 너무나 아름다워서 그 누구도 다른 여자들에게 관심을 두지 않았다.
> = She was so beautiful that no one gave _____ thought to _____ girls.

➡ _____

[44~45] 다음 괄호 안의 단어를 우리말에 맞게 바르게 배열하여 문장을 완성하시오.

★★★

44

> Lily는 새로운 업무 때문에 쉽게 피로를 느낀다.
> (Lily / tired / because / of / feels / easily / a / task / new)

➡ _____

★★★

45

> 시험 문제 중 몇몇은 쉬웠지만 나머지는 너무 어려웠다.
> (Some of / were / easy / difficult / the test questions / but / the others / were)

➡ _____

05

Chapter
수동태

Point Check I

◆ **수동태**: 어떤 일이 어떻게 발생되거나 일어나게 되었는지에 초점이 맞춰진 문장을 말한다. 사물이 스스로 행동을 할 수 없기 때문에 수동태 문장을 사용할 경우가 많다. 'be동사＋과거분사'의 형태를 지닌다.

1. 수동태의 시제와 형태: [be동사 + 과거분사 + by 목적격]

시제	평서문	부정문	의문문	목적격
현재	am, are, is + 과거분사	am, are, is not + 과거분사	Am, Are, Is + 주어 + 과거분사	+ by 목적격
과거	was, were + 과거분사	was, were not + 과거분사	Was, Were + 주어 + 과거분사	
미래	will be + 과거분사	will be not + 과거분사	Will + 주어 + be + 과거분사	

2. 능동태에서 수동태 문장 만들기

① 능동태의 동사가 현재형 ⇒ 수동태의 **be동사(am/are/is) + 과거분사**
② 능동태의 동사가 과거형 ⇒ 수동태의 **be동사(was/were) + 과거분사**
③ 능동태의 불특정 주어 ⇒ 수동태 'by + 행위자' 생략 가능
• I clean the bathroom every Sunday. [능동태]
➡ The bathroom is cleaned by me every Sunday. [수동태]

3. 수동태의 종류

종류	평서문	부정문	의문문
진행형	주어 + be동사 + **being** + 과거분사 + by 목적격	주어 + be동사 + **not** being + 과거분사 + by 목적격	• be동사 + 주어 + **being** + 과거분사 ～? • 의문사 + be동사 + **being** + 과거분사 ～?
완료형	주어 + **have/has been** + 과거분사 + by 목적격	주어 + **have/has not been** + 과거분사 + by 목적격	• **Have/Has** + 주어 + **been** + 과거분사 ～? • 의문사 + **have/has been** + 과거분사 ～?
조동사	주어 + **조동사** + be + 과거분사 + by 목적격	주어 + **조동사 not** be + 과거분사 + by 목적격	• **조동사** + 주어 + be + 과거분사 ～? • 의문사 + **조동사** + be + 과거분사 ～?

일반적인 수동태

• **수동태**: 어떤 일이 발생되거나 일어나게 되었는지에 초점이 맞춰진 문장으로 주로 스스로 무언가를 할 수 없는 사물을 주어로 수동태 문장을 만든다.

1. 수동태 만들기

[능동태] Sally **makes** a model house.

[수동태] A model house **is made** by Sally.

➡ ① 능동태의 동사가 현재형 → 주어의 인칭에 따라 'am, are, is' 중 하나를 선택 + 과거분사
② 능동태의 동사가 과거형 → 주어의 인칭에 따라 'was, were' 중 하나를 선택 + 과거분사
③ 능동태의 주어가 'people'처럼 누구나 알거나, 'somebody'처럼 말하지 않아도 되는 경우 수동태에서 'by + 행위자'는 생략이 가능

2. 수동태의 시제: [be동사로 나타낸다.]

시제	형태	예문
현재	am, are, is + 과거분사	• The song is sung by the famous singer.
과거	was, were + 과거분사	• The song was sung by the famous singer.
미래	will be + 과거분사	• The song will be sung by the famous singer.

3. 'by + 목적격'의 생략

(1) 행위자가 일반인일 때
• English **is spoken (by people)** in many countries.

(2) 행위자를 알 수 없을 때
• That building **was built (by someone)** in the 15th century.

Check up!

Answer Keys p. 18

A 다음 주어진 문장과 같은 뜻이 되도록 빈칸에 알맞은 말을 쓰시오.

1 She cleans her room every evening.
➡ Her room ____is cleaned____ by her every evening.

2 Someone found my wallet last night.
➡ My wallet _____ by someone last night.

3   All age groups loved the animated movie.
    ➡ The animated movie _____ by all age groups.

4   The police officer saw the wanted criminal at the bus station.
    ➡ The wanted criminal _____ by the police officer at the bus station.

5   Andy will open the grocery store next year.
    ➡ The grocery store _____ by Andy next year.

6   The plumber fixed the broken pipe.
    ➡ The broken pipe _____ by the plumber.

7   Hundreds of people use the train every morning.
    ➡ The train _____ by hundreds of people every morning.

8   My mom bought this microwave fifteen years ago.
    ➡ This microwave _____ by my mom fifteen years ago.

9   Somebody stole my laptop in the classroom.
    ➡ My laptop _____ in the classroom.

10 They built this palace in the 16th century.
    ➡ This palace _____ in the 16th century.

B 다음 능동태 문장을 수동태로 전환해서 문장을 완성하시오.

1   The author wrote another interesting detective novel.
    ➡ *Another interesting detective novel was written by the author.*

2   The manager refused to accept this proposal.
    ➡ _____

3   Her beautiful smile attracts some people.
    ➡ _____

4   The band will perform a live concert this evening.
    ➡ _____

5   They will bring some cookies for the party.
    ➡ _____

6   Jim and Tim made the kite yesterday.
    ➡ _____

수동태의 부정문과 의문문

- **수동태의 부정문**: be동사 뒤에 'not'을 붙여서 'be not + 과거분사 + by목적격'으로 만든다.
- **수동태의 의문문**: 'Be + 주어 + 과거분사 ～?'의 형태가 된다.

1. 수동태의 부정문: [be동사 + not + 과거분사 + by 목적격]

- He **does not** take the Korean history class.
  = The Korean history class **is not taken** by him.

- She **did not** teach English writing.
  = English writing **was not taught** by her.

2. 수동태의 의문문: [be동사 + 주어 + 과거분사 + by목적격～?]

- **Do** you write a diary every night?
  = **Is** a diary **written** by you every night?

- **Did** the students clean the classroom?
  = **Was** the classroom **cleaned** by the students?

3. 의문사가 있는 의문문의 형태

의문사가 목적어일 경우	[의문사 + be동사 + 과거분사 + by목적격～?]

- What did she watch on TV?
  ➡ What was watched by her on TV?

의문사가 부사일 경우	[의문사 + be동사 + 주어 + 과거분사 + by목적격～?]

- When did he play tennis?
  ➡ When was tennis played by him?

의문사가 주어일 경우	[By + 의문사 + be동사 + 주어 + 과거분사～?]

- Who broke the window yesterday?
  ➡ By whom was the window broken yesterday?

A   다음 문장을 수동태로 바꾸어 쓰시오.

1   What did she find in the room?

➡ _____ *What was found by her in the room?* _____

2   Do many students take the graduation test?

➡ _____

3   Which pen does Hana use every day?

➡ _____

4   Did Tom break the windows?

➡ _____

5   Harry and his son did not make the table.

➡ _____

6   Does Lina keep the iguana in her room?

➡ _____

7   What kind of movie will they watch tonight?

➡ _____

8   Did Sam draw any pictures on the wall?

➡ _____

9   Whom did Max invite to the big party?

➡ _____

10   Thomas will not pick her up because he is so busy.

➡ _____

11   Where did Suho make the minicar model?

➡ _____

12   Does the organization help many abandoned dogs?

➡ _____

13   When did he dig the hole?

➡ _____

14   They did not run the flower shop.

➡ _____

15   Why did the community cancel the conference?

➡ _____

5-3 진행형 수동태

• 진행형 수동태: be동사로 진행형 'be being'을 만들고, '과거분사'를 써서 'be being + 과거분사'의 수동태 진행형을 만든다.

1. 진행형의 평서문: [주어＋be동사＋being＋과거분사＋by 목적격]

• A cook **is cooking** some special food.
= Some special food **is being cooked** by a cook.

2. 진행형의 부정문: [주어＋be동사＋not＋being＋과거분사＋by 목적격]

• Harry **is not practicing** the violin.
= The violin **is not being practiced** by Harry.

3. 진행형의 의문문:

(1) 의문사가 없는 경우: [be동사 + 주어 + being + 과거분사 + by목적격～?]

• **Is** she **teaching** children?
= **Are** children **being taught** by her?

(2) 의문사가 있는 경우: [의문사 + be동사 + being + 과거분사 + by목적격～?]

• **What are** the students **doing** in the hall?
= **What is being done** by the students in the hall?

★Check up!

Answer Keys p. 18

A 우리말 해석에 맞게 주어진 단어를 이용하여 빈칸을 채우시오.

Note
• televise 텔레비전으로 방송하다

1 어떤 종류의 영화가 상영 중이니? (show)
➡ What kind of movies ___are being shown___ ?

2 그 차는 지금 수리 중이니? (repair)
➡ Is the car _____ now?

3 그 콘서트는 지금 TV에서 방송되고 있지 않다. (televise)
➡ The concert isn't _____ on TV now.

4 몇몇 중요한 이슈들이 회의실에서 토의되고 있다. (discuss)
➡ Some important issues are _____ in the meeting room.

Answer Keys p. 18

5 지금 내가 가장 좋아하는 곡이 Sally에 의해 연주되고 있다. (play)
➡ My favorite song is _____ by Sally right now.

6 그 접시들은 물로 세척되고 있었다. (wash)
➡ The dishes are _____ with water.

7 아이들을 위한 맛있는 점심식사가 요리되고 있다. (cook)
➡ A delicious lunch is _____ for children.

8 그 리더를 통해 몇 가지 가능한 대안들이 추천되고 있다. (recommend)
➡ Several possible alternatives _____ by the leader.

9 실험실에서 David는 무엇을 하고 있니? (do)
➡ What _____ by David in the laboratory?

10 Jane과 Tom은 타워를 건설하고 있는 중이 아니다. (build)
➡ The tower _____ not _____ by Jane and Tom.

11 그녀는 서랍에 수건을 쌓고 있다. (place)
➡ The towels _____ in the drawer by her.

12 그 편지는 많은 이들에 의해 읽히고 있다. (read)
➡ The letter _____ by many people.

13 낡은 냉장고는 수리공에 의해 수리되고 있다. (fix)
➡ The old refrigerator _____ by the repairman.

14 그 소년은 어린 양을 치료해 주고 있는 중이다. (treat)
➡ The young sheep _____ by the boy.

15 그 폭력적인 연극은 비평가들에게 비난받고 있는 중이니? (criticize)
➡ Is the violent play _____ by the critics?

완료형 수동태

- 완료형 수동태: 'have been + 과거분사'의 형태를 가지고 있다.

1. 완료형의 평서문: [주어 + have/has been + 과거분사 + by 목적격]

- The old woman **has planted** various flowers.
  = Various flowers **have been planted** by the old woman.

2. 완료형의 부정문: [주어 + have/has not been + 과거분사 + by 목적격]

- Kelly **hasn't finished** the story yet.
  = The story **has not been finished** by Kelly.

3. 완료형의 의문문:

(1) 의문사가 없는 경우: [Have/Has + 주어 + been + 과거분사 + by목적격 ~?]

- **Have** they **traveled** around Europe?
  = **Has** Europe **been traveled** by them?

(2) 의문사가 있는 경우: [의문사 + have/has been + 과거분사 + by목적격 ~?]

- **What have** you and Mary **seen** at Namsan Tower?
  = **What has been seen** by you and Mary at Namsan Tower?

Answer Keys p. 18

A 우리말과 뜻이 같도록 주어진 말을 이용하여 빈칸을 채우시오.

1 그 전염병의 원인은 아직 밝혀지지 않았다. (reveal)

➡ The cause of the epidemic ____*has not been revealed*____ yet.

2 그 문제가 벌써 Helen에 의해 풀렸니? (solve)

➡ _____ the problem already _____ by Helen?

3 근로자들은 그에 의해 임금을 지불 받았니? (pay)

➡ _____ the workers _____ by him?

4 문제들은 아직 다 출제되지 못했다. (set)

➡ The questions _____ yet.

5 얼마나 많은 사람들이 공연에 초대되었니? (invite)

➡ How many people _____ to the performance?

6 아직 내가 기다리는 영화가 개봉되지 않았다. (release)

➡ The movie that I am waiting for _____

   yet.

7 그 그림들은 그 젊은 남자에 의해 그려졌다. (draw)

➡ The pictures _____ by the young man.

B 다음 문장을 수동태로 전환할 때 빈칸에 알맞은 말을 쓰시오.

1 She has used this camera since last week.

➡ This camera ___*has been used*___ by her since last week.

2 The volunteers have helped the poor.

➡ The poor _____ by the volunteers.

3 Helen has painted her daughter's portrait.

➡ Her daughter's portrait _____ by Helen.

4 The teacher has postponed the test several times.

➡ The test _____ by the teacher several

   times.

5 The company has invented a new type of coffee.

➡ A new type of coffee _____ by the company.

6 Some people have used the information provided Mr. Park.

➡ The information provided Mr. Park _____ by

   some people.

7 My family has celebrated the holiday.

➡ The holiday _____ by my family.

8 I have already returned the books to the library.

➡ The books _____ to the library by

   me.

9 Has Sara recycled all the items?

➡ _____ all the items _____ by Sara?

10 What have the people prepared for the party?

➡ What _____ for the party?

Note

• **be released** 개봉되다

• **volunteer** 자원봉사자

• **portrait** 초상화

• **postpone** 연기하다, 미루다

• **provide** 제공하다, 주다

5-5 조동사의 수동태

• **조동사의 수동태**: 조동사 다음에 be동사와 과거분사를 사용하여 '조동사＋be＋과거분사' 형태로 나타낸다.

1. 평서문: [주어＋조동사＋be＋과거분사＋by 목적격]

• Thomas **can get** first prize this time.
= First prize **can be gotten** by Thomas this time.

2. 부정문: [주어＋조동사 not be＋과거분사＋by 목적격]

• Amy **may not allow** the children to go camping.
= The children **may not be allowed** to go camping by Amy.

3. 의문문:

(1) 의문사가 없는 경우: [조동사＋주어＋be＋과거분사＋by 목적격～?]

• **Should** we **give up** the prize this time?
= **Should** the prize **be given up** by us this time?

(2) 의문사가 있는 경우: [의문사＋조동사＋be＋과거분사＋by 목적격～?]

• **What can** he do to go abroad?
= **What can be done** by him to go abroad?

✪Check up!

Answer Keys p. 19

A 다음 밑줄 친 부분을 어법에 맞게 고쳐서 문장을 바르게 완성하시오.

Note

• **do one's best** 최선을 다하다
• **scold** 야단치다, 꾸짖다

1 The coat <u>will buy</u> by my mom.
➡ The coat ____*will be bought*____ by my mom.

2 Your English skills <u>will improve</u> if you do your best.
➡ Your English skills _____ if you do your best.

3 The boys <u>may not scold</u> by their parents.
➡ The boys _____ by their parents.

4 A sofa <u>will bring</u> by Jane.
➡ A sofa _____ by Jane.

5 This promise <u>must keeping</u> by us forever.
➡ This promise _____ by us forever.

6 These seeds <u>will plant</u> next to the tree.
➡ These seeds _____ next to the tree.

7 My design <u>must not copy</u> by others.

➡ My design _____ by others.

8 <u>Should it finish</u> by tomorrow?

➡ _____ it _____ by tomorrow?

9 When <u>can</u> the work <u>start</u> by him?

➡ When_____ the work _____ by him?

10 Thirty points <u>can score</u> in the game by the team.

➡ Thirty points _____ in the game by the team.

B 다음 문장을 수동태로 전환할 때 빈칸에 알맞은 말을 쓰시오.

1 The professor may accept Tim's proposal.

➡ Tim's proposal ___*may be accepted*___ by the professor.

2 How often should you take the medicine?

➡ How often should the medicine _____ by you?

3 The students will bring cans and bottles.

➡ Cans and bottles _____ by the students.

4 What can John do to save money?

➡ What _____ by John to save money?

5 Do I have to take care of the dog until four o'clock?

➡ Does the dog _____ until four o'clock by me?

6 Can you repair the broken watch?

➡ Can the broken watch _____ by you?

7 He might have rescued the sick animals last night.

➡ The sick animals might _____ by him last night.

Practice More I

Answer Keys p. 19

A 빈칸에 알맞은 말을 써 넣으시오.

1 The movie _____is (was) directed_____ by Peter. (direct)

2 The competition _____ won by a young girl. (be)

3 A lot of problems _____ by the final contest. (cause)

4 I want to know what monthly magazines _____ by the store. (sell)

5 Coffee beans _____ when I entered the room. (roast)

6 Unfortunately, she _____ by her opponent. (defeat)

7 Some servants have _____ cruelly by Mr. Kim. (treat)

8 When was the special message _____? (announce)

9 Several storybooks have _____ for us by my aunt. (write)

10 A lot of endangered animals have _____ by the park. (protect)

B 주어진 문장을 수동태 문장으로 바꾸어 쓰시오.

1 He delivered the pizza to me.
   ➡ _____ *The pizza was delivered to me by him.* _____

2 The students have already solved the riddle.
   ➡ _____

3 You should not forget the deadline for the reports.
   ➡ _____

4 The robot isn't moving the box.
   ➡ _____

5 The lady ought to clean all the hotel rooms.
   ➡ _____

> **Note**
> • **defeat** 패배시키다
> • **opponent** 상대
> • **servant** 하인, 고용인
> • **cruelly** 잔인하게, 무심하게
> • **endangered** 위험에 처한
> • **deadline** 기한, 마감 시간
> • **ought to** ~해야 한다

6 Sam's words broke my heart.

➡ _____

7 The factory does not follow the rules.

➡ _____

8 When did she find this file?

➡ _____

9 The company did not produce this special chocolate.

➡ _____

10 Do they hold the final game in the stadium?

➡ _____

C 다음 문장에서 어법상 어색한 것을 찾아 바르게 고치시오.

1 Your ID card has read successfully.

_____read_____ ➡ ___been read___

2 The scientists have been used the machine.

_____ ➡ _____

3 What has been seeing during the trip?

_____ ➡ _____

4 The island has explored many times.

_____ ➡ _____

5 Can the garbage be recycling?

_____ ➡ _____

6 The large room is not be used now.

_____ ➡ _____

7 The students may be not scolded by their moms.

_____ ➡ _____

8 Valuable lessons must be learning by all the students.

_____ ➡ _____

9 What can being done to prevent such traffic accidents?

_____ ➡ _____

10 We have being helped by Sam until now.

_____ ➡ _____

D 다음 단어를 알맞게 배열하여 문장을 완성하시오.

1 (the, is, being, the repairman, broken, by, printer, fixed)

➡ *The broken printer is being fixed by the repairman.*

2 (the, is, the, by, container, being, large helicopter, moved)

➡ _____

3 (the walls, by, Ann's house, being, of, volunteers, painted, were)

➡ _____

4 (a new business, by, is, being, James, developed)

➡ _____

5 (a, was, question, he, stupid, such, asked)

➡ _____

6 (a wooden hut, made, Harry, will, be, by his father, for)

➡ _____

7 (cheating, never, has, by, been, the teacher, accepted)

➡ _____

8 (delicious, being, for, dinner, prepared, Minji, was, a)

➡ _____

9 (used, on the street, were, sold, cars, being, the)

➡ _____

10 (the, by, old, being, washing machine, is, fixed, Tom)

➡ _____

Point Check II

◆ **수동태** : 어떤 일이 어떻게 발생되거나 일어나게 되었는지에 초점이 맞춰진 문장을 말한다. 사물이 스스로 행동을 할 수 없기 때문에 수동태 문장을 사용할 경우가 많다. 'be동사+과거분사'의 형태를 지닌다.

1. 4형식과 5형식 문장의 수동태

4형식 문장	5형식 문장

• Juliet gave him a handkerchief. [능동태]
 간목   직목
 	
➡ ① He was given a handkerchief.
   [간접목적어의 수동태]
   ② A handkerchief was given to him by
   Juliet. [직접목적어의 수동태]
	• Lorry heard a man shouting(shout) in the building.
	  ➡ A man was heard shouting(to shout) in the building by Lorry.

2. 부정사와 동명사의 수동태

to부정사의 수동태	[to be + 과거분사]	동명사의 수동태	[being + 과거분사]

3. that이 이끄는 문장의 수동태

주절과 that절의
시제가 같은 경우
	[It is ~ that...] / [~ is + 과거분사 + to부정사]
	• Cathy believes **that** Robby loves her so much.
	  ➡ **It** is believed **that** Robby loves her so much by Cathy.
	  ➡ Robby **is believed to love** her so much by Cathy.

that절의 시제가
이전인 경우
	[It is ~ that...] / [~ is + 과거분사 + 완료부정사(to have + 과거분사)]
	• I know **that** the earthquake destroyed the buildings.
	  ➡ **It** is known **that** the earthquake destroyed the buildings.
	  ➡ The earthquake **is known to have destroyed** the buildings.

4. 수동태에 자주 쓰이는 동사구

• ask for	~을 요청하다	• bring up	~을 기르다
• catch up with	~을 따라잡다	• laugh at	~을 비웃다
• look after	~을 돌보다	• look down on	~을 멸시하다
• look up to	~을 존경하다	• make use of	~을 이용하다
• run over	~을 치다	• take care of	~을 돌보다
• put off	~을 미루다		

Lesson 5-6 4형식 문장의 수동태

• **4형식 문장의 수동태**: '주어 + 동사 + 간접목적어 + 직접목적어'로 이루어진 4형식 문장은
목적어가 두 개이기 때문에 수동태 문장을 두 개 만들 수 있다.

1. 4형식 문장의 수동태 만들기

• Lina sent me a gift. [능동태]
　　　　　 간목　직목
➡ ① I **was sent** a gift by Lina. [간접목적어의 수동태]

　 ② A gift **was sent** to me by Lina. [직접목적어의 수동태]

➡ 직접목적어가 수동태의 주어가 될 경우에는 간접목적어 앞에 'to, for, of'와 같은 전치사를 붙여준다.

2. 직접목적어만을 수동태의 주어로 하는 동사

to + 간접목적어	sell, pass, bring, write, read
for + 간접목적어	buy, make, get, find, cook, choose, do

• She **buys** her daughter a new dress.
➡ A new dress **is bought** for her daughter by her. (O)
　 Her daughter **is bought** a new dress by her. (X)

3. 간접목적어 앞에 쓰이는 전치사와 동사

to + 간접목적어	give, lend, show, tell, teach, send, sell, pass, bring, read, write
for + 간접목적어	buy, make, get, find, cook, choose, do
of + 간접목적어	ask

☆Check up!

Answer Keys p. 19~20

A 괄호 안에서 알맞은 것을 고르시오.

1 The letter will be sent ((to) / for) you.

2 The soccer ball was given (to / of) Sam by his sister.

3 A nice house was built (for / to) my family.

4 A few difficult questions were asked (of / to) Cindy.

5 The old chair has already been sold (to / for) Jane.

6 A green dress was bought (to / for) my daughter.

7 Some think the secret has not been told (to / for) anyone.

8 A mountain bike was brought (for / **to**) me by my father.

9 A suitable shelter should be found (**to** / for) the disabled.

10 Some delicious food will be cooked (**for** / to) the guests.

B 다음 문장을 수동태로 바꿀 때 빈칸에 알맞은 말을 쓰시오.

1 James will give her a pink hat.
→ She _____*will be given a pink hat*_____ by her.
→ A pink hat _____*will be given to James*_____ by her.

2 I didn't show my mother my report card.
→ My mother _____ by me.
→ My report card _____ by me.

3 The story gave us valuable lessons.
→ We _____ by the story.
→ Valuable lessons _____ by the story.

4 She asked him some stupid questions.
→ He _____ by her.
→ Some stupid questions _____ by her.

5 The teacher told her students interesting news.
→ Her students _____ by the teacher.
→ Interesting news _____ by the teacher.

C 다음 문장을 수동태 표현으로 완성하시오

1 My mother bought us a birthday present.
→ _____*A birthday present was bought for us*_____ by my mother.

2 The people will help the poor.
→ _____ by the people.

3 That guy will bring us two raincoats.
→ _____ by that guy.

4 Minju taught me English grammar.
→ _____ by Minju.

5 The house owner rented those visitors the rooms.
→ _____ by the house owner.

Lesson 5-7

5형식 문장의 수동태

• **5형식 문장의 수동태:** 목적격보어가 명사나 형용사일 경우 'be동사 + 과거분사' 뒤에 'by + 목적격'을 이어서 써 준다.

1. 5형식 문장의 수동태

목적격보어가 명사일 때	• People call New York the Big Apple. ➡ New York is called the Big Apple (by people).
목적격보어가 형용사일 때	• I have painted the walls of my room blue. ➡ The walls of my room have been painted **blue** by me.
목적격보어가 to부정사일 때	• I told Noboru to keep in touch. ➡ Noboru was told **to keep** in touch by me.

2. 지각동사와 사역동사의 수동태

동사	목적격보어의 형태	예문
지각동사	원형부정사 ➡ to부정사 현재분사 ➡ 현재분사	• I saw a girl play (playing) the guitar. ➡ A girl was seen to play (playing) the guitar.
사역동사	원형부정사 ➡ to부정사	• The king made the knight leave. ➡ The knight was made to leave by the king.
	[예외] 수동태 구문에서 사역동사는 'make, help, let'이 주로 사용되며, **'let'은 'be allowed to'로** 나타낸다. • The owner let me exchange the jeans. ➡ I was allowed to exchange the jeans by the owner.	

Check up!

Answer Keys p. 20

A 다음 주어진 문장을 수동태로 바꾸어 쓰시오.

1 I named my dog Alex.

➡ *My dog was named Alex by me.*

2 They elected her leader.

➡ ______________________

Answer Keys p. 20

3　We should keep this room clean.

　　➡ _____

4　He heard her singing some sad songs.

　　➡ _____

5　We will call the new plane Last Glory.

　　➡ _____

6　I asked the students to keep quiet.

　　➡ _____

7　We have left the dog alone in the garden.

　　➡ _____

8　I saw some girls dancing on the stage.

　　➡ _____

9　My father calls me little princess.

　　➡ _____

10　The coach usually told us to do our best.

　　➡ _____

B　빈칸에 알맞은 말을 고르시오.

1　The cat was ((seen) / looked) sleeping on the sofa.

2　Many people were (to make / made) to build a high tower.

3　We will be made (to join / be joined) the soccer club.

4　My mother was helped to (learned / learn) how to make kimchi.

5　Tom was allowed (to go / going) hiking with his friends this week.

6　Sujin heard the boy (singing / sang) loudly in his room.

7　John and I have been made (to bring / brought) a raincoat by him.

5-8 기타 수동태 (1)

- 동명사의 수동태: 'be' 뒤에 'ing'를 붙여서 'being + 과거분사'의 형태를 만든다.
- to부정사의 수동태: 'to be + 과거분사'의 형태로 나타낸다.
- that절이 있는 수동태: 'that'이 이끄는 문장이 목적어인 경우, 가주어 it을 이용하거나 that절의 주어를 수동태의 주어로 하여 문장을 만들 수 있다.

1. 부정사와 동명사의 수동태

to부정사의 수동태 [to be + 과거분사]	• Lisa wants the members in the club to choose her as leader. ➡ Lisa wants to be chosen as leader by the members in the club.
동명사의 수동태 [being + 과거분사]	• Mia hates being treated like a child.

2. that이 이끄는 문장의 수동태

주절과 that절의 시제가 같은 경우	[It is ~ that...] / [~ is + 과거분사 + to부정사] • People <u>say</u> **that** she is the best actress. ➡ It is said that she is the best actress. ➡ She is said to be the best actress.
that절의 시제가 이전인 경우	[It is ~ that...] / [~ is + 과거분사 + 완료부정사(to have + 과거분사)] • The scholar <u>says</u> **that** the moon moved around the earth. ➡ It is said that the moon moved around the earth by the scholar. ➡ The moon is said to have moved around the earth by the scholar.

 Check up!

Answer Keys p. 20

A 다음 주어진 말을 이용하여 빈칸을 완성하시오.

1 She really doesn't like _being talked_ to while she is asleep. (talk)

2 There are a lot of things ＿＿＿＿＿＿ by tomorrow. (do)

3 It was said that John ＿＿＿＿ the best actor in the film festival. (be)

4 ＿＿＿＿＿ alone at home is really sad. (leave)

5 The boys want ＿＿＿＿＿ to the graduation party. (invite)

6 Jessica hates ＿＿＿＿＿＿ when she's studying. (disturb)

기타 수동태 (2)

- **동사구의 수동태**: 동사구로 수동태를 만들 경우 함께 묶어 써야 한다.
  수동태가 될 때 맨 앞의 동사만 'be동사 + 과거분사'의 형태로 만든다.
- **수동태를 쓰지 않는 경우**: 목적어를 갖지 않는 자동사들은 수동태로 바꿀 수 없고, 목적어를
  갖는 타동사 중에도 일부는 수동태로 바꿀 수 없다.

1. 자주 쓰이는 동사구

• ask for	~을 요청하다	• bring up	~을 기르다
• catch up with	~을 따라잡다	• laugh at	~을 비웃다
• look after	~을 돌보다	• look down on	~을 멸시하다
• look up to	~을 존경하다	• make use of	~을 이용하다
• run over	~을 치다	• take care of	~을 돌보다
• put off	~을 미루다		

2. 수동태를 쓰지 않는 경우

(1) 자동사의 문장: 1형식, 2형식 문장이 해당된다.

- The bus **arrived** at the station just now.
  ➡ 목적어가 없는 1형식 문장으로, 수동태를 만들 수 없다.

(2) 상태를 나타내는 동사들의 경우 수동태로 쓰지 않는다.

- **상태동사**: have, become, resemble, weigh, fit, cost 등
- The millionaire **has** expensive sports cars.
  ➡ '가지다'의 뜻으로 소유의 상태를 나타내는 문장으로, 수동태를 만들 수 없다.

Check up!

Answer Keys p. 20

A 다음 문장을 수동태로 바꿀 때 빈칸에 알맞은 말을 쓰시오.

1 Most of the girls laughed at the performance.
➡ The performance ___*was laughed at*___ by most of the girls.

2 I took care of some sick dogs.
➡ Some sick dogs _____ by me.

3 I think she should put off her trip until next month.
➡ I think her trip _____ until next month.

4 He looks down on the poor.
➡ The poor _____ by him.

Answer Keys p. 20

5 They make use of this flower to decorate their room.

➡ This flower _____ by them to decorate their room.

6 Brent turned off the radio because his baby was sleeping.

➡ The radio _____ by Brent because his baby was sleeping.

7 He couldn't catch up with her.

➡ She _____ by him.

8 Lisa looked after the sick baby.

➡ _____ by Lisa.

9 The teacher threw the game magazine away in the morning.

➡ The game magazine _____ by the teacher in the morning.

10 Which topic did the members talk about last night?

➡ Which topic _____ by the members last night?

'by' 이외의 전치사를 사용하는 수동태

- 일반적으로 수동태의 행위자는 'by + 행위자'로 쓰이지만 때로는 'by' 대신 다른 전치사가 쓰이기도 한다.

◈ 'by'이외의 전치사를 사용하는 수동태

수동태 + 전치사 at		수동태 + 전치사 of/from	
• be surprised at	~에 놀라다	• be tired of	~에 싫증나다
• be shocked at	~에 충격을 받다	• be composed of	~로 구성되다
• be disappointed at	~에 실망하다	• be made of	~로 만들어지다
• be excited at	~에 흥분하다		(재료의 성질 변화가 없음)
		• be made from	~로 만들어지다
			(재료가 화학적으로 변함)
수동태 + 전치사 with		기타	
• be filled with	~로 가득 차다	• be interested in	~에 관심 있다
• be satisfied with	~에 만족하다	• be involved in	~에 연루되다, 관여하다
• be covered with	~로 덮이다	• be known as	~로 알려지다
• be pleased with	~에 기뻐하다	• be married to	~와 결혼하다

 Check up!

Answer Keys p. 20

A 주어진 단어를 이용하여 빈칸을 완성하시오. (be동사는 과거형으로 쓰시오.)

1 The boys __were surprised at__ the accident. (surprise)

2 The conference room will _____ a lot of people. (crowd)

3 Seven girls _____ the incident. (involve)

4 He is _____ playing soccer. (tire)

5 I _____ meeting you again. (please)

6 The restaurant _____ its delicious Italian food. (know)

7 The bowl _____ oranges and apples. (fill)

8 They _____ the result. (satisfy)

9 Our coach _____ the score. (disappoint)

10 My daughter _____ making dolls by herself. (interest)

B 다음 문장을 수동태로 바꿀 때 빈칸에 알맞은 말을 쓰시오.

1   A lot of dust covered the road. (with)

➡ _____

2   My test result disappointed my parents. (at)

➡ _____

3   I heard that people made the doll out of chocolate. (out of)

➡ _____

4   Tomorrow's math test worries me. (about)

➡ _____

5   The game made people excited. (at)

➡ _____

Practice More II

A 괄호 안에서 알맞은 것을 고르시오.

1   The special medal was ((given) / giving) to the winners.

2   I remember that the picture was sent (to / for) my daughter two days ago.

3   We have not been (told to leave / told to been left) this area.

4   Every child in the store was (made happy / been made happy) by the comic books.

5   The boy was seen (being played / to play) soccer with his brother.

6   I (was told / was been told) the rules of the game by the leader of our team.

7   They (were shown / were showing) a sad documentary by their history teacher.

8   A letter of invitation will be (written / writing) to the class presidents.

9   Edward wants to (be chosen / be being chosen) as a coach.

10 People would like to (treated / be treated) kindly.

B 주어진 문장을 수동태 문장으로 바꾸어 쓰시오.

1   They brought their mom a bunch of flowers.
    ➡ A bunch of flowers _____*was brought to their mom*_____ by them.

2   The professor told me the rules of the test.
    ➡ The rules of the test _____ by the professor.

3   My mom asked me the same question several times.
    ➡ I _____ several times by my mom.

4   Mary will make John a robot.
    ➡ _____ by Mary.

5   He turned on the light in his study.
    ➡ The light _____ in his study.

6   The news surprised us.
    ➡ We _____ the news.

7   The storm worries me.
    ➡ I _____ the storm.

8   I saw the boy play the drums.
    ➡ The boy _____ by me.

9   We saw the woman enter the house yesterday.
    ➡ The woman _____ the house
      yesterday by us.

10 I saw a strange person knock on the door.
    ➡ A strange person _____ on
      the door by me.

C 다음 문장에서 어법상 어색한 것을 찾아 바르게 고치시오.

1   The room was crowded in people yesterday.
                    _____in_____ ➡ _____with_____

2   Our team is composed for twelve members.
                    _____ ➡ _____

3   I asked the students keep quiet.
                    _____ ➡ _____

4   They were tired for taking exams every day.
                    _____ ➡ _____

5   A lot of leaves was covering the road.
                    _____ ➡ _____

6   Many fans have been disappointed for the accident.
                    _____ ➡ _____

7   The teacher will be satisfied to her grade.
                    _____ ➡ _____

8   She said to be the best player.
                    _____ ➡ _____

9   The rock used to be calling the gold rock by people.
                    _____ ➡ _____

10 Were you been advised to study hard for your future?
                    _____ ➡ _____

Practice More II

Answer Keys p. 20~21

D 다음 주어진 단어를 알맞게 배열하여 문장을 완성하시오.

1   (the, has, painted, old, green, roof, been)

➡ _____*The old roof has been painted green.*_____

2   (her, ring, made, pearls and diamonds, is, of)

➡ _____

3   (a moving story, our mom, is, us, read, by, to)

➡ _____

4   (a birthday card, given, me, will, be, by Jane, to)

➡ _____

5   (the players, for, are, choose, expected, the game, to, their leader)

➡ _____

6   (my son, named, my mother, has, by, been, John)

➡ _____

7   (the game, called, the rain, was, because of, off)

➡ _____

8   (he, the drama, was, death, bored, with, to)

➡ _____

9   (lily, in, was, red dress, dressed, a)

➡ _____

10   (a doghouse, my mother, being, is, by, made)

➡ _____

내신 최다 출제 유형

01 다음 밑줄 친 부분이 옳은 것을 고르시오.

[출제 예상 90%]

① Cell phones should be turn off at a theater.
② Only English should be spoken in class.
③ Books should be return on time.
④ Food should not be ate in the bus.
⑤ Homework must be do before class.

02 다음 우리말을 영어로 바르게 옮긴 것을 고르시오.

[출제 예상 85%]

> 그녀는 3년 전에 사고를 당했다고 말해진다.

① It is said to she has had an accident three years ago.
② She is said to have had an accident three years ago.
③ She is said that have had an accident three years ago.
④ She said that she has an accident three years ago.
⑤ She is said to have an accident three years ago.

03 다음 문장을 수동태로 바꿔 쓸 때 빈칸에 들어갈 말이 알맞게 짝지어진 것을 고르시오.

[출제 예상 90%]

> Because you can make a mistake when you say it, you must think about it one more time.
> = Because a mistake _____ when you say it, it _____ one more time.

① can made - must think of
② can be made - must be think of
③ can be made - must be thought about
④ can make - must think of
⑤ can be making - must be thinking about

04 다음 우리말과 뜻이 같도록 빈칸에 알맞은 말을 고르시오.

[출제 예상 90%]

> 아빠는 내게 크리스마스 선물로 자전거를 사 주셨다.
> = A bicycle _____ me as a Christmas present by dad.

① was bought
② was bought for
③ is bought
④ has bought for
⑤ had bought for

[01~02] 다음 문장의 빈칸에 들어갈 말이 알맞게 짝지어진 것을 고르시오.

01

- English is taught _____ us by Mr. Jackson.
- The room was made tidied _____ my sister.

① to − for   ② to − of   ③ of − for
④ by − for   ⑤ for − to

02

- Mountains are covered _____ snow in winter.
- She was worried _____ his grade.

① with − in   ② with − over
③ of − at   ④ for − about
⑤ with − about

[03~04] 다음 중 밑줄 친 부분의 쓰임이 잘못된 것을 고르시오.

03
① The last puzzle can't be solved.
② All the tickets have been sold out.
③ The good students must had praised.
④ My brother's car is being repaired.
⑤ His opinion should be considered.

04 ★★★
① We are taught not to make noise in class.
② Left-handed people are not considering normal in every country.
③ Icebergs are melting in the polar regions.
④ To be honest, Jerry was cheating on the test.
⑤ Mary and Tom were seen standing by the fence.

05 다음 빈칸에 들어갈 말이 나머지 넷과 다른 것을 고르시오.
① Every night, a fairy tale was read _____ me by my mom when I was young.
② Science is taught _____ us by Mr. Han.
③ The basketball was given _____ Harry.
④ The dictionary was lent _____ her.
⑤ The pretty doll was bought _____ my sister by my dad.

06 다음 중 밑줄 친 전치사의 쓰임이 옳은 것을 고르시오.
① The letter was written for me by the poet.
② Directions were asked of the old woman.
③ The technology was brought for the company.
④ Pizza and salad were cooked to the children by their mom.
⑤ A new sweater was made to me by my mom.

[07~08] 다음 중 어법상 옳은 것을 <u>모두</u> 고르시오.

07 ① The stories has been known for 500 days.
② The trumpet have been played since this morning.
③ We will train by the coach.
④ The wedding will be held on November 7th.
⑤ She was being punished when her mom visited her school.

08 ① The singer was given a huge picture of himself printed on a screen by his fans.
② Some workers are paid their wages weekly.
③ Her friends were cooked special Thai food by Jeje.
④ I was bought a computer by my parents.
⑤ He was chosen a nice tie by his girlfriend.

[09~10] 다음 두 문장의 빈칸에 들어갈 말이 바르게 짝 지어진 것을 고르시오.

09
• The hunters saw the tigers _____ the young deer.
➡ The tigers were seen _____ the young deer by the hunters.

① kill − to kill
② kill − killed
③ kill − being killed
④ killing − being killed
⑤ killing − to be killed

★★★
10
• The crew helped the old lady _____ her seat belt.
➡ The old lady was helped _____ her seat belt by the crew.

① fasten − fasten
② fastened − to fasten
③ fasten − to fasten
④ be fastening − to fasten
⑤ to be fastened − to fasten

[11~12] 다음의 빈칸에 들어갈 말로 알맞지 <u>않은</u> 것을 고르시오.

11
All the people were _____ to enjoy the party by the host.

① ordered ② told ③ made
④ had ⑤ allowed

12
My little daughter _____ by her grandmother.

① is looked after ② will be educated
③ is not resembled ④ wasn't cared for
⑤ will be raised

[13~14] 다음 문장을 수동태로 바꿀 때 빈칸에 알맞은 말을 넣으시오.

13

> The coach says that we ought to do something to win the game.
> = The coach says that something _____ to win the game.

① ought to done   ② ought to doing
③ ought to did   ④ ought be to do
⑤ ought to be done

14

> The committee may not choose her story as the best one.
> = Her story _____ as the best one by the committee.

① may be not chosen
② may not be chosen
③ may not by choose
④ may be not chose
⑤ may not be chose

15 다음 밑줄 친 부분의 쓰임이 잘못된 것을 고르시오.

① I was satisfied <u>with</u> the result.
② We are interested <u>in</u> dancing in the group.
③ His name is well-known <u>to</u> all of us.
④ She was surprised <u>at</u> the news.
⑤ My room was filled <u>of</u> so many comic books.

★★★
16 다음 능동태 문장을 수동태 문장으로 바꾼 것 중 잘못된 것을 고르시오.

① His father is making a doghouse.
   → A doghouse is being made for his father.
② You must keep your words.
   → Your words must be kept by you.
③ She saw me standing in front of the school.
   → I was seen standing in front of the school by her.
④ I heard him playing the guitar.
   → He was heard playing the guitar by me.
⑤ They laughed at someone.
   → Someone was laughed at by them.

★★★
17 다음 중 빈칸에 들어갈 단어가 나머지 넷과 다른 것을 고르시오.

① They are not interested _____ music.
② I didn't want to be interrupted _____ anybody.
③ The palace is located _____ the center of the city.
④ Jade's teacher is disappointed _____ him.
⑤ The queen was dressed _____ a green dress.

18 다음 빈칸에 알맞은 말을 모두 고르시오.

> _____ was the series of fifteen stamps published?

① What   ② Where   ③ When
④ Which   ⑤ Whom

[19~21] 다음 문장을 바꿔 쓸 때 빈칸에 들어갈 알맞은 표현을 고르시오.

19

He didn't let us sleep in the subway station.
➡ We _____ in the subway station.

① didn't let them sleep
② were not allowed sleep
③ were not allowed to sleep
④ were allowed to sleep
⑤ didn't let sleep

20

Do we have to download the music file again?
➡ Does the music file _____ again?

① must be downloaded
② must being downloaded
③ had to be downloaded
④ have to be downloaded
⑤ has to be downloaded

21

What did you see in the art gallery?
➡ What _____ by you in the art gallery?

① seen   ② was seen
③ were seen   ④ have been seen
⑤ has been seen

22 다음 보기 의 문장을 수동태로 바르게 고친 것을 고르시오.

보기
Did she borrow the books from the library?

① Did she borrowed the books from the library?
② Were the books borrowing from the library by her?
③ Did she be borrowed the books from the library?
④ Was she borrowed the books from the library?
⑤ Were the books borrowed from the library by her?

23 다음 중 어법상 틀린 문장을 고르시오.

① We are given much information by the news.
② This skirt was made for me by my mom.
③ A delicious meal was cooked to me by my mom.
④ A pictorial book was bought for me by Peterson.
⑤ A toy robot was presented to him as a gift.

★★★
24 다음 중 어법상 옳은 것을 모두 고르시오.

① The novel was based on a true story.
② She was satisfying with her presents.
③ Korea is filled of wonderful sightseeing places.
④ We were ashamed of losing the game.
⑤ I was disappointed of my history score.

05. 수동태 **167**

25 다음 [보기]의 문장과 의미가 가장 가까운 것을 고르시오.

> **[보기]**
>
> Nobody has handed in the report yet.

① The report hasn't been handed in yet.
② The report haven't been handed in yet.
③ The report wasn't handed in yet.
④ The report shouldn't be handed in yet.
⑤ The report mustn't be handed in yet.

[26~29] 다음 빈칸에 알맞은 말을 고르시오.

26

> The man was asked _____ the place as soon as possible.

① leave   ② to leave   ③ to be left
④ leaving   ⑤ being left

27

> He was sad _____ punished by his father.

① be   ② being   ③ been
④ to be   ⑤ have been

28

> I didn't study at all. So, I'm afraid _____ asked many questions by the teacher.

① being   ② to be   ③ of being
④ of been   ⑤ been

29 다음 밑줄 친 부분 중 어법상 올바르지 <u>않은</u> 것을 <u>모두</u> 고르시오.

① The tall tower <u>was build</u> in 1998.
② The baggage <u>is weighed</u> 50 kilograms.
③ Chinese <u>is learned</u> in many countries.
④ The cake <u>will be bake</u> by Anna.
⑤ Many accidents <u>are caused</u> by drunk drivers.

30 다음 중 어법상 틀린 문장을 고르시오.

① By whom was the book wrote?
② Was my room cleaned by you?
③ Where were the lost books found?
④ Was the camera fixed by Jack?
⑤ What was stolen from the department store?

◇◇◇◇◇◇◇◇◇ **서술형 평가** ◇◇◇◇◇◇◇◇◇

[31~33] 다음 문장을 수동태로 바꿀 때 빈칸에 알맞은 말을 쓰시오.

31

> I will practice the drums starting next week.

➡ The drums _____ _____ _____ starting next week.

32

> The mayor is trying to change the city into a popular tourist destination.

➡ The city _____ _____ _____ to change into a popular tourist destination.

★★★
33

I have baked blueberry muffins since early this morning.

➡ Blueberry muffins _____

_____ _____ _____ _____

since early this morning.

[34~35] 다음의 문장을 두 가지 형식의 수동태 문장으로 바꿀 때 빈칸에 알맞은 말을 쓰시오.

34

Mary told me some funny stories.

➡ I _____ _____ some funny stories _____ _____.

➡ Some funny stories _____ _____

_____ _____ _____ _____.

★★★
35

A pretty woman asked Jim the direction to the museum.

➡ Jim _____ _____ the directions to the museum _____ _____

_____ _____.

➡ The direction to the museum _____

_____ _____ _____

_____ _____.

[36~38] 다음의 문장을 수동태로 고쳐 쓰시오.
★★★
36

Most people laughed at the man.

➡ _____

★★★
37

Jimmy has put off the deadline for a long time.

➡ _____

★★★
38

People say that the musician is a genius.

➡ _____ is a genius.

➡ The musician _____

[39~40] 다음 괄호 안의 단어를 우리말에 맞게 바르게 배열하여 문장을 완성하시오.
★★★
39

나는 그들에 의해 편하게 떠날 수 있었다.
(I / allowed / leave / to / was / them / by / comfortably)

➡ _____

40

그에 의해 피아노가 연주된 곳은 어디니?
(the / piano / played / was / where / by / him)

➡ _____

Note

06
Chapter
부정사

◆ **부정사:** 동사원형 앞에 to를 붙이면 'to부정사', to가 없으면 '원형부정사'라고 한다. 명사처럼 쓰여 주어, 목적어, 보어 역할을 하며, 형용사, 부사처럼 쓰이기도 한다.

◆ **명사적 용법:** 명사처럼 쓰여 문장에서 주어, 목적어, 보어 역할을 한다.

◆ **형용사적 용법:** 문장에서 형용사처럼 쓰이며 명사, 대명사를 꾸며주는 역할을 한다.

1. 부정사의 명사적 용법

명사적 용법	예문
주어 역할 [~하는 것은]	• To travel gives you with broad outlook on life. [주어]
목적어 역할 [~하는 것을, ~하기를]	• Tom managed to find a good job. [목적어]
보어 역할 [~하기, ~하는 것]	• She hopes that everyone is to be happy. [보어]
의문사 + to부정사	• We didn't <u>know</u> who(m) to go with. [의문사 + to부정사 : 주로 동사 뒤에서 동사의 목적어로 쓰인다.]

2. 부정사의 형용사적 용법

형용사적 용법 [~할, ~하는]	예문
명사 수식	• Students have a lot of work to do.
대명사 수식	• I just want something to drink.
전치사의 목적어일 경우	• Jacky needs some paper to write on.

3. 부정사의 부사적 용법

부사적 용법	예문
목적, 의도 [~하기 위해서(=in order to)]	• They went to London to watch the soccer game.
감정 [~해서, ~하게 되어]	• I am so happy to get a new laptop computer.
판단 [~하는 것을 보니]	• He must be a doctor to examine the patients.
결과 [~해서(결국) ...되다]	• I grew up to be a famous cook.
조건 [~한다면 (=if)]	• To buy these drinks, you would get one more.

6-1 부정사의 형태

• **to부정사**: 'to부정사'는 동사의 성질을 가지고 있기 때문에 부정, 진행, 수동의 역할을 할 수 있다.

1. 평서문: [to + 동사원형]

• Jiho studies English very hard **to go** to America.

2. 부정문: [not / never + to부정사]

• We tried **not(never) to make** our teacher upset.

3. 진행형: [to be + 동사-ing] – 주어가 하고 있는 행동이 강조된다.

• <u>Henry</u> seems **to be studying** Korean very hard.

4. 수동형: [to be + 과거분사] – 주어가 동작의 대상이 된다.

• <u>These</u> are the things **to be finished** by this Friday.

☆Check up!

Answer Keys p. 23

A 다음 괄호 안의 말을 이용하여 문장을 완성하시오.

1 I think she should study hard ___*not to fail the exam*___ . (not, fail the exam)

2 My daughter seems _____ festivals. (enjoy)

3 They expect all the work _____ by Friday. (do)

4 I'm so excited _____ the parade with you. (watch)

5 Minhyuk did his best _____ the competition. (not, lose)

6 Jane told me _____ for tomorrow's meeting. (not, late)

7 He decided _____ a taxi there. (never, take)

8 The wall seems _____ black. (paint)

9 She wanted the watch _____ . (fix)

10 The girl appears _____ a lot of fun. (have)

6-2 부정사의 명사적 용법

• **명사적 용법**: 명사처럼 쓰여 문장에서 주어, 목적어, 보어 역할을 한다.

1. 주어와 주격보어의 역할

(1) 주어: to부정사가 문장의 맨 앞에서 주어의 역할을 한다. 이때 to부정사의 주어가 길 경우 'it ~ to' 용법의 문장으로 바꿔 쓸 수 있다.

• **To pronounce** English word correctly is not easy.
  [to부정사-주어]

= It is not easy **to pronounce** English word correctly.
  [It: 가짜 주어]　　　　　　　[to부정사 이하: 진짜 주어]

(2) 주격보어: 주어에 대해 보충 설명하는 보어 역할을 한다.

• The right way to make friends is **to be** honest with other people.
　　　　　　　　　　　　　　　　　　[to 부정사-보어]

2. 목적어와 목적격보어의 역할

(1) 목적어: to부정사가 목적어의 역할을 한다.

want, agree, choose, decide, expect, fail, hope, learn, plan, wish pretend, manage, promise, refuse, aim, would like, would love	＋to부정사 (to＋동사원형)

• We **agreed to stop** fighting each other.

• Sally **promised to be** polite to everyone, but she wasn't.

(2) 목적격보어: to부정사가 목적어를 보충 설명하는 보어 역할을 한다.

tell, ask, want, allow, expect, enable, invite, advise, would like	＋목적어	＋to부정사 (to＋동사원형)

• It will **enable you to understand** our present condition.

• **Would you like** me **to order** Mexican food?

☆Check up!

Answer Keys p. 23

A　다음 밑줄 친 부분이 문장에서 어떤 역할을 하는지 쓰시오.

1　To watch the game was boring.　　　　　　[주어]

2　My dream is to be a medical doctor.　　　＿＿＿＿＿

3　To stop eating fast food makes you healthier.　＿＿＿＿＿

4　Mary asked him to check her schedule.　　＿＿＿＿＿

5　Mr. Park decided to quit his job.　　　　　＿＿＿＿＿

B 주어진 문장을 it ~ to 구문으로 바꾸어 쓰시오.

1 To live a happy life is my dream.

➡ _____ *It is my dream to live a happy life.* _____

2 To exercise regularly is important.

➡ _____

3 To travel around the world is my special goal.

➡ _____

4 To know yourself is not easy.

➡ _____

5 To get an A on the science test is really hard.

➡ _____

C 다음 주어진 단어를 알맞게 배열하여 문장을 완성하시오.

1 The solution is (return, by, to, these books, six)

➡ The solution is _____ *to return these books by six* _____.

2 Actually, we would like (this, quit, project, to)

➡ Actually, we would like _____.

3 Helen's dream is (write, novels, to, interesting)

➡ Helen's dream is _____.

4 The girls want (take, a, class, to, swimming)

➡ The girls want _____.

5 The man allowed us (to, a nap, for, take, a while)

➡ The man allowed us _____.

6 He refused (confess, he, to, Hana's ring, stole, why)

➡ He refused _____.

7 It is difficult (prepare, alone, for, to, a party)

➡ It is difficult _____.

8 I asked the teacher (to, sheet, me, the answer, show)

➡ I asked the teacher _____.

9 My sister's wish is (model, become, a, to, world-famous)

➡ My sister's wish is _____.

10 What she wants is (to, make, a scholarship, happy, get, and, her parents)

➡ What she wants is _____.

6-3 의문사 + to부정사

• 의문사 + to부정사: '의문사 + 주어 + should + 동사원형'의 문장과 같은 의미로 사용된다.

1. '의문사 + to부정사'와 함께 쓰이는 동사

know, show, tell, learn decide, teach, explain, talk about, think about	+ 의문사	+ to부정사 (to + 동사원형)

(1) how to + 동사원형: 어떻게 ~할지

   • Sophia wanted to **know how to make** glass marbles.

(2) what to + 동사원형: 무엇을 ~할지

   • We don't **know what to do** for Jackson.

(3) where to + 동사원형: 어디에서 ~할지

   • Can you **tell me where to take** a shower?

(4) when to + 동사원형: 언제 ~할지

   • Jessy and Robert talked about **when to go** on a picnic.

2. [의문사 + to부정사] = [의문사 + 주어 + should + 동사원형]

   • Mina and Tom didn't know **what to say** for Angie.
   = Mina and Tom didn't know **what they should say** for Angie.

☆Check up!

Answer Keys p. 23

A 주어진 단어를 이용하여 빈칸에 알맞은 말을 쓰시오.

1   I have decided _where to go_ this summer vacation. (where, go)

2   She doesn't know ＿＿＿＿＿＿＿. (when, leave)

3   Please tell me ＿＿＿＿＿＿＿ at tomorrow's party. (which pants, wear)

4   Can I show her ＿＿＿＿＿＿＿ the blue box? (how, open)

5   Tim didn't know ＿＿＿＿＿＿＿ about the matter. (what, should, say)

6   I can't decide ＿＿＿＿＿＿＿ for lunch. (what, eat)

7   Do they know ＿＿＿＿＿＿＿ this game? (how, should, play)

8   The expert taught us ＿＿＿＿＿＿＿ much money. (how, save)

9   He was thinking about ＿＿＿＿＿＿＿ when he grew up. (what, should, do)

6-4 부정사의 형용사적 용법

- **형용사적 용법**: 형용사처럼 쓰여 명사, 대명사를 꾸며주는 역할을 한다.
  '～할' 이라는 뜻으로 쓰이며, 꾸며주는 명사 뒤에 위치한다.

1. 명사를 꾸미는 to부정사

(1) '명사 + to부정사': 뒤에서 명사를 꾸며 준다.

- Jenny bought some <u>books</u> **to read** on the trip.
  = Jenny bought some <u>books</u> that she would read on the trip.

(2) '명사구 + to부정사 + 전치사': 'to부정사+전치사'에서 수식받는 명사구는 전치사의 목적어가 된다.

- We found <u>a cheap and nice hotel</u> **to stay in**.

  [in의 목적어 ➡ a cheap and nice hotel]

(3) '대명사 + 형용사 + to부정사': '-thing, -body, -one' 등의 대명사 뒤에 수식어구가 있을 경우
  to부정사는 뒤에 나온다.

- I'm so cold and hungry. I really need <u>something</u> **warm to eat**.

2. 'be + to부정사'

운명	～할 운명이다	• Come to think of it, I was to meet you in my whole life.
명령/의무	～해야 한다	• You are not to eat on the subway.
예정	～할 예정이다	• We are to go to Caribbean Bay in Everland this Saturday.
의도/의지	～하려고 하면	• If you are to lose weight, you have to exercise regularly.
가능	～할 수 있다	• They are to be famous dancers in the future.

Answer Keys p. 23

A 주어진 단어를 알맞게 배열하여 문장을 완성하시오.

1 She has _____*a lot of books to read*_____.
(a lot of, to, books, read)

2 There were _____.
(many toys, with, to, play)

3 Here is _____.
(some, drink, to, juice)

06. 부정사 **177**

4 He bought _____.

(some, to, dinner, noodles, cook, for)

5 Why don't you start _____?

(lose, to, exercising, weight)

6 Is there _____?

(anybody, her, move, help, the boxes, to)

7 The officer has _____.

(animals, to, rules, protect, make, to)

8 He is _____.

(a nice person, teach, the, to, students)

9 Please bring me _____.

(to, on, put, desk, these things, a)

10 The lonely woman needed _____.

(a friend, to, talk, to)

B 주어진 문장을 'be to' 구문을 사용한 문장으로 바꾸어 쓰시오.

1 Jane and I are going to go hiking this weekend.

➡ _____ *Jane and I are to go hiking this weekend.* ____

2 I think you must not make any noise in this place.

➡ I think _____

3 The wine festival is going to be held next week.

➡ _____

4 Always do your best if you want to achieve your goal.

➡ Always do your best _____

5 We are going to meet tomorrow morning in front of the bus stop.

➡ _____ in front of the bus stop.

6 He was destined to die in World War I.

➡ _____

7 You should hand in the report by next week.

➡ _____ by next week.

8 The salad on the table couldn't be eaten.

➡ The salad on the table _____

9 Harry is going to come back home tomorrow.

➡ _____ home tomorrow.

부정사의 부사적 용법

· **부사적 용법**: 부사처럼 쓰여 동사, 형용사, 다른 부사 또는 문장 전체를 수식하면서 더욱 자세히 설명하는 것을 말한다. to부정사는 '왜 ~하는지, ~하기 위해서, ~해서'라는 뜻으로 해석된다.

1. 부사적 용법 – 목적

(1) to + 동사원형: ~하기 위해 = [in order to], [so that + 주어 + can + 동사원형]

· Jane met counselor **to talk** to about her future.

= Jane met a counselor **in order to** talk about her future.

= Jane met a counselor **so that she could talk** about her future.

(2) not + to부정사: ~하지 않기 위해 = [in order not to~], [so as not to~]

· I washed the dishes **not to hear** her scolding.

= I washed the dishes **in order not to hear** her scolding.

= I washed the dishes **so as not to hear** her scolding.

(3) 'for + 명사': to부정사의 '목적 역할'을 대신

· Iwan went home early **to take care of** the little puppies.

= Iwan went home early **for** the little puppies.

2. 부사적 용법 – 원인 : to부정사가 감정을 나타내는 형용사를 수식할 때 '~해서, ~하니'의 뜻으로 감정의 원인을 나타낸다.

happy pleased delighted excited glad surprised sorry sad disappointed	**+to부정사** **(to + 동사원형)**

· She was so surprised **to hear** the bad news.

3. 그 외의 부사적 용법

근거	~하다니	· Tim must be lazy to move so slowly.
결과	~해서 결국 ...되다	· He grew up to be the best actor in the world.
조건	~한다면	· My parents will be proud of me to get the honorable prize.

A 다음 문장과 뜻이 통하도록 주어진 말을 이용하여 문장을 쓰시오.

1 He went to the subway station to pick her up. (in order to)

➡ _____He went to the subway station in order to pick her up._____

2 They went out to do volunteer work. (so as to)

➡ _____

3 Tim turned off the light to go to bed. (so that)

➡ _____

4 I opened the window to ventilate the room. (so as to)

➡ _____

5 I checked out some reports to write my graduation thesis. (for)

➡ _____

6 I dropped by his house to give him a birthday present. (so that)

➡ _____

7 She will call Mary to let her know the facts. (in order to)

➡ _____

8 Mr. Kim sent me an email to remind me of the proposal. (so as to)

➡ _____

9 They are going to go to the market to buy milk and cheese. (for)

➡ They are going to go to the market _____

B 주어진 단어를 알맞게 배열하여 문장을 완성하시오.

1 He was _____disappointed to see his test result_____.
(test result, disappointed, see, to, his)

2 They were _____.
(sorry, the same, to, mistake, make)

3 Jim must be _____.
(a genius, without, solve, hints, to, the problem)

4 She _____.
(to, grew, designer, up, be, fashion, a)

5 I think Cindy must be _____.
(that, to, honest, like, act)

> **Note**
> • **ventilate** 환기시키다
> • **check out** ~을 확인하다, ~을 조사하다
> • **thesis** 논문, 학위
> • **drop by** (=stop by) ~에 잠깐 들리다
> • **proposal** 제안
> • **competition** 경쟁, 대회
> • **disappointed** 실망한
> • **solve** 풀다, 해결하다
> • **honest** 정직한

Practice More I

Answer Keys p. 24

A 괄호 안에서 알맞은 것을 고르시오.

1   The boy promised (to volunteer / volunteering) at the event.

2   Our goal is (to save / save) the environment.

3   I can't decide (where / what) to write about.

4   As it was very hot, we planned (to go / going) swimming.

5   Why did the lady (talks / tell) him to buy that shirt?

6   I would (like her / her like) to participate in the beauty contest.

7   I don't know (how / what) to eat for lunch.

8   Helen ordered us (to fix / fix) the chair and the table.

9   It's difficult (to correct / corrected) ungrammatical sentences.

10   The girl grew up to (being / be) a great actress.

B 보기와 같이 문장을 바꾸어 쓰시오.

> 보기
>
> They didn't know where to go.
> ➡ They didn't know where they should go.

1   Sam asked what to buy for his daughter's graduation present.
   ➡ _____

2   Let's discuss where to go this holiday.
   ➡ _____

3   The boys have learned how to direct a movie.
   ➡ _____

4   Tell me which cup to choose among these.
   ➡ _____

5   I didn't know where to visit first during the trip.
   ➡ _____

6   Sorry, I can't remember when to turn left or right.

⇒ _____

7   Helen asked the waiter where to borrow an umbrella.

⇒ _____

8   Please tell mc which phone to buy.

⇒ _____

9   The students wanted to learn how to play that computer game.

⇒ _____

10 Bill showed me how to solve the riddle.

⇒ _____

C   다음 문장에서 어법상 <u>어색한</u> 것을 찾아 바르게 고치시오

1   The teacher was angry found that Lisa lied to her.

___found___ ⇒ ___to find___

2   We are to having a party this Saturday.

_____ ⇒ _____

3   I went out as so to investigate the place.

_____ ⇒ _____

4   Nothing is to not be found in the room.

_____ ⇒ _____

5   This is a nice bench to sit.

_____ ⇒ _____

6   We bought a magazine to be read.

_____ ⇒ _____

7   People agreed going to the concert on Friday.

_____ ⇒ _____

8   He advised me studied English and math every day.

_____ ⇒ _____

9   All the people expect us to got first prize.

_____ ⇒ _____

10 The teacher allowed us using the computer.

_____ ⇒ _____

D 다음 주어진 단어를 알맞게 배열하여 문장을 완성하시오.

Note

· audition 몡오디션
        동오디션을 보다

1 (was, the, I, documentary, sad, watch, to)

➡ *I was sad to watch the documentary.*

2 (she, is, that, to, said, believe, see, to)

➡ _____

3 (let's, hotel, in, find, stay, to, a)

➡ _____

4 (the princess, him, was, seventeen, marry, to, at)

➡ _____

5 (they, join, agreed, next, to, semester, our community)

➡ _____

6 (Lily, ask, will, she, you, tries, not, her, to, before, help, it)

➡ _____

7 (her job, some, on, is, street, hand out, samples, the, to)

➡ _____

8 (if, to, somebody, audition, our dance team, they, is, must, join)

➡ _____

9 (I, succeed, you, want, everything, to, do, in, you)

➡ _____

10 (James, a marathon, started, so, run, exercising, that, could, regularly, he)

➡ _____

Point Check II

◆ **부정사**: 'to+동사원형'을 'to부정사'라고 하고, 동사원형만이 있는 경우 '원형부정사'라고 한다.

◆ **대부정사**: 앞의 말에 대한 반복을 피하기 위해 'to부정사'에서 동사원형을 생략하고 'to'만 사용하는 것을 말한다.

1. 대부정사

• You can <u>go to the concert</u> with Jenny if you want **to** (go to the concert).

2. 부정사의 시제

단순부정사 [to + 동사원형]	완료부정사 [to + have + 과거분사]
• It seems that the man is very kind. ➡ The man <u>seems</u> to be very kind.	• It appeared that Jessica had solved the problems. ➡ Jessica <u>appeared</u> to have solved the problems.

3. 목적격보어로 쓰이는 to부정사 (5형식 문장)

동사+목적어+to부정사	동사+목적어+원형부정사
want, ask, tell, allow, get advise, expect +to부정사	사역동사: have, let, make 지각동사: hear, feel, see watch, notice +원형부정사
• Mr. Smith <u>expected</u> them to have a great time.	• She <u>had</u> me boil the water. ➡ 원형부정사(동사원형)는 사역동사와 지각동사의 목적격보어 역할을 한다.

4. to부정사의 의미상의 주어

(1) for + 목적격

• It was a little difficult **for us** <u>to get</u> the first prize.

(2) of + 목적격: to부정사가 사람의 성격을 나타내는 형용사를 꾸며줄 때 사용한다.

• It was <u>foolish</u> **of you** to make that mistake.

to부정사의 시제

• **to부정사의 시제**: '단순부정사 (to＋동사원형)'와 '완료부정사 (to＋have＋과거분사)'가 있다.

1. 단순부정사: [to ＋ 동사원형]

주절과 종속절의 시제가 동일하거나, 종속절의 시제가 이후인 경우 단순부정사를 사용한다.

• It **seems** that the woman over there **is** a professional model.

= The woman over there <u>seems</u> **to be** a professional model.

• It is likely that he **will win** the quiz show.

= He is likely **to win** the quiz show.

2. 완료부정사: [to ＋ have ＋ 과거분사]

종속절의 시제가 주절보다 이전인 경우 사용한다.

• It **seems** that Maria **felt** something on her head.

= Maria <u>seems</u> **to have felt** something on her head.

• It **appeared** that Tom **had found** the correct answer.

= Tom <u>appeared</u> **to have found** the correct answer.

Check up!

Answer Keys p. 24

A 밑줄 친 부분을 주어로 하여 주어진 문장과 뜻이 같게 빈칸에 알맞은 말을 쓰시오.

1   It seems that <u>the woman</u> is a professional pianist.
  ➡ The woman ___*seems to be*___ a professional pianist.

2   It is likely that <u>the competition</u> will be postponed.
  ➡ The competition _____.

3   It appeared that <u>Inho</u> had made a big mistake.
  ➡ Inho appeared _____.

4   It is likely that <u>she</u> will go to America to study English.
  ➡ She is likely _____.

5   It seems that <u>they</u> ate up all the cakes.
  ➡ They seem _____.

6   It appeared that <u>the boys</u> had met each other.
  ➡ The boys seemed _____.

원형부정사와 대부정사

- **원형부정사**: 'to' 없는 동사원형을 '원형부정사'라고 한다.
- **대부정사**: 앞의 나온 말의 반복을 피하기 위해 to부정사에서 동사원형을 생략하고 'to'만 사용하는 것을 말한다.

1. 원형부정사의 동사

(1) 지각동사: 5형식 문장에서 지각동사의 목적격보어로 부정사가 올 때 원형부정사가 쓰인다.

see watcht hear feel notice listen to look at	+ 목적어	+ 원형부정사 (동사원형)

- I saw the athlete **jump** high on TV.
- I looked at a girl **crying** loudly on the street.

➡ 동작이 진행 중인 것을 강조할 때는 원형부정사 대신에 현재분사를 쓰기도 한다.

(2) 사역동사

make let have (help)	+ 목적어	+ 원형부정사 (동사원형)

- Laura **made** us **bring** some cookies.
- Jin will have her car **washed**.

→ 목적어가 동작의 대상이 되는 경우 과거분사가 쓰인다.

※ help : 준사역동사로써 원형부정사와 to부정사 모두 목적격 보어로 사용할 수 있다.

- Marian helped him **find** a pharmacy.
= Marian helped him **to find** a pharmacy.

2. 대부정사

- You may use my paints if you want **to** (use my paints).
- He cleaned the house before I came home because I told him **to** (clean the house).

A 주어진 단어를 빈칸에 알맞은 형태로 바꾸어 쓰시오.

1   Let me _____show_____ you some pictures that he drew. (show)

2   The crowd saw the man _____ well. (dance)

3   She noticed some flowers _____ in the street. (plant)

4   The boy heard someone _____ his name. (call)

5   Didn't listen to James _____ the guitar? (play)

6   Look at the two dogs _____ on the sofa. (lie)

7   Mary helped me _____ the problem. (solve)

8   Mom made me _____ the car. (clean)

9   Kate will have her watch _____. (fix)

10 Mrs. Kim had her secretary _____ the file. (find)

11 The storm makes our plan _____. (change)

12 I noticed the man _____ me. (follow)

13 Amy will have her house _____. (remodel)

14 Jack had me _____ all the English sentences. (memorize)

15 We heard someone _____. (cry)

부정사의 의미상의 주어

• 의미상의 주어: 'to부정사'의 의미상의 주어는 to부정사가 나타내는 동작의 주체를 의미한다.

1. 의미상의 주어를 사용하는 경우

(1) 'for+목적격': 부정사의 의미상의 주어가 문장의 주어나 목적어와 일치하지 않을 때

• It is very important **for you to take** a literature lesson.

• It was bad **for you to cheat** on the test.

(2) 'of+목적격': [부정사 앞에 사람의 성질이나 특징을 나타내는 형용사가 있을 때]

• It is so **kind of her to offer** her seat to the old lady.

2. 의미상의 주어를 쓰지 않는 경우

(1) 일반 사람이거나 문맥상 주어가 뚜렷한 경우

• It is not easy **to run** a marathon.

• His dream is **to be** the best in his field.

(2) 문장의 주어가 같은 경우

• I wish **to major** in Chinese literature.

(3) 문장의 목적어가 같은 경우

• She wants me **to work** much harder.

 **Check up!**

Answer Keys p. 25

A 다음 빈칸에 알맞은 말을 쓰시오.

1 It is impossible ___for___ me to quit working here right now.

2 It is nice _____ you to go to the conference tomorrow.

3 It was good _____ me to see you again.

4 It is so stupid _____ him to act like that.

5 It is generous _____ her to invite me to the party.

6 It is very important _____ you to take a taxi.

7 It is such a pleasure _____ me to buy the bag.

8 It was brave _____ him to save the children from the accident.

9 It was foolish _____ you to forget the test.

6-9 자주 쓰이는 부정사 표현

1. too... to~ : 너무 ...해서 ~하지 못하다

- Jenny is **too** young **to** write the alphabet.

   = Jenny is **so** young **that** she **can't** write the alphabet.

   ➡ 'too... to ~'는 'so that cannot'으로 바꿔 쓸 수 있다.

2. ...enough to~ : ~하기에 충분히 ...하다

- Anna is smart **enough to** understand the problem.

   = Anna is **so** smart **that** she **can** understand the problem.

   ➡ '...enough to~'는 'so that can'으로 바꿔 쓸 수 있다.

3. in order (not) to~, so as (not) to~ : ~하기 위하여 (~하지 않기 위하여)

- We got up early **in order to arrive** at the airport on time.
- I prepared very hard **in order not to** mess up the interview.

 **Check up!**

Answer Keys p. 25

A 각 문장의 뜻이 같도록 'too ~ to' 또는 'enough to'를 이용해 문장을 바꾸어 쓰시오.

1 Brian is so tall that he can reach the shelf.

➡ *Brian is tall enough to reach the shelf.*

2 Kate is so tired that she can't go hiking.

➡ _____

3 Jane is so smart that she can solve any problems.

➡ _____

4 Emily is so lazy that she can't clean her room every day.

➡ _____ every day.

5 The statue is so heavy that we can't move it.

➡ _____

Practice More II

A 다음 밑줄 친 부분을 어법상 바르게 고치시오.

1 It isn't easy <u>of</u> him to get the scholarship this semester.

➡ _____for_____

2 It is <u>importantly</u> for you to finish your homework by six.

➡ _____

3 It was very kind <u>to</u> you to invite all of us.

➡ _____

4 It was very careless <u>for</u> you not to follow the traffic rules.

➡ _____

5 He waved his hands cheerfully <u>of</u> the people to notice him.

➡ _____

6 I think it might be <u>danger</u> for you to go out alone at night.

➡ _____

7 The crowd saw the boys <u>to play</u> soccer.

➡ _____

8 Jina helped me <u>finding</u> my dog.

➡ _____

9 I tried <u>to not</u> make the same mistake.

➡ _____

B 주어진 단어를 빈칸에 알맞은 형태로 써 넣으시오.

1 Let me _____add_____ some sugar to this bowl. (add)

2 She heard someone _____ in the room. (cry)

3 They made her _____ their ideas. (use)

4 It was so hot that we _____ go out yesterday. (can)

5 The man seems _____ a dentist. (be)

6 I'm so happy _____ the parade now. (watch)

7 It was foolish _____ to forget the meeting. (he)

8 Mom told me _____ writing in my dairy. (not, put off)

9 It is not easy _____ to take care all of the students. (we)

10 Sharon wants the watch _____ right now. (repair)

C   'too ~ to' 또는 'enough to'를 이용하여 의미가 통하도록 문장을 바꾸어 쓰시오.

1   Jack is very busy. He can't go with us.

    ➡ *Jack is too busy to go with us.*

2   Sara is smart. She can teach us how to solve the problem.

    ➡ _____

3   My laptop is really old-fashioned. It can't run the application.

    ➡ _____

4   Linda was so nervous that she couldn't sit still.

    ➡ _____

5   Our team is so strong that we can win this game.

    ➡ _____

6   I was very sick. I couldn't exercise.

    ➡ _____

7   Kate is so ambitious that she can't be satisfied with the result.

    ➡ _____

8   Adam is so young that he can't travel alone.

    ➡ _____

9   It was so cloudy that we can't see stars.

    ➡ _____

10 The book was so interesting that I read it overnight.

    ➡ _____

Practice More II

Answer Keys p. 25

D 다음 주어진 단어를 알맞게 배열하여 문장을 완성하시오.

1 (the, is, untie, to, knot, easy)

➡ _____ *The knot is easy to untie.* _____

2 (the cookie, bite, hard, to, me, is, for)

➡ _____

3 (she, question, to, answer, my, refused)

➡ _____

4 (it, of, save, in the fire, was, the dog, brave, her, to)

➡ _____

5 (it, for, easy, her name, was, remember, to, us)

➡ _____

6 (the children, have, appeared, wrong answer, found, the, to)

➡ _____

7 (told, never, the teacher, the box, his students, open, to)

➡ _____

8 (my brother, enough, first prize, to, the olympiad, in, smart, is, get)

➡ _____

9 (Mr. Park, the workers, that, had, tower, build)

➡ _____

10 (your pizza, delicious, it, sold out, is, so, that)

➡ _____

내신 최다 출제 유형

01 다음의 주어진 문장과 의미가 같은 것을 고르시오.

[출제 예상 85%]

> To make true friends is good for your life.

① It is good to your life to make true friends.
② It is good to your life make true friends.
③ It is good for your life to make true friends.
④ It is good for your life make true friends.
⑤ It is good for your life that to make true friends.

02 다음 우리말을 바르게 영작한 것을 고르시오.

[출제 예상 80%]

> 나는 그에게 언제 떠나야 할지를 말해 주었다.

① I told him when does he go to leave.
② I told him when to leave.
③ I told him that when he leaves.
④ I tell him when to leave.
⑤ I tell him to leave.

03 다음 빈칸에 들어갈 말이 나머지 넷과 다른 것을 고르시오.

[출제 예상 90%]

① It was very silly _____ him to lose his cell phone again.
② It is natural _____ him to love Jennifer.
③ It was difficult _____ us to play tennis.
④ It is hard _____ me to get an A on math test.
⑤ It wasn't easy _____ her to learn rap music.

04 다음 빈칸에 공통으로 들어갈 알맞은 단어를 고르시오.

[출제 예상 85%]

> • I have many comic books _____.
> • Her hobby is _____ books.

① read   ② reading
③ reads   ④ to be read
⑤ to read

05 다음 중 어법상 틀린 것을 고르시오. [출제 예상 90%]

① We asked him to help us out.
② Jinho saw his sister enter the theater.
③ He listened to me to sing in my room.
④ Our teacher made us be quiet.
⑤ She saw her friend crying alone.

06 다음 중 어법상 옳은 것을 고르시오. [출제 예상 85%]

① She asked him answer the questions.
② I told him fix the door.
③ She felt a kitten touched her leg.
④ He heard a dog bark.
⑤ I saw her to watch TV.

07 다음 밑줄 친 부분을 바르게 고쳐 쓰시오.

[출제 예상 85%]

> My little brothers watched me to clean my car.

_____ ➡ _____

[01~02] 다음 문장의 빈칸에 들어갈 동사의 형태가 바른 것을 고르시오.

01

I'm so tired now. I don't want _____ on the field trip.

① gong ② go
③ to have gone ④ gone
⑤ to go

02

The boy told me _____ any friends help him.

① not have ② not to have
③ have not ④ to have not
⑤ to not have

[03~05] 다음 빈칸에 들어갈 말로 알맞은 것을 고르시오.

03

I didn't know _____ to do at first. Because I was so nervous.

① how ② when ③ where
④ what ⑤ why

04

It will be fun _____ you to learn how to fix the machine.

① of ② for ③ to
④ by ⑤ at

05

Kelly told me that the food made her _____ of her mother's cooking.

① thinking ② to think ③ of thinking
④ thought ⑤ think

06 다음 빈칸에 들어 갈 수 있는 것을 고르시오.

Someone _____ him to take my dictionary without my permission.

① let ② made ③ saw
④ watched ⑤ told

07 다음 중 주어진 문장과 의미가 같은 것을 고르시오.

The police arrived so late that they couldn't catch the robber.

① The police arrived too late can't catch the robber.
② The police arrived too late to catch the robber.
③ The police arrived so late to catch the robber.
④ The police arrived so late not to catch the robber.
⑤ The police arrived too late that to catch the robber.

★★★
08 다음 밑줄 친 be to 용법이 나머지 넷과 다른 것을 고르시오.

① She <u>is to</u> stay here until he comes back home.

② They <u>are to</u> finish the project before they go on vacation.

③ He can go to the party, but he <u>is not to</u> be back too late.

④ Since the date <u>is to</u> be in an hour, I have to be ready for it.

⑤ Nobody <u>is to</u> take a break without his permission.

[09~10] 다음 중 어법상 어색한 것을 고르시오.

09 ① You must do what your parents told you to do.

② I'll have her study English after class.

③ I felt something to tickle my toes.

④ She saw a man walking with a big dog.

⑤ I tried my best not to grow stout.

> **Note** grow stout 살이 찌다 (주로 여성에게 사용함)

10 ① I don't know how to surf the Internet well.

② I'd like you think about my idea.

③ Let her decide what to do with old clothes.

④ She wants to improve her speaking skills.

⑤ Do they know how to make a homepage?

[11~12] 다음 to부정사의 용법이 나머지 넷과 다른 것을 고르시오.

11 ① I grew up <u>to be</u> an English teacher.

② They planted many trees <u>to protect</u> the forest.

③ She did her best <u>to lose</u> weight.

④ It's helpful <u>to get</u> some advice on the test.

⑤ Peter must be silly <u>to believe</u> such a foolish rumor.

★★★
12 ① I put my hand out of the window <u>to throw</u> out the garbage.

② Would you please give me something <u>to eat</u>?

③ Some of my friends stopped by <u>to pick</u> me up.

④ Sara and I went to the shopping mall <u>to buy</u> new shoes.

⑤ She parked her car <u>to look</u> at the map.

★★★
13 다음 중 어법상 옳은 것을 고르시오.

① What are you planning to do this summer vacation?

② I decided forming a band like theirs.

③ The outdoor activities you choose do will help you get healthy.

④ She expected see Lim again.

⑤ He wanted me find out who broke the window.

14 다음 중 밑줄 친 부분의 올바른 형태들끼리 짝지어진 것을 고르시오.

> • They won't let their daughter <u>go</u> out late at night.
> • I asked my husband <u>fix</u> the vacuum cleaner.

① going – fix
② gone – fixed
③ goes – to fix
④ going – fixed
⑤ go – to fix

15 다음 두 문장에 공통으로 들어갈 알맞은 단어를 고르시오.

> • We didn't have _____ money to buy a big house.
> • My speech is always slow _____ for everyone to understand.

① so
② enough
③ too
④ such
⑤ rather

16 다음 중 to부정사가 명사적 용법으로 쓰이지 <u>않은</u> 것을 고르시오.

① It isn't easy to know whether the news is true.
② She wants to be the best dancer.
③ Wouldn't it be better to visit your grandmother?
④ The fisherman put the nets in the sea to catch fish.
⑤ Helen's hobby is to collect old post cards.

17 ★★★ 다음 밑줄 친 부분과 바꿔 쓸 수 있는 것을 고르시오.

> She <u>was to</u> take a trip with her friends, but one of them canceled.

① was able to
② must
③ was supposed to
④ was sure to
⑤ liked to

[18~19] 다음 빈칸에 들어갈 말로 알맞은 것을 고르시오.

18
> A piece of paper is not enough for me _____.

① to write
② to write on
③ to write with
④ writing
⑤ writing on

19
> Lina asked her oldest sister _____ her some funny stories about her school life.

① to tell
② tell
③ told
④ to be told
⑤ telling

[20~21] 다음 중 주어진 문장의 밑줄 친 부분과 쓰임이 같은 것을 고르시오.

20

> Jim came to my house <u>to borrow</u> my car.

① The family decided <u>to take</u> a trip to Europe.
② The postman came home <u>to deliver</u> the letters.
③ She didn't expect <u>to read</u> the book.
④ I didn't choose <u>to join</u> the dance club.
⑤ She agreed <u>to help</u> them do homework.

★★★
21

> Here are some books <u>to read</u> in the train.

① They need something sweet <u>to drink</u>.
② The new game is very interesting <u>to play</u>.
③ Henry and Jimmy planned <u>to take</u> a trip.
④ Did you decide <u>to make</u> a study group?
⑤ There are too many things <u>to do</u> these days.

[22~23] 다음 중 어법상 어색한 것을 고르시오.

22 ① It won't be easy to do those puzzles.
② It's strange for an actress to be a comedian.
③ It isn't hard to fix the MP3 player.
④ It may be interest to take a walk with dogs.
⑤ It's easy to answer the questions.

23 ① He promised to develop his talent.
② Can you help me carry these bags?
③ The project will help you learning to deal with other people.
④ She has wanted to make a trip around the world.
⑤ I know that he managed to take care of his pets.

24 다음 중 어법상 옳은 것을 <u>모두</u> 고르시오.

① It's time of you to make up your mind about it.
② The hat is too dark for me to wear.
③ It is wise for you not to buy that old computer.
④ It is hard of me to learn to ride a bicycle.
⑤ It was rude of him to leave without a word.

25 다음 괄호 안에 주어진 단어들을 어법에 맞게 배열한 것을 고르시오.

> Beacause of the development of transportation, people think the world is _____ everywhere they want in a day.
> (to, go, small, enough)

① enough small go to
② enough small to go
③ small enough to go
④ small enough go to
⑤ go to small enough

26 다음 우리말을 영어로 바르게 옮긴 것을 고르시오.

> 이제는 우리가 영웅을 찾기 시작할 시간이다.

① It is time of us to start searching for a hero.
② It is time for us to start searching for a hero.
③ It is time to start searching for a hero.
④ It is time to us to start searching a hero.
⑤ It is time for us to start searching for a hero.

27 다음 중 나머지 넷과 의미가 다른 것을 고르시오.

① I got up early in order to go jogging.
② I got up early in order that I would go jogging.
③ I got up early so that I would go jogging.
④ I got up early to go jogging.
⑤ I got up so early that I was able to go jogging.

28 다음 밑줄 친 부분의 쓰임이 틀린 문장을 고르시오.

① She needed a chair to sit with.
② They found a good place to stay in.
③ That is a nice toy robot to play with.
④ I have some good friends to rely on.
⑤ There are some dead flowers we need to cut off.

29 다음의 빈칸에 알맞지 않은 단어를 고르시오.

> It is _____ for us to be able to draw pictures.

① difficult   ② careless   ③ easy
④ impossible ⑤ important

30 다음 중 문장의 전환이 잘못된 것을 고르시오.

① Jack was so sick that he couldn't go to work.
　→ Jack was too sick to go to work.
② He is so weak that he can't carry the box.
　→ He is too weak to carry the box.
③ It is so expensive that we can't buy it.
　→ It is to expensive for us to buy it.
④ She is so short that she can't reach it.
　→ She is too short to reach it.
⑤ The test was so hard that I couldn't pass it.
　→ The test was too hard to pass.

◇◇◇◇◇◇◇◇◇ 서술형 평가 ◇◇◇◇◇◇◇◇◇

[31~33] 다음 중 어법상 틀린 곳을 찾아 고쳐 쓰시오.

31

> Some questions which she asked him are difficult too for him to understand.

_____ ➡ _____

32

The building seemed be bigger than it looked in the picture.

_____ ➡ _____

33

Preparing your schedule in advance helped you booked the tickets for the concert.

_____ ➡ _____

[34~36] 다음 두 문장이 같은 뜻이 되도록 빈칸에 알맞은 말을 쓰시오.

34

Andy was so tired that he couldn't finish his work yesterday.
= Andy was _____ tired _____ finish his work yesterday.

➡ _____

35

I'm supposed to teach her how she should paint the wall.
= I'm supposed to teach her _____ _____ paint the wall.

➡ _____

36

Harry should be able to dance well so that he can become a good dancer.
= Harry must be able to dance well _____ _____ _____ become a professional dancer.

➡ _____

[37~38] 다음 괄호 안의 주어진 동사를 알맞은 형태로 바꾸어 쓰시오.

37

She decided when _____ _____ her foreign friends to her house. (invite)

➡ _____

38

The exercise will enable you _____ _____ healthy and feel fresh. (keep)

➡ _____

[39~41] 다음 주어진 문장과 같은 뜻이 되도록 문장을 알맞게 고쳐 쓰시오. 단, 각 빈칸에 하나의 단어만 들어갈 수 있음 ('I'm'은 한 단어로 함)

★★★
39

> Actually, I'm so busy that I can't think about anything else.

➡ Actually, _____ _____ _____
_____ _____ _____ _____
_____.

★★★
40

> She is so smart that she can decide what she wants to be in the future.

➡ She is _____ _____ _____
_____ _____ _____ _____
_____ in the future.

★★★
41

> It seems that Kevin and Hatty are surprised at the accident.

➡ _____ _____ _____ _____
_____ _____ _____ at the
accident.

[42~43] 다음 괄호 안의 단어를 우리말에 맞게 바르게 배열하여 문장을 완성하시오.

★★★
42

> 어떤 이들에게는 그들 자신들의 결정을 내리는 것이 쉽지 않다.
> (it / not / for / to / make / easy / is / someone / own / their / decisions)

➡ _____
_____

★★★
43

> 그들이 이곳에 도착하는 데 5시간이 걸렸다.
> (took / it / hours / to / get / here / for / them / five)

➡ _____

07
Chapter
동명사

◆ **동명사:** '동사＋ing'의 형태로 명사 역할을 한다.

'~함, ~하기'의 뜻을 가지며, 문장에서 주어, 보어, 목적어의 역할을 한다.

1. 동명사의 형태 : 평서문 '동사원형 + ing' / 부정문 'not (never) + 동명사'

2. 동명사의 역할

동명사 용법	예문
주어 역할 ~하는 것은	• Smiling is good to everyone. = It is good to smile to everyone. ➡ 동명사 문장은 'It ~ to부정사' 용법으로 전환할 수 있다.
보어 역할 ~하기, ~하는 것	• Tobby's hobby is playing soccer.
목적어 역할 ~하는 것을, ~하기를	• He imagines taking a trip to Europe.

3. 동명사를 목적어로 쓰는 동사

• enjoy	즐기다	• mind	신경을 쓰다	• keep	유지하다	• finish	끝내다
• practice	연습하다	• deny	부정하다	• imagine	상상하다	• quit	그만두다

4. 동명사와 to부정사의 사용에 따라 의미가 달라지는 동사들

• try + 동명사	(시험 삼아)~해 보다	• forget + 동명사	~한 것을 잊다 (이미 완료된 행동)
• try + to부정사	~하려고 노력하다, 애쓰다	• forget + to부정사	~할 것을 잊다 (완료되지 않은 것)
• remember + 동명사	~한 것을 기억하다 (이미 완료된 행동)	• stop + 동명사	~하는 것을 멈추다
• remember + to부정사	~할 것을 기억하다 (완료되지 않은 것)	• stop + to부정사	~하기 위해 멈추다

5. 동명사와 현재분사

동명사	현재분사
• There is a woman left in the waiting room. [용도, 목적]	• The falling leaves make me sad. [상태, 동작의 진행]
• His job is teaching science at school. [보어]	• They are playing hide-and-seek in the park. [진행형]
• Jane doesn't like swimming in the pool. [목적어]	• I sat listening to music. [동시동작]

7-1 동명사의 형태와 역할

- **동명사**: 동사가 명사가 된 형태를 말한다. 문장의 주어, 보어, 목적어로 쓰이며, 동사의 성질도 가지고 있으므로 뒤에 목적어나 보어를 가질 수 있다.

1. 동명사의 형태

⑴ 평서문: [동사 + ing]

- Her job is **designing** mural patterns.

⑵ 부정문: [not (never) + 동명사]

- He dislikes **not putting** things in its place.

2. 동명사의 역할 [동사 + ing]

⑴ 주어 [~하는 것은]

- **Preparing lessons** before class is so important.

  = **It** is so important **preparing (to prepare)** lessons before class.

  [가주어]   [진주어]

  ➡ 가주어 it을 사용할 때는 동명사보다 to부정사를 주로 사용한다.

⑵ 보어 (주격보어) [~하기, ~하는 것]

- Her job is **counseling** people.

  = Her job is **to counsel** people.

  ➡ 주격보어는 to부정사로 바꿀 수 있다.

⑶ 목적어 [~하는 것을, ~하기를]

- 동사의 목적어
- Miranda enjoys **watching** romantic TV show.
- 전치사의 목적어
- Jenny's grandmother is interested in **gardening**.

A   보기 에서 맞는 말을 골라 빈칸에 알맞은 형태로 바꾸어 쓰시오.

> 보기
>
> be   make   pass   watch   learn   run   wear   travel
> come   get   talk   correct   drink   sell   overeat

1   _____*Being*_____ a good parents is really difficult.

2   My sister is interested in _____ bread.

3   I'm not sure of _____ the final exam.

4   _____ how to swim is exciting but hard.

5   Miranda said, "Thank you for _____ to my party."

6   My mother enjoys _____ dramas.

7   Linda likes _____ with her neighbors.

8   _____ all over the world is my dream.

9   Jane doesn't like _____ contact lenses.

10   _____ his report takes a lot of time.

11   _____ an A on the English test is too difficult.

12   _____ too much coffee is harmful.

13   I always heard that _____ was not good for my health.

14   Her wish is _____ a Korean restaurant in LA.

15   The woman's job is _____ handmade cupcakes on the street.

동명사를 목적어로 하는 동사

• 동명사가 목적어 역할을 할 때 동명사만을 취하는 동사들이 있다.

◈ 동명사만을 목적어로 사용하는 동사

admit	avoid	consider	deny	dislike	enjoy
finish	imagine	mind	postpone	practice	quit
suggest	understand	give up	go on	keep on	put off

• Mansu **suggested cleaning** the park.

• Have you **imagined flying** in the sky like Icarus?

• I really wanted to **avoid having** a singing test.

• John **postponed replying** to her suggestion.

Grammar Plus +

• **to** 부정사만을 목적어로 갖는 동사

want, hope, expect, decide, need, plan, promise, refuse, earn, agree, wish, would like

Check up!

Answer Keys p. 27

A 주어진 말을 이용하여 빈칸을 완성하시오.

1   The girl gave up _____hiding_____ Tim's birthday present. (hide)

2   We denied _____ his proposal. (accept)

3   He suggested _____ fishing this weekend. (go)

4   I don't mind _____ the door. (close)

5   I disliked _____ at home, so I went shopping. (stay)

6   Have you finished _____ your homework? (do)

7   Let's go on _____ the issue. (discuss)

8   She considered _____ a new cell phone. (buy)

9   I can't imagine _____ without my family. (live)

10 He put off _____ his summer trip. (plan)

11 I started _____ how to swim in the sea. (learn)

12 They postponed _____ the seminar because of the storm. (hold)

13 The students have practiced _____ for three weeks. (sing)

7-3 동명사와 to부정사를 목적어로 하는 동사

동명사와 to부정사를 모두 목적어로 쓰면서 뜻이 같은 동사들도 있고 뜻이 달라지는 동사들도 있다.

1. '동명사 문장' = 'to부정사 문장'

begin	start	hate	like	love	prefer	continue	intend

- Dabin **started learning** English in elementary school.

    = Dabin **started to learn** English in elementary school.
- Cherry **hates making** a mess in the house.

    = Cherry **hates to make** a mess in the house.

2. '동명사 문장' ≠ 'to부정사 문장'

• **remember** + 동명사 (과거에) ~했던 것을 기억하다	• **remember** + **to부정사** (미래에) ~할 것을 기억하다
• **forget** + 동명사 (과거에) ~했던 것을 잊다	• **forget** + **to부정사** (미래에) ~할 것을 잊다
• **regret** + 동명사 (과거에) ~했던 것이 유감스럽다	• **regret** + **to부정사** (미래에) ~하게 되어 유감이다
• **try** + 동명사 (시험 삼아) 한번 ~해보다	• **try** + **to부정사** ~하려고 노력하다

- Ray **remembered singing** in front of the people. [remember + 동명사]
- Ray **remembered to do** the laundry this afternoon. [remember + to부정사]

Grammar Plus +

- **stop**

    stop + 동명사: ~하는 것을 그만두다 [동명사가 목적어]

    stop + to부정사: ~하기 위해 (동작을) 멈추다 [to부정사가 목적을 나타내는 부사어]

Answer Keys p. 27

A 괄호 안에서 알맞은 것을 모두 고르시오.

1   David couldn't imagine ((meeting) / to meet) her again.

2   I can't wait (to go / going) hiking with him tomorrow.

3   You should practice (posing / to pose) more naturally.

4   They intend (to plan / planning) their summer vacation trip.

5   He didn't like (eating / to eat) only vegetables.

6   I think Tim doesn't like (dancing / to dance) in front of others.

7   She enjoys (writing / to write) novels than watching TV.

8   The princess loved (making / to make) floral arrangements.

9   They have continued (fighting / to fight) each other.

10   I consider (moving / to move) to another city.

B 주어진 단어를 알맞은 형태로 바꾸어 빈칸을 채우시오.

1   They remember ___watching___ this movie last week. (watch)

2   He forgot _____ the door. (lock)

3   Please, you should stop _____ now. (complain)

4   I know that he tried _____ an A on the math test. (get)

5   Does he regret _____ our discussion group? (join)

6   John stopped _____ his train schedule. (check)

7   My mother remembers _____ the boys yesterday. (see)

8   We regret _____ that you failed the audition. (say)

9   She tried _____ those strange shirts. (buy)

10   I forget _____ the paper to the English teacher. (turn in)

7-4 동명사와 현재분사

- **동명사**: 명사의 역할을 하며 목적, 용도를 나타낸다.
- **현재분사**: 형용사의 역할을 하며 상태, 동작을 나타낸다.

◈ 동명사와 현재분사

동명사	현재분사
[용도, 목적] '동명사 + 명사' • The sleeping bag is warm and comfortable for outdoors activities.	[상태, 동작의 진행] '현재분사 + 명사' • The crying girl is my younger sister.
[보어] 'be동사 + 동명사' ~하는 것 • Mandy's hobby **is** riding a bicycle.	[진행형] 'be동사 + 현재분사' ~하고 있다 • Eric **is** making a clay doll now.
[목적어] '일반동사 + 동명사' ~하는 것 • They **practice** playing the recorder for the test.	[동시동작] '일반동사 + 현재분사' ~하면서 • She **wrote** a letter while listening to music.

★Check up!

Answer Keys p. 27

A 밑줄 친 부분의 쓰임이 동명사인지 현재분사인지 구별하시오.

1 Let's not wake up the <u>sleeping</u> girl. _____[현재분사]_____

2 He is <u>running</u> down the street. _____

3 My hobby is <u>going</u> shopping. _____

4 My mom listened to radio while <u>cooking</u>. _____

5 The <u>swimming</u> pool is large but dirty. _____

6 They are <u>having</u> lunch together. _____

7 They thought that <u>breaking</u> the window was the only way to escape. _____

8 There is a woman <u>crying</u> in the rain. _____

9 I sometimes take a <u>sleeping</u> pill whenever I can't sleep.

_____

10 The movie that I wanted to watch is <u>playing</u> at the theater.

_____

Practice More Ⅰ

Answer Keys p. 27~28

A 보기 에서 맞는 말을 골라 빈칸에 알맞은 형태로 바꾸어 쓰시오.

> 보기
> help   bother   persuade   watch   give
> be   repair   buy   have   turn off

1   His wish is ____helping____ the abandoned animals.

2   _____ others is usually difficult.

3   Stop _____ him. He is tired of studying all night.

4   I like _____ TV over the weekends.

5   _____ positive is important for happiness.

6   The woman's next task is _____ her watch.

7   _____ presents to others makes me happy.

8   Would you mind _____ the TV?

9   I plan on _____ a great time with Helen in Busan.

10   They have postponed _____ concert tickets because of the storm.

B 다음 밑줄 친 부분을 어법에 맞게 고치시오.

1   We denied <u>was saw</u> him last night.   ➡   _having seen_

2   You should remember <u>locking</u> the door when you go out.
                                                     ➡   _____

3   They couldn't imagine <u>to live</u> here.   ➡   _____

4   He stopped <u>to eat as much</u> and started exercising for his health.
                                                     ➡   _____

5   Answering all the questions <u>are</u> hard.   ➡   _____

6   She doesn't mind <u>to go</u> outside despite of the bad weather.
                                                     ➡   _____

7   Why don't you go on <u>discuss</u> today's issue? ➡   _____

8　I made my daughter happy by <u>to give</u> her some presents.

➡ _____

9　Let's keep on <u>to work out</u> together.　➡ _____

10　She said she wanted to buy a pair of <u>run</u> shoes.

➡ _____

C　주어진 문장을 한 문장으로 바꾸어 쓰시오.

1　Moving the box on the table + They began it.

➡ _____ *They began moving the box on the table.* _____

2　Putting off my promise + I hate it.

➡ _____

3　Doing homework at night + John likes it.

➡ _____

4　Making him cry + Sorry, we didn't intend it.

➡ _____

5　Watching movies on weekends + My sister prefers it.

➡ _____

6　Cleaning your classroom + Have you finished it?

➡ _____

7　Meeting him here + I couldn't imagine it.

➡ _____

8　Visiting a nursing home + We intend it.

➡ _____

9　Playing the drums + Her hobby is it.

➡ _____

10　Reading detective novels + He enjoys it.

➡ _____

D 주어진 단어를 알맞게 배열하여 문장을 완성하시오.

1 (don't, Monday, to, forget, uniform, next, wear, your)

➡ _____ *Don't forget to wear your uniform next Monday.* _____

2 (they, bag, would, buy, a, to, sleeping, like)

➡ _____

3 (my father, a, is, considering, new, buying, house, family, for, our)

➡ _____

4 (I, regret, the party, really, early, leaving, so)

➡ _____

5 (Then, interesting, something, try, find, to, ?)

➡ Are you bored? _____

6 (you, stop, here, should, swimming)

➡ _____

7 (we, mistake, have, the same, making, to, avoid)

➡ _____

8 (the, whole, rain, continued, weekend, falling)

➡ _____

9 (his father, shows, enjoys, comedy, watching)

➡ _____

10 (let's, singing, on, together, go)

➡ _____

Point Check II

◆ **동명사:** '동사+ing'의 형태로 명사 역할을 한다.

'~함, ~하기'의 뜻을 가지며, 문장에서 주어, 보어, 목적어의 역할을 한다.

1. 동명사의 의미상의 주어

의미상의 주어를 사용하지 않는 경우	의미상의 주어를 사용하는 경우
일반 사람이 주어인 경우	문장의 주어와 동명사의 주어가 다른 경우 ➡ 소유격 또는 목적격으로 표현
문장의 주어와 같은 경우	① 의미상의 주어가 부정대명사, 무생물, 추상명사일 경우 목적격
문장의 목적어와 같은 경우	② 의미상의 주어가 all, both, this, those 등일 경우 목적격

2. 동명사의 시제

⑴ 완료동명사: [having + 과거분사].

• Jessie is proud of **having won** first prize.

⑵ 수동형 동명사: 단순 수동형 – [being + 과거분사], 완료 수동형 – [having been + 과거분사]

• She looks forward to **being kept** in touch her friends.

• He was ashamed of **having been scolded** by his teacher.

◆ 동명사의 관용 표현

1	be excited about -ing	~에 대해 흥분하다
2	be good at -ing	~을 잘하다
3	be interested in -ing	~에 관심 있다
4	be responsible for -ing	~에 책임이 있다
5	be surprised at -ing	~에 대해 놀라다
6	be tired of -ing	~을 지겨워하다
7	be worried about -ing	~에 대해 걱정하다
8	feel like -ing	~하고 싶다
9	look forward to -ing	~을 고대하다
10	on -ing	~하자마자

동명사의 의미상의 주어

• **의미상의 주어**: 동명사는 동사의 성질을 갖고 있기 때문에 문장 안에서 행위자를 갖게 되는데 이를 동명사의 의미상의 주어라고 한다. 문장의 주어와 동명사의 주어가 다른 경우가 있다.

1. 의미상의 주어를 사용하는 경우

⑴ 소유격 또는 목적격: 문장의 주어와 동명사의 주어가 다른 경우 소유격 또는 목적격의 형태로 나타낸다.

➡ 문어체에서는 소유격을, 구어체에서는 목적격을 주로 사용한다.

• Mary forgot **his (him) giving** her his phone number last night.

= Mary forgot that he gave her his phone number last night.

⑵ 목적격: ① 의미상의 주어가 부정대명사, 무생물, 추상명사일 경우 목적격으로 나타낸다.
② 의미상의 주어가 all, both, this, those 등일 경우 목적격으로 나타낸다.

• I dislike <u>someone</u> calling **me** friendly.

• They are sure of **this being** faulty.

2. 의미상의 주어를 사용하지 않는 경우

⑴ 일반 사람이 주어인 경우

• **Making noise** in a public place is not polite.

⑵ 문장의 주어와 같은 경우

• She likes **reading** old stories.

⑶ 문장의 목적어와 같은 경우

• He praised them for **working** very hard.

Answer Keys p. 28

A 주어진 말을 의미가 통하도록 배열하여 문장을 완성하시오.

1 I don't mind _____*my sister's using my laptop*_____. (using, my, laptop, sister's, my)

2 She forgets _____. (telling, information, some, his)

3 They don't understand _____. (being, meeting, his, the, for, late)

4 Jane felt bad about _____. (the, losing, Minho's, game)

B   보기 와 같이 동명사를 이용한 문장으로 완성하시오.

보기

   I like that Tim dances on the stage.
   ➡ I like Tim's dancing on the stage.

1   I don't like that he goes to such a dangerous place.

   ➡ _____

2   Do you mind if I borrow your car?

   ➡ _____

3   I am sure that he is James.

   ➡ _____

4   He is certain that Cindy will come back home soon.

   ➡ _____

5   Everybody remembers that she wins the game.

   ➡ _____

6   The teacher suggests that Peter participate in the competition.

   ➡ _____

7   They are disappointed that Yuna breaks the rule.

   ➡ _____

8   I want Mr. Lee to be the coach of our team.

   ➡ _____

9   Sam is certain that the movie will be famous.

   ➡ _____

10 She is proud that her son having a doctorate.

   ➡ _____

Lesson 7-6 동명사의 시제

- **완료동명사**: 동명사의 시제가 문장 동사의 시제보다 앞서 있을 경우 사용한다.
- **수동형 동명사**: 동명사의 의미상의 주어가 행위를 받는 수동의 관계일 때 사용한다.

1. 단순동명사: [동사+ing]

- He is proud of **getting** first prize.
  → He is proud that he gets first prize.
- She regretted **not cleaning** the basement.
  → She regretted that she did not clean the basement.

2. 완료동명사: [having+과거분사]

- She enjoyed **having swum** in the river when she was young.
  → She enjoyed that she had swum in the river when she was young.

3. 수동형 동명사: 단순 수동형 – [being+과거분사], 완료 수동형 – [having been+과거분사]

- Most teenagers don't like **being told** what to do.
- The woman is sure of her car **having been broken** into again.

Check up!

Answer Keys p. 28

A 다음 문장을 보기 와 같이 바꾸어 쓰시오.

> 보기
>
> They denied that they had seen the girl.
> ⇒ They denied having seen the girl.

1 Thomas admits that he is guilty.
⇒ _____

2 Jieun suggests that she will invite us to her wedding party.
⇒ _____

3 I am proud that I got first prize.
⇒ _____

4 They were ashamed that they had been late for the meeting.
⇒ _____

5 She is sure that she will get an A on the final exam.
⇒ _____

6 He admits that he stole the necklace.
⇒ _____

7-7 동명사의 관용 표현

1	be excited about -ing	~에 대해 흥분하다
2	be good at -ing	~을 잘하다
3	be interested in -ing	~에 관심있다
4	be responsible for -ing	~에 책임이 있다
5	be surprised at -ing	~에 대해 놀라다
6	be tired of -ing	~을 지겨워하다
7	be worried about -ing	~에 대해 걱정하다
8	feel like -ing	~하고 싶다
9	look forward to -ing	~을 고대하다
10	on -ing	~하자마자
11	thank ... for -ing	~에 대해 ...에게 감사하다
12	object to -ing	~에 반대하다
13	need -ing = need to be + 과거분사	~할 필요가 있다
14	How (What) about -ing? = What do you say to -ing?	~하는 것이 어때?
15	keep (prevent / stop) A from -ing	A가 ~하는 것을 막다 (못하게 하다)
16	be used to -ing	~하는 데 익숙하다
17	be busy -ing	~하느라 바쁘다
18	be worth -ing	~할 만한 가치가 있다
19	go -ing	~하러 가다
20	It's no use -ing	~해 봐야 소용없다
21	There is no -ing = It is impossible to + 동사원형	~하는 것은 불가능하다
22	spend + 시간(돈) (in) -ing	~하느라 ...을 쓰다
23	have trouble (difficulty / a hard time) (in) -ing	~하는 데 어려움을 겪다
24	cannot help -ing = cannot but + 동사원형	~하지 않을 수 없다

A 다음 주어진 말을 이용하여 우리말을 영어로 완성하시오.

1 그녀는 그 소식을 듣자마자 울기 시작했다. (hear, the news)
➡ _____*On hearing the news*_____, she began to cry.

2 나는 화장품을 사는 데 너무 많은 돈을 썼다. (money, buy)
➡ I spent too _____ cosmetics.

3 우리는 John을 사랑하지 않을 수 없다. (love)
➡ We _____ John.

4 Jane은 새로 태어난 조카를 보기를 고대하고 있다. (meet)
➡ Jane _____ her newborn nephew.

5 그들은 잃어버린 자동차 키를 찾느라 고생했다. (find)
➡ They _____ the lost car key.

6 엄마는 내가 하이킹 가는 것을 막으려고 했다. (hike)
➡ Mom would try to prevent me _____.

7 나는 Jim의 자전거가 수리될 필요가 있다고 생각한다. (repair)
➡ I think Jim's bike _____.

8 난 잘 때마다 창문을 열어 둔다. (open)
➡ I never go to bed _____ the window.

9 내일 무슨 일이 일어날지 아는 것은 불가능하다. (know)
➡ _____ what will happen tomorrow.

10 그녀는 영어로 일기를 쓰는 데 익숙하다. (write)
➡ She _____ in her dairy in English.

11 나와 Tim은 기말 고사를 준비하느라 바빴다. (prepare)
➡ Tim and I _____ for the final exam.

12 Andy는 밤에 혼자서 그 숲에 들어가고 싶지 않았다. (go)
➡ Andy didn't feel _____ to the forest alone at night.

13 이 영화는 다른 사람들에게 추천할 가치가 있다. (recommend)
➡ The movie _____ to others.

14 엎질러진 물이다. (cry)
➡ _____ over spilt milk.

15 내가 도착했을 때 그들은 막 떠나려는 참이었다. (leave)
➡ When I arrived, they _____.

Practice More II

A 괄호 안에 주어진 단어를 이용하여 빈칸에 쓰시오.

1 I remember _____*her telling*_____ a lie to me. (she, tell)

2 We are proud of _____ the contest. (you, win)

3 Do you mind _____ the window? (I, open)

4 There is no doubt of _____ true. (this, be)

5 My parents will be happy about _____ with honors. (my sister, graduate)

6 I'm looking forward to _____ his best at the audition. (he, do)

7 Are you certain of _____ here? (John, come)

8 We remembered _____ the building when we were having dinner. (the woman, enter)

9 I'm in favor of _____ the class president. (Minji, be)

10 He is not used to _____ like that. (you, talk)

B 다음 문장에서 어법상 <u>어색한</u> 것을 찾아 바르게 고치시오.

1 He admitted to lived in the blue house.

     _____*lived*_____ ➡ _____*living*_____

2 Jane didn't regret being sold that wooden chair.

     _____ ➡ _____

3 I dislike having bothered by the noise.

     _____ ➡ _____

4 We are sure of found the right solution.

     _____ ➡ _____

5 I admit to be guilty.   _____ ➡ _____

6 They are happy about praised by their parents.

     _____ ➡ _____

7 Do you feel like to go to the theater?

     _____ ➡ _____

8 Sam is busy to prepare for his wedding.

     _____ ➡ _____

9   What you should remember is never caused trouble?

_____ ➡ _____

10   There's no to know what comes next.

_____ ➡ _____

C   보기 와 같이 문장을 바꾸어 쓰시오.

보기

I am sorry for not coming to your birthday party.
➡ I am sorry that I can't come to your birthday party.

1   We are sorry for being late.

➡ _____

2   She was worried about missing her train.

➡ _____

3   They are afraid of failing the exam.

➡ _____

4   I am sorry for not having answered your questions quickly.

➡ _____

5   I am sure of Paul's breaking the world record.

➡ _____

6   Mina was proud of having entered the university.

➡ _____

7   The girl denied having seen the accident.

➡ _____

8   I was nervous of having forgotten his birthday.

➡ _____

9   She remembered his calling her that day.

➡ _____

10   We are proud of her succeeding in this field.

➡ _____

Practice More Ⅱ

Answer Keys p. 28~29

D 다음 우리말 해석에 맞게 주어진 단어를 이용하여 문장을 완성하시오.

1 나는 내 딸의 졸업식에 가는 것을 기대한다.
(looking forward to, graduation ceremony)

➡ *I'm looking forward to going to my daughter's graduation ceremony.*

2 Cindy는 학교에서 새 친구들을 사귀느라고 바빴다.
(busy, make, at school)

➡ _____

3 그들은 그 영화를 이번 주 목요일에 개봉하는 데 어려움을 겪고
있다. (difficulty, release, this Thursday)

➡ _____

4 Sara는 그 드레스를 사는 데 많은 돈을 썼다.
(spend, buy, the dress)

➡ _____

5 그는 내게 차를 빌려주었던 것을 잊고 있었다. (lend, his car)

➡ _____

6 그녀는 요새 밤에 잠드는 것에 어려움을 겪고 있다. (trouble, sleep)

➡ _____

7 나는 그런 이상한 모자를 쓰고 싶지 않다. (wear, strange hat)

➡ _____

8 주말마다 봉사를 할 가치가 있다. (volunteer, worth)

➡ _____

9 그는 아침마다 부모님에게 전화하는 것을 잊지 않는다.
(not, forget to, every morning)

➡ _____

10 아버지는 내가 머리를 짧게 자르는 것을 막았다.
(prevent, have, cut)

➡ _____

내신 최다 출제 유형

01 다음 중 어법상 <u>어색한</u> 것을 고르시오. [출제 예상 85%]

① The musical was worth watching.
② On hearing about his success, we started to shout with joy.
③ It is no use crying over the broken window.
④ The people in Russia are used to live in a cold climate.
⑤ I was very busy preparing for my son's birthday party.

02 다음 빈칸에 알맞은 말이 바르게 짝지어진 것을 고르시오.

> • Keep _____ for 20 to 30 minutes.
> • They pretended _____ about it.

① running − know
② run − knowing
③ running − to know
④ to run − to know
⑤ running − knowing

03 다음 주어진 문장의 밑줄 친 부분과 쓰임이 <u>다른</u> 것을 고르시오.

> Swimming in the rain is exciting.

① He went out without <u>saying</u> goodbye.
② He is <u>playing</u> the guitar for me.
③ At last he finished <u>carving</u> the ice sculpture.
④ My way of <u>helping</u> him is writing a letter.
⑤ What I want to do is not <u>being</u> alone.

04 다음 주어진 문장의 밑줄 친 부분과 쓰임이 같은 것을 고르시오.

> I have met the woman <u>making</u> a big kite over there.

① <u>Doing</u> extreme sports is certainly more exciting.
② Her job is <u>teaching</u> science at school.
③ He sometimes takes <u>sleeping</u> pills.
④ <u>Holding</u> hot drinks without a cup holder is dangerous.
⑤ I remember the boy <u>waiting</u> for her.

05 다음 밑줄 친 부분 중 어법상 <u>틀린</u> 것을 고르시오.

> I'm Jinwoo. I enjoy not only ① <u>listening</u> to music, but also ② <u>composing</u> music.
> I like ③ <u>to read</u> books, too.
> This year, I planned ④ <u>writing</u> my own story. This is the first step to getting closer to my dream. I hope ⑤ <u>to become</u> a writer.

06 다음 우리말을 영어로 바르게 옮긴 것을 고르시오.

> 그는 따돌림을 당하는 것도 두려워했다.

① He was also afraid of to be left out.
② He was also afraid of leaving out.
③ He was also afraid of being leave out.
④ He was also afraid of be left out.
⑤ He was also afraid of being left out.

[01~04] 다음 빈칸에 알맞은 말을 고르시오.

01

Mia gave up _____ the MP3 player and decided to borrow her brother's.

① fix   ② to fix   ③ fixing
④ to be fixed ⑤ being fix

02

I looked forward to _____ a trip to America. Because I've never been there before.

① have taken ② to take   ③ take
④ be taking   ⑤ taking

03

She was not only fond of reading poems, but also capable of _____ good poems.

① make   ② making   ③ made
④ be making ⑤ to be made

04

They cannot help _____ for entering private land without any permission.

① apologize   ② to apologize
③ apologized   ④ apologizing
⑤ for apologize

05 다음 빈칸에 들어갈 수 없는 것을 고르시오.

People _____ talking about the hostages in IS.

① avoided   ② wanted   ③ stopped
④ began   ⑤ continued

[06~07] 다음 밑줄 친 부분의 용법이 나머지 넷과 다른 것을 고르시오.

06
① Having good friends is good for you.
② Taking too many naps makes you dizzy.
③ Seeing is believing.
④ Judging from her behavior, she seems a nurse.
⑤ Jogging every morning makes me healthy.

07
① Her goal is getting first prize in the contest.
② My wish is being a great editor.
③ Seon's uncle is coming now.
④ Every salaryman's routine is coming back to work on Monday.
⑤ His hobby is playing baseball.

[08~09] 다음 중 밑줄 친 부분의 쓰임이 <u>어색한</u> 것을 고르시오.

08 ① We suddenly began <u>to laugh</u> at his joke.
② She enjoys <u>assembling</u> the model ship.
③ I decided <u>to apply</u> for the interview.
④ He stopped <u>drinking</u> coke a year ago.
⑤ Would you mind <u>to step</u> aside a little bit?

★★★
09 ① John and Max considered <u>going</u> on a backpack trip to Canada.
② Kate put off <u>to buy</u> a new hat and shorts.
③ We agreed <u>to extend</u> the time limit.
④ Because he was nervous, he refused <u>to speak</u>.
⑤ Mary understood them <u>to be</u> satisfied.

Note   a backpack trip 배낭여행

10 다음 두 문장을 같은 뜻이 되도록 할 때 빈칸에 알맞은 말을 고르시오.

> She could not help smiling at the caricature of her.
> = She could not _____ _____ at the caricature of her.

① for smiling ② to smile   ③ but smile
④ and smile   ⑤ of smiling

11 다음 괄호 안에 주어진 단어들을 바르게 배열한 것을 고르시오.

> I missed the entertainment show 'Muhandojeon' because I _____. (doing / busy / was / my homework)

① my homework doing was busy
② doing my homework was busy
③ was doing my homework busy
④ busy was doing my homework
⑤ was busy doing my homework

[12~13] 다음 중 어법상 <u>어색한</u> 것을 고르시오.
★★★
12 ① His life has been devoted to helped the poor.
② My sister and I are used to going shopping late at night.
③ She is accustomed to being a leader.
④ I could not but accept the suggestion.
⑤ I am looking forward to seeing the march.

13 ① She spent most of her time cooking dinner.
② She doesn't enjoy to be friends with strangers.
③ We have trouble making decisions.
④ She's been busy looking for a new job.
⑤ I had difficulty focusing on the test.

[14~15] 다음 중 어법상 올바른 것을 고르시오.

14
① Jude wants to sleep instead of eat something.
② Nobody could imagine to meet the actor.
③ Jessy wanted to avoid argue about the topic.
④ Jane and Harry prefer dying to living in dishonor.
⑤ I feel like to taking a walk in the park.

★★★
15
① I started learn to play tennis last month.
② He imagined to live in Norway.
③ We apologized for not joining their study group.
④ They planned taking the first train.
⑤ She seems to dislike make noise in public places.

★★★
16 다음 밑줄 친 부분의 쓰임이 올바른 것을 <u>모두</u> 고르시오.

① Parents are <u>worried of</u> their daughters going outside at night.
② He was responsible <u>of breaking</u> the window.
③ She felt <u>like cry</u> when she heard the sad news.
④ Tim left her <u>without saying</u> anything.
⑤ He apologized <u>for being</u> mean to them.

[17~19] 다음 우리말과 같은 뜻이 되도록 빈칸에 알맞은 단어를 고르시오.

17

| 매일 30분 정도 달리는 것은 너의 건강을 더 좋게 만들어 줄 수 있다. |
| = _____ for about thirty minutes can make you healthier. |

① Run   ② Ran   ③ To be ran
④ Running   ⑤ Have running

18

| 올해 첫날 나는 다이어트를 하기로 결심했다. |
| = On the first day of this year, I decided _____ on a diet. |

① to go   ② going   ③ go
④ go to   ⑤ be

19

| 외출할 때 불 끄는 것을 잊지 마라. |
| = Don't forget _____ off the light when you go out. |

① turned   ② turning   ③ to turn
④ turn   ⑤ have turned

20 다음 우리말을 영어로 바르게 옮긴 것을 고르시오.

> 그들은 내가 시험에 실패할 것이라고 상상하지 않았다.

① They didn't imagine I was failing the test.
② They didn't imagine my failing the test.
③ They didn't imagine their failing the test.
④ They didn't imagine I fail the test.
⑤ They didn't imagine my failed the test.

★★★
21 다음 주어진 문장과 뜻이 같은 것을 고르시오.

> It's impossible to live without water.

① There is not livings without water.
② There is no living without water.
③ There are no living without water.
④ There is no water without living.
⑤ There is no live without water.

★★★
22 다음 짝지어진 문장들의 의미가 <u>다른</u> 것을 고르시오.

① I like to travel by bus alone.
  = I like traveling by bus alone.
② Tina continued to help them.
  = Tina continued helping them.
③ I started to learn how to swim last week.
  = I started learning how to swim last week.
④ Please remember to send me a post card.
  = Please remember sending me a post card.
⑤ It began to snow yesterday.
  = It began snowing yesterday.

23 다음 대화의 빈칸에 들어갈 말이 바르게 짝지어진 것을 고르시오.

> A What do you plan _____ this winter vacation?
> B I'm thinking of _____ to America with my brother. I just want to visit Rocky Mountain National Park. Can you join us?
> A That sounds great! I'm looking forward to _____ the beautiful scenery.

① doing – going – seeing
② to do – to go – see
③ to do – going – seeing
④ do – going – see
⑤ doing – go – seeing

24 다음 밑줄 친 부분의 쓰임이 올바른 것을 고르시오.

① I had to postpone <u>to meet</u> his family.
② We consider <u>to move</u> to Colorado.
③ He remembers <u>to see</u> me yesterday.
④ Sora dislikes <u>to be</u> a lawyer.
⑤ He continued <u>to search</u> for unique plants.

25 다음 중 어법상 어색한 것을 모두 고르시오.

① The gentleman stopped to help a little girl.

② She forgot booking a ticket for the movie.

③ Suzie really regrets cheating on the test last time.

④ I remembered turn off the TV before I went out.

⑤ Learning foreign languages is not easy.

[26~27] 다음 주어진 문장의 밑줄 친 부분과 쓰임이 같은 것을 고르시오.

26

Jane's hobby is making hand-knitted dolls.

① The woman stood reading the notice.

② Brandon finished doing his project perfectly.

③ I am playing the piano.

④ Why are you waiting for him so long?

⑤ The girl is wearing diamond earrings.

27

She sat talking to her mother.

① They admitted cheating on the test.

② His problem is talking too much.

③ The player practiced running faster than the others.

④ She avoids going to the swimming pool.

⑤ Her mother is listening to rock music.

28 다음 두 문장의 의미가 같도록 할 때 빈칸에 알맞은 것을 고르시오.

She is willing to eat pizza tonight.
= She _____.

① dislikes eating pizza tonight

② hates eating pizza tonight

③ doesn't mind eating pizza tonight

④ doesn't like to eat pizza tonight

⑤ doesn't like eating pizza tonight

[29~30] 다음 두 문장의 의미가 같도록 할 때 빈칸에 알맞은 말을 고르시오.

29

She remembered that she talked to the man at the cafe.
= She remembered _____ to the man at the cafe.

① to talk   ② talking   ③ talked
④ being talk   ⑤ having been talked

30

I want to postpone our appointment until next Saturday.
= I want to _____ off our appointment until next Saturday.

① get   ② take   ③ turn
④ cut   ⑤ put

◇◇◇◇◇◇◇◇ 서술형 평가 ◇◇◇◇◇◇◇◇◇

[31~33] 다음 두 문장이 같은 의미가 되도록 할 때 빈칸에 알맞은 말을 쓰시오.

31

Henry's character needs changing.
= Henry's character needs to _____
_____.

➡ _____

32

The movie was not worth seeing due to the poor story.
= It is not _____ _____
_____ the movie due to the poor story.

➡ _____

33

Hatty couldn't go out of the house because it was raining.
= The rain prevented her _____ going out of the house.

➡ _____

[34~35] 다음 문장에서 틀린 곳을 찾아 바르게 고쳐 쓰시오.

34

I remembered visit my aunt's house in LA. I went to Universal Studio and saw some actors and actresses.

_____ ➡ _____

35

Mr. Smith has lung cancer. He stopped to smoke for his health.

_____ ➡ _____

[36~37] 다음 대화의 내용과 일치하도록 괄호 안의 단어를 이용하여 알맞은 말을 쓰시오.

36

A What's up, Jay?
B Vicky borrowed my new dress a week ago and she didn't give it back to me.
A Oh, I think she forgot about it. Why don't you call her?

➡ Jay is upset because Vicky forgot
_____ _____ _____ _____
a week ago and didn't give it back to her. (borrow)

Answer Keys p. 29~30

37

A Yo, Chris. I heard your band is looking for a new member.
B Oh, Jenny. Yeah, we need a singer.
A Can I join your band, then? I really want to sing in your band.

➡ Jenny is looking forward _____ _____ _____ _____. (join)

★★★
38 보기 의 단어 중 알맞은 것을 골라 빈칸에 알맞게 변형하여 쓰시오.

보기
meet　win　help　exchange

➡ (1) Jamie and I will try _____ the game.
(2) Neil gave up trying to _____ his jacket for a bag.

[39~40] 다음 우리말과 뜻이 같도록 괄호 안의 단어를 바르게 배열하시오.

39
좋은 친구들을 사귀는 것은 중요하다.
(good / is / making / friends / important)

➡ _____

40
그녀는 내가 책을 잘 쓸 것을 확신했다.
(she / well / sure / was / my / writing / book / a / of)

➡ _____

[41~42] 다음 우리말과 같은 뜻이 되도록 괄호 안의 말을 이용하여 문장을 완성하시오.

41
너는 내 신발을 본 것을 기억하니?
(see, my shoes)

➡ Do you _____ _____ _____ _____?

42
그녀는 일을 열심히 하지 않은 것을 부인한다.
(not, deny)

➡ She _____ _____ _____ hard.

08
Chapter
분사

Point Check I

◆ **분사:** '동사원형＋ing' 또는 '동사원형＋ed(과거분사)'의 형태로 나타낼 수 있다.
　　　　명사를 수식하거나 주어와 목적어의 상태를 설명하는 형용사 역할을 한다.

1. 현재분사와 과거분사

	현재분사	과거분사
형태	동사원형＋ing ～하고 있는 (진행) / ～하게 하는 (능동)	동사원형＋ed, 불규칙 과거분사 ～한 (완료) / ～된, ～해진 (수동)
예문	• Emily watched some girls dancing on the stage.	• Tom has cut his finger on the broken glass.

2. 분사의 한정적 용법과 서술적 용법 : 명사를 수식하거나 보어 역할을 한다.

한정적 용법	명사 앞	• That running dog is my uncle's.
	명사 뒤	• The woman wearing glasses is my older sister Kelly.
서술적 용법	주격보어	• Alice is playing the flute on the stage.
	목적격보어	• They looked around the restaurant decorated with antique furniture.

3. 현재분사와 동명사: [동사원형 + ing]

	현재분사	동명사
역할	형용사로서 명사를 수식하거나 보어 역할을 한다.	명사로서 주어나 보어로 쓰이며, 동사나 전치사의 목적어 역할을 한다.
예문	• That crying boy is Jenny's brother.	• Mr. Jackson's job is teaching English literature at the university.

분사의 종류

• 분사: 명사를 수식하거나 주어나 목적어의 상태를 설명하는 형용사 역할을 한다. 동사원형에 '-ing'를 붙이면 현재분사, '-ed'를 붙이면 과거분사가 된다.

◆ 현재분사와 과거분사

	현재분사	과거분사
형태	동사원형 + ing	동사원형 + ed, 불규칙 과거분사
쓰임	[진행] ~하고 있는 • Jenny is singing and dancing. • They watched a girl singing in the square. [능동] ~하게 하는 • I found an interesting game on the Internet. • Learning new things is so interesting.	[완료] ~한 • Hyerin folded the dried laundry. • Grandmother has dried the shrimps. [수동] ~된, ~해진 • Jim's arm is broken from the accident. • There are pieces of a broken vase on the floor.

Answer Keys p. 31

A 괄호 안에서 알맞은 것을 고르시오.

1 Be careful, there are some ((broken) / breaking) pieces of glass.

2 The movie is very (moved / moving).

3 An (excited / exciting) crowd of people started to shout.

4 When we got there, some dancers were (performing / performed).

5 Do not wake up the (sleeping / slept) baby.

6 I picked up some (fallen / falling) leaves.

7 The amount of money (stolen / stealing) is about three thousand dollars.

8 Let's pick up those (broken / breaking) pieces of ice.

9 She is afraid that the washing machine is not (working / worked) properly.

10 I decided to sell the (using / used) car.

8-2 한정적 용법과 서술적 용법

- **한정적 용법**: 명사를 꾸며주는 역할을 하며, 분사가 다른 수식어구와 함께 쓰이면 명사의 뒤에서 수식한다.
- **서술적 용법**: 문장에서 주격보어 또는 목적격보어의 역할을 한다.

1. 한정적 용법

(1) 명사 앞에서 수식: 분사가 단독으로 쓰일 경우
- He didn't know there were so many **abandoned** children. (abandoned → children 수식)
- The old woman collected **forsaken** dolls. (forsaken → dolls 수식)

(2) 명사 뒤에서 수식: 분사가 구를 이루어 수식하는 경우
- The lady **standing over there** is the May Queen this year. (standing over there → the lady 수식)
  = The lady **(who is) standing over there** is the May Queen of this year.
- Jayeong and I watched a movie **directed by Choi Donghun**.
  (directed by Choi Donghun → a movie 수식)

2. 서술적 용법: '주어와 보어', '목적어와 보어'의 관계에 따라 '현재분사'와 '과거분사'를 사용한다.

주격보어	능동 – [현재분사] ~하면서, ~하게 하는
	• I was seated knitting a scarf.
	수동 – [과거분사] ~한, ~된, ~해진
	• **Mike's backyard was** destroyed **by the heavy rain.**
목적격 보어	능동 – [현재분사] ~하는 것을
	• They saw a big star shinning in the night sky.
	수동 – [과거분사] ~되는 것을
	• My mother will leave **the door** unlocked for me.

3. 주격보어와 목적격보어의 동사

분사를 주격보어로 갖는 동사	come, go, become, sit, stand, remain, stay, keep
분사를 목적격보어로 갖는 동사	keep, leave, find, get, have, make, 지각동사

A 주어진 단어를 알맞은 형태로 빈칸에 쓰시오.

1 The boys chased the _____*running*_____ thief. (run)

2 The roof was _____ because of the storm. (damage)

3 Linda stood _____ to music. (listen)

4 The woman was _____ out loud looking for her daughter. (cry)

5 Put the _____ dough into the bowl and add some sugar. (mix)

6 The lady _____ in front of the door is my aunt. (stand)

7 I introduced my pet _____ Bob to him. (call)

8 She said the accident was a _____ experience. (terrify)

9 We should keep the fire _____ for a week. (burn)

10 The barking dog was _____ to the stake. (tie)

B 분사를 이용하여 두 문장을 한 문장으로 연결하시오.

1 Look at the tower. It is built by the workers.

➡ _____*Look at the tower built by the workers.*_____

2 Do you know the girl? She is picking up some fallen leaves.

➡ _____

3 Students came here to do their homework.They are having lunch.

➡ _____

4 The man is my English teacher. He is preparing for the lesson in his office.

➡ _____

5 There are some houses. Those are covered with snow.

➡ _____

6 I see a small bird. It is standing on the branch.

➡ _____

현재분사와 동명사

• 현재분사와 동명사: 모두 동사 뒤에 -ing가 붙기 때문에 문장 안에서 쓰인 의미와 역할의 차이로 구분한다.

◈ 현재분사와 동명사

	현재분사	동명사
역할	형용사로서 명사를 수식하며, 주어나 목적어의 보어 역할을 한다.	명사로서 주어나 보어로 쓰이며, 동사나 전치사의 목적어 역할을 한다.
뜻	~하고 있는, ~하게 하는	~하기 위한, ~하는 것
형태	동사원형 + ing	동사원형 + ing
쓰임	• That singing girl is so cute. [상태, 동작] • Jane is writing a letter in English. [진행]	• Olivia bought a new swimming suit. [목적, 용도] • Sally's job is nursing sick people. [주격보어]

Check up!

Answer Keys p. 31

A 밑줄 친 부분이 보기의 A와 같으면 A를, B와 같으면 B를 표시하시오.

보기
A He is waiting for me in the living room.
B Does she know the girl walking down the street?

1 Who is the woman singing in the room?   [B]

2 There is no waiting room in this building.   _____

3 I am proud of being your daughter.   _____

4 This movie is so embarrassing.   _____

5 He decided to buy a new washing machine.   _____

6 Kate was taking a picture of the lake.   _____

7 John is making the dress for his daughter.   _____

8 His dream is selecting the national soccer team.   _____

9 The monster attacking the city in the movie was realistic.

_____

10 I think they are really good at speaking French.   _____

8-4 감정을 나타내는 분사

감정을 나타내는 현재분사와 과거분사는 형용사로 쓰인다.

- **현재분사 형용사**: 사물을 꾸미거나 사물인 주어의 상태를 나타낼 때 사용한다.
- **과거분사 형용사**: 사람을 꾸미거나 사람인 주어의 상태를 나타낼 때 사용한다.

현재분사 (-ing) ~한 감정을 느끼게 하는		과거분사 (-ed, 불규칙과거분사) ~한 감정을 느끼는	
· boring	지루하게 하는	· bored	지루함을 느끼는
· confusing	혼란하게 하는	· confused	혼란스러운
· surprising	놀라운	· surprised	놀란
· tiring	지치게 하는	· tired	피곤한, 지친
· depressing	우울하게 하는	· depressed	우울한
· moving	감동을 주는	· moved	감동 받은
· satisfying	만족스러운	· satisfied	만족한
· amazing	놀라운	· amazed	놀란
· pleasing	기쁘게 하는	· pleased	기쁜
· amusing	즐겁게 하는	· amused	즐거워진
· disappointing	실망스러운	· disappointed	실망한
· embarrassing	당황하게 하는	· embarrassed	당황한
· frightening	무섭게 하는	· frightened	무서워진
· terrifying	두렵게 하는	· terrified	두려워진

☆Check up!

Answer Keys p. 31

A 주어진 낱말을 알맞은 형태로 빈칸에 쓰시오.

1 He looked so _____satisfied_____ with the result. (satisfy)

2 It was very _____ that you lied to me. (disappoint)

3 I was really _____ to hear that Mary failed the exam. (surprise)

4 After the game, they were so _____. (depress)

5 We were _____ to hear that we would go hiking. (excite)

6   It was _____ that they were married. (shock)

7   The dancers were _____ at the performance. (amaze)

8   Tom was deeply _____ by the speech. (move)

9   Last night, there was a _____ noise in the room. (fright)

10   I was _____ when I hear the direction. (confuse)

11   She told us a lot of _____ stories. (interest)

12   Jimmy was _____ because he had nothing to do last night. (bore)

13   The report about the universe was so _____. (fascinate)

14   We were _____ when we got back home. (tire)

15   The children were terrified because of the _____ dog. (bark)

Practice More I

Answer Keys p. 31~32

A 다음 문장에서 어법상 <u>어색한</u> 것을 찾아 바르게 고치시오.

1 She has no fixing schedule. So, she can join us.

                            fixing ➡ *fixed*

2 The girl danced on the stage is my sister.

                            ➡

3 Amy is interesting in the movie.

                            ➡

4 There were some people ran in the park.

                            ➡

5 They shouldn't eat any fish catching in the place.

                            ➡

6 I saw a lot of jumped dolphins in the show.

                            ➡

7 Do you see the man stood in front of the door?

                            ➡

8 The race was interesting. I was really fascinating by it.

                            ➡

9 There are children played in the mud.

                            ➡

10 I saw a wounding soldier lying on the bed.

                            ➡

B 다음 주어진 말을 이용하여 빈칸에 알맞은 말을 쓰시오.

1 His behavior embarrasses many people.

  ➡ His behavior _____ *is embarrassing* _____.

  ➡ Many peopler _____ *are embarrassed* _____ by his behavior.

2 The difficult lecture exhausts students.

  ➡ The difficult lecture _____.

  ➡ Students _____ by the difficult lecture.

3 A lot of homework annoys him.

  ➡ A lot of homework _____.

  ➡ He _____ by a lot of homework.

Practice More I

4   The bad smell disgusts most people.

➡ The bad smell _____.

➡ Most people _____ by the bad smell.

5   His song fascinates many girls.

➡ His song _____.

➡ Many girls _____ by his song.

C   다음 두 문장을 완전한 한 문장으로 만드시오.

1   Can you see the girl over there? She is holding some books.

➡ ____*Can you see the girl holding some books over there?*____

2   Look at the cat. It is lying on the sofa.

➡ _____

3   There is a woman. She is crying in the rain.

➡ _____

4   There is a car. It is parked next to the park.

➡ _____

5   Do you know about the book? It was written by Mr. Han.

➡ _____

6   They found a box. It was covered with black paper.

➡ _____

7   I saw Peter. He was painting the wall.

➡ _____

8   Who is the handsome boy? He is eating lunch on the grass.

➡ _____

9   Linda saw some workers. They moved heavy bricks.

➡ _____

10   I heard my name. It was called in the crowd.

➡ _____

D 다음 주어진 말을 알맞게 배열하여 문장을 완성하시오.

1 (the, a speech, the stage, Amy, girl, on, is, making)

➡ *The girl making a speech on the stage is Amy.*

2 (they, going, school, were, about, to, depressed, back)

➡ _____

3 (she, floor, sat, on, cross-legged, the)

➡ _____

4 (I, pictures, colors, love, dark, in, painted)

➡ _____

5 (my friends, the result, and, with, are, disappointed, I)

➡ _____

6 (we, us, could, a big bird, above, flying, see)

➡ _____

7 (I, the family, house, know, the, in, living)

➡ _____

8 (Jane, India, a film, saw, in, made)

➡ _____

9 (Kelly, her stuff, paper, had, in, wrapped)

➡ _____

10 (got, he, the game, his leg, during, broken)

➡ _____

Point Check Ⅱ

◆ **분사구문**: 접속사가 있는 부사절의 접속사와 주어를 생략하고 동사를 분사 형태로 만들어 사용하는 문장을 말한다.

◆ **형용사로서의 분사**: 사물이 주어일 때 현재분사를 사용하며, 사람이 주어일 때 과거분사를 사용한다.

1. 분사구문 만들기

[평서문] As I didn't have breakfast, I was very hungry in the morning.

[분사구문] ➡ **Not having** breakfast, I was very hungry in the morning.

① 접속사와 주어를 지운다. (부사절과 주절의 주어가 다를 경우에는 주어를 생략하지 않는다.)
② 부정형일 경우, 'Not'을 문장 맨 앞으로 뺀다.
③ '동사+ing' 형태를 만든다. (be동사일 경우 'be+ing')
④ 부사절의 be동사 뒤에 분사가 형용사 역할을 할 때, 분사구문에서 'being'은 생략이 가능하다.
   • **When** I was tired, I went to bed early. ➡ **(Being) Tired**, I went to bed early.

2. 분사구문의 용법

시간	when, while, after, as	원인, 이유	because, as, since
조건	if, unless	동시동작	while, when, and
연속동작	and	양보	although, though, even if

3. 분사구문의 시제

수동형 분사구문 [being+과거분사]	• As I was left alone, I felt free. ➡ (Being) Left alone, I felt free.
완료형 분사구문 [having+과거분사]	• Although he had gotten some good advice, he didn't do the right things. ➡ Having gotten some good advice, he didn't do the right things.

4. with + 명사 + 분사

(1) 명사와 분사의 관계가 능동 → 현재분사
   • He did his homework while Jane was cooking food.
   ➡ He did his homework **with Jane cooking** food.

(2) 명사와 분사의 관계가 수동 → 과거분사
   • The boy looked at me and his arms were folded.
   ➡ The boy looked at me **with his arms folded**.

8-5 분사구문

• **분사구문**: 접속사가 있는 부사절의 접속사와 주어를 생략하고 분사를 사용한 형태를 말한다.

1. 분사구문의 기본 형태: 부사절과 주절의 주어가 같은 경우

① 접속사 As 삭제	• ~~As~~ I saw him again, I couldn't say anything at all.
② 부사절의 주어 삭제	• ~~I~~ saw him again, I couldn't say anything at all.
③ 부사절의 동사는 분사 형태로 바꿈 (동사가 수동태일 경우 be+ing)	• ~~saw~~ him again, I couldn't say anything at all. saw → seeing

= Seeing him again, I couldn't say anything at all. [분사구문]
그를 다시 봤을 때 나는 아무런 말도 할 수 없었다.

2. 주어가 있는 분사구문 (독립분사구문): 부사절과 주절의 주어가 일치하지 않는 경우 분사 앞에 주어를 쓴다.

| ① 접속사 Because 삭제 | • ~~Because~~ it is Jerry's assignment, Henry can take a break now. |
| ② 부사절의 동사는 분사 형태로 바꿈 (동사가 be동사일 경우 be+ing) | • it ~~is~~ Jerry's assignment, Henry can take a break now.
is → being |

= It being Jerry's assignment, **Henry** can take a break now. [분사구문]
그것들은 Jerry가 할 부분이기 때문에 Henry는 이제 쉴 수 있다.

3. 접속사가 있는 분사구문: 부사절의 의미를 정확하게 나타내기 위해 접속사를 써 주기도 한다.

① 접속사 삭제하지 않음	• Before we watched the movie, we prepared some pizza and coke.
② 부사절의 주어 삭제	• Before ~~we~~ watched the movie, we prepared some pizza and coke.
③ 부사절의 동사는 분사형태로 바꿈 (동사가 be동사일 경우 be+ing)	• Before ~~watched~~ the movie, we prepared some pizza and coke. watched → watching

= Before watching the movie, we prepared some pizza and coke. [분사구문]
영화를 보기 전에 우리는 약간의 피자와 콜라를 준비했다.

A 다음 문장을 분사구문으로 바꾸어 빈칸을 채우시오.

1 When she was on vacation, she went hiking with John.

　➡ _____*Being on vacation*_____ , she went hiking with John.

2 While I was studying English, mom came back home.

　➡ Mom came back home, _____.

3 Because the baby felt hungry, she started to cry.

　➡ _____, the baby started to cry.

4 If he takes a taxi, he can arrive at the conference on time.

　➡ _____, he can arrive at the conference
　on time.

5 Since we don't have enough time, we have to hurry up.

　➡ _____, we have to hurry up.

6 Although she did her best, she failed to get first place.

　➡ _____, she failed to get first place.

7 If she opens the box, she will be scolded by her father.

　➡ _____, she will be scolded by her
　father.

8 When Tim doesn't know what to do, he asks his grandfather
for advice.

　➡ _____, Tim asks his grandfather
　for advice.

9 Though I hear that the rumor was wrong, I still don't believe
her.

　➡ _____, I still don't believe her.

10 After he watched the drama, he started to cook dinner.

　➡ _____, he started to cook dinner.

Answer Keys p. 32

B   다음 주어진 말을 이용하여 분사구문을 절로 바꾸시오.

1   Being so tired, she went to bed early. (because)

➡ _____*Because she was so tired*_____, she went to bed early.

2   Turning to the right, you'll find the post office on the street. (if)

➡ _____, you'll find the post office on the street.

3   All students stood up, giving a big hand to her. (and)

➡ All students stood up, _____

4   Not being tall enough, he became a great basketball player. (although)

➡ _____, he became a great basketball player.

5   Jake cleaned his room, talking with his girlfriend on the phone. (while)

➡ Jake cleaned his room _____

_____

6   Having nothing to drink, I went to the market. (because)

➡ _____, I went to the market.

7   Turning to the right, you can find a bank. (if)

➡ _____, you can find a bank.

8   She being innocent, nobody believed her. (though)

➡ _____, nobody believed her.

9   Opening her eyes, she could see everything around her. (when)

➡ _____, she could see everything around her.

10   Watching the movie, I was so moved. (when)

➡ _____, I was so moved.

8-6 분사구문의 쓰임

> • **분사구문의 용법**: 분사구문은 접속사에 따라 '시간, 원인, 조건, 양보, 동작' 등의 의미를 가진다.

1. 시간: when, while, after, as, as soon as

- **When** I <u>got</u> first prize, I was so happy.
  = **Getting** first prize, I was so happy.

2. 원인, 이유: because, as, since

- **Because** he <u>didn't have</u> enough money, he couldn't buy a sports car.
  = **Not having** enough money, he couldn't buy a sports car.

3. 조건: if, unless

- **If** she <u>wanted</u> to do this task, she needed to try harder.
  = **Wanting** to do this task, she needed to try harder.

4. 동시동작: while, when, and

- **While** he is taking a bath, he listens to music.
  = **Taking** a bath, he listens to music.
  ➡ 부사절에 진행형이 포함되어 있을 경우 'Being 동사 -ting'로 표현하지 않는다.
  Being taking a bath, he listens to music. (**X**)

5. 연속동작: and

- She came back home, **and** she went into her room.
  = She came back home, **going** into her room.
  = **Coming** back home, she went into her room.

6. 양보: although, though, even if

- **Although** he was nervous, he told them what he wanted to do.
  = **Being** nervous, he told them what he wanted to do.

A 다음 분사구문의 쓰임을 구분하시오.

1 Taking a taxi, they can arrive at the concert on time.
_____[조건]_____

2 Being happy, she didn't smile.
_____

3 Graduating from college, I went to America to get a job.
_____

4 Jane watched the movie, eating some popcorn.
_____

5 Not living in Korea, she doesn't know about Korean culture.
_____

6 Feeling tired, he kept studying in the library.
_____

7 Waiting for a bus, he met his old friend.
_____

8 Turning to the right, you can find my house.
_____

B 다음 괄호 안의 단어를 우리말에 맞게 바르게 배열하여 문장을 완성하시오.

1 나는 열이 나서 약을 조금 먹었다. (fever, a, I, took, having, medicine, some)
➡ _____ _Having a fever, I took some medicine._ _____

2 열심히 공부한다면 너는 좋은 성적을 얻을 거야. (harder, you, good, will, grades, studying, get)
➡ _____

3 무엇을 할지 모르겠다면 너의 부모님께 물어 보아라. (not, what, ask, knowing, to do, parents, your)
➡ _____

4 좌회전을 하면 그 초등학교를 찾을 수 있을 것이다. (to the left, you'll, find, turning, elementary school, the)
➡ _____

5 눈을 감으면 바람을 느낄 거야. (closing, the wind, your, feel, you'll, eyes)
➡ _____

8-7 분사구문의 시제

> • 분사구문의 시제: 부사절의 시제와 주절의 시제가 같을 때는 단순 분사구문을 사용하며, 부사절의
> 시제가 앞서 있을 경우 완료 분사구문을 사용한다.

1. 단순 분사구문과 완료 분사구문

시제	단순 분사구문	완료 분사구문
형태	[현재분사]	[having + 과거분사]
긍정문	• If you <u>read</u> the article closely, you can find the answer. ➡ Reading the article closely, you can find the answer.	• If you <u>had read</u> the article closely, you could find the answer. ➡ Having read the article closely, you could find the answer.
부정문	• As she <u>doesn't finish</u> her homework, she can't watch TV. ➡ Not finishing her homework, she can't watch TV.	• As she <u>hadn't finished</u> her homework, she couldn't watch TV. ➡ Not having finished her homework, she couldn't watch TV.

2. 수동형의 분사구문

단순 수동형 [being + 과거분사]	• As the novel was written in Chinese, it was difficult to read. ➡ (Being) Written in Chinese, it was difficult to read.
완료 수동형 [having been + 과거분사]	• If the wallet had been stolen, she might not know what to do. ➡ (Having been) Stolen the wallet, she might not know what to do.

➡ 수동형 분사구문에서 'Being'과 'Having been'은 생략이 가능하다.
➡ 분사구문의 부정형은 시제에 관계없이 'not (never)'이 문장 맨 앞에 온다.

☆Check up!

Answer Keys p. 32

A 부사절은 분사구문으로, 분사구문은 부사절로 바꾸시오.

1 After she had finished preparing for the party, she took a rest.

➡ ___*Having finished preparing for the party*___ , she took a rest.

2 If you had taken Tim's advice, you wouldn't fail the exam.

➡ _____ , you wouldn't

fail the exam.

3 Having failed to reach the final round, James prepares for the game again.

➡ _____, James prepares for the game again.

4 When he was praised for his project, he felt really excited.

➡ _____, he felt really excited.

5 Having lost my camera, I couldn't take a picture of her.

➡ _____, I couldn't take a picture of her.

6 As Linda was left alone at home, she felt lonely.

➡ _____, Linda felt lonely.

7 If you had not read the book, you had trouble finding the answer.

➡ _____, you had trouble finding the answer.

8 Being invited to my birthday party, he didn't come.

➡ _____, he didn't come.

9 After I had written the letter, I posted it.

➡ _____, I posted it.

10 (Having been) built seventy years ago, the tower is now a ruin.

➡ _____, the tower is now a ruin.

11 When it was seen from the plane, the island was beautiful.

➡ _____, the island was beautiful.

12 Before she heard the truth, she didn't expect her to act like that.

➡ _____, she didn't expect her to act like that.

8-8 'with' 분사구문

> • 'with + 명사 + 분사': '~을 ...한 채로'의 뜻으로 동시동작을 나타낸다. 명사와 분사의 관계가 능동이면 현재분사를, 수동이면 과거분사를 사용하며, 분사 대신에 형용사나 부사를 쓸 수도 있다.

1. 'with + 명사 + 분사'

(1) 현재분사: 명사와 분사의 관계가 능동일 경우

- I had dinner while Jenny was using my smartphone.
   = I had dinner **with** Jenny **using** my smartphone. (Jenny : using = 능동)

(2) 과거분사: 명사와 분사의 관계가 수동일 경우

- I thought about it while I was crossing my arms.
   = I thought about it **with** my arms **crossed**. (my arms : crossed = 수동)

2. 'with + 명사 + 형용사'

- Please don't say anything as I am sad.
   = Please don't say anything **with me (being) sad.** (being 생략 가능)

3. 'with + 명사 + 부사'

- The deer looked at the hunter sadly when its leg was in a trap.
   = The deer looked at the hunter sadly **with its leg (being) in a trap.** (being 생략 가능)

☆Check up!

Answer Keys p. 32~33

A   with를 이용하여 두 문장을 한 문장으로 완성하시오.

1   I was reading the book. Mom was sewing beside me.

➡   *I was reading the book with mom sewing beside me.*

2   Mary studied English. Linda was using my laptop.

➡ _____

3   The girl looked at me. Her leg was shaking.

➡ _____

4   John was sleeping. His arms were stretched.

➡ _____

5   Max kept on running. His face was all sweaty.

➡ _____

6   All students got out of the classroom. The light was on.

➡ _____

7   The woman was sitting on the sofa. Her arms crossed.

➡ _____

8   Harry was walking home. His daughter was following him.

➡ _____

9   Kate went to sleep. Her dog was sleeping beside her.

➡ _____

10 Sue was watching TV. Her daughter was lying on the sofa.

➡ _____

B   다음 중 어법상 어색한 부분을 찾아 바르게 고쳐 쓰시오.

1   With her eye bandage, she could not read well.

   _____bandage_____ ➡ _____bandaged_____

2   He was talking on the phone with her writes a memo.

   _____ ➡ _____

3   The badger ran away with its leg broke.

   _____ ➡ _____

4   I fell asleep with the lights turn on.

   _____ ➡ _____

5   They were walking in the park with their dog followed.

   _____ ➡ _____

Practice More II

A   다음 문장에서 어법상 <u>어색한</u> 것을 찾아 바르게 고치시오.

1   Having afraid of barking dogs, she has never had a dog.

        <u>   Having   </u> ➡ <u>   Being   </u>

2   Repairing well, the watch works right.

        <u>   </u> ➡ <u>   </u>

3   Being read the sad novel, she shed tears.

        <u>   </u> ➡ <u>   </u>

4   They being so cold outside, I canceled the hike.

        <u>   </u> ➡ <u>   </u>

5   He listened to the radio, tapped his finger to the music.

        <u>   </u> ➡ <u>   </u>

6   Having washed several times, the shoes look clean.

        <u>   </u> ➡ <u>   </u>

7   Felt a little cold, Mina closed the door.

        <u>   </u> ➡ <u>   </u>

8   Knowing not where to go, he asked her for advice.

        <u>   </u> ➡ <u>   </u>

9   Please don't talk with your mouth fulled.

        <u>   </u> ➡ <u>   </u>

10 Leaving alone, she can take a rest peacefully.

        <u>   </u> ➡ <u>   </u>

B   괄호 안에서 알맞은 것을 고르시오.

1   The boy looked at me with his arms (crossed / crossing).

2   (Having / Being) a lot of time, we can go anywhere.

3   (Having finished / Finished) our project, we went to the party.

4   He was standing there with his finger (pointed / pointing) the window.

5   (Turned in / Turning in) the report, she begins to sleep.

6   (Surprising / Surprised) at the news, we had nothing to say.

7 (Been on vacation / Being on vacation), John went to the beach.

8 (Having found / Having been found) the ring, he brought it to the police officer.

9 (Not having seen / Having not seen) Max before, she couldn't recognize him.

10 (Having been / Being) so busy yesterday, I must do my homework today.

C 밑줄 친 부분을 분사구문 또는 평서문으로 고쳐 쓰시오.

1 When we heard the news, we felt sad.
   ➡ _____Hearing the news_____, we felt sad.

2 If you exercise regularly, you will be much healthier.
   ➡ _____, you will be much healthier.

3 As Brian doesn't like noodles, he usually eats rice.
   ➡ _____, he usually eats rice.

4 Because she had been sick for three days, the girl looked unhealthy.
   ➡ _____, the girl looked unhealthy.

5 I close one of my eyes, and I tried to walk straight.
   ➡ I tried to walk straight _____

6 After she had walked her cat, she gave it some sausages.
   ➡ _____, she gave it some sausages.

7 Because the book had been written in Chinese, it was so hard to read.
   ➡ _____, the book was so hard to read.

8 Although Tim was sick in bed, he sent an email to us.
   ➡ _____, Tim sent an email to us.

9 Having been treated by Mrs. White, he got better.
   ➡ _____, he got better.

10 Having been nervous, I couldn't say anything.
   ➡ _____, I couldn't say anything.

Practice More Ⅱ

Answer Keys p. 33

D 주어진 단어를 알맞게 배열하여 문장을 완성하시오.

1 (hearing, I, outside, the strange, stood up, looked, sound, and)

➡ *Hearing the strange sound, I stood up and looked outside.*

2 (Jack, first, was, prize, excited, the contest, in, getting)

➡ _____

3 (with, the dog, its, looked, sadly, tied, at, mouth, the sky)

➡ _____

4 (having, he, anywhere, go, lost, his car, couldn't)

➡ _____

5 (not, where, they, summer trip, deciding, their, had, to, planning, go, trouble)

➡ _____

6 (on, the English test, embarrassed, cheating, were, they, been, caught, having)

➡ _____

7 (was, turned off, watching, with, John, the lights, the news)

➡ _____

8 (my, failed, doing, to, class president, best, I, elected, be)

➡ _____

9 (being, became, he, a, young, scientist, great)

➡ _____

10 (done, to, he, homework, having, else, has, do, nothing, his)

➡ _____

내신 최다 출제 유형

01 다음 빈칸에 알맞은 말을 고르시오. [출제 예상 85%]

> Pooh Bear is _____ in getting the honey.

① interest
② interesting
③ interested
④ be interested
⑤ be interesting

02 다음 빈칸에 알맞지 <u>않은</u> 것을 고르시오. [출제 예상 80%]

> The lunch menu was steak. It made us _____.

① excited
② pleased
③ happy
④ surprised
⑤ interesting

03 다음 문장 중 어법상 <u>잘못된</u> 것을 고르시오.
[출제 예상 90%]

① He was deeply moving.
② I was born and raised in the country.
③ She was afraid that movie would be boring.
④ Her dancing was really impressing.
⑤ Joy was confused about what is true and false.

04 다음 주어진 문장의 밑줄 친 부분과 바꿔 쓸 수 있는 것을 고르시오. [출제 예상 85%]

> <u>While I'm writing a poem</u>, I listen to Bach.

① Being write a poem
② Writing a poem
③ Write a poem
④ Having write a poem
⑤ To write a poem

05 다음 두 문장의 의미가 같지 <u>않은</u> 것을 <u>모두</u> 고르시오. [출제 예상 85%]

① Not throwing the ball, I can't hit it.
  = If you don't throw the ball, I can't hit it.
② Leaving now, you can catch the train.
  = While you leave now, you can catch the train.
③ Turning left, you'll find the bank.
  = As you turn left, you'll find the bank.
④ Being kind, she could make many friends.
  = Since she was kind, she could make many friends.
⑤ Eating less food, he becomes fatter and fatter.
  = As he eats less food, he becomes fatter and fatter.

[01~03] 다음 밑줄 친 동사의 알맞은 형태를 고르시오.

01

> Long ago, our ancestors believed that God was <u>control</u> the weather.

① control   ② controlled
③ controls   ④ controlling
⑤ has controlled

02

> During the Gold Rush, jeans were <u>make</u> for miners.

① make   ② making   ③ made
④ is making   ⑤ to make

03

> In many English dictionaries <u>publish</u> lately, we can find what we need.

① publishes   ② published
③ publishing   ④ are published
⑤ have published

[04~05] 다음 빈칸에 들어갈 말이 바르게 짝지어진 것을 고르시오.

04

> • She imagined _____ the flute in front of the audience.
> • I worked with my nephews for a year, _____ them to speak English.

① played − teaching
② played − taught
③ playing − taught
④ playing − teaching
⑤ play − teaching

05

> • Do you know that man standing with his arms _____?
> • We saw an excursion boat _____ under the Golden Gate Bridge.

① fold − pass   ② folding − passing
③ folded − passed   ④ fold − passed
⑤ folded − passing

[06~07] 다음 중 밑줄 친 동사의 형태가 올바른 것을 <u>모두</u> 고르시오.

06 ① There lived a kind girl <u>naming</u> Konggi.
② The boy <u>played</u> on the court is Brandon.
③ She likes the boy <u>sitting</u> on the bench.
④ They bought me an MP3 player <u>made</u> in Japan.
⑤ I want to buy a <u>using</u> car at a low price.

07 ① We have to read the book <u>written</u> in Chinese.
② The movie directed by Steven Spielberg was <u>moving</u>.
③ Who is that woman <u>danced</u> on the stage?
④ The boy <u>helped</u> an old lady is my brother.
⑤ Look at the boy <u>played</u> with his dog over there.

08 다음 중 어법상 <u>어색한</u> 것을 고르시오.

① I decided to take a trip for a month.
② I read 'The Good Earth,' and I was very moving.
③ She spent her vacation preparing for the presentation.
④ She was surprised at what she saw with her friends.
⑤ We noticed her wallet lying on the floor under the table.

> **Note** 'The Good Earth' 펄 벅의 소설 '대지'

09 다음 분사구문을 부사절로 바꿀 때 빈칸에 들어갈 알맞은 말을 고르시오.

> Being good at drawing, he became a cartoonist.
> = _____ he was good at drawing, he became a cartoonist.

① Before ② Though ③ When
④ Because ⑤ While

10 다음 괄호 안의 동사를 알맞은 형태로 바꾼 것끼리 짝지어진 것을 고르시오.

> • Kelly always sings (wash) the dishes.
> • The broken window makes her (embarrass).

① washing − embarrassing
② washing − embarrassed
③ washed − embarrassed
④ washes − embarrasses
⑤ wash − embarrassing

[11~12] 다음 밑줄 친 부분의 쓰임이 나머지 넷과 <u>다른</u> 것을 고르시오.

11 ① <u>Learning</u> something new is exciting.
② How about <u>joining</u> the reading club?
③ I am <u>making</u> some paper flowers for my boyfriend.
④ Although she was poor, she never stopped <u>helping</u> others.
⑤ She had to earn money to buy <u>dancing</u> shoes.

12 ① <u>Knowing how to get there</u>, he pretended not to know.
② <u>Being poor</u>, he was a very talented writer.
③ <u>Drawn by a child</u>, the picture was good and moving.
④ <u>Reading a book on the sofa</u>, I fell asleep.
⑤ <u>Being nice</u>, she is not popular.

[13~15] 다음 중 빈칸에 들어갈 알맞은 말을 고르시오.

13
> I couldn't read this story _____ in Japanese characters.

① write ② written ③ writing
④ is writing ⑤ has written

14

There are many false rumors that made us _____.

① confused
② confusing
③ confuse
④ to be confused
⑤ was confusing

15

I have to catch cockroaches as fast as I can because they make me _____.

① scared
② scaring
③ scare
④ be scared
⑤ be scaring

16 다음 밑줄 친 부분 중 어법상 옳은 것을 고르시오.

① The party must have been excited.
② The documentary film was very moved.
③ If you meet him later, you'll be surprising.
④ I was so disappointing to hear the result.
⑤ The vacation was quite interesting for me.

[17~18] 다음 중 어법상 어색한 것을 고르시오.

17

① Jacky's humor is so interesting.
② The result of math test was satisfying.
③ She was surprised at the price of the antique furniture.
④ My neighbor's noise was very annoyed to me.
⑤ Ally heard shocking news from her friends.

18

① My father was surprised at my dirty room.
② I'm interested in cooking Korean food.
③ It's amazing that you became a teacher.
④ The map is confusing. We don't know where we are.
⑤ I was disappointing at the movie.

[19~20] 다음 주어진 분사구문을 부사절의 문장으로 바르게 바꾼 것을 고르시오.

★★★
19

Not having enough time, he couldn't go to the party.

① As he doesn't have enough time, he couldn't go to the party.
② As he didn't have enough time, he couldn't go to the party.
③ Because he doesn't have enough time, he couldn't go to the party.
④ Because he didn't have enough time, he hasn't gone to the party.
⑤ As he doesn't have enough time, he can't go to the party.

★★★
20
Finishing her homework, she went shopping with her friends.

① If she finished her homework, she went shopping with her friends.
② Although she finished her homework, she went shopping with her friends.
③ Unless she finished her homework, she went shopping with her friends.
④ After she finished her homework, she went shopping with her friends.
⑤ Though she finished her homework, she went shopping with her friends.

[21~22] 다음 문장의 밑줄 친 부분과 쓰임이 같은 것을 고르시오.

21
There is a girl <u>reading</u> a magazine in the waiting room.

① <u>Reading</u> many books is good for us.
② Hannah's dream is <u>being</u> a famous ballerina.
③ A <u>barking</u> dog seldom bites.
④ <u>Working</u> as a teacher was a nice job.
⑤ Would you mind <u>following</u> this rule?

22
We need to be quiet because of the <u>sleeping</u> baby.

① Where did you see a doll <u>moving</u> itself?
② Do you know that woman <u>wearing</u> a yellow dress?
③ After <u>punishing</u> me, she let me go home.
④ People enjoy <u>eating</u> sausages in buns.
⑤ Some people are <u>crying</u> in the theater.

[23~25] 다음 빈칸에 들어갈 말이 차례대로 바르게 짝 지어진 것을 고르시오.

23
A lot of famous pictures were _____ by Vincent van Gogh. He was famous for _____ self-portraits.

① painted − painted
② painted − painting
③ painting − painted
④ painting − painting
⑤ painted − paint

★★★
24
Green and blue have a _____ effect, while black and other dark colors have a _____ effect.

① relaxing − depressing
② relaxing − depressed
③ relaxed − depressing
④ relax − depress
⑤ relaxed − depressed

25

Judy was listening to music with her eyes _____. Listening to music and _____ TV are very exciting.

① closing − watching
② closed − watched
③ closed − watching
④ close − watch
⑤ closed − watch

26 다음 밑줄 친 부분이 어법상 어색한 것을 고르시오.

① We study with the music on.
② Dave spoke with tears rolling down his face.
③ Sally waited for him with her back against the fence.
④ I read a book with my legs crossing.
⑤ Please speak with your eyes contacted.

[27~28] 다음 주어진 문장과 분사구문의 용법이 같은 것을 고르시오.

27

Crossing the street, we should be careful.

① Watching TV, she was playing games with her cell phone.
② Walking to school, I listened to the radio.
③ Working hard, she didn't get the project.
④ Being old, she never stopped learning something new.
⑤ Traveling in England, she saw many historical places.

★★★
28

Listening to the speech, Jane translated it into English.

① Living near the park, I could arrive first.
② Getting up late, you'll be late for school again.
③ Meeting Steven, you'll like him.
④ Watching a movie, I drank coke and ate a hot-dog.
⑤ Being sick, he couldn't make an appointment.

★★★
29 다음 주어진 문장과 뜻이 같은 것을 고르시오.

Tony went to bed early last night, but he woke up in the afternoon.

① Go to bed early last night, he woke up in the afternoon.
② Going to bed early last night, he woke up in the afternoon.
③ Going to bed early last night, he wakes up in the afternoon.
④ Going to bed early last night, and he woke up in the afternoon.
⑤ Going to bed early last night, but he woke up in the afternoon.

30 다음 밑줄 친 부분의 우리말 해석이 바르지 못한 것을 고르시오.

① <u>Having lunch</u>, we talked about our new classroom teacher.
(점심을 먹으면서)

② <u>Eating pizza</u>, I'm still hungry.
(피자를 먹었기 때문에)

③ <u>Using the electronic dictionary</u>, you can find the words easily.
(전자 사전을 이용한다면)

④ <u>Being young</u>, they can do their best.
(젊기 때문에)

⑤ <u>Playing soccer</u>, Hojun hurt his legs.
(축구를 하는 도중에)

★★★
31 다음 밑줄 친 부분 중 어법상 옳은 것을 모두 고르시오.

① <u>Open the window</u>, the dust blew into my room.

② <u>Feeling not well</u>, I went back home early.

③ <u>Seeing her</u>, I waved my hands.

④ <u>It being painted by the famous artist</u>, I don't understand what it means.

⑤ <u>Living in Canada before</u>, I go skiing often.

[32~33] 다음 글에서 어법상 어색한 부분을 고르시오.

32
① When Lucy ② arrived, her husband was ③ cleaning the house ④ with the radio ⑤ turning on.

★★★
33
The people ① <u>shouted</u> in the ② <u>public place</u> were very ③ <u>rude</u>. They looked ④ <u>shocked</u> about ⑤ <u>something</u>.

◇◇◇◇◇◇◇◇◇ **서술형 평가** ◇◇◇◇◇◇◇◇◇

[34~36] 다음 우리말과 같은 뜻이 되도록 빈칸에 알맞은 말을 쓰시오.

34
서쪽을 향해 달려가고 있는 소년이 Tommy 이다.

➡ The boy _____ towards the west is Tommy.

35
Harry는 양손을 들고서 창문 옆에 서 있었다.

➡ Harry was _____ next to the window _____ his hands up.

36
삼일 후 우리에게 남은 음식은 전혀 없었다.

➡ After three days, we had no _____ _____.

[37~39] 다음 문장을 분사구문으로 바꿀 때 빈칸에 들어갈 알맞은 말을 쓰시오.

37

> As he was surprised at the news, he fell down on the floor.

➡ _____ _____ _____ _____,

he fell down on the floor.

38

> Because we didn't know where to go, we searched for a place on the Internet.

➡ _____ _____ _____ _____

_____, we searched for a place on the Internet.

39

> As she finished her report, she has nothing else to do.

➡ _____ _____ _____ _____,

she has nothing else to do.

[40~41] 다음 밑줄 친 부분과 뜻이 같도록 접속사를 이용하여 바꿔 쓰시오.

40

> <u>Arriving home</u>, I noticed I hadn't taken my school bag.

➡ _____,

I noticed I hadn't taken my school bag.

41

> Not spending much money on himself, he bought a diamond ring for his wife on their wedding anniversary.

➡ _____

_____, he bought a diamond ring for his wife on their wedding anniversary.

★★★
42 다음 글의 밑줄 친 ⓐ ~ ⓒ를 어법상 바르게 고쳐 쓰시오.

> When I traveled to London, I tried to find a ⓐ <u>talk</u> bird. There is a famous festival in London that finds the best bird. One bird ⓑ <u>name</u> Prudle was well-known for talking. She can mimic the ⓒ <u>speak</u> language of humans.

➡ ⓐ _____ ⓑ _____ ⓒ _____

43 다음의 주어진 동사를 어법에 맞게 변형하여 쓰시오.

(1) The man _____ the garden is my father. (water)

(2) John Hancock Center was _____ in 1970. (build)

(3) The idol star had his picture _____. (take)

44 다음의 주어진 우리말과 같도록 빈칸에 알맞은 말을 쓰시오.

(1) 나는 미소 짓는 모나리자를 보았다.
➡ I saw the _____ Mona Lisa.

(2) 저 망가진 로봇들은 누구의 것이지?
➡ Whose are those _____ robots?

45 다음 우리말과 뜻이 같도록 빈칸에 알맞은 말을 쓰시오.

> 그녀는 자신의 상황을 고려하여 결정을 내릴 것이다.
> _____, she will make a decision.

➡ _____, she will make a decision.

[46~48] 다음 괄호 안의 단어를 우리말에 맞게 바르게 배열하여 문장을 완성하시오.

46

> 6시 정각이므로 그녀는 퇴근을 했다.
> (six o'clock / being / it / she / left / office / the)

➡ _____

★★★
47

> 우리는 그녀를 만난 적이 없어서 친절한지 어떤지 몰랐다.
> (not / met / her / didn't / having / know / before / she / was / or not / kind / we / whether)

➡ _____
_____

★★★
48

> 그들은 시간이 없으므로 서둘러야 했다.
> (no / having / hurry / they / up / had to / time)

➡ _____

Note

Chapter

형용사와 부사

Point Check I

◆ **형용사:** 사람이나 사물의 성질, 특징 등을 나타내는 말로, 명사 앞뒤에서 꾸며 주기도 하고, 동사 뒤에 와서 주어나 목적어의 상태를 설명해 주기도 한다.

1. 형용사의 쓰임

한정적 용법	형용사 + 명사	• Most models are tall women.
	명사 + 형용사	• I desire to meet someone helpful for me.
서술적 용법	주격보어	• His dream is so huge.
	목적격보어	• This books made me powerful.

2. 형용사의 어순

서수	기수	성질	크기	신/구	색깔	국적	재료
first	one	good	middle	new	white	Korean	wooden
second	two	bad	huge	old	black	American	rock

3. 수량 형용사

	셀 수 있는 명사 (수)	셀 수 없는 명사 (양)	공통으로 쓰는 수량 형용사
매우 많은 수(양)의	a great number of	a great deal of	a lot of, lots of plenty of
꽤 많은 수(양)의	quite a few, not a few	not a little, no little	
많은	many	much	
조금, 약간	a few	a little, a small amount of	some, any
거의 ~없는	few, very few, only a few	little, very little	

4. 숫자 읽기

정수	278	two hundred (and) seventy-eight
분수	$4\frac{3}{5}$	four and three fifths
소수	14.37	fourteen point three seven
연도	2012	two thousand (and) twelve
날짜	11월 7일	November (the) seventh (= the seventh of November)
시간	11:25	eleven twenty-five (= twenty-five after eleven)

9-1 형용사

형용사의 역할과 쓰임

· **형용사**: 형용사는 사람이나 사물의 생김새, 성질 등을 나타내는 말이다. 명사 앞에서 꾸며주거나, 동사 다음에 와서 주어, 목적어가 어떤 상태인지 알려주는 보어 역할을 한다.

1. **한정적 용법**: 명사의 앞이나 뒤에 위치해 명사의 모습이나 성질을 나타낸다.

  (1) 형용사 + 명사

  · Yuna Kim is a **famous** figure skater.

  · Brad is a **handsome** actor.

  (2) -thing, -one, -body로 끝나는 대명사의 경우 형용사가 뒤에 위치

  · They want to do something **special** to celebrate their success.

◆ 한정적 용법으로 쓰이는 형용사

· only	· elder	· lone	· live
· former	· major	· golden	· wooden

2. **서술적 용법**: 주격보어나 목적격보어의 자리에서 주어나 목적어의 상태를 알려준다.

  (1) 주격보어: 2형식 문장에서 사용된다.

  · Michael's behavior was so **polite**.

  (2) 목적격보어: 5형식 문장에서 사용된다.

  · His songs make me **calm**.

◆ 서술적 용법으로 쓰이는 형용사

· afraid	· alone	· asleep	· alike
· alive	· awake	· glad	

 **Check up!**

Answer Keys p. 35

A 괄호 안에서 알맞은 단어를 고르시오.

1 We met a lot of (ⓢtrange / strangely) travelers there.

2 James was the (only / alone) student who passed the exam.

3 Both of the boys are (like / alike).

4   My older sister is (tall / **taller**) than your brother.

5   She is (afraid / scaring) of many insects.

6   While my daughter was (sleep / asleep), I started to clean the house.

7   Mom always said that I should do something (meaning / meaningful).

8   It was such a (great / greatly) outdoor activity!

9   The (mainly / main) event will be held after lunch.

10 The man sitting next to Tim is our (former / form) class president.

B   주어진 형용사를 어법이나 문맥상 알맞은 곳에 넣어 문장을 다시 쓰시오.

1   She prepared well to avoid making the mistake. (the same)
    ➡   *She prepared well to avoid making the same mistake.*

2   Helen was the person we met at last night's party. (only)
    ➡ _____

3   We put all the books on the table. (interesting)
    ➡ _____

4   There is no one who could move the statue. (heavy)
    ➡ _____

5   How can I buy a dog? (cute)
    ➡ _____

6   Thomas will recommend somewhere for you to go. (great)
    ➡ _____

7   Everyone was surprised when they heard about Harry's accident. (sudden)
    ➡ _____

9-2 형용사의 어순

• 형용사의 어순: 2개 이상의 형용사를 나열할 때 사용하는 순서를 말한다.

1. 형용사 어순

서수	기수	성질	크기	신/구	색깔	국적	재료
first	one	nice	big	new	green	Korean	wooden
second	two	pretty	large	old	pink	American	rock
third	three	smart	small	young	purple	English	metal

• Samantha bought a **little white** puppy.

2. 형용사 앞에 다른 수식어가 올 때

all both double half	+	정관사	the	+(형용사) 명사
		지시형용사	this that these those	
		소유격	my your his her its our their	

• They love **all their daughters and sons** so much.

Check up!

Answer Keys p. 35

A 다음 주어진 말을 알맞게 배열하시오.

1 I didn't know that this is ___Tim's favorite American___ food. (favorite, Tim's, American)

2 James grew up to be a _____. (young, famous, bassist)

3 He thinks he should move _____ chair outside. (small, black, this, new)

4 We're going to throw away _____ shirts. (dirty, all, green, these)

5 _____ are walking down the street. (girls, three, pretty)

6 My daughter used to like to wear _____ shorts.
(those, blue, pairs of, three)

7 _____ boys are playing basketball.
(the, Japanese, both of, tall)

8 I saw _____ dogs in the room.
(small, three, white)

9 She bought _____ shelves.
(nice, wooden, four, green, old)

10 Nick read _____ lines of the page and was
fascinated by the book. (four, the, first)

11 _____ guys are my friends.
(Korean, both of, big, the)

12 She choose to buy _____ tower.
(green, the, tallest, second, new)

13 My son bought _____ scarf for me.
(silk, a, black, big)

14 Do you see _____ garden? I love it.
(beautiful, large, the, green)

15 There used to be _____ house on this street.
(blue, a, old, small)

B 다음 우리말에 맞게 빈칸에 알맞은 말을 쓰시오.

1 Jennifer는 똑똑한 어린 영국 소녀이다.
➡ Jennifer is _____*a smart young English girl*_____.

2 Mary는 커다란 녹색 연을 만들었다.
➡ Mary _____.

3 그는 그녀를 위해 아름다운 큰 다이아몬드 반지를 샀다.
➡ He bought _____.

9-3 형용사의 형태

- **명사 / 동사 + 접미사:** 현재분사와 과거분사처럼 형용사 역할을 하는 것도 있고, 명사나 동사 뒤에 접미사가 붙어 형용사로 쓰이기도 한다.
- **the + 형용사:** 형용사 앞에 정관사 'the'를 붙여 '~한 사람들'이라는 뜻으로 명사처럼 사용할 수 있다.

1. 명사 / 동사 + 접미사

	접미사	단어			
동사	-able, -ible	admirable	believable	desirable	flexible
명사	-al	cultural	emotional	natural	national
	-(a)n	American	European	Asian	Korean
	-ful	careful	helpful	powerful	wonderful
	-less	careless	helpless	useless	hopeless
	-(l)y	friendly	lovely	healthy	wealthy
	-ous	famous	dangerous	curious	generous
	-ive, -ish	active	passive	foolish	childish

2. 분사의 형용사 역할: 현재분사와 과거분사 모두 문장에서 형용사처럼 사용

- They had a **disappointing** time on this trip. [현재분사]
- I was so **satisfied** with the result. [과거분사]

3. the + 형용사: 항상 복수 취급

- Sometimes, **the young** lack the courage to do something.
  (the young = young people)
- **The rich** sometimes seem to be unhappy.
  (the rich = rich people)

A 주어진 단어를 알맞은 형태로 바꾸어 빈칸에 쓰시오.

1 The beginning of the movie was really ___*impressive.*___ . (impress)

2 I think the rumor is _____. (believe)

3 People experienced some _____ differences when they visited other countries. (culture)

4 You broke your leg again! How _____ you are! (care)

5 They were really _____ to us. I love them. (friend)

6 I don't think it is _____ because it has a safety cap. (danger)

7 _____ usually read books that contain special raised letters. (blind)

8 Tim said he wanted to invent some _____ metals. (flex)

9 It is _____ to hear the news that they got married last month. (shock)

10 She thought the situation was _____. She was so depressed. (hope)

B 다음 우리말에 맞게 괄호 안의 단어를 이용하여 문장을 완성하시오.

1 그는 내게 친절한 조언을 약간 해 주었다. (friendly, advice)
  ➡ He gave _____*me some friendly advice*_____ .

2 조심성 없는 운전자들 때문에 교통사고가 난다. (careless, traffic accidents)
  ➡ Because of _____, _____.

3 대통령의 연설은 감동적이었다. (emotional)
  ➡ The president's speech _____.

4 Maria는 항상 회의에서 소극적인 태도를 보인다. (passive, attitude)
  ➡ Maria always _____ in meeting.

5 Ben은 가끔 쓸모없는 것을 만든다. (useless, sometimes)
  ➡ Ben _____ things.

9-4 수량 형용사

Lesson

• **수량 형용사:** 수와 양을 나타내는 형용사로서 셀 수 있는 명사에 쓰는 수량 형용사, 셀 수 없는 명사에 쓰는 수량 형용사, 둘에 함께 쓰는 수량형용사로 구분할 수 있다.

1. 셀 수 있는 명사와 셀 수 없는 명사의 수량 형용사

	셀 수 있는 명사 (수)	셀 수 없는 명사 (양)
매우 많은 수(양)의	a great number of	a great deal (amount) of
꽤 많은 수(양)의	quite a few, not a few	not a little, no little
많은	many	much
조금, 약간	a few	a little, a small amount of
거의 ~없는	few, very few, only a few	little, very little

➡ 셀 수 없는 명사: '많은'의 뜻을 가진 'so much, too much'는 긍정문에, 'much'는 부정문, 의문문에 사용한다.

• **A great number of** mice followed the man and jumped into a river.

• We need **a great deal of** time to do this project.

Grammar Plus +

• **a number of + 복수명사 / the number of + 복수명사 구분하기**

- 'a number of'는 자체로 뒤의 명사를 꾸미는 한정사이므로 복수 동사가 오며 복수 취급을 해 준다.
  A number of people buy the special chocolate. 많은 사람들이 그 특별한 쵸코렛을 산다.

- 'the number of'는 뒤의 명사가 'the number'을 꾸며 주기 때문에 복수 명사가 와도 단수 동사가 오며 단수 취급해 준다는 의미로 사용된다.
  The number of people buys the special chocolate. 사람들의 수가 그 특별한 쵸코렛을 산다.

2. 둘 모두 사용하는 수량 형용사

많은	lots of, a lot of, plenty of	약간의, 조금의	some, any
충분한	enough	전혀 없는	no

➡ 'some'은 긍정문에, 'any'는 부정문, 의문문에 사용한다.

• **A lot of** people came to his concert.

• There was **enough** rain last summer.

• He has already bought **plenty of** books.

• There are **some** melons on the table.

• There wasn't **any** soup left in the pot.

09. 형용사와 부사 **271**

Answer Keys p. 35

A 주어진 말을 이용하여 빈칸에 알맞은 말을 쓰시오.

1 그 건물에는 꽤 많은 식당들이 있다. (a great number of)
➡ There are ___a great number of restaurants___ in the building.

2 이 강의를 이해할 학생들이 꽤 적을 것이다. (few)
➡ _____ will understand this lecture.

3 나는 그 기록을 깨려고 꽤 많이 도전했다. (so many)
➡ I tried _____ to break the record.

4 몇몇 학생들이 영어 숙제를 했다. (several)
➡ _____ did their English homework.

5 컵에는 거의 물이 없었다. (little)
➡ There was _____ in the cup.

6 방 안에 있는 사람들의 수는 13명이다. (the number of)
➡ _____ in the room is thirteen.

7 그 영화 동아리에는 John을 아는 사람이 거의 없다. (very few)
➡ There are _____ who know John.

8 꽤 많은 사람들이 그를 응원했다. (more than a few)
➡ _____ cheered for him.

> **Note**
> • more than a few(little)
> 적잖은

B 밑줄 친 부분을 바르게 고치시오.

1 I had a few doubt about him.
_____ *a little*

2 Tim threw out a large number of oil.
_____

3 Too many time was spent on repairing his watch.
_____

4 She stayed in Linda's house a great number of time last week.
_____

5 Only a little people lived in the village at that time.
_____

숫자 읽기 (1)

• 수사: 기수와 서수, 배수사 등을 통틀어 말한다.

1. 기수와 서수

수	기수	서수	수	기수	서수
1	one	first	20	twenty	twentieth
2	two	second	21	twenty-one	twenty-first
3	three	third	22	twenty-two	twenty-second
4	four	fourth	23	twenty-three	twenty-third
5	five	fifth	24	twenty-four	twenty-fourth
6	six	sixth	25	twenty-five	twenty-fifth
7	seven	seventh	30	thirty	thirtieth
8	eight	eighth	40	forty	fortieth
9	nine	ninth	50	fifty	fiftieth
10	ten	tenth	60	sixty	sixtieth
11	eleven	eleventh	70	seventy	seventieth
12	twelve	twelfth	80	eighty	eightieth
13	thirteen	thirteenth	90	ninety	ninetieth
14	fourteen	fourteenth	100	a hundred	a hundredth
15	fifteen	fifteenth	1,000	a thousand	a thousandth

2. 정수
세 자리씩 끊어 읽고, 백 자리 수 뒤에는 'and'를 써서 연결하지만 구어체에서는 생략하기도 한다. 수를 읽을 때 'hundred, thousand, million' 앞에 복수를 나타내는 숫자가 오더라도 복수형으로 쓰지 않는다.

• 135	a (one) hundred (and) thirty-five
• 1,837	a thousand, eight hundred (and) thirty-seven
• 56,781	fifty-six thousand, seven hundred (and) eighty-one
• 246,457	two hundred (and) forty-six thousand, four hundred (and) fifty-seven
• 7,256,052	seven million, two hundred (and) fifty-six thousand, (and) fifty-two

3. 분수와 소수

분수: 분자는 기수로, 분모는 서수로 읽고, 분자가 2 이상이면 분모에 '-s'를 붙인다.

• $\frac{1}{3}$	a third (one third)	• $\frac{5}{8}$	five eighths
• $3\frac{3}{5}$	three and three fifths	• $2\frac{1}{2}$	two and a half (one half)

소수: 모두 기수로 읽되, 소수점 이하는 한 자리씩 읽는다.

• 0.25	zero point two five	• 32.89	thirty-two point eight nine

Answer Keys p. 36

A 다음의 숫자의 기수와 서수 형태를 쓰시오.

1 30 ➡ _____thirty_____ / _____thirtieth_____

2 79 ➡ _____ / _____

3 1,054 ➡ _____ / _____

4 487 ➡ _____ / _____

5 230 ➡ _____ / _____

6 716 ➡ _____ / _____

7 9,802 ➡ _____ /

_____

8 114 ➡ _____ / _____

9 91 ➡ _____ / _____

10 63 ➡ _____ / _____

B 다음 주어진 표현을 영어로 읽을 때의 표기법을 쓰시오.

1 86,240 ➡ _eighty-six thousand, two hundred forty_

2 $\dfrac{3}{6}$ ➡ _____

3 5,987,145 ➡ _____

4 $\dfrac{4}{7}$ ➡ _____

5 10.15 ➡ _____

6 3,774,854 ➡ _____

7 60,315 ➡ _____

8 63.198 ➡ _____

9 280,268 ➡ _____

10 $\dfrac{2}{9}$ ➡ _____

9-6 숫자 읽기 (2)

· 수사: 기수와 서수, 배수사 등을 통틀어 말한다.

1. 연도와 날짜

연도: 두 자리씩 끊어 읽는다.			
· 1995	nineteen ninety-five	· 2015	two thousand (and) fifteen
날짜: 서수를 이용한다.			
· 5월 23일	May (the) twenty-third = the twenty-third of May		
· 2007년 7월 12일	July (the) twelfth, two thousand seven = the twelfth of July, two thousand seven		

2. 배수사: quarter (1/4), half (반), once (1배, 한 번), twice (2배, 두 번), 3배 (세 번)부터는 '숫자 + times'로 배수를 표현한다.

· I have taken a trip with my boyfriend's family **four times**.

· My oldest sister's room is **twice** <u>as large as</u> my room.
= My oldest sister's room is **twice** <u>larger than</u> my room.

3. 시각

(1) 시간과 분을 끊어서 읽는다.

· 5:30	five thirty	· 7:35	seven thirty-five	· 12:47	twelve forty-seven
· 2:07	two oh seven	· 1:15	one fifteen	· 3:55	three fifty-five

(2) after (past)와 to

after ~을 지나서	30분 이전을 나타내는 분에 사용	· 7:10	ten after seven
to ~전에	30분 이후를 나타내는 분에 사용	· 8:45	fifteen to nine (= a quarter to nine)
past ~을 지나서	30분에 사용	· 11:30	half past eleven

➡ 'after (past)'와 'to'는 주로 분을 'a quarter (15분), half (30분)'로 표현할 때 함께 쓰인다.

A 다음 표현들을 영어로 읽을 때의 표기법을 쓰시오.

1 1989년 ➡ _nineteen eighty-nine_

2 3:13 ➡ _____

3 2015년 8월 6일 ➡ _____

4 1:23 ➡ _____

5 11월 25일 ➡ _____

6 1789년 ➡ _____

7 5:48 ➡ _____

8 7:20 ➡ _____

9 2035년 7월 18일 ➡ _____

10 2월 25일 ➡ _____

11 1990년 ➡ _____

12 11:25 ➡ _____

13 4:03 ➡ _____

14 1884년 ➡ _____

15 1994년 1월 2일 ➡ _____

B 우리말과 같은 뜻이 되도록 빈칸에 알맞은 말을 쓰시오.

1 그는 Helen의 집에 3번 다녀온 적이 있다.
   ➡ He has been to Helen's house ___three times___.

2 Billy의 머리 길이는 내 머리 길이의 반이다.
   ➡ Billy's hair is _____ as long as my hair.

3 우리는 오늘 Tim과 5번 싸웠다.
   ➡ We fought with Tim _____.

4 그녀는 파스타의 3/4을 버렸다.
   ➡ She threw away three _____ of the pasta.

5 우리 엄마는 한 달에 7번 수영을 하러 가신다.
   ➡ My mom goes swimming _____ a month.

Practice More Ⅰ

Answer Keys p. 36

A 다음 주어진 말을 알맞은 형태로 바꾸어 빈칸에 쓰시오.

1 I gave her some advice for staying ____*healthy*____. (health)

2 The woman is a writer and she has a lot of _____ works. (interest)

3 This is a really _____ device for finding tiny things. (use)

4 The _____ people started to discuss how to find a solution. (surprise)

5 I think _____ behavior is very important when you have a job interview. (nature)

6 These days, Tim exercises hard to get _____ muscles. (strength)

7 Helen was _____ and shy, but she became an extremely different person. (passively)

8 I was really angry because she made a _____ mistake again. (fool)

9 John is a _____ actor in Korea. (fame)

10 My baby is really _____ about everything. (curiosity)

B 다음 문장에서 어법상 어색한 것을 찾아 바르게 고치시오.

1 We have a great number of time to play. Let's go!

____*number*____ ➡ ____*deal*____

2 Quite a few oil is in the bottle.

_____ ➡ _____

3 I didn't spend many money on this.

_____ ➡ _____

4 She walks with a pretty white small cat.

_____ ➡ _____

5 I have been to Paris a time.

_____ ➡ _____

6 It will rain tomorrow. So, little people will visit here.

_____ ➡ _____

Note

- **natural** (사람, 태도 등이) 자연스런, 꾸밈없는
- **passive** 소극적인
- **passively** 소극적으로
- **extremely** 매우
- **curious** 호기심이 강한
- **curiosity** 호기심

7   I want to learn special something.

_____ ➡ _____

8   Jane watched this movie three time.

_____ ➡ _____

9   There is many milk in the refrigerator.

_____ ➡ _____

10   Mary was disappointing when she heard the news.

_____ ➡ _____

C   보기 에서 알맞은 단어를 찾아 빈칸에 써 넣으시오.

보기
> little   few   much   many   amount   number

1   I just had a ___little___ soup because I wasn't hungry.

2   The bus leaves in a _____ minutes.

3   Wow, you spent too _____ money! You should save your money.

4   Why are very _____ people there? I don't expect this situation.

5   They have spent a great _____ of time in LA.

6   Only a _____ men will buy this car.

7   They have _____ hope of survival.

8   A _____ of people are gathered in the meeting room.

9   We tried _____ times to solve the problem.

10   _____ people understand her speech. It's so terrible.

D 주어진 단어를 알맞게 배열하여 문장을 완성하시오.

1 (a, plate, small, metal)

➡ There is _____*a small metal plate*_____ on the table.

2 (these, of, movies, both, horrible)

➡ I'm going to watch _____ tonight.

3 (plastic, these, fifteen)

➡ I have to clean _____ dishes.

4 (large, a, American, chair, old, lovely, pink)

➡ She bought _____

5 (number, every, festival, large, people, a, of, year, to, came, the)

➡ _____

6 (great, to, a, needed, time, the car, deal, is, of, fix)

➡ _____

7 (read, homework, she, more, to, her, a few, do, books)

➡ _____

8 (a, will, students, tomorrow, rafting, few, go)

➡ _____

9 (was, face, there, little, in, happiness, people's)

➡ _____

10 (he, three, used, black, wear, big, to, these, skirts)

➡ _____

Point Check Ⅱ

◆ **부사**: 동사, 형용사, 다른 부사, 또는 문장 전체를 꾸며 더 자세한 정보를 준다. '형용사, 명사, 동사'의 형태를 바꿔 부사로 만드는 경우도 있다.

1. 부사의 위치

동사 + 부사	• The wind blows gently.	부사 + 부사	• She sings very well.
부사 + 형용사	• A yellow bird is so cute.	부사 + 문장 전체	• Luckily, I got the last one.

2. 형용사로 부사 만들기

규칙		단어	
대부분의 경우	-ly	slow – slowly	moral – morally
-y로 끝나는 경우	y를 i로 바꾸고 -ly	happy – happily	heavy – heavily
-le로 끝나는 경우	e를 없애고 -y	possible – possibly	terrible – terribly

3. 뜻이 다른 부사

• late	늦게	• lately	최근에
• hard	열심히	• hardly (= rarely)	거의 ~않다
• high	높이	• highly	매우, 높이 평가하여
• near	가까이에	• nearly (= almost)	거의

4. 빈도부사: '일반동사 앞 / be동사 뒤 / 조동사 뒤'에 위치

always	usually	often	sometimes	seldom	rarely	never
항상	보통, 대개	종종, 자주	가끔, 때때로	드물게	거의 ~않는	결코 ~않는

◄─────────────────────────────────────►
100%   0%

5. 이어동사: '타동사 + 부사'

(1) [타동사 + 부사 + 명사] = [타동사 + 명사 + 부사]

• Sam **saw off** his friends. = Sam **saw** his friends **off**.

(2) [타동사 + 대명사 + 부사]

• **Give** it **up** if you can't catch those bugs.

9-7 부사

부사의 쓰임

- **부사**: 동사, 형용사, 다른 부사, 또는 문장 전체를 꾸며 더 자세한 정보를 준다. 주로 꾸며주는 말의 앞이나 뒤에 쓴다.

1. 부사의 위치

(1) [동사 + 부사]

- The deer **runs** away **quickly** from the lion.

(2) [부사 + 형용사]

- Two little pigs were **very depressed**.

(3) [부사 + 부사]

- She can speak Chinese **very well**.

(4) [부사 + 문장 전체]

- **Unfortunately, she couldn't pass the exam.**

2. 부사의 종류

1. 방법, 방식	quickly, softly, heavily
2. 장소	here, there, upstairs, downstairs, abroad, inside, outside
3. 시간	tomorrow, yesterday, now, then, already, recently
4. 빈도, 횟수	once, twice, sometimes, usually, rarely
5. 정도, 강조	completely, nearly, entirely, really, quite

3. 부사의 형태

	규칙	단어	
대부분의 경우	-ly	• great − greatly	wide − widely
-y로 끝나는 경우	y를 i로 바꾸고 -ly	• happy − happily	heavy − heavily
-le로 끝나는 경우	e를 없애고 -y	• simple − simply	gentle − gently
-ic로 끝나는 경우	-ally를 붙임	• basic − basically	scientific − scientifically
-ll로 끝나는 경우	-y	• full − fully	dull − dully

A 주어진 말을 알맞은 위치에 넣어 문장을 다시 쓰시오.

1 The child nodded his head. (bravely)

➡ *The child nodded his head bravely.*

2 All of us passed the graduation exam. (fortunately)

➡ _____

3 My little sister talked with her friend. (quietly)

➡ _____

4 She was pleased that she could buy the house. (very)

➡ _____

5 They are looking for the ring. (carefully)

➡ _____

6 It's not true. (certainly)

➡ _____

7 The gallery was not damaged by the storm. (luckily)

➡ _____

8 He does his best to speak English. (fluently)

➡ _____

9 The stone was slippery to pick up. (too)

➡ _____

10 I think James is having dinner. (too quickly)

➡ _____

B 주어진 말을 알맞은 형태로 바꾸어 빈칸에 쓰시오.

1 The cost of that coat has ___greatly___ decreased recently. (great)

2 He solved the problem _____. (simple)

3 This dress was _____ made for my daughter. (special)

4 Could you _____ give me some advice about the project? (possible)

5 They had a baby, and lived _____ ever after. (happy)

6 I saw the man who _____ prepared for the party. (busy)

7 She opened the window _____. (wide)

9-8 부사 파악하기

- 단어 자체가 부사이지만, '형용사＋ly' 형태의 부사들도 많다.
- '-ly'의 형태이지만 뜻이 완전히 다른 부사들도 있다.

1. 형용사와 모양은 같으나 뜻이 다른 부사

단어		단어		단어	
• late	형 늦은 부 늦게	• high	형 높은 부 높이, 높게	• last	형 마지막인 부 마지막으로
• hard	형 열심인, 어려운 부 열심히	• long	형 긴 부 오래, 길게	• near	형 가까운 부 가까이
• early	형 이른 부 일찍	• enough	형 충분한 부 충분히	• right	형 옳은 부 바르게
• fast	형 빠른 부 빠르게	• most	형 가장 많은 부 가장 많이	• well	형 건강한 부 잘, 능숙하게

- Brandon was **late** again this morning. [형용사]
- Alice stayed up **late** last night. [부사]

2. 뜻이 다른 부사

• late	늦게	• lately	최근에
• hard	열심히	• hardly (= rarely)	거의 ~않다
• high	높이	• highly	매우, 높이 평가하여
• near	가까이에	• nearly (= almost)	거의

- She had to clean the house **late** at night.
- Have you seen any movies **lately**?

Grammar Plus +

- lively, lonely, lovely, friendly, manly, yearly, monthly 등은 원래 '-ly'로 끝나는 형용사 단어들이며, 부사 형태는 따로 없다.

A 다음 밑줄 친 부분을 우리말로 해석하시오.

1. a. The boy was wearing <u>a pretty hat</u>.

   _____ *[예쁜 모자]*

   b. It's <u>pretty hot</u> outside.

   _____ *[아주 더운]*

2. a. We have to <u>practice hard</u> to win the game.

   _____

   b. This rock is <u>so hard</u>. We can't break it.

   _____

3. a. He played the piano <u>quite well</u>.

   _____

   b. Jane had an accident, but she is <u>well</u> now.

   _____

4. a. She said, "Your answer is <u>right</u>."

   _____

   b. We should <u>turn right</u> to get to the station.

   _____

5. a. <u>Most</u> people think she is the best player on the team.

   _____

   b. What kind of movie do you like <u>most</u>?

   _____

B 주어진 단어를 알맞게 바꾸어 빈칸에 알맞은 말을 쓰시오.

1. ___*Lately,*___ my friends have been worrying about their future. (late)

2. They sat _____ together on the bench. (close)

3. It took _____ thirty minutes to finish our homework. (near)

4. John became a _____ successful actor. (high)

5. He says that he has to work _____ tonight. (late)

6. I can _____ believe the rumor. (hard)

7. The machines are _____ used in Europe. (most)

8. The bird flow _____ in the sky. (high)

9. Their mom watched them _____. (close)

9-9 빈도부사

· 빈도부사: 어떤 일이 얼마나 빈번하게 일어나는지를 알려주는 부사를 말한다.

1. 빈도부사의 종류

always	usually	often	sometimes	seldom	rarely	never
항상	보통, 대개	종종, 자주	가끔, 때때로	드물게	거의 ~않는	결코 ~않는
100%	90~99%	75~89%	30~74%	10~29%	1~9%	0%

➡ rarely = hardly 거의 ~않는 (부정의 의미)

2. 빈도부사의 위치

(1) 일반동사 앞: [주어 + 빈도부사 + 일반동사]

· Phillip **often** goes to the bookstore with his girlfriend.

(2) be동사 뒤, 조동사 뒤: [주어 + be동사 + 빈도부사], [주어 + 조동사 + 빈도부사]

· The old man was **sometimes** watering the garden when I saw him.

· Jessy will **never** go swimming again.

➡ 'never'는 뜻 자체에 부정의 의미가 있으므로 'not'과 함께 쓰일 수 없다.

Grammar Plus +

· 조동사와 be동사가 함께 쓰이면 빈도부사는 그 사이에 들어간다.
She promised me that she **would always be** with me.
· 'usually, sometimes, normally, occasionally'는 강조를 위해 문장의 맨 앞에 위치할 수 있다.
Occasionally, James plays tennis with his sister.

 Check up!

Answer Keys p. 37

A 다음 밑줄 친 부분을 어법에 맞게 바르게 고치시오.

1 The movie that Helen always watches <u>is too sadly</u>.

➡ _____ *is too sad.* _____

2 I <u>feel sometimes</u> uncomfortable with James.

➡ _____

3 He <u>got often lost</u> while he was traveling in LA.

➡ _____

Answer Keys p. 37

4   Her team <u>never will win</u> the game without her.

  ➡ _____

5   It <u>sometimes is easy</u> to understand what she is saying.

  ➡ _____

6   Nick <u>shakes usually hands</u> when he meets someone new.

  ➡ _____

7   We <u>often are able to</u> see people who break traffic rules.

  ➡ _____

8   She <u>drinks seldom</u> water at night.

  ➡ _____

9   The word <u>used is usually</u> to encourage people.

  ➡ _____

10 They <u>will forget never</u> today's experience.

  ➡ _____

B 다음 우리말과 같은 뜻이 되도록 빈칸에 알맞은 말을 쓰시오.

1   그녀는 가끔 아이들과 함께 극장에서 영화를 본다. (watch)
  ➡ She _____*sometimes watches movies*_____ with her children
    at the theater.

2   큰 개 때문에 그 모퉁이를 돌 때면 나는 항상 긴장한다. (be)
  ➡ I _____ when I turn the
    corner because of a big dog.

3   Jessy는 거의 연습을 하지 않는데도 불구하고 피아노를 잘 친다.
    (practice)
  ➡ Though _____, she plays the
    piano very well.

4   Peter는 대개 방과 후에 두 시간씩 친구들과 농구를 한다. (play)
  ➡ Peter _____ with his friends
    for two hours after school.

5   우리는 자주 독서 모임에서 토론을 하곤 했다. (used to)
  ➡ We _____ on current events
    in our reading group.

여러 부사의 용법

• 부사는 보다 자세한 정보를 주기 위하여 여러 가지 형태와 용법으로 사용할 수 있다.

◈ 여러 부사의 쓰임

already 이미, 벌써	– 긍정문과 놀람을 나타내는 의문문에 사용된다. • Mom has already eaten dinner.
yet 아직, 벌써	– 의문문과 부정문에 사용되며, 주로 문장의 끝에 위치한다. • David might not know her true character yet.
still 여전히, 아직도	– 긍정문과 의문문에 사용된다. • Is she still angry about your mistake? ➡ 계속되는 행위를 강조할 때 부정문에도 쓰이기도 하며, 이때 'still'은 부정어 앞에 위치한다. • Jim still didn't understand the question.
too 또한, 역시	– 긍정문에 사용된다. • Marilyn is wise and pretty, too.
either 또한 (아니다)	– 부정문에 사용된다. • Mark doesn't like to eat vegetables, either. ➡ 'not~ either' = 'neither' • Jane won't leave, I won't, either. = Jane won't leave, neither will I.
very 매우	– 형용사와 부사의 원급을 수식한다. • She has very little free time.
much 훨씬	– 형용사와 부사의 비교급을 수식한다. • Dictionaries are much thicker than the other textbooks.
else 그, 그 밖에	– 수식하는 말 뒤에 위치한다. • I couldn't see anyone else in the gym. • What else do you want to do? ➡ 'else'가 의문대명사, 부정대명사 뒤에 올 때는 '형용사'로 쓰인다.
even ~조차	– 수식하는 말 앞에 위치한다. • He didn't know even that I really like Jenny.
ago ~전에	– 시간을 나타내는 말과 함께 쓰이고, **과거시제와 함께 사용**된다. • Luna wrote a lot of letters to him ten years ago.
before ~전에	– 과거 시점을 기준으로 그 이전에 일어난 일을 나타낼 때 쓰며, **완료시제와 함께 사용**된다. • The street froze because it had snowed before.

A 괄호 안에서 알맞은 것을 고르시오.

1   They haven't seen Bill for three hours. Did he go back home (already / still)?

2   If you don't accept our proposal, we won't accept your proposal, (neither / either).

3   Most of us don't have our own cameras (still / yet).

4   The eagles are (still / even) flying to find some prey.

5   Don't act like that. Nick is having a hard time, (either / too).

6   The fact that (even / else) he criticized me makes me depressed.

7   Jane and Mr. Lee got married three months (ago / before).

8   Mom usually cleans the house (very / much) quickly.

9   What (else / even) do you want her to do?

10   I heard that he traveled to Russia a few months (before / ago).

11   She won't leave, and (neither / either) will we.

12   Tina moved to another city three years (ago / before).

13   How (yet / else) can they get there in an hour?

14   Be kind to others, and they will be kind to you, (even / too).

15   **A** I should not have spicy food. **B** Me, (even / neither).

이어동사

- 이어동사: 목적어가 명사인지 대명사인지에 따라서 그 위치가 달라진다.

1. [타동사 + 부사 + 명사] = [타동사 + 명사 + 부사]
- **Put on** the raincoat. = **Put** the raincoat on.

2. [타동사 + 대명사 + 부사]
- **Turn** it **off** when you go out. **(O)**
- Turn off it when you go out. **(X)**

3. [타동사 + 부사]로 쓰이는 동사

• turn on/off	(TV, 스위치 등을) 켜다/끄다	• turn down	(소리, 온도 등을) 줄이다
• take off	(옷, 모자 등을) 벗다	• give up	포기하다
• put on	(옷, 모자 등을) 입다	• pick up	집어 들다, 차로 데리러 가다
• try on	시험 삼아 해보다, 옷을 입어보다	• put off	연기하다, 미루다
• see off	배웅하다	• throw away	내버리다, 던지다

Grammar Plus +

- [자동사 + 전치사]: '자동사+전치사'는 두 단어가 합쳐 **하나의 타동사**로 쓰인다.
  두 단어는 분리 될 수 없으며, 목적어가 명사인지 대명사인지 상관없이 전치사 뒤에 위치한다.
◈ [자동사 + 전치사]로 쓰이는 동사

    look for   look at   listen to   talk about   depend on   agree with

    I'm **looking for** my pen. (O) / I'm **looking** my pen **for**. (X)

Answer Keys p. 37

A   괄호 안에 들어갈 알맞은 말을 고르시오.

1   He wished that you wouldn't (give it up / give up it).

2   She tried to (put it on / put on it), but it was too tight.

3   David ironed (out the wrinkles / out them) on his son's black shirt.

4   You should not put (it off / off it). Trust is important.

5   Does she remember when she handed (in the paper / in them)?

6   Please check (out the weather / out it) before leaving.

7   We don't agree (him with / with him).

8   She stopped to fill (up her car / up it).

9   The man throw (away it / it away) carelessly.

10 I looked (the books for / for the books) for my homework.

B   다음 우리말과 같은 뜻이 되도록 빈칸에 알맞은 말을 쓰시오.

1   이 바지를 입어 봐도 될까요?
    ➡ Can I _____try on_____ these pants?

2   나중에 다시 걸겠습니다.
    ➡ I will _____.

3   기상 악화 때문에 소풍은 일주일간 미루어졌다.
    ➡ Because of the bad weather, the picnic has been _____
    for a week.

4   그녀는 정원을 가꾸는 것을 포기했다.
    ➡ She _____ working in the garden.

5   외출을 해야 하기 때문에 나는 집 안의 불을 껐다.
    ➡ Because I have to go out, I _____ all the lights
    _____ in the house.

6   이를 닦을 때 물을 잠가라.
    ➡ When you brush your teeth, _____ the water.

7   라디오 소리 좀 줄여 줄래요?
    ➡ Could you _____ the radio _____, please?

Practice More Ⅱ

Answer Keys p. 38

A 다음 괄호 안에서 알맞은 것을 고르시오.

1   I think Max will arrive (soon / before).

2   (Lately / Late), she has started to learn how to ride a bike.

3   The teacher watched the babies (close / closely).

4   She (is always / always is) smiling. It makes people happy.

5   I can (hardly / mostly) believe the professor's explanation.

6   The dolphin jumps (highly / high).

7   My parents (take often / often take) a walk after dinner.

8   Would you please (turn it off / turn off it)?

9   It took (near / nearly) thirty minutes to finish the race.

10 The boy got the (mostly / most) votes.

B 다음 문장에서 어법상 어색한 것을 찾아 바르게 고치시오.

1   How do often you call your mother?

    _____do often_____ ➡ _____often do_____

2   The baby smiled and it made me happily.

    _____ ➡ _____

3   I'm hard ever late for school. I am proud of it.

    _____ ➡ _____

4   Do not go nearly the dog. It usually barks at people.

    _____ ➡ _____

5   Jane is responsible for making a seriously mistake.

    _____ ➡ _____

6   Mostly students go to school by bus.

    _____ ➡ _____

7   I will be always with you.

    _____ ➡ _____

8   We can move the box easy.

_____ ➡ _____

9   The young girl became a high experienced dancer.

_____ ➡ _____

10 Minji colored that picture beautiful.

_____ ➡ _____

C   괄호 안에서 알맞은 것을 고르시오.

1   The rain has stopped, but it's (still / yet) humid outside.

2   His question was (too / so) foolish that everyone laughed at him.

3   It's (pretty / little) hard to solve the problem without any hints.

4   Have you finished doing the dishes (still / yet)?

5   I'm so bored lately. I want to try something (else / even).

6   I've never seen those pictures (ago / before).

7   Did she (turn off it / turn the TV off)?

8   We're waiting (for our turn / our turn for).

9   I stopped to fill (up my water bottle / up it).

10 Moody (still / yet) feels sleepy though she slept for almost ten hours.

D 주어진 단어를 바르게 배열하여 문장을 완성하시오.

1 (often, we, the, together, go, movies, to)

⟹ _____ *We often go to the movies together.* _____

2 (Jane, hope, I, next, and, abroad, month, study, to)

⟹ _____

3 (and, not, hand in, Jina's, her report, am, going, I, to, neither)

⟹ _____

4 (do, still, husband, to, your, you, for, need, wait)

⟹ _____

5 (she, already, for, making, has, daughter, finished, dress, her, a)

⟹ _____

6 (am, I, upset, mistake, still, about, John's)

⟹ _____

7 (Mary, spicy, but, kimchi, dislikes, often, she, food, eats)

⟹ _____

8 (think, than, I, much, mine, your room, bigger, is)

⟹ _____

9 (could, my, I, believe, eyes, hardly)

⟹ _____

10 (my sister, enough, middle school, is, enter, to, old)

⟹ _____

내신 최다 출제 유형

01 다음 밑줄 친 부분의 쓰임이 나머지 넷과 다른 것을 고르시오. [출제 예상 85%]

① This book is <u>hard</u> to read.
② Tommy's new school days are very <u>hard</u>.
③ I have a <u>hard</u> time finding the hospital.
④ She studied <u>hard</u> to pass the exam.
⑤ This bread is too <u>hard</u> to eat.

02 다음의 빈칸에 공통으로 들어갈 알맞은 말을 고르시오. [출제 예상 80%]

- Would you like to drink _____ more juice?
- There were _____ mangoes in the basket.

① any   ② some   ③ a little
④ little   ⑤ much

03 다음 중 밑줄 친 부분이 어법상 틀린 것을 고르시오. [출제 예상 85%]

① We have <u>lots of</u> friends.
② She wants <u>some</u> water to drink.
③ He stored <u>much</u> rice in his storeroom.
④ We had <u>few</u> volunteers to work on the farm.
⑤ I need <u>a little</u> more minutes to mark the answers on the answer card.

04 다음 주어진 단어 중 틀린 한 곳을 고쳐서 우리말에 맞게 다시 쓰시오. [출제 예상 85%]

read, interesting, story, she, a few, us
그녀는 우리에게 몇몇 흥미로운 이야기를 읽어 주었다.

➡ _____

05 다음 대화의 빈칸에 알맞은 말을 쓰시오. [출제 예상 85%]

A I can't sing well.
B _____ _____ _____. I'm not good at singing.

➡ _____

06 다음 각 문장에서 어법상 틀린 부분을 찾아 고쳐 쓰시오. [출제 예상 85%]

(1) Don't be lately for school.
(2) Please study hardly.

(1) _____ ➡ _____
(2) _____ ➡ _____

[01~02] 다음의 빈칸에 들어갈 알맞은 것을 고르시오.

01
> **A** John, hurry up!
> **B** I'm not ready _____. Can you wait for a little longer?

① still   ② seldom   ③ already
④ even   ⑤ yet

02
> I haven't noticed _____ about this book yet.

① interesting something
② anything interesting
③ interesting anything
④ something interesting
⑤ interesting thing

03 다음 중 짝지어진 단어의 관계가 나머지 넷과 <u>다른</u> 것을 고르시오.

① effective − effectively
② constant − constantly
③ friend − friendly
④ nice − nicely
⑤ heavy − heavily

[04~05] 다음 밑줄 친 부분 중 그 쓰임이 <u>어색한</u> 것을 고르시오.

04
① Where did you buy <u>all those lovely accessories</u>?
② Raise <u>left your hand</u> and sing along with me.
③ I did well for <u>my first two years</u> of middle school.
④ The restaurant is famous for <u>its good service</u>.
⑤ <u>Another five more pages</u> have been added.

05
① There is <u>nothing comparable</u> to his job.
② You are blessed with <u>something valuable</u>.
③ I have eaten <u>everything imaginable</u>.
④ She has <u>something unique</u> from other women.
⑤ <u>Things bad</u> do not happen to good people.

06 다음 중 어법상 옳은 것을 고르시오.

① Put off it and you don't have to care about it.
② Put it off and you don't have to care about it.
③ Put off it and you don't have to care it about.
④ Put it off and you haven't to it care about.
⑤ Put it off and you don't care about it have to.

07 다음 주어진 우리말을 영어로 바르게 옮긴 것을 고르시오.

> 그녀 역시 할 말을 찾지 못하는 것 같았다.

① She couldn't seem to find any words, either.
② She couldn't seem to find any words, too.
③ She couldn't seem to find any words, neither.
④ She couldn't seems to find any words, also.
⑤ She couldn't seems to find any words, too.

08 다음 중 밑줄 친 부분의 용법이 나머지 넷과 다른 것을 고르시오.

① The kind man helped me find the subway station.
② More jobs need to be made for the jobless.
③ Seats for the disabled are also available.
④ The clever are not greedy and the greedy are not clever.
⑤ The young tend to be idealistic.

[09~10] 다음 밑줄 친 부분의 뜻이 나머지 넷과 다른 것을 고르시오.

09 ① We already have too much to do.
② Fortunately, they have much food left.
③ How much money do you need?
④ It takes much time to build a real relationship.
⑤ I thought the medicine was invented much earlier.

10 ① The material is still used in making fans.
② Jinah still goes to law school seminars.
③ Minsu sat still looking out of the window.
④ Are you still waiting for him?
⑤ She still has a question about the problem.

[11~13] 다음 빈칸에 들어갈 말이 바르게 짝지어진 것을 고르시오.

11
> A How _____ money do you have?
> B I have one hundred dollars.
> A Is it _____ to buy an MP3 player?

① many – some
② much – enough
③ much – any
④ many – enough
⑤ many – some

12

Because Jason had _____ particular to do, he walked along the street looking for _____ exciting.

① much – anything
② something – anything
③ nothing – anything
④ nothing – something
⑤ something – nothing

13

- Have you _____ been to North America?
- I _____ lived in Canada.

① once – still   ② ever – once
③ never – once   ④ ever – before
⑤ ever – already

[14~15] 다음 중 어법상 어색한 것을 고르시오.

14
① Both his parents are proud of him.
② All the students looked happy.
③ Who gave you those red roses?
④ I don't need this big old blue skirt.
⑤ Let me introduce my Chinese three friends.

15
① We don't know about it at all.
② Our boss called off the meeting again.
③ She looks gorgeous dressed up like that.
④ Larry didn't agree us with.
⑤ I have to pick up the girl who will clean this office.

16 다음 중 어법상 옳은 것을 고르시오.

① I think David is very taller than Jim.
② The woman is much happy than she was last month.
③ She predicts that life will be very different in a century.
④ She has bought the book a week ago.
⑤ I agreed that this was a much nice garden.

17 다음 밑줄 친 부분 중 쓰임이 올바른 것을 모두 고르시오.

① He is a pleased boy satisfied with everything.
② English is one of main subjects in every school.
③ I heard the afraid people shout for help.
④ The former president is ashamed of his mistake.
⑤ Don't wake up an asleep baby.

18 다음 우리말을 영어로 표현한 것 중 바르지 못한 것을 고르시오.

오후 2시 45분

① two and three fourths
② fifteen to three
③ a quarter to three
④ two forty-five
⑤ forty-five past two

19 다음 중 영어로 읽을 때의 표기법이 <u>틀린</u> 것을 고르시오.

① 2008년 9월 2일: September the second, two thousand eight

② 1시 15분: a quarter after one

③ 25.19: two five point one nine

④ $7\frac{3}{5}$: seven and three fifths

⑤ 수십 만: hundreds of thousands

[20~21] 다음 중 어법상 <u>어색한</u> 것을 고르시오.

20 ① Sometimes Jinny forgets it.

② Mike's sister often came to the game.

③ The picture has caught people's imaginations.

④ When I touch it, it feels usually slippery.

⑤ I have never thought about it.

21 ① I worked until late at night.

② People are trying very hardly to save water.

③ Jenny thinks Sara is the most beautiful girl in her school.

④ The park is close to the downtown area.

⑤ A long time ago, only a few houses had televisions.

22 다음 문장의 빈칸에 들어갈 수 <u>없는</u> 단어를 고르시오.

> On his way home, he saw a _____ girl in pink.

① cute   ② blind   ③ strange
④ pretty   ⑤ glad

23 다음 빈칸에 들어갈 형용사로 알맞은 것을 고르시오.

> My phone bill is very expensive. Do you think that the price is _____ it?

① worthy   ② worth   ③ valuable
④ valued   ⑤ worthwhile

24 다음 중 빈칸에 공통으로 들어갈 알맞은 말을 고르시오.

> • Would you like to have _____ snacks before the movie starts?
> • My Canadian friends like _____ Korean food.

① any   ② little   ③ few
④ a little   ⑤ some

25 다음 문장의 밑줄 친 부분의 쓰임이 잘못된 것을 고르시오.

① Most of them don't know what they want to do <u>yet</u>.

② He found they did not use spoons <u>even</u> when they ate soup.

③ Have you finished your work <u>still</u>?

④ It's <u>already</u> been two months since she left.

⑤ What <u>else</u> can you tell me about the boy?

26 다음 밑줄 친 hard의 뜻이 나머지 넷과 <u>다른</u> 것을 고르시오.

① The miners worked <u>hard</u> to make a living.

② He came to know that it was <u>hard</u> to be kind.

③ New school days were <u>hard</u> and made me nervous.

④ We have had a <u>hard</u> time settling in here.

⑤ The weather is <u>hard</u> to predict.

27 다음 문장의 밑줄 친 부분 중 어법상 어색한 곳을 고르시오.

If you don't ① <u>clean</u> the house, I ② <u>won't</u>, ③ <u>neither</u>. I'm ④ <u>tired</u> of ⑤ <u>doing</u> it alone.

◇◇◇◇◇◇◇◇◇ **서술형 평가** ◇◇◇◇◇◇◇◇◇

[28~30] 다음 문장에서 어법상 틀린 곳을 찾아 바르게 고쳐 쓰시오.

28
> When I first began Kung Fu, I learn how to sit and breathe good.

_____ ➡ _____

29
> Judy kept me outside too longest in the cold weather, so I caught a cold.

_____ ➡ _____

30
> Some students began to show on as early as 6 o'clock.

_____ ➡ _____

[31~33] 다음 우리말과 같은 뜻이 되도록 괄호 안의 단어를 바르게 배열하여 쓰시오.

31
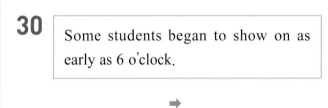
> 나는 보통 저녁식사 후에 숙제를 한다.
> I _____ after dinner.
> (usually / my / homework / do)

➡ _____

Answer Keys p. 38~39

32

사막에는 거의 비가 오지 않고 햇볕이 계속 내리쬔다.

_____ and the sun keeps shining in the desert.
(rains / it / rarely)

➡ _____

33

이 게임에서 당신은 같은 방에 여러 번 들어갈 수 있다.

In this game, you can step into the

_____.

(times / room / same / several)

➡ _____

[34~35] 다음 주어진 문장을 괄호 안의 지시어대로 고쳐 쓰시오.

34

His band has twice as many fans as mine.

➡ [비교급]

_____

35

It's eleven thirty.

➡ [시간: past 사용]

_____

10

Chapter
비교구문

Point Check I

◆ **비교구문:** 형용사와 부사의 형태를 변화시켜 두 개 이상의 것을 비교하는 것을 말한다.
비교구문은 '원급, 비교급, 최상급'으로 나눌 수 있다.

1. 비교급과 최상급의 형태

	비교급 [~보다 ~한]	최상급 [가장 ~한]
대개의 경우	• 형용사 / 부사 er + than	• the 형용사 / 부사 est
2음절 이상의 형용사	• more 형용사 / 부사 + than	• the most 형용사 / 부사

2. 원급, 비교급, 최상급 표현

as 원급 as	[as + 형용사/부사 + as + A]	A만큼 ~한(하게)
	[not as (so) + 형용사/부사 + as + A]	A만큼 ~하지 않은(않게)
	[배수사 + as + 형/부 + as + A]	A보다 몇 배 ~한(하게)
	[as ~ as possible (one can)]	가능한 한 ~한(하게)
비교급 than	[형용사/부사 비교급 + than...]	...보다 더 ~한
	[not + 형용사/부사 비교급 + than...]	...보다 더 ~하지 않은
	[less 형/부 + than...]	보다 덜 ~한(하게)
	[비교급 and 비교급]	점점 더 ~한(하게)
	[the + 비교급, the + 비교급]	~하면 할수록 더 ...한(하게)
the 최상급	[the + 서수 + 최상급]	~번째로 가장 ...한
	[the least 원급]	가장 덜 ~ 한
	[one of the 최상급 + 복수명사]	가장 ~한 ...중의 하나
	[There is nothing ~ 비교급 + than...]	...보다 더 ~한 것은 없다
	[No (other) ~ as(so) + 원급 + as + A]	A만큼 ~한(다른) 것은 없다
	[No (other) ~ 비교급 + than A]	A보다 ~한(다른) 것은 없다
	[A~비교급 + than any other + 단수명사]	A는 다른 어떤 (단수명사)보다 ~하다
	[A~비교급 + than all the other + 복수명사]	A는 다른 어떤 (복수명사)보다 ~하다

비교급과 최상급 만들기

- **비교급:** [형용사(부사)-er/-r+than] ~보다 더 ...한
- **최상급:** [the+형용사(부사)-est/-st] 가장 ~한

* 2음절 이상의 단어들은 '-er/-r' 대신에 'more'를, '-est/-st' 대신에 'most'를 앞에 붙여준다.

1. 비교급과 최상급의 규칙변화

대개의 경우	-er, -est	• cold – colder – coldest
'-e'로 끝나는 경우	-r, -st	• close - closer - closest
자음+y	y를 'i'로 바꾸고 +-er, -est	• dirty – dirtier – dirtiest
단모음+단자음	자음 +-er, -est	• big – bigger – biggest
2음절 이상의 형용사	more, most + 원급	• famous – more famous – most famous
분사 형태의 형용사		• exciting – more exciting – most exciting
형용사+ly형태의 부사		• exactly – more exactly – most exactly

2. 비교급과 최상급의 불규칙변화

원급	비교급	최상급	뜻	원급	비교급	최상급	뜻
• good	better	best	좋은	• late	latter	last	(순서) 늦은
• well	better	best	건강한, 잘	• far	farther	farthest	(거리) 먼
• bad	worse	worst	나쁜	• far	further	furthest	(정도) 먼
• ill	worse	worst	병든	• many	more	most	(수) 많은
• old	older	oldest	나이든, 늙은	• much	more	most	(양) 많은
• old	elder	eldest	연장의 손위의	• few	fewer	fewest	(수) 적은
• late	later	latest	(시간) 늦은	• little	less	least	(양) 적은

➡ 'badly (나쁘게) – worse – worst'로 나타낸다.

➡ 'elder – eldest'는 주로 가족 관계에서만 쓰이며, 한정용법에 쓰인다.

☆Check up!

Answer Keys p. 40

A 다음 형용사의 비교급, 최상급을 쓰시오.

1 cheap – _cheaper_ – _cheapest_

2 good – _____ – _____

3 far   – _____ – _____ / _____ – _____

4 small   – _____ – _____

5 late   – _____ – _____ / _____ – _____

6 large   – _____ – _____

7 wide   – _____ – _____

8 narrow   – _____ – _____

9 little   – _____ – _____

10 nice   – _____ – _____

11 famous   – _____ – _____

12 lucky   – _____ – _____

13 strange   – _____ – _____

14 bad   – _____ – _____

15 pretty   – _____ – _____

16 sad   – _____ – _____

17 safe   – _____ – _____

18 near   – _____ – _____

19 kindly   – _____ – _____

20 happily   – _____ – _____

B   주어진 단어를 알맞게 변형하여 빈칸을 채우시오.

1   Our company tried to make a _____*better*_____ product. (good)

2   This is the _____ situation I've ever experienced. (bad)

3   Chris had _____ chicken than I did. (little)

4   His performance is _____ than mine. (practice)

5   I saw the drama, but it was the _____ one I've ever
    seen. (bore)

6   The new action movie is _____ than the movie I saw
    last week. (interest)

7   For _____ information, just contact us. (far)

8   Max is the _____ of my four brothers. (old)

10-2 원급비교(동등비교)

• **as 원급 as**: 'as ~ as' 사이에는 형용사 또는 부사의 원형이 들어간다. 비교하는 두 대상이 비슷하거나 같을 때 사용하며, '...만큼(처럼) ~한'이라고 해석한다.

1. as + 형/부 + as + A : A만큼 ~한(하게)

➡ 원급비교의 비교 대상은 '인칭대명사 + 동사' 또는 '목적격'으로 나타낼 수 있다.

• Jasmine is **as clever as** Helen (is). [형용사]

• I eat food **as slowly as** Harry (eats). [부사]

• Jude has **as little juice as** me (I have). [명사구]

2. not as(so) + 형/부 + as + A : A만큼 ~하지 않은(않게)

➡ 원급비교의 부정문은 비교 대상을 바꿔서 비교급으로 표현할 수 있다.

• Harry is **not as(so) fast as** you.
  = You are **faster than** Harry.

• Jennifer did **not** play the violin **as (so) well as** you.
  = You played the violin **better than** Jennifer.

3. 배수사 + as + 형/부 + as + A : A보다 몇 배 ~한(하게)

(1) '배수사 + the + 단위명사 + of~'로 바꿀 수 있다.

• This dress is **twice as big as** that one.
  = This dress is **twice the size of** that one.

단위명사	size, height, length, number, amount 등

(2) 'three times' 이상의 표현은 비교구문으로 바꿀 수 있다.

• This bag is **three times as heavy as** that one.
  = This bag is **three times heavier than** that one.

(3) 배수사 + 명사

• Toby watched **five times as many movies as** Sam.

**Check up!**

Answer Keys p. 40

A 보기 와 같이 문장을 완성하시오.

보기
> Harry is 175 cm. Minhyuk is 180 cm.
> ➡ _____ Harry is not as tall as Minhyuk. _____

1 The blue basket weighs 5 kg. The red basket weighs 7 kg.
➡ The blue basket is _____ the red basket.

2   Billy scored two goals. Nick scored six goals.
    ➡ Nick scored _____ Billy.

3   The man ate three bananas. I ate three bananas.
    ➡ The man ate _____ me.

4   Brian got an A on the test. You got an A, too.
    ➡ You are _____ Brian.

5   Mary created five new bags. Jinsu created five new bags.
    ➡ Jinsu created _____ Mary.

6   Tim runs 100 meters in 13 seconds. Peter runs that for in
    10 seconds.
    ➡ Tim runs _____ Peter.

7   Jane has 12 notebooks. I have 7 notebooks.
    ➡ I don't have _____ Jane.

8   My sister went to sleep at eleven. Father went to sleep at ten.
    ➡ My sister did not go to sleep _____ father.

9   The scarf is 5 dollars. The pants are 5 dollars, too.
    ➡ The scarf is _____ the pants.

10 He drank 2 liters of water. She drank 1.5 liters of water.
    ➡ She didn't drink _____ him.

B 우리말 해석에 알맞게 문장을 완성하시오.

1   Amy는 자기의 여동생보다 3배의 음식을 더 먹었다.
    ➡ Amy ate three times ___*as much food as*___ her sister.

2   나비는 모기보다 위험하지 않다.
    ➡ A butterfly is _____ a mosquito.

3   그 탑은 그 건물의 절반 높이다.
    ➡ The tower is _____ the building.

4   Brandon은 Max보다 2배 점프를 높게 할 수 있다.
    ➡ Brandon can jump _____ Max can.

5   그의 방은 내 방보다 4배가 더 크다.
    ➡ His room is _____ my room.

10-3 원급의 여러 표현

- **원급의 관용표현**: 'as ~ as'를 이용한 여러 가지 표현을 외워두자.
- **원급의 강조어구**: 형용사와 부사의 원형 앞에 쓰여 '매우'의 뜻을 가지며, 형용사나 부사를 강조하기 위해 사용한다.

1. 원급의 관용 표현

• **as ~as possible (one can)**	가능한 한 ~한(하게)

- Please reply to me as soon as possible.
  = Please reply to me as soon as you can.

➡ 'as ~ as one can'으로 바꿔 쓸 때는 인칭과 시제를 일치시킨다.

- I tried to start as fast as possible.
  = I tried to start as fast as I could.

• **as long as**	~하는 한 (시간)

- As long as it rains, we can't go on a picnic.

• **as(so) far as**	~하는 한(정도)

- As (So) far as I'm concerned, there's no place we can hide.

• **as good as**	거의 (= almost, nearly), ~나 마찬가지인

- The electronic dictionary is as good as a tutor.

Grammar Plus +

- **어떠한 일을 잘 했다고 표현할 때는 무엇을 쓸까?**
- : **as well as**

When the project was finished, we ourselves praised that we did the job **as well as** we could.

'as~ as'를 빼고도 앞 문장이 말이 될 수 있어야 하기 때문에 'good' 대신 'well'이 들어간다.
즉, 'We did the job well.'의 형식이 되어 부사가 와야 한다.

2. 원급의 강조: very, so, pretty는 형용사나 부사 원형 앞에서 '매우'라는 뜻으로 사용된다.

- Maria felt **so** embarrassed.
- Jack was **pretty** hungry and he ate the hamburgers **very** fast.

Answer Keys p. 40

A 다음 우리말 해석에 맞게 빈칸을 채우시오.

1 그가 여기에 있는 한 아무것도 걱정할 것이 없을 것이다.
➡ ___As long as___ he's here, there will be nothing to worry about.

2 James는 도둑을 가능한 한 빠르게 쫓아갔다.
➡ James ran after the thief _____.

3 이 책은 조금 젖었지만 거의 새 것이다.
➡ This book is _____ although it is a little bit wet.

4 우리가 아는 한 그는 매운 것을 못 먹는다.
➡ _____, he can't eat spicy food.

5 교수님은 가능한 한 빨리 리포트를 제출하라고 말했다.
➡ The professor said we should turn in the report
_____.

6 Mr. Kim은 매우 피곤함을 느꼈다.
➡ Mr. Kim felt _____ tired.

7 그 낡은 카메라는 거의 쓸모가 없었다.
➡ The old camera was _____.

8 밖에 비가 내리는 한 우리는 소풍을 갈 수 없다.
➡ _____, we can't have a picnic.

9 Mary는 살 수 있는 만큼 많은 꽃을 샀다.
➡ Mary bought as many flowers _____.

10 그 유리창은 거의 깨져 있었다.
➡ The window was _____.

비교급 비교

• **비교급의 비교**: 비교급은 형용사 또는 부사 뒤에 '-er' 또는 앞에 'more'를 붙여 'than'과 함께 사용한다. 우리말로는 '더 ~한(하게)'라는 뜻으로 쓰인다.

1. (more) 형/부-er than... : ...보다 더 ~한(하게)

• A blue whale is **larger than** a sea lion.

• An anaconda is **more dangerous than** a normal snake.

2. less 형/부 than... : ...보다 덜 ~한(하게)

• A train ticket is **less expensive** than a plane ticket.

= A train ticket is **not as(so) expensive as** a plane ticket.

= A plane ticket is **more expensive than** a train ticket.

3. 비교급 and 비교급: 점점 더 ~한(하게)

• I was getting **fatter and fatter**.

• The man ran **faster and faster**.

4. the 비교급, the 비교급: ~하면 할수록 더 ...한(하게)

→ 접속사를 사용하여 '접속사 + 주어 + 동사 ~, 주어 + 동사 ~'로 바꾸어 쓸 수 있다.

• **The harder** you exercise, **the healthier** you will be.

= If you exercise **harder**, you will be **healthier**.

• **The more** junk food he had, **the less healthy** he became.

= As he had **more** junk food, he became **less healthy**. ('less + 원급' 주의)

5. 비교급 강조어구: '매우, 훨씬'이라는 의미로 비교급 앞에 위치해서 의미를 강조한다.

강한 의미	much, even, far, still, a lot
훨씬 더 ~한 (하게)	• I think that she'll be much better next time.
약한 의미	a little, a bit, slightly, somewhat
약간/조금 더 ~한 (하게)	• This car feels a little more comfortable than the other cars.

Grammar Plus +

• 비교 대상이 주어와 같은 종류일 경우 소유대명사로 나타낼 수 있다.

My skirt is prettier than hers.

Answer Keys p. 40

A 다음 밑줄 친 부분을 바르게 고치시오.

1 Max is <u>more tall</u> than his brother.

taller

2 She was walking slower and <u>slow</u>.

_____

3 John is <u>more smarter</u> than Jim.

_____

4 His answer sounds less <u>sillier</u> than hers.

_____

5 She looks <u>thin</u> than she is.

_____

6 I think Max is less <u>smarter</u> than Paul.

_____

7 Sally is less <u>diligence</u> than her brother.

_____

8 The eagle is <u>more fast</u> than the pigeon.

_____

9 Sam is <u>little</u> smart than Tim.

_____

10 The sooner, the <u>good</u>.

_____

B 다음 우리말 해석에 맞게 문장을 완성하시오.

1 이 자동차는 예전 것보다 훨씬 낫다. (far, good)
  ➡ This car is _____far better_____ than the old one.

2 더 높이 올라갈수록 날씨는 더 추워질 것이다. (high, cold)
  ➡ _____ you climb,_____ it will be.

3 나의 코트가 그녀의 것보다 조금 더 길다. (a little, long)
  ➡ My coat is _____ than hers.

4 그녀의 요리 실력은 점점 더 좋아지고 있다. (good)
  ➡ Her cooking is getting _____.

5 이 침대가 조금 더 편안하게 느껴진다. (a little, comfortable)
  ➡ This bed feels _____.

10-5 최상급 비교

- **최상급**: 셋 이상을 비교할 때 쓰이며 '가장 ~한'이라는 뜻을 가진다. 형용사나 부사 뒤에 '-est/ -st' 또는 앞에 'most'를 붙여 최상급 형태를 만들며, 정관사 'the'와 함께 쓰인다.

1. the (most) 형/부-est

in + 장소	• Peter is the most diligent student in the class.
of + 복수명사	• Marilyn is the prettiest of her friends.
관계사절	• This movie is the most boring (that) I've watched.

2. 부사의 최상급: 대개 the를 생략한다.
- Sammy acts **(the) most mischievously** in the class.

3. one of the 최상급 + 복수명사: 가장 ~한 ...중의 하나
- Ironman is **one of the most popular heroes** in movies.

4. the + 서수 + 최상급: ~번째로 가장 ...한
- The Shanghai Tower is **the second tallest** building in the world.

5. the least 원급: 가장 덜 ~한
- Jenny found **the least expensive** shoes in the shop.
  = Jenny found **the cheapest** shoes in the shop.

 Check up!

Answer Keys p. 40~41

A 주어진 말을 최상급으로 바꾸어 빈칸에 쓰시오.

1 Nick knows the history of the picture ___*the most exactly.*___ . (exactly)

2 He took us to _____ in the city. (a good restaurant)

3 What is _____ in your country? (a tall tower)

4 _____ is that I got an A on the test. (a happy news)

5 He is _____ in his company. (a diligent worker)

6 I think it might be _____ I have. (a thick book)

7   The Coast Redwood is _____ in the world.
    (a big tree)

8   We think it is the _____ in the night sky.
    (a bright star)

9   This story is _____ I've ever heard. (a move story)

10 James thought it was _____ ever. (a good album)

B   우리말과 같은 뜻이 되도록 문장을 완성하시오.

1   "Old Boy"는 내가 본 최고 영화들 중 하나이다.
    ➡ "Old Boy" is _____*one of the best movies*_____ I've seen.

2   Busan은 한국에서 2번째로 인기가 많은 도시이다.
    ➡ Busan is _____ in Korea.

3   그는 매장에서 가장 비싼 펜을 샀다.
    ➡ He bought _____ in the store.

4   축구는 우리 반에서 3번째로 인기 있는 운동이다.
    ➡ Soccer is _____ in our class.

5   Lily는 가장 덜 어려운 영어 시 조차 외우지 못했다.
    ➡ Lily could not even memorize _____ poem.

6   Won Bin은 한국에서 가장 인기 있는 배우 중 한 명이다.
    ➡ Won Bin is _____ in Korea.

7   그녀의 이야기는 모든 이야기 중에서 가장 재미가 없다.
    ➡ Her story is _____ of all stories.

8   그 책은 역사상 가장 오래된 책 중에 하나다.
    ➡ The book is _____ in history.

9   나는 방 안에서 가장 덜 더러운 모자를 찾았다.
    ➡ I found _____ in the room.

10 Harry는 학교에서 3번째로 인기있는 학생이다.
    ➡ Harry is _____ in the school.

10-6 최상급의 다른 표현

• 원급과 비교급을 이용하여 최상급의 표현을 할 수 있다.

1. There is nothing + 비교급 + than... : ...보다 더 ~한 것은 없다

• There is nothing lovelier than Leeds Castle in England
= Leeds Castle is the loveliest castle in England.

2. 원급/비교급을 이용한 최상급 표현

the + 최상급
The Nile River is the longest river in the world.

= [No (other) ~ as(so) + 원급 + as + A] A만큼 ~한 (다른) 것은 없다
• No (other) river is as long as the Nile River in the world.

= [No (other) ~ 비교급+than A] A보다 ~한 (다른) 것은 없다
• No (other) river is longer than the Nile River in the world.

= [A ~ 비교급+than any other + 단수명사] A는 다른 어떤 (단수명사) 보다 ~하다
• The Nile River is longer than any other river in the world.

= [A ~ 비교급+than all the other + 복수명사] A는 다른 어떤 (복수명사) 보다 ~하다
• The Nile River is longer than all the other rivers in the world.

 **Check up!**

Answer Keys p. 41

A 보기 와 같이 There is nothing ~ 비교급 + than 구문을 이용하여 문장을 완성하시오.

> 보기
>
> She enjoys snowboarding the most.
>   There is nothing she enjoys more than snowboarding.

1 A challenge is the most important thing in my life.

➡ _____

2 She worries most about her kids living in China.

➡ _____

3 Regular exercise and a good diet are the most helpful for losing weight.

➡ _____

4 Waiting for someone is the most boring thing to do.

➡ _____

5 He wants a new laptop the most as his graduation gift.

➡ _____

6 To be what your mother wants you to be is the most difficult thing.

➡ _____

B 다음 문장들이 같은 뜻이 되도록 빈칸에 알맞은 말을 쓰시오.

1 This shirt was the most expensive thing in my room.

➡ *No (other) shirt in my room was as expensive as this shirt.*

➡ *No (other) shirt in my room was more expensive than this shirt.*

➡ *This shirt was more expensive than any other shirt in my room.*

➡ *This shirt was more expensive than all the other shirts in my room.*

2 Mt. Everest is the highest mountain.

➡ _____

➡ _____

➡ _____

➡ _____

3 This is the oldest fossil.

➡ _____

➡ _____

➡ _____

➡ _____

4 Mr. Kim is the richest person in Korea.

➡ _____

➡ _____

➡ _____

➡ _____

5 Kate is the smartest student in our class.

➡ _____

➡ _____

➡ _____

➡ _____

Practice More Ⅰ

Answer Keys p. 41~42

A 다음 문장에서 어법상 <u>어색한</u> 것을 찾아 바르게 고치시오.

1 Kelly's joke is more funny than yours.

  more funny ➡ _funnier_

2 It is as higher as that tower.

  _____ ➡ _____

3 The more hard you study, the better your grades will be.

  _____ ➡ _____

4 They are little and little interested in this movie.

  _____ ➡ _____

5 She is one of the most important person in Japan.

  _____ ➡ _____

6 This is more expensive than any other books in the shop.

  _____ ➡ _____

7 We got to the station the most early of all the people.

  _____ ➡ _____

8 Amy is as not healthy as her sister.

  _____ ➡ _____

9 This rope is two times as long as that rope.

  _____ ➡ _____

10 Please come back as soon as you possible.

  _____ ➡ _____

B 주어진 단어를 알맞은 형태로 바꾸어 빈칸을 채우시오.

1 The black coat looks ____better____ than the white one. (good)

2 The river was _____ river in Korea. (long)

3 She said love was _____ than money. (important)

4 The more he smoked, _____ healthy he became. (little)

5 Who ever can shout _____ will be the winner. (loud)

6 No other country in the world is _____ than Russia. (large)

7 Tim is much _____ than me. (tall)

8   Mr. Lee behaved more _____ than I did. (polite)

9   This is _____ time of Jane's life. (sad)

10 I think this device is _____ than others. (useful)

C 주어진 문장과 뜻이 같도록 비교급과 최상급을 이용하여 빈칸을 채우시오.

1   Mary says drawing pictures is more pleasant than cooking.
    ➡ Mary says cooking is ___*less pleasant*___ than drawing pictures.

2   I did not behave as bravely as Brandon did.
    ➡ Brandon behaved _____ than I did.

3   Tim was not as honest as John.
    ➡ John was _____ than Tim.

4   The English test is not as difficult as the math test.
    ➡ The math test is _____ than the English test.

5   The pasta doesn't taste as delicious as the pizza.
    ➡ The pizza tastes _____ than the pasta.

6   This is the shortest scarf in the shop.
    ➡ No other scarf is as _____ this in the shop.

7   My brother is taller than me. I'm 175 and he is 177.
    ➡ My brother is _____ than me.

8   I think trust is the most precious thing of all.
    ➡ I think nothing is _____ than trust.

9   Seoul and Busan are the most popular cities in Korea.
    ➡ Seoul is _____ cities in Korea.

10 No (other) teacher is more generous than Mr. Brown in our school.
    ➡ Mr. Brown is _____ than any other teacher in our school.

D 다음 우리말 해석에 맞게 주어진 단어를 알맞게 배열하여 문장을 완성하시오.

1 Lina는 그 고양이를 본 이후로 점점 더 빠르게 걷기 시작했다.
(Lina, faster, to, faster, began, and, walk)

➡ _Lina began to walk faster and faster_ after she saw the cat.

2 가격이 더 싸질수록 물건의 질은 더 떨어진다.
(the, becomes, lower, quality, the product's)

➡ The cheaper the price becomes, _____

_____

3 이 마을의 공기가 도시의 공기보다 덜 오염되었다.
(the, in the city, was, in this village, than, less, air, polluted, the air)

➡ _____

4 태풍의 피해는 사람들이 생각했던 것보다 더 심각하다.
(the damage, thought, more, is, people, of, serious, the storm, than)

➡ _____

5 이것은 내가 읽었던 소설 중에 가장 무서운 것이다.
(this, scariest, read, is, ever, novel, I've, the)

➡ _____

6 Jack은 우리가 만났던 사람 중에 가장 친절한 사람 중에 한 명이다.
(Jack, met, one, we've, is, people, kindest, of, the)

➡ _____

7 그는 학교 선거에서 가장 많은 표를 획득했다.
(he, election, in, got, the school, the, votes, most)

➡ _____

8 그녀가 그 일을 애써 잊으려 할수록 그 일은 또렷이 더 기억날 것이다.
(the, forget, the, harder, it, more, she, clearly, tries to, remembers, the thing, she)

➡ _____

9 그는 나이가 들수록 점점 더 관대해졌다.
(he, generous, more, became, more, and)

➡ As he got older, _____

9 Jina는 자기의 이모보다 아기를 더 잘 돌보았다.
(Jina, did, care, her aunt, took, than, the baby, better, of)

➡ _____

중간 기말고사 예상문제

내신 최다 출제 유형

01 다음 중 어법상 틀린 것을 고르시오. [출제 예상 90%]

① I thought a trip by train would be far cheaper.
② What is the longer river in the world?
③ He needs a bigger size.
④ No one is more important than myself.
⑤ The is the best festival I have ever had.

02 다음 중 주어진 문장과 의미가 같은 것을 고르시오. [출제 예상 85%]

> Math isn't so easy as science.

① Science is more difficult than math.
② Science is the easiest subject.
③ Science is not easier than math.
④ Science is as easy as math.
⑤ Science is easier than math.

03 다음 두 문장의 의미가 서로 다른 것을 고르시오. [출제 예상 85%]

① I am better at English than John.
  → John is not as good at English as me.
② Most of the girls are more worried than boys about their looks.
  → Boys are less worried about their looks than most of girls.
③ I probably behave more gently with ladies.
  → I probably don't behave as gently with men as I do with ladies.
④ Boys are as sensitive as girls.
  → Girls are less sensitive than boys.
⑤ Tony is noisier than Jack.
  → Jack is not as noisy as Tony.

04 다음 글의 ⓐ ~ ⓒ에 알맞은 단어들이 바르게 짝지어진 것을 고르시오. [출제 예상 80%]

> The elephant is one of the ⓐ smart / smarter / smartest animals on land. It is almost as ⓑ smart / smarter as a dolphin. The elephant ⓒ hard / hardly ever forgets its experiences.

① smarter – smart – hardly
② smartest – smarter – hardly
③ smartest – smart – hardly
④ smartest – smart – hard
⑤ smartest – smarter – hard

05 다음 대화의 빈칸 ⓐ ~ ⓒ에 들어갈 말이 바르게 짝지어진 것을 고르시오. [출제 예상 90%]

> **A** I think dogs are _____ ⓐ _____ than cats. Dogs are man's best friends.
> **B** You're right. But cats are _____ ⓑ _____ than dogs.
> **A** You're right, however, among all the different kinds of pets, dogs are the _____ ⓒ _____.

① trustworthy – interesting – popular
② more trustworthy – more interesting – most popular
③ more trustworthy – interesting – most popular
④ trustworthier – more interesting – popularest
⑤ more trustworthy – most interesting – more popular

318   Grammar Master Level 3

[01~03] 다음 중 형용사 또는 부사의 비교가 잘못 연결된 것을 고르시오.

01
① small − smaller − smallest
② tired − more tired − most tired
③ hot − hotter − hottest
④ exciting − excitinger − excitingest
⑤ well − better − best

02
① funny − funnier − funniest
② nice − niceer − niceest
③ many − more − most
④ boring − more boring − most boring
⑤ little − less − least

03
① difficult − more difficult − most difficult
② easy − easier − easiest
③ curious − curiouser − curiousest
④ slowly − more slowly − most slowly
⑤ bad − worse − worst

[04~06] 다음 빈칸에 들어갈 알맞은 것을 고르시오.

04

> If you eat _____ calories than you use, you will lose weight.

① little   ② less   ③ least
④ few   ⑤ fewer

05

> She thought he would love riding a bike _____ riding a motorcycle.

① much as she as
② as much as she enjoyed
③ as did much as she
④ as much she enjoy as
⑤ as she did as much

06

> If you follow that advice, you will become _____ than you are now.

① healthier   ② so healthy
③ healthy   ④ more healthy
⑤ most healthy

★★★
07 다음 중 밑줄 친 much의 쓰임이 나머지 넷과 다른 것을 고르시오.

① Thank you so <u>much</u> for replying me.
② If we had no body language, it would be <u>much</u> harder to communicate.
③ I was able to learn <u>much</u> about different cultures.
④ Be careful not to buy too <u>much</u> clothes.
⑤ She said that she had a habit of eating candies too <u>much</u>.

08 다음 중 어법상 옳은 것을 고르시오.

① She is one of the best singer in Korea.

② I prefer watching TV to play outside.

③ He is smartest student at his school.

④ Fortunately, the little bird got good and good.

⑤ Her son was in the most famous soccer player.

★★★
09 다음 문장 중 나머지 넷과 의미가 다른 것을 고르시오.

① No country in the world is as small as Vatican City.

② No country in the world is smaller than Vatican City.

③ Vatican City is not as small as any other country in the world.

④ Vatican City is the smallest country in the world.

⑤ Vatican City is smaller than any other country in the world.

10 다음 중 어법상 어색한 것을 고르시오.

① I think line A is longer than line B.

② I think your doll is cuter than hers.

③ People might use genetic engineering to make it stronger.

④ Left-handed people tend to better at art.

⑤ Tony is much shorter than any other boy in his class.

11 주어진 문장과 의미가 같은 것을 모두 고르시오.

> Soybean paste soup is the best dish at this restaurant.

① Soybean paste soup is not as good as any other dish at this restaurant.

② Soybean paste soup is better than any other dish at this restaurant.

③ Nothing is better than soybean paste soup at this restaurant.

④ Soybean paste soup is very good at this restaurant.

⑤ Nothing is not as good as soybean paste soup at this restaurant.

Note soybean paste soup 된장국

12 다음 문장의 빈칸에 들어갈 수 없는 것을 고르시오.

> In the country, farmers want _____ higher prices for their goods.

① very   ② even   ③ far
④ much   ⑤ still

13 다음 문장의 밑줄 친 부분과 바꿔 쓸 수 있는 것을 고르시오.

> Lucy decided to go to school as fast as she could.

① possible   ② she can   ③ able
④ could   ⑤ ability

★★★
14 다음 중 짝지어진 두 문장의 의미가 서로 같지 <u>않은</u> 것을 고르시오.

① English is harder than Chinese.
= Chinese is less hard than English.

② She was so pretty that she could be an actress.
= She was so pretty enough to be an actress.

③ I don't know what to do.
= I don't know what I should do.

④ He is too short to reach the top.
= He is so short that he can reach the top.

⑤ No matter what I want, he'll get it for me.
= Whatever I want, he'll get it for me.

[15~16] 다음 두 문장의 의미가 같도록 빈칸에 알맞은 것을 고르시오.

15
Junho is bigger than Max.
= Max is _____ big _____ Junho.

① as — as
② so — as
③ not so — as
④ not less — than
⑤ not so — than

16
He is the most popular singer in Korea.
= He is _____ than _____ other singer in Korea.

① popular — any
② more popular — some
③ the most popular — any
④ popular — some
⑤ more popular — any

[17~19] 다음 빈칸에 들어갈 말로 알맞은 것을 고르시오.

17
I think the world will be much _____ than it is now.

① good
② well
③ best
④ better
⑤ worst

18
As the China is becoming stronger, people need to use Chinese _____ more than before.

① a lot of
② a lot
③ too
④ many
⑤ else

19
On the final exam report, most of the subjects' grades got _____ by 10 percent.

① worst
② much
③ better
④ more
⑤ best

20 다음 주어진 문장과 의미가 같은 것을 고르시오.

> New York is the most crowded city in America.

① Every city in America is as crowded as New York.
② New York is as crowded as other cities in America.
③ New York is not so much crowded as other cities in America.
④ Every city in America is more crowded than New York.
⑤ No city in America is as crowded as New York.

[21~22] 다음 우리말과 같은 뜻이 되도록 빈칸에 들어갈 알맞은 말을 고르시오.

21

> 날씨가 추워질수록 나는 기분이 더 좋아진다.
> = _____ the weather is, _____ I feel.

① Cold − good
② Coldest − best
③ Colder − better
④ The colder − the better
⑤ The coldest − the better

22

> 너의 이야기는 가능한 한 구체적으로 쓰여야 한다.
> = Your story should be written as _____ as _____.

① specifically − can
② specifically − can be
③ specifically − possible
④ specific − can
⑤ specific − could

23 다음 우리말을 영어로 잘못 옮긴 것을 고르시오.

① 그녀는 200달러나 가지고 있다.
 → She has as much as 200 dollars.
② 나는 공부를 더 열심히 할수록 더 스트레스를 받는다.
 → The harder I study, the most stressed I get.
③ 이 프로그램은 저것보다 인기가 덜하다.
 → This program is less popular than that one.
④ Judy는 나보다 예쁘다.
 → Judy is prettier than I am.
⑤ 그의 자전거가 나의 것보다 훨씬 좋다.
 → His bike is much better than mine.

24 다음 중 주어진 문장의 밑줄 친 부분과 의미가 같은 것을 고르시오.

> Bulgoggi tastes as good as rib eye steak.

① Boys are good at English as well as math.
② Some of the men are noisy as well as talkative.
③ Husbands do the dishes as well as clean the house.
④ I play soccer as well as John.
⑤ Boys as well as girls can play badminton.

25 다음 빈칸에 들어갈 알맞은 것을 고르시오.

> The nicer you are, _____.

① the better everyone felt
② the best you make everyone
③ the better everyone feels
④ the better you felt
⑤ to be best you are

[26~27] 다음 빈칸에 알맞은 것을 고르시오.

26

> This stone tower is _____ tower in this temple.

① the second tallest
② the second tall
③ a second tallest
④ the second taller
⑤ second tallest

27

> The lake, Black Pool, is _____ than all the other lakes in the world.

① less frightening
② frightened
③ frightening
④ more frightening
⑤ most frightening

◇◇◇◇◇◇◇◇◇ 서술형 평가 ◇◇◇◇◇◇◇◇◇

[28~30] 다음 우리말과 같은 뜻이 되도록 빈칸에 알맞은 말을 쓰시오.

28

> 더욱 스릴이 있을수록 Tom은 그것을 더 즐긴다.

➡ _____ the activity, the more Tom enjoys it.

29

> 화가가 그녀를 방문할 때마다 그녀는 점점 더 긴장했다.

➡ _____ a painter visited her, she was _____ nervous.

30

> Jenny의 정원은 David의 정원보다 세 배나 큰 정원이다.

➡ Jenny's garden is a big garden. It is _____ David's.

10. 비교구문   **323**

중간 기말고사 예상문제

[31~33] 다음 두 문장이 같은 뜻이 되도록 빈칸에 알맞은 말을 쓰시오.

★★★
31

This is the most expensive dress in the world.

➡ This is _____ _____ than _____ _____ _____ _____ in the world.

32

Her favorite food is kimchi soup.

➡ There's _____ _____ that she likes _____ _____ kimchi soup.

33

Designing a wedding dress is not as easy as I thought.

➡ Designing a wedding dress is _____ _____ _____ I thought.

[34~36] 우리말과 같은 뜻이 되도록 괄호 안의 단어를 바르게 배열하여 쓰시오.

★★★
34

나는 5권의 책을 사는 데 겨우 10달러를 썼다.
(I / no / spent / than / more / to / buy / books / five / ten / dollars)

➡ _____

35

Rachel은 평균체중 보다 과체중이다.
(Rachel / average weight / is / more / than / overweight / the)

➡ _____

36

더 많은 그림을 그릴수록 더욱 잘 그림을 그리게 될 거야.
(The / more / you'll / you / draw ×2 / pictures ×2 / the / better)

➡ _____

★★★
37 다음 최상급의 문장을 괄호 안의 지시어대로 바꿔 쓰시오.

Mt. Everest is the highest mountain in the world.

(1) _____
_____
(no ~ as ~ as)

(2) _____
_____
(~ than all the other)

(3) _____
_____
(~ than any other)

11

Chapter
가정법

Point Check I

◆ **가정법:** 어떤 일이 일어날 가능성이 없을 때 그 반대의 의미를 가정해 나타낼 때 사용한다.

1. 가정법의 종류

if	조건	• If William comes back, we will go camping together.
	과거	• If it rained now, we couldn't go hiking.
	과거완료	• If it had stormed yesterday, we would have canceled the flight.
I wish	과거	• I wish he asked me a date.
	과거완료	• I wish you had bought it yesterday.
as if	과거	• He acted af if he didn't understand the question.
	과거완료	• She talked as if Tom had left recently.

2. Without (But for) 가정법

과거 ~이 없다면	**Without (But for) ..., 주어 + 조동사 과거 + 동사원형** Without her help, I could not solve this problem. = But for her help, I could not solve this problem.
과거완료 ~이 없었다면	**Without (But for) ..., 주어 + 조동사 과거 + have 과거분사** Without this cell phone, I wouldn't have called to my mom. = But for this cell phone, I wouldn't have called to my mom.

가정법 과거

• **가정법 과거**: 현재의 사실과 반대되는 일이나 현재에 일어날 것 같지 않은 일을 가정해서 말할 때 사용한다.

1. 가정법 과거: 현재의 사실과 반대되는 가정을 말한다.

의미	만약 …한다면(…라면) ~일 텐데
형태	If + 주어 + 과거형…주어 + would (could / should / might) + 동사원형~
예문	• If I were tall and thin, I could be a model. 　= As I am not tall and thin, I can't be a model. [직설법 현재형] 　= I am not tall and thin, so I can't be a model.

➡ 직설법의 긍정은 가정법에서 부정으로 표현하고, 직설법의 부정은 가정법에서 긍정으로 표현

➡ 가정법 과거는 현재 사실에 대한 반대를 나타내기 때문에 직설법으로 전환할 때 시제 역시 한 시제 후의 것으로 나타낸다.

• **If** you **didn't want to** go there, your friends **might** be disappointed.
　= **As** you **want to** go there, your friends **may not** be disappointed.

2. 단순 조건절 'if'와 가정법 과거의 비교

단순 조건절	• If we finish work late at night, we will have to take a taxi. 　= Maybe we'll finish work late at night, so maybe we'll have to take a taxi. ➡ 단순 조건은 앞으로 그럴 수도 있는 가능성을 나타내는 표현으로 'if' 조건절에는 현재형을, 주절에는 미래형을 사용한다.
가정법 과거	• If we finished the work late at nigh, we would have to take a taxi. 　= We don't finish the work late at night, so we won't have to take a taxi. ➡ 가정법 과거는 주절과 조건절에 모두 과거형을 사용한다.

3. 가정법 과거의 be동사: If절의 be동사는 인칭에 상관없이 'were'를 사용한다.

• **If** he **were** kind, everyone **would** like him.
　= He **is not** kind, so everyone **doesn't** like him.

➡ 구어체(회화)에서는 인칭에 따라 'was'를 사용하기도 한다.

 Answer Keys p. 44

A   다음을 가정법 문장으로 바꾸어 쓰시오.

1   As she's tired, she can't study all night.

➡ _____ *If she were not tired, she could study all night.* _____

2   As I'm sick, I can't participate in the contest.

➡ _____

3   As he doesn't like Italian food, he won't join us for lunch.

➡ _____

4   As it snows heavily, the baseball game won't be held.

➡ _____

5   As they don't know her address, they can't visit her.

➡ _____

6   Harry doesn't miss the bus, so he'll not take a taxi.

➡ _____

7   As we have more time, we can play with our daughter.

➡ _____

8   As Mary doesn't speak Korean, she doesn't talk to people.

➡ _____

9   As I don't have a sister, I can't play dolls with her.

➡ _____

10   As we go to the party, we can enjoy the holiday.

➡ _____

가정법 과거완료

- **가정법 과거완료:** 과거의 사실과 반대되는 일이나 일어날 것 같지 않은 과거의 일을 가정해서 말할 때 사용한다.
- **혼합 가정법:** 'if'가 있는 조건절에서는 과거의 사실과 반대되는 일을 가정하고, 주절에서는 현재의 사실을 나타내는 문장을 말한다.

1. 가정법 과거완료: 과거 사실과 반대되는 가정을 말한다.

의미	만약 ...했었다면(...이었다면) ~했었을(이었을) 텐데
형태	If + 주어 + had + 과거분사...주어 + would (could / should / might) + have + 과거분사~ ➡ if 절에서 과거보다 이전 과거인 대과거 시제를 사용한다.
예문	• If I had listened to him, I wouldn't have made a mistake. = As I didn't listen to him, I made a mistake. [직설법 과거형] = I didn't listen to him, so I made a mistake.

➡ 가정법 과거완료의 조건절은 '과거완료 (had p.p.)'를 사용한다.

2. 혼합 가정법: 조건절은 과거 사실과 반대, 주절은 현재의 사실을 나타낸다.

의미	(과거에) 만약 ~했다면, (지금) ...일텐데
형태	If + 주어 + had + 과거분사...주어 + would (could / should / might) + 동사원형~
예문	• If she had practiced hard, she would get first prize in the contest. = As she didn't practice hard, she doesn't get first prize in the contest.

➡ 혼합 가정법은 과거의 사실이 현재까지 영향을 미치는 경우에 사용한다.

Grammar Plus +

- **혼합 가정법에서 직설법 문장으로 전환할 때**
  ① 'if'절의 'had+과거분사' → 과거형
  ② 주절의 '조동사 과거+동사원형' → 현재형
  ③ 긍정 (부정) → 부정 (긍정)

If I **had worn** the life vest, I **could play** in the pool now.
➡ **As** I **didn't wear** the life vest, I **can't play** in the pool now.

➡ 혼합 가정법에서 보통 if 절에는 과거, 주절에는 현재를 나타내는 부사(구)를 사용한다.

Answer Keys p. 44

A 다음을 가정법 과거완료 문장으로 바꾸어 쓰시오.

1 As I didn't move to Seoul last month, I couldn't meet her.

➡ *If I had moved to Seoul last month, I could have met her.*

2 As he wasn't careful, he made a big mistake.

➡ _____

3 As it rained, Tim couldn't go hiking.

➡ _____

4 As she saw a horror movie alone that night, she couldn't sleep well.

➡ _____

5 As I didn't have a serious problem, I didn't call her for help.

➡ _____

6 As we didn't play the piano well, the orchestra would not accept us.

➡ _____

7 As Mina didn't write the letter in English, I could read it.

➡ _____

8 As he didn't try to keep his promise, people didn't like him.

➡ _____

9 As I didn't make a different choice, the situation didn't change.

➡ _____

10 As she wasn't sleepy, she started to read a book.

➡ _____

Answer Keys p. 44

B 다음을 혼합 가정법 문장으로 바꾸어 쓰시오.

1   As she spent all her money, she can't buy a wallet.

➡   *If she hadn't spent all her money, she could buy a wallet.*

2   As John didn't study hard, he can't pass the exam.

➡   _____

3   As Alice lost my key, I can't enter the room.

➡   _____

4   As the girl didn't bring her book, the teacher is angry.

➡   _____

5   As Tim left, we feel so lonely.

➡   _____

6   As I broke my brother's laptop, he can't play games.

➡   _____

7   As Cindy didn't read the book, she can't complete the report.

➡   _____

8   As Nick called her this morning, she is not late for the meeting.

➡   _____

9   As he didn't exercise regularly, he isn't healthy now.

➡   _____

10   As he didn't register for the course, he can't take the exam.

➡   _____

• **I wish 가정법**: 과거, 현재, 미래에 실현 불가능하거나 이루기 힘든 소망을 표현할 때 'I wish' 가정법을 사용한다.

1. I wish 가정법 과거: 현재나 미래에 이룰 수 없는 것을 소망할 때 사용한다.

의미	～라면 좋을 텐데 (➡ 하지만 아니다)
형태	I wish (that) + 주어 + 과거형
예문	• I wish I lived in a house with a big garden. = I'm sorry I don't live in a house with a big garden. ➡ 'I wish 가정법'은 'I'm sorry + 직설법'으로 바꿔 쓸 수 있다.

➡ 미래에 있을 일에 대한 소망을 나타낼 때는 종속절에 'will' 대신 'would'를 사용한다.

• I **wish** we **would** take a trip to Europe for a month.
  = I'**m sorry** we **will not** take a trip to Europe for a month.

2. I wish 가정법 과거완료: 과거에 실현 불가능한 일이나 이루기 힘든 것을 소망할 때 사용한다.

의미	～였더라면 (했더라면) 좋았을 텐데 (➡ 그런데 아니었다)
형태	I wish (that) + 주어 + 과거완료(had+p.p)
예문	• I wish Jennifer had taken a trip. = I'm sorry Jennifer didn't take a trip.

 **Check up!**

Answer Keys p. 44~45

A 다음을 I wish 가정법 문장으로 바꾸어 쓰시오.

1 I'm sorry you are feeling lonely today.

➡ I wish _____*you were not feeling lonely today.*_____

2 I'm sorry they are not here with us.

➡ I wish _____

3 I don't have money to buy that luxurious bag.

➡ I wish _____

4   I'm sorry he didn't go to the wine festival with us.

⇒ I wish _____

5   I laughed at one of our classmates. I regret it.

⇒ I wish _____

6   I'm sorry my sister ate too much salad for breakfast.

⇒ I wish _____

7   I'm sorry the teacher didn't give us information related to the test.

⇒ I wish _____

8   We don't live in a world free from disease.

⇒ I wish _____

9   I'm sorry Jane didn't take a taxi.

⇒ I wish _____

10   I regret that I did not start preparing for the party earlier.

⇒ I wish _____

11   I'm sorry I couldn't make your dress early.

⇒ I wish _____

12   I didn't travel around the country when I was young.

⇒ I wish _____

13   I regret that I did not pay attention to the people around me.

⇒ I wish _____

14   There are not enough restrooms in the park.

⇒ I wish _____

15   I regret that I didn't call him last night.

⇒ I wish _____

as if 가정법

• **as if 가정법**: 과거나 현재의 사실과 반대되는 일 또는 일어날 것 같지 않은 과거나 현재의 일을 가정해서 말할 때 사용한다.

1. as if + 가정법 과거: 현재의 사실과 반대되는 것을 그러한 것처럼 표현한다.

의미	마치 ...처럼 ~하다
형태	[주어＋동사의 현재형 ~ as if(as though)＋주어＋과거형]
예문	• David acts as if he were popular at school. 　= In fact, David isn't popular at school.

→ 'as if 가정법 과거'는 <u>주절의 시제와 가정의 상황이 동시적일 경우</u>에 사용한다.

2. as if + 가정법 과거완료: 과거의 사실과 반대되는 것을 그랬던 것처럼 표현한다.

의미	마치 ...였던 것처럼 ~하다
형태	[주어＋동사의 현재형 ~ as if(as though)＋주어＋과거완료]
예문	• Jessica talks as if she had gone to Africa to help sick people. 　= In fact, Jessica didn't go to Africa to help sick people.

→ 'as if 가정법 과거완료'는 <u>주절의 시제보다 가정의 상황이 이전인 경우</u>에 사용한다.

3. as if + 직설법: 사실과 반대가 아니라 그럴 가능성이 있을 경우 직설법 문장을 사용한다.

• Oliver looks **as if** <u>he has no money at all</u>. [➡ 사실 돈이 많을 수도 있다.]

4. 가정법의 명사절: '제안, 명령, 요구, 주장' 등을 의미하는 동사의 목적어로 'that'절이 오면 동사는 'should ＋ 동사원형'의 형태가 된다. (should는 생략이 가능하다)

suggest, order, demand, insist request, require, recommend	＋	that＋주어＋(should)＋동사원형

• Nicole ordered **that** her children **(should) stay** at home today.

Answer Keys p. 45

A 주어진 문장과 뜻이 같도록 빈칸에 알맞은 말을 쓰시오.

1 In fact, he wasn't a very famous actor in America.

➡ He sounds _as if he had been a very famous actor in America._

2 In fact, the boys don't like to play soccer.

➡ The boys act _____

3 In fact, she didn't study English literature in college.

➡ She pretended _____

4 In fact, the man was not a scientist.

➡ The man behaved _____

5 In fact, she doesn't go to church.

➡ She pretends _____

6 In fact, Mijin didn't witness the car accident.

➡ Mijin talked _____

7 In fact, the police had not made much effort to find the lost dog.

➡ The police pretended _____

8 In fact, James is not a professional photographer.

➡ James acts _____

9 In fact, the boy likes her very much.

➡ The boy behaves _____

10 In fact, we had made the same mistake again.

➡ We pretended _____

B 다음 괄호 안의 동사의 올바른 형태를 빈칸에 쓰시오.

1 I suggested that he _____ at once. (가다)

2 The captain ordered that the soldiers _____ the building.
(파괴하다)

3 It is necessary that everyone _____ in the report by Tuesday.
(제출하다)

4 The doctor recommends that she _____ the medicine twice
a day. (먹다)

5 The teacher ordered him _____ finish his homework. (끝내다)

Grammar Plus +

• 'as if+주어+과거형'을
쓰는 경우

① 주절의 동사가 현재이고,
가정의 상황이 같은 시제일 때
ex) In fact, she <u>likes</u> to eat
chocolate ice cream.
→ She <u>acts</u> as if she
<u>didn't like</u> to eat chocolate
ice cream.

② 주절의 동사와 가정의 상황의
동사가 동시 발생일 때
ex) In fact, I'm not a
princess in a movie.
→ I felt as if I were a
princess in a movie.

• 'as if+주어+had+과거분사'
를 쓰는 경우

① 주절의 동사가 현재이고, 가정
의 상황이 과거일 때
ex) In fact, I <u>didn't finish</u>
my homework.
→ I <u>act</u> as if I <u>had finished</u>
my homework.

② 주절의 동사가 과거이고, 가정
의 상황이 같은 시제일 때
ex) In fact, he <u>was not</u> a
doctor.
→ He <u>acted</u> as if he <u>had
been</u> a doctor.

③ 주절이 과거이고, 가정의 상황
이 과거완료일 때
ex) In fact, they <u>had drunk</u>
apple juice.
→ They <u>acted</u> as if they
<u>had not drunk</u> apple juice.

'if' 이외의 가정법 표현

• 'if'를 사용하지 않고, 'without', 'but for'로 가정법을 나타낼 수도 있다.

1. Without (But for) + 명사 + 가정법 과거: 현재의 사실과 반대되는 경우에 사용한다.

의미	～이 없다면
형태	Without (But for) ..., 주어 + would (could, should, might) + 동사원형
예문	• Without water and air, we could not live. = But for water and air, we could not live. = If it were not for water and air, we could not live.

2. Without (But for) + 명사 + 가정법 과거완료: 과거의 사실과 반대되는 경우에 사용한다.

의미	～이 없었다면
형태	Without (But for) ..., 주어 + would (could, should, might) + have + 과거분사
예문	• Without his advice, Marilyn wouldn't have become a movie star. = But for his advice, Marilyn wouldn't have become a movie star. = If it had not been for his advice, Marilyn wouldn't have become a movie star.

Answer Keys p. 45

A 다음 두 문장의 뜻이 같도록 빈칸에 알맞은 말을 채우시오.

1 Without her advice, I couldn't have accomplished it.

➡ _____If it had not been for her advice,_____, I couldn't have accomplished it.

2 What would have happened without this device?

➡ What would have happened _____

3 But for this map, we couldn't find our base camp.

➡ _____, we couldn't find our base camp.

4 Without the book, students couldn't have finished their homework.

➡ _____, students couldn't have finished their homework.

5 But for the dictionary, she couldn't write the letter in English.

➡ _____ she couldn't write the letter in English.

Practice More I

Answer Keys p. 45

A 주어진 문장과 의미가 같도록 빈칸을 채우시오.

1   I'm sorry I'm not a professional model.
    ➡ I wish _____ *I were a professional model.* _____

2   As she's not young, she can live alone.
    ➡ If _____ young, _____ alone.

3   As Amy didn't take the medicine, she has a stomachache.
    ➡ If Amy _____ she _____
    a stomachache.

4   As he earns enough money, he can buy the house.
    ➡ If _____ enough money, he _____
    the house.

5   I regret that I didn't pay attention to the dangerous situation.
    ➡ I wish _____

6   In fact, John didn't have much money to buy a car.
    ➡ John pretended _____

7   As I finished the project, I took a nap for a while.
    ➡ If I _____ the project, I _____
    a nap for a while.

8   As he stayed up last night, he is really tired now.
    ➡ If he _____ last night, he _____
    really tired now.

9   As Mike didn't own a car, he didn't drive to school.
    ➡ If Mike _____ a car, he _____
    to school.

10 Without this guide, I couldn't find our destination.
    ➡ _____ I couldn't find our destination.

B 다음 문장에서 어법상 <u>어색한</u> 부분을 찾아 바르게 고치시오.

1   If she is a famous model, she could travel all around the world.
    _____ *is* _____ ➡ _____ *were* _____

2   If I speak Chinese well, I would go and live there.
    _____ ➡ _____

3   If the team had won the game, they would be the top team in
     Korea.   _____ ➡ _____

4   He talks as if he is brave.   _____ ➡ _____

5   Linda behaves as if she knows nothing.
                               _____ ➡ _____

6   I wish my brother listened to what my parents say.
                               _____ ➡ _____

7   He ordered that the work is finished.
                               _____ ➡ _____

8   I wish I have a brother or a sister.
                               _____ ➡ _____

9   If they hadn't studied hard, they couldn't pass the test.
                               _____ ➡ _____

C   다음을 가정법 문장으로 다시 쓰시오.

1   I'm sorry she won't stop eating too much.
     ➡   _____ *I wish she would stop eating too much.* _____

2   As he broke his leg, he can't go skating with us.
     ➡ _____

3   As she was the only child, she felt lonely.
     ➡ _____

4   I'm sorry that their best album doesn't sell well.
     ➡ _____

5   In fact, Sara couldn't afford to buy the newest car.
     ➡ Sara behaved _____

6   As I have the device, I can repair my watch by myself.
     ➡ _____ I couldn't repair my watch by myself.

7   But for the Internet, we would have confronted many terrible
     problems.
     ➡ _____ we would have confronted many
        terrible problems.

8 I regret that I didn't take the graduation exam last semester.

➡ _____

9 I'm sorry that I didn't accept his proposal last week.

➡ _____

10 But for the rope, we couldn't have survived.

➡ _____ we couldn't have survived.

D 주어진 단어를 알맞게 배열하여 문장을 완성하시오.

1 (she, as if, her sister, pretended, with, had, a good relationship, she)

➡ *She pretended as if she had a good relationship with her sister.*

2 (if, loved, she, the cooking book, Kate, have decided, buy, hadn't, Italian food, wouldn't, to)

➡ _____

3 (she, as if, by, pretends, the novel, herself, wrote, she)

➡ _____

4 (I, as if, English, feel, real, teacher, were, a, I)

➡ _____

5 (if, the lottery, we, of, each, we, have given, had won, would, to, one, 1,000 dollars, you)

➡ _____

6 (it, the leader, important, the game, is, the rules, change, that, of)

➡ _____

7 (if, a great professor, I, a good teacher, could, hadn't, become, I, met, not, have)

➡ _____

8 (I, the weather, freezing, wish, cold, not, be, would)

➡ _____

내신 최다 출제 유형

01 다음 우리말을 영어로 바르게 옮긴 것을 고르시오.

[출제 예상 85%]

> 네가 시험에 합격했더라면 좋았을 텐데.

① I wish you passed the exam.
② I wish you pass the exam.
③ I wish you had passed the exam.
④ I wish you were passed the exam.
⑤ I wish you will pass the exam.

02 다음 두 문장이 같은 뜻이 되도록 할 때 빈칸에 들어갈 알맞은 말을 고르시오.

[출제 예상 90%]

> I stayed at home because the weather was so bad.
> = If the weather _____ so bad, I _____ at home.

① are not – will not stay
② were not – wouldn't stay
③ had been – would have stayed
④ hadn't been – would stay
⑤ hadn't been – wouldn't have stayed

03 다음 중 빈칸에 알맞지 않은 것을 고르시오.

[출제 예상 85%]

> _____, we wouldn't have anything to do for the concert.

① Without her
② If it had not been for her
③ If it were not for her
④ Were it not for her
⑤ But for her

04 다음 주어진 문장과 의미가 같은 것을 고르시오.

[출제 예상 90%]

> If it had been rainy, we would have canceled the picnic.

① We didn't cancel the picnic because it wasn't rainy.
② We didn't cancel the picnic because it isn't rainy.
③ We doesn't cancel the picnic because it wasn't rainy.
④ We canceled the picnic because it was rainy.
⑤ We doesn't cancel the picnic because it isn't rainy.

05 다음 중 어법상 어색한 것을 고르시오. [출제 예상 85%]

① If they had left early, they wouldn't have missed the train.
② Julie would be nervous if Kevin refused her request.
③ If he had taken your advice last year, he would have passed the exam.
④ If I had a time machine, I would travel to the future.
⑤ If she asked me then, I would have helped her.

06 우리말과 같도록 괄호 안의 단어들을 바르게 배열하여 문장을 완성하시오.

[출제 예상 85%]

> 나는 마치 내가 그 영화 속의 공주인 것처럼 느껴졌다.
> (as / were / princess / if / a / in / movie / a / I)

➡ I felt _____.

[01~02] 다음 밑줄 친 부분의 쓰임이 <u>잘못된</u> 것을 고르시오.

01
① I wish I <u>could</u> speak Japanese well.
② He insisted that he <u>follows</u> Justin.
③ If you <u>have</u> some money, you can buy that bike.
④ She stood there as if she <u>were</u> a model.
⑤ If he <u>climbs</u> the top, he'll know what happened there.

★★★
02
① If I were you, I <u>would not make</u> that mistake.
② She pretends as if she <u>knew</u> nothing at all.
③ I wish my father <u>could be</u> here with me now.
④ If he <u>had wanted</u> to, he could have become an actor.
⑤ She wouldn't be what she is if her mother <u>didn't support</u> her when she was young.

03 다음 중 밑줄 친 <u>if</u>의 용법이 나머지 넷과 <u>다른</u> 하나를 고르시오.

① I'll be happy <u>if</u> you accept our invitation.
② I still wonder <u>if</u> she really loved her job.
③ <u>If</u> my sister is sick, I will take care of her.
④ You can choose her <u>if</u> you think she's the best.
⑤ <u>If</u> you want to be a model, you must exercise regularly.

★★★
04 다음 주어진 문장을 가정법 문장으로 바르게 바꾼 것을 고르시오.

> As she was not qualified for the job, she could not get it.

① If she had been qualified for the job, she couldn't have gotten it.
② If she had qualified for the job, she could have gotten it.
③ If she had been qualified for the job, she could have gotten it.
④ If she was qualified for the job, she could have gotten it.
⑤ If she was qualified for the job, she could got it.

[05~06] 다음 빈칸에 들어갈 알맞은 말을 고르시오.

05
> I wish I _____ a decision last night.

① had made   ② made   ③ make
④ makes   ⑤ to make

06
> If she _____ closer to the office, she could walk there.

① had lived   ② live   ③ lived
④ would live   ⑤ have lived

07 다음 문장의 밑줄 친 부분 중 쓰임이 올바른 것을 고르시오.

① My life would be different now if I <u>had not worked</u> hard.

② I'll tell him everything when he <u>will come</u> back here.

③ It is important that she <u>keeps</u> her word.

④ If I <u>am</u> a goddess, I would make the world happy.

⑤ She doesn't know if he <u>helps</u> her move tomorrow.

08 다음 중 밑줄 친 부분과 바꿔 쓸 수 있는 것을 고르시오.

> <u>Without her</u>, we couldn't finish the project.

① If it is not for her

② If it were for her

③ If it had not been for her

④ If it has not been for her

⑤ If it were not for her

★★★
09 다음 중 어법상 어색한 것을 고르시오.

① Keep silent, or you might find yourself out of work.

② I wish you had come to this place with me.

③ My teacher advised that we follow the rule.

④ I am walking as if I had been a model on the stage.

⑤ Catch me if you can.

[10~11] 다음 가정법 문장을 직설법 문장으로 바르게 바꾼 것을 고르시오.

10
> She talks as if she had read the book.

① In fact, she read the book.

② In fact, she didn't read the book.

③ In fact, she reads the book.

④ In fact, she doesn't read the book.

⑤ In fact, she had read the book.

11
> I pretend as if I were not interested in the rumor.

① In fact, I am not interested in the rumor.

② In fact, I was interested in the rumor.

③ In fact, I am interested in the rumor.

④ In fact, I was not interested in the rumor.

⑤ In fact, I'll be interested in the rumor.

[12~13] 다음 우리말을 영어로 바르게 옮긴 것을 고르시오.

★★★
12
> 만약 내가 너의 전화번호를 알았더라면 그때 너에게 전화를 했을 텐데.

① If I had known your phone number, I would call you then.

② If I had known your phone number, I would have called you then.

③ If I knew your phone number, I would call you then.

④ If I knew your phone number, I have called you then.

⑤ If I had known your phone number, I would had called you then.

13 만약 내가 더 어리다면 중국어 공부를 할텐데.

① If I have been younger, I would have studied Chinese.

② If I was young, I would study Chinese.

③ If I had been younger, I would had studied Chinese.

④ If I were younger, I would have studied Chinese.

⑤ If I were younger, I would study Chinese.

[14~15] 다음 밑줄 친 부분 중 어법상 어색한 것을 고르시오.

14 ① Jane would have been late but for my help.

② If I were you, I would look for another job.

③ I wish she had been a little bit more quiet.

④ I would buy that bike if it is cheaper.

⑤ If you had taken the subway, you would have arrived on time.

15 ① I asked that they looked for the missing cat.

② Mr. Jackson insisted that we trust other people.

③ It is necessary that the law be followed by all people.

④ The general ordered that the flag be raised.

⑤ It is important that the hostages are still alive.

[16~17] 다음 글의 밑줄 친 부분 중 어법상 어색한 것을 고르시오.

16 ① When the young woman ② talks to her friends, she always ③ acts ④ as if she ⑤ is an old woman.

17 ① If he ② studied English ③ when he ④ was young, his pronunciation ⑤ would be better now.

[18~19] 다음 빈칸에 알맞은 말을 고르시오.

18 I don't have any older brother. I wish _____.

① I have no older brother

② I had an older brother

③ I didn't have an older brother

④ I have an older brother

⑤ I have had an older brother

19

> He speaks as if he were my boyfriend.
> In fact, _____.

① I am not his girlfriend
② he is my boyfriend
③ he was my boyfriend
④ he isn't my boyfriend
⑤ I was his girlfriend

20 다음 빈칸에 공통으로 들어갈 말로 알맞은 것을 고르시오.

> • _____ his help, I would have failed the interview.
> • _____ air, no one could live.

① With   ② Without   ③ But
④ In   ⑤ Because of

21 다음 주어진 문장과 의미가 같은 것을 고르시오.

> I wish she had not gone back to Canada.

① I'm sorry she has not gone back to Canada.
② I'm sorry she didn't go back to Canada.
③ I'm sorry she goes back to Canada.
④ I'm sorry she would go back to Canada.
⑤ I'm sorry she went back to Canada.

22 다음 대화의 빈칸에 들어갈 말이 바르게 짝지어진 것을 고르시오.

> **A** If you could bring five items with you to a deserted island, what _____ you choose?
> **B** A firestone, a lantern, a knife, my boyfriend, and whatever he wants to _____.
> **A** It sounds nice. And you know what? James wishes he _____ your boyfriend.

① will − take − is
② would − bring − were
③ will − brought − were
④ would − brought − is
⑤ will − brought − were

◇◇◇◇◇◇◇◇◇ 서술형 평가 ◇◇◇◇◇◇◇◇◇

[23~25] 다음 주어진 문장을 괄호 안의 지시어대로 바꿔 쓰시오.

23

> In fact, she didn't cook the food by herself.

➡ She talks _____.
  (as if 가정법)

24

Kelly didn't come to my party because of her work schedule.

➡ I wish _____ in spite of her work schedule. (I wish 가정법)

★★★
25

As I didn't take your advice then, I'm not happy now.

➡ If _____, I _____ happy now. (혼합 가정법)

[26~28] 다음 우리말과 같은 뜻이 되도록 빈칸에 알맞은 말을 쓰시오.

26

만약 어제 눈이 오지 않았다면 우리는 지금 등산을 할 수 있을 텐데.

➡ If it _____ _____ yesterday, we _____ _____ the mountain now.

27

내 여동생은 마치 지난밤에 유령을 보았던 것처럼 말한다.

➡ My sister _____ _____ _____ _____ _____ _____ a ghost last night.

28

만약 네가 괜찮다면 그는 너와 스키 타러 갈 텐데.

➡ If you _____ _____, he _____ _____ skiing with you.

[29~30] 다음 우리말과 같은 뜻이 되도록 괄호 안의 단어를 이용하여 문장을 쓰시오.

★★★
29

내가 억만장자라면 좋을 텐데.

➡ _____ a billionaire. (be)

★★★
30

그녀는 마치 유명한 사람처럼 행동한다.

➡ _____ a famous person. (act)

11. 가정법 **345**

Note

12

Chapter
관계사

Point Check I

◆ **관계대명사:** 두 개의 문장에서 중복되는 내용을 합쳐 연결하는 역할을 하는 것을 말한다. 선행사에 따라 쓸 수 있는 관계대명사가 다르다.

◆ **선행사:** 관계대명사가 이끄는 절이 설명하는 명사를 선행사라고 한다.

1. 관계대명사의 종류

선행사 　　격	주격	목적격	소유격
사람	who	who(m)	whose
사물, 동물	which	which	whose (= of which)
사람, 사물, 동물	that	that	–
선행사 없음	what (～하는 것)	what (～하는 것)	–

2. 관계대명사의 생략

(1) 목적격 관계대명사: 'who(m), which, that'의 경우 생략이 가능하다.
 • He was a teacher (**whom**) my mom met yesterday.
 ➡ He was a teacher. My mom met him yesterday.

(2) 주격 관계대명사 + be동사 + 분사: '주격 관계대명사 + be동사'는 생략이 가능하다.
 • The girl (**who is**) **crying** under the tree is my little sister.

3. 복합관계대명사

복합 관계대명사	명사절		부사절	
who(m)ever	anyone who(m)	누구든지	no matter who(m)	누가 ～하더라도
whichever	anything that	어느 것이든지	no matter which	어느 것을 ～하더라도
whatever	anything that	무엇이든지	no matter what	무엇을 ～하더라도

4. 관계대명사의 계속적 용법과 한정적 용법

계속적 용법	① 선행사 다음에 '콤마(,)'가 있다. ② 관계절은 선행사에 대한 부가 설명이기 때문에 순서대로 해석한다. ③ 의미에 따라 '접속사 + 대명사'로 바꿀 수 있다. ④ '(콤마) + 관계대명사 (who, which)'의 형태이다.
한정적 용법	① 선행사 다음에 '콤마(,)'가 없다. ② '선행사 + 관계대명사 (that, what)'의 형태이다.

Lesson 12-1 관계대명사

• **관계대명사**: 관계대명사는 두 문장을 하나로 연결하는 접속사이면서 앞에 나온 명사를 대신하는 대명사의 역할을 한다. 관계대명사에는 'who, what, which, that'이 있으며, 선행사에 따라 다르다.

1. 관계대명사의 종류: 선행사에 따라 사용할 관계대명사가 결정되며, 그 격에 따라 주격, 소유격, 목적격의 역할을 한다.

선행사 　　격	주격	목적격	소유격
사람	who	who(m)	whose
사물, 동물	which	which	whose (= of which)
사람, 사물, 동물	that	that	–
선행사 없음	what (~하는 것)	what (~하는 것)	–

➡ 관계대명사 'that'은 선행사가 사람, 사물, 동물에 상관없이 모두 쓰일 수 있다.

➡ 관계대명사절은 앞에 있는 명사를 꾸며주는 형용사절이며, 꾸밈을 받는 명사를 선행사라고 한다.

2. 의문사와 관계대명사의 차이

의문사 who, which, what	관계대명사 who, which, what
'누구, 어떤 것, 무엇'의 뜻을 갖는다.	선행사를 수식하면서 '접속사＋대명사'의 역할을 한다.
• Who knows Tom's sister? [누가]	• I know the girl who is dancing over there. [the girl = who]
• Which do you want to eat, bibimbap or gimbap? [어느 것]	• Peggy is making a doll which she'll give to Jenny. [a doll = which]
• What is your email address? [무엇]	• What Fred wants to do is watching this movie. [what – ~하는 것]

Answer Keys p. 47

A 보기 에서 알맞은 것을 골라 빈칸에 쓰시오.

보기

who　　　whom　　　which　　　whose

1　Mary is a Korean. She loves her country.
　➡ Mary is a Korean ___who___ loves her country.

Answer Keys p. 47

2 I will meet Tim. His mother is a designer.

→ I will meet Tim _____ mother is a designer.

3 Guhong is one of my friends. I met him last year.

→ Guhong _____ I met last year is one of my friends.

4 No one followed the rules. They were made by Minjae.

→ No one followed the rules _____ were made by Minjae.

5 I haven't seen the woman. She lives next door.

→ I haven't seen the woman _____ lives next door.

6 The rabbits live in the zoo. They are eating some carrots.

→ The rabbits _____ are eating some carrots live in the zoo.

7 The police have caught the thief. He stole my new car.

→ The police have caught the thief _____ stole my new car.

8 Some of my friends couldn't come to my house. I invited them.

→ Some of my friends _____ I invited couldn't come to my house.

9 Hana is reading the book. Its cover is covered with feathers.

→ Hana is reading the book _____ cover is covered with feathers.

10 The new camera was bought by Sam. I broke it.

→ I broke the new camera _____ was bought by Sam.

B 우리말 해석에 맞게 빈칸을 채우시오.

1 저 남자가 내가 어제 공원에서 만났던 축구선수이다.

→ The man is the soccer player *whom I met in the park yesterday.*

2 그것은 내가 겪었던 것 중에 가장 무서운 경험이었다.

→ It was the most terrifying experience _____.

3 나에게 전화한 소년은 Kate의 남동생이었다.

→ The boy _____ was Kate's brother.

4 우리에게 중요한 것은 내일 그가 떠난다는 것이다.

→ _____ is that he will leave tomorrow.

5 그녀에게는 이 가게에서 가장 비싼 시계가 있다.

→ She has a watch _____ in this shop.

Lesson

12-2 관계대명사 which, who

- 관계대명사 which: 선행사가 사물이나 동물로 주어 역할을 할 때는 주격으로, 목적어 역할을 할 때는 목적격으로 'which'를 사용한다.
- 관계대명사 who: 관계대명사가 설명해 주는 선행사가 '사람'일 경우 사용한다.

1. 관계대명사 which

격	의미 및 예문
주격 which	• Luke bought a new shirt. It is fashionable. = Luke bought a new shirt which is fashionable.
소유격 whose (= of which)	• We have a cat. Its fur is white and shaggy. = We have a cat whose (of which) fur is white and shaggy.
목적격 which	• Colin hasn't finished the report yet. He has to finish it tomorrow. = Colin hasn't finished the report which he has to finish tomorrow.

2. 관계대명사 who

격	의미 및 예문
주격 who	• Sandra is an actress. She performs well. = Sandra is an actress who performs well.
소유격 whose	• I know a girl. Her sister is a famous model. = I know a girl whose sister is a famous model.
목적격 who(m)	• We are middle school students. Mr. Park teaches us. = We are middle school students who(m) Mr. Park teaches.

Check up!

Answer Keys p. 47

A   보기 에서 알맞은 관계대명사를 골라 문장을 완성하시오.

보기
| who | whom | whose | which |

1   They know a Korean girl. She is interested in traditional dance.
➡ They know a Korean girl _who is interested in traditional dance._

2   Jane is the girl. Her electronic dictionary was stolen yesterday.
➡ Jane is the girl _____

3   The students go to this concert. They should bring a ticket.
    ➡ The students _____

4   He and I visited the amusement park. It was completed in
    2014.
    ➡ He and I visited the amusement park _____

5   The foreigner was very rude. We met him yesterday.
    ➡ The foreigner _____

6   The vase was one of the most expensive ones in the shop. He
    broke it.
    ➡ The vase _____

7   The boy was my classmate. He helped the poor woman.
    ➡ The boy _____

8   The singer won first prize in the contest. Her song made
    people happy.
    ➡ The singer

    _____

9   We think this is an issue. It requires more detailed information.
    ➡ We think this is an issue _____

10 Minhyuk is one of my friends. My sister likes him.
    ➡ Minhyuk is one of my friends _____

12-3 관계대명사 that, what

- 관계대명사 that : 선행사가 '사람＋사물', '사람+동물', '최상급, 서수, the only' 등이 오는 경우에는 관계대명사 'that'만을 쓸 수 있다.
- 관계대명사 what : 다른 관계대명사들과 달리 'what'은 스스로 선행사를 가지고 있다. 명사 역할을 하면서 주어, 목적어, 보어로 쓰이며, '~하는 것'의 뜻을 가진다.

1. 관계대명사 that

격	의미 및 예문
주격 that	• The man is my tennis coach. He found you. = The man that (who) found you is my tennis coach. ➡ 선행사가 사람이나 사물일 경우, 'who'나 'which'를 대신 사용할 수 있다.
목적격 that	• She is a doctor. Sam met her last weekend. = She is a doctor that (whom) Sam met last weekend.

2. 관계대명사 that을 사용하는 경우

복합적 선행사	'사람 + 사물', '사람 + 동물'
강조적 선행사	최상급, 서수, the only, the same, the very, all, no, little, much, '-thing'으로 끝나는 대명사

3. 관계대명사 what : 선행사가 없다.

명사 역할	예문
주어	• What I want to eat is salmon sushi. = The thing that I want to eat is salmon sushi.
목적어	• They didn't want to do what he suggested. = They didn't want to do the thing that he suggested.
보어	• A photographer is what I want to be. = A photographer is the thing that I want to be.

➡ 관계대명사 'what'은 'the thing that'으로 바꿔 쓸 수 있다.

A that, what을 사용하여 다음 문장을 완성하시오.

1　They are the vets. They work in the animal hospital.

➡ They are the vets _____*that work in the animal hospital.*_____

2.　The thing matters to me. It is the result of the final exam.

➡ _____

3　I saw something. It was shining under the water.

➡ I saw something _____

4　James and the cat were saved. They fell into the sea.

➡ James and the cat _____ were saved.

5　I will watch the movie. It is directed by my brother.

➡ I will watch the movie _____

6　The album of the year is Britney's album. People voted for the album.

➡ The album of the year _____ is
Britney's album.

7　Please show me the thing. You bought it yesterday.

➡ Please show me _____ yesterday.

8　A hero is a person. He helps the poor and the disabled.

➡ A hero is a person _____

9　There were no vacant rooms. We could stay in a room during the day.

➡ There were no vacant rooms _____

B 괄호 안에서 알맞은 것을 고르시오.

1　The woman is a writer (what / (who)) wrote a lot of interesting novels.

2　Look at the dog (whose / that) tail is short. It's so cute.

3　Don't go near the machine (that / who) makes a lot of noise.

4　(Which / What) he wants to try is not flying a kite but playing soccer.

5　The book (whose / which) cover is green is my favorite one.

6　The boy (that / whose) called you is my cousin.

7　His polite attitude was (that / what) made me happy.

복합관계대명사

· whoever, whichever, whatever : 주어 또는 목적어로 쓰여 '~이든지'의 뜻을 가지며, 문장의
앞에서 부사로 쓰여 '~할지라도'의 뜻을 가지기도 한다.

◈ 복합관계대명사

복합관계대명사	명사절		부사절	
who(m)ever	anyone who(m)	누구든지	no matter who(m)	누가 ~하더라도
whichever	anything that	어느 것이든지	no matter which	어느 것을 ~하더라도
whatever	anything that	무엇이든지	no matter what	무엇을 ~하더라도

1. whoever

· **Whoever** visits here will be welcomed. ^(누구든지)
= **Anyone who** visits here will be welcomed.

· **Whoever** visits, be kind to the person. ^(누가 ~하더라도)
= **No matter who** visits, be kind to the person.

2. whichever

· We can buy **whichever** we want here. ^(어느 것이든지)
= We can buy **anything that** we want here.

· **Whichever** you take, your English skills will improve. ^(어느 것을 ~하더라도)
= **No matter which** you take, your English skills will improve.

3. whatever

· I tried to experience **whatever** I saw. ^(무엇이든지)
= I tried to experience **anything that** I saw.

· **Whatever** he touched, it was turned into gold. ^(무엇을 ~하더라도)
= **No matter what** he touched, it was turned into gold.

Grammar Plus +

· **복합관계형용사**: [whichever, whatever + 명사] – 형용사 역할을 하여 뒤의 명사를 꾸며준다.
Whatever books you read, they may give you wisdom.
= **No matter what** books you read, they may give you wisdom.

Answer Keys p. 47

A 다음 우리말 해석에 맞게 빈칸을 채우시오.

1 누구든지 그 문제를 푸는 사람이 1등 상을 받을 것이다.
➡ ___*Whoever*___ solves the problem will get first prize.
➡ ___*Anyone who*___ solves the problem will get first prize.

2 그녀가 걱정하는 것은 무엇이든지 우리가 없애주겠다.
➡ We will get rid of _____ she is worried about.
➡ We will get rid of _____ she is worried about.

3 어느 누구든지 공을 먼저 잡으면 우승자가 될 것이다.
➡ _____ grabs the ball first will be the winner.
➡ _____ grabs the ball first will be the winner.

4 그는 Helen이 원하는 것은 무엇이든지 고를 수 있다고 말했다.
➡ He said that Helen could choose _____
➡ He said that Helen could choose _____

5 그 사람들이 누구일지라도 우리는 그들을 존중해야 한다.
➡ We should respect them, _____ they are.
➡ We should respect them, _____ they are.

6 그가 누구와 사랑에 빠질지라도 그녀는 신경쓰지 않았다.
➡ _____ he falls in love with, she didn't mind.
➡ _____ he falls in love with, she didn't mind.

7 무슨 일을 하든지 네가 하는 일을 사랑하라.
➡ _____ you do, love what you are doing.
➡ _____ you do, love what you are doing.

8 네가 어떤 것을 주더라도 나는 행복할 것이다.
➡ _____ you give me, I will be happy.
➡ _____ you give me, I will be happy.

9 어느 버튼을 누르더라도 폭탄은 터질 것이다.
➡ The bomb will explode, _____ button you may push.
➡ The bomb will explode, _____ button you may push.

10 그가 무슨 말을 들을지라도 그는 신경 쓰지 않는다.
➡ _____ he hears, he doesn't care about it.
➡ _____ he hears, he doesn't care about it.

관계대명사의 용법

• **관계대명사의 용법**: 선행사에 대해 부가적인 설명을 덧붙일 때는 관계대명사 앞에 '콤마(,)'를 쓰며, 문장의 순서대로 해석하는 것을 관계대명사의 계속적 용법이라고 한다.

1. 계속적 용법과 한정적 용법

계속적 용법	① 선행사 다음에 '콤마(,)'가 있다. ② 관계절은 선행사에 대한 부가 설명이기 때문에 순서대로 해석한다. ③ 의미에 따라 '접속사 + 대명사'로 바꿀 수 있다. ④ 형태는 '콤마(,) + 관계대명사 who, which'이다.
한정적 용법	① 선행사 다음에 '콤마(,)'가 없다. ② 형태는 '(선행사) + 관계대명사 that, what'이다.

(1) 계속적 용법: who, which

• Tonny and Emma helped a man. **He** was Mel Gibson.

= Tonny and Emma helped a man, **who** was Mel Gibson.

= Tonny and Emma helped a man, **and he** was Mel Gibson.

• Maria had drawn a portrait of her mother. **It** became famous.

= Maria had drawn a portrait of her mother, **which** became famous.

= Maria had drawn a portrait of her mother, **and it** became famous.

(2) 한정적용법: that, what

• It was a jewelry box decorated with pearls. We looked for **it** in Insadong.

= It was a jewelry box decorated with pearls **that** we looked for in Insadong.

2. 관계대명사절이 문장 가운데 있을 경우: 앞뒤에 '콤마(,)'를 붙여준다.

• Judy started to take art lessons. She is good at painting.

➡ Judy, **who started to take art lessons**, is good at painting.

A   보기와 같이 알맞은 관계대명사를 이용하여 한 문장으로 바꾸어 쓰시오.

> 보기
>
> She helped the woman. She was Katie's grandmother
> ➡ She helped the woman, ___who___ was Katie's grandmother.

1   The man had two books. They were written by Harry.

   ➡ _____

2   There are three more people. They are waiting for John.

   ➡ _____

3   We met Jane. She seemed to need help.

   ➡ _____

4   I lied to him again. It made him angry.

   ➡ _____

5   I like the paintings. They were painted by father.

   ➡ _____

6   He missed the bus. It meant we might be late.

   ➡ _____

7   We will fly to London. It means we won't have to worry
     about the plan.

   ➡ _____

8   An old woman gave me some apples. She lives next door.

   ➡ _____

9   The game was shown on TV. It attracted many people.

   ➡ _____

10   A nurse didn't wear a uniform. She was taking care of a sick
     child.

   ➡ _____

관계대명사의 생략

- **목적격 관계대명사**: 관계대명사가 목적어의 역할을 하는 것으로 목적격 관계대명사는 문장에서 항상 생략할 수 있다.

- **주격 관계대명사**: 주어 역할을 하는 주격 관계대명사 뒤에는 동사가 오는데, 'be동사'가 오면 '주격관계대명사+be동사'는 생략할 수 있다.

1. 목적격 관계대명사: 목적어 역할을 하는 'who(m), which, that'은 생략할 수 있다.

- The woman **(whom)** you saw is my English teacher.

- Thomas didn't answer the questions **(which)** Jenny asked.

- We watched the movie **(that)** you recommended.

Grammar Plus +

- 관계대명사 앞에 전치사가 쓰인 경우 목적격 관계대명사는 생략할 수 없다.

Where can I buy the gift **about which** you explained to me?

2. 주격 관계대명사 + be동사: [주격관계대명사 + be동사 + 분사(현재/과거)]

- Does Andy know that girl **(who is)** **playing** the violin over there?

- I have some books **(which are)** **read** in the train.

☆Check up!

Answer Keys p. 48

A 다음 문장에서 생략해도 되는 부분을 쓰시오.

1 The man whom we met is not a famous actor. ___whom___

2 He can solve the problem which I made. _____

3 Have you found the luggage that you lost? _____

4 The people whom I met in LA were very handsome.

_____

5 The song that Jane is singing is the best song. _____

6 You can't cancel the conference that you arranged.

_____

7 Who was the lady whom I saw in the hall? _____

8 Alex who was injured yesterday was taken to hospital.

_____

전치사 + 관계대명사

> • **전치사＋관계대명사**: 관계대명사가 전치사의 목적어일 경우 전치사는 관계대명사의 앞이나 관계대명사절의 끝에 위치하며, '전치사＋관계대명사'의 형태일 경우 'that'은 쓸 수 없다.

1. 전치사 + 관계대명사

- Diana was the prettiest at the party. + Her parents were proud of her.
  = Diana was the prettiest at the party **of whom** her parents were proud.
  = Diana was the prettiest at the party **who(m) (that)** her parents were proud **of**.

➡ 전치사가 관계대명사 바로 앞에 위치 할 경우 'whom' 대신 'who'를 사용할 수 없다.

➡ 관계대명사 앞에 전치사가 없는 경우에는 'that'을 사용할 수 있다.

2. 한정사 + 전치사 + 관계대명사: '한정사 + of + 관계대명사 목적격'일 경우 계속적 용법으로 쓰인다.

- The king had three daughters, **all of whom** were beautiful and wise.

◈ 한정사

all	both	each	some	many	most	any	neither	none

★Check up!

Answer Keys p. 48

A 관계대명사를 이용하여 다음을 한 문장으로 바꾸시오.

1 Do you know the girl? Jane is talking to her with a smile. (whom)

➡ *Do you know the girl whom Jane is talking to with a smile?*

➡ *Do you know the girl to whom Jane is talking to with a smile?*

2 This is the house. James was born in it. (which)

➡ _____

➡ _____

3 The woman is a candidate. Many people work for her. (whom)

➡ _____

➡ _____

4 This is a nice guidebook. I found good information in it.

➡ _____ (that)

➡ _____ (which)

Practice More I

Answer Keys p. 48

A 빈칸에 알맞은 말을 쓰시오.

1 I know the people __who__ live next to me.

2 Jim is the foreigner _____ we met at yesterday's party.

3 All _____ we want to know is the boy's name.

4 You can invite anyone _____ you like.

5 I didn't understand _____ he said.

6 The girls visited the wise woman, _____ gave them useful advice.

7 The woman didn't tell me about _____ she was about to say.

8 Can you describe the tower _____ walls are red?

9 The scholars have found some dinosaur fossils, _____ will be displayed in the museum.

10 Mr. Park is a mentor _____ I can rely on.

B 다음 문장에서 어법상 어색한 것을 찾아 바르게 고치시오.

1 I think the boy whose sent her the letter is John.

   whose ➡ _who_

2 My father says which Sally needs is rest.

   _____ ➡ _____

3 Tom plays tennis, that is similar to badminton.

   _____ ➡ _____

4 It is a building what was built about sixty years ago.

   _____ ➡ _____

5 Someone which comes here will be treated well.

   _____ ➡ _____

6 This is the camera with that he took the photo.

   _____ ➡ _____

7 There are twelve students, most of them come from India.

   _____ ➡ _____

Practice More I

8　We saw a lot of dolls, some of that were made by Cindy.

　　　_____ ➡ _____

9　No matter what tries he, it makes his parents angry.

　　　_____ ➡ _____

10　You can invite anything who you like.

　　　_____ ➡ _____

C　주어진 두 문장을 하나의 문장으로 바꾸어 쓰시오.

1　The student was scolded. She didn't do homework.
　➡　_The student who didn't do homework was scolded._

2　What is the title of the novel? John told me about it last night.
　➡　_____

3　Look at those dogs. They are lying on the ground peacefully.
　➡　_____

4　We couldn't go to the beach party. We weren't invited to it.
　➡　_____

5　I've never seen Minhyuk. Jane went to the theater with him two days ago.
　➡　_____

6　My mother gave me this letter. It has influenced me a lot.
　➡　_____

7　The bag is expensive. He's looking at it.
　➡　_____

8　He was a very friendly writer. I met him last year in Mexico.
　➡　_____

9　The woman bought the coat. I see her every morning in the park.
　➡　_____

10　Andy can't trust some people. He worked with them.
　➡　_____

D   주어진 단어를 알맞게 배열하여 문장을 완성하시오.

1   (no, I, he, didn't, anything, matter, say, what, asked)

➡   *No matter what I asked, he didn't say anything.*

2   (I, the boy, all the food, the table, know, ate, who, on)

➡   _____

3   (last week, Alice, two years, I, hadn't, whom, for, saw, seen, I)

➡   _____

4   (remember, ran down, do, the street, you, who, the girl)

➡   _____

5   (whoever, the game, the riddle, the winner, solves, will, of, be)

➡   _____

6   (basketball, a sport, is, and, my friends, that, I, like)

➡   _____

7   (whichever, choose, it, you, won't, you, regret)

➡   _____

8   (what, the test, matters, is, to, the result, me, of)

➡   _____

9   (please, want, let, you, know, me, what)

➡   _____

10 (I, decide, follow, will, you, whatever)

➡   _____

Point Check Ⅱ

◆ **관계부사**: 선행사를 수식하는 절을 이끌면서 '접속사＋부사'의 역할을 하는 것을 말하며,
'전치사＋관계대명사'로 바꿔 쓸 수 있다.

1. 관계부사의 종류

	선행사	관계부사	전치사+관계대명사
when (시간)	the time, the day, the month, the year	when	at/in/to which
where (장소)	the place, the house, the town, the city	where	at/in/to which
why (이유)	the reason	why	for which
how (방법)	the way	how	in which

2. 복합관계부사

복합관계부사	선행사		양보의 부사절	
whenever	at any time (when)	～할 때는 언제나	no matter when	언제 ～하더라도
wherever	at any place (where)	～하는 어디서든지	no matter where	어디에서 ～하더라도
however	in any way (that), in whatever way	어떤 식으로든	no matter how	아무리 ～하더라도

3. 관계부사와 선행사의 생략 : 관계부사나 선행사 중 하나를 생략할 수 있다.

관계사	선행사
when	the time, the day, the month, the year
where	the place, the house, the town, the city
why	the reason

➡ **how** : 'how'와 선행사(the way) 둘 중 하나만 사용한다.

4. 관계부사의 계속적 용법

규칙	① 'when, where'만 계속적 용법이 가능하다. ② 선행사 앞에 '콤마(,)'를 붙인다. ③ 앞에서 뒤로 해석한다. ④ '접속사＋부사(there, then)'의 의미를 가진다.

관계부사

- 관계부사: 시간, 장소, 이유, 방법 등을 나타내는 선행사를 꾸며주는 역할을 하며,
  '전치사＋관계대명사'를 대신 사용하기도 한다.

◆ 관계부사의 종류

	선행사	관계부사	전치사+관계대명사
시간	the time, the day, the month, the year	when	at/in/to which
장소	the place, the house, the town, the city	where	at/in/to which
이유	the reason	why	for which
방법	the way	how	in which

1. when : 시간

- I remember the day. ＋ We first met on the day.

  ＝ I remember the day **and** we first met on the day.

  ➡ I remember the day **when** we first met.

  ➡ I remember the day **on which** we first met.

2. where : 장소

- Paris is a romantic city. ＋ I lived in the city last year.

  ＝ Paris is a romantic city **and** I lived in the city last year.

  ➡ Paris is a romantic city **where** I lived last year.

  ➡ Paris is a romantic city **in which** I lived last year.

3. why : 이유

- She knew the reason. ＋ Tonny didn't say any excuse.

  ＝ She knew the reason **why** Tonny didn't say any excuse.

  ➡ She knew the reason **for which** Tonny didn't say any excuse.

4. how : 방법

- He'll tell us the way. ＋ We will debate in that way.

  ＝ He'll tell us the way **and** we will debate in that way.

  ➡ He'll tell us **how** we will debate.

  ➡ He'll tell us **the way** we will debate.

  ➡ He'll tell us **the way in which** we will debate.

➡ 'the way'와 'how'를 같이 사용하지 않는다.

A 다음 두 문장이 같은 뜻이 되도록 관계대명사나 관계부사를 이용하여 빈칸을 채우시오.

1   He can clearly remember the day when Helen and he first met.
   ➡ He can clearly remember the day *on which Helen and he first met*.
   ➡ He can clearly remember the day *when Helen and he first met*.

2   How large was the house? Many people stayed at the house.
   ➡ How large was the house _____?
   ➡ How large was the house _____?

3   This is her birthday. We visited her house today.
   ➡ This is her birthday _____.
   ➡ This is her birthday _____.

4   Emma can't guess the reason. He couldn't attend the meeting for the reason.
   ➡ Emma can't guess the reason _____.
   ➡ Emma can't guess the reason _____.

5   I like the way. The teacher deals with his students in the way.
   ➡ I like the way _____.
   ➡ I like _____.

6   This museum is the biggest. I have ever visited the place.
   ➡ This museum is the biggest place _____.
   ➡ This museum is the biggest place _____.

7   Timmy remembered the day. His big brother went to the army the day.
   ➡ Timmy remembered the day _____.
   ➡ Timmy remembered the day _____.

8   I taught them the way. They speak Japanese well in the way.
   ➡ I taught them the way _____.
   ➡ I taught them _____.

관계부사로 쓰이는 that

> • **that**: 관계부사 when, why, how를 대신할 수 있다. 문장의 끝에 전치사가 올 경우에는 '관계
> 대명사'의 역할을 한다.

1. 관계부사 that

- Jenny remembered the day **when** she went to Europe.
  = Jenny remembered the day **that** she went to Europe.

- This is **the way** they made the machine.
  = This is **how** they made the machine.
  = This is **the way that** they made the machine.

➡ 'the way how'는 불가능하지만, 'the way that'은 가능하다.

2. that + 전치사

- That's the house **that** Mr. and Mrs. White live **in**.
  (= which)

  = That's the house **where** Mr. and Mrs. White live.

➡ 장소를 나타내는 'where' 대신 'that'을 쓸 경우 항상 전치사가 온다.

Check up!

Answer Keys p. 49

A 다음 빈칸에 알맞은 말을 보기 에서 모두 골라 쓰시오.

보기
that   when   where   why   how   the way

1 March is the month ___when / that___ I got married.

2 The park _____ my daughter plays tennis was closed.

3 That's the restaurant _____ we usually have dinner.

4 Tell her the reason _____ he left without saying goodbye.

5 Tomorrow is the day _____ my family take a rest at home.

6 Sam explained everything in a way _____ I could understand.

7 This is the way _____ the team could win the national soccer league.

8 Tim shows _____ people can make tomato stew easily.

- **복합관계부사**: 'whenever, wherever, however'는 자체에 선행사가 있으며, '시간, 장소, 양보'를 나타내는 문장을 이끈다.

◈ 복합관계부사

복합관계부사	선행사		양보의 부사절	
whenever	at any time (when)	~할 때는 언제나	no matter when	언제 ~하더라도
wherever	at any place (where)	~하는 곳은 어디서든지	no matter where	어디에서 ~하더라도
however	in any way (that) in whatever way	어떤 식으로든	no matter how	아무리 ~하더라도

1. whenever

- You can ask me **whenever** you wonder about something. (~할 때는 언제나)
  = You can ask me **at any time when** you wonder about something.

- **Whenever** she wants ice cream, he buys it for her. (언제 ~을 하더라도)
  = **No matter when** she wants ice cream, he buys it for her.

2. wherever

- We can't eat lunch **wherever** we want. (~하는 곳은 어디서든지)
  = We can't eat lunch **at any place where** we want.

- **Wherever** you go, I will follow you. (어디에서 ~하더라도)
  = **No matter where** you go, I will follow you.

3. however

- They can do it **however** they want. (어떤 식으로든)
  = They can do it **in any way that** they want.

- **However** hard he works, his boss will not be satisfied. (아무리 ~하더라도)
  = **No matter how** hard he works, his boss will not be satisfied.

Answer Keys p. 49

A 우리말 해석에 맞게 빈칸에 알맞은 말을 쓰시오.

1 그녀가 원할 때는 언제나 떠나도 좋다.
➡ She may leave ___*whenever*___ she wishes.
➡ She may leave ___*at any time*___ she wishes.

2 가격이 아무리 비싸더라도 사람들은 그 자동차를 샀다.
➡ _____ high the price was, people bought the car.
➡ _____ high the price was people bought the car.

3 나는 그들이 가는 곳은 어디라도 함께 할 것이다.
➡ I will be with them _____ they go.
➡ I will be with them _____ they go.

4 그 소파를 엄마가 마음에 드는 곳에 어디든지 놔둬라.
➡ Put the sofa _____ mom likes.
➡ Put the sofa _____ mom likes.

5 아무리 많이 벌더라도 너는 돈을 모아야 한다.
➡ _____ much you earn, you should save money.
➡ _____ much you earn, you should save money.

B 다음 빈칸에 알맞은 관계부사를 쓰시오.

1 How do you feel ___*whenever*___ you go to the beach?

2 People can sit _____ they want.

3 _____ tired she may be, she must attend school.

4 I feel sad _____ I see the photo.

5 We got good service _____ we visited.

6 You can visit us _____ you want.

관계부사의 생략과 계속적 용법

- **관계부사의 생략:** 관계부사와 선행사가 나란히 있을 경우 관계부사나 선행사를 생략할 수 있다.
- **관계부사의 계속적 용법:** 선행사 뒤에 콤마를 써 계속적 용법을 나타낼 수 있다.

1. 관계부사와 선행사의 생략: 선행사 다음의 관계부사는 생략이 가능하다.
선행사가 일반적인 날짜, 장소, 이유를 나타내는 경우 생략이 가능하다.

관계부사	선행사	예문
when (시간)	the day, the time, the year	• December 28th is (the day) when he was born. = December 28th is the day (when) he was born.
where (장소)	the place, the city, the country	• This is (the place) where I met him for the first time. = This is the place (where) I met him for the first time.
why (이유)	the reason	• He doesn't know (the reason) why Mary was angry. = He doesn't know the reason (why) Mary was angry.

➡ **how**: 원래 'how'와 '선행사'는 함께 쓰이지 않는다.

2. 관계부사의 계속적 용법

규칙	① 'when, where'만 계속적 용법이 가능하다. ② 선행사 앞에 '콤마(,)'를 붙인다. ③ 앞에서 뒤로 해석한다. ④ '접속사 + 부사(there, then)'의 의미를 가진다.

(1) when

- He visited Emily at nine. she wasn't home then.
  ➡ He visited Emily at nine, **when (but then)** she wasn't home.

(2) where

- We went to the concert. We watched a wonderful musical there.
  ➡ We went to the concert, **where (and there)** watched a wonderful musical.

Answer Keys p. 49

A 주어진 말을 알맞은 위치에 넣어 문장을 완성하시오.

1 May 15th is the day we thank our teachers. (when)

→ _____ *May 15th is the day when we thank our teachers.* _____

2 Let's go to the store you bought the bike. (where)

→ _____

3 This is the place I used to work with my boyfriend. (where)

→ _____

4 2002 was when Korea hosted the World Cup. (the year)

→ _____

5 The bakery I bought the bread is next to the flower shop. (where)

→ _____

6 That is why she left us without any explanation. (the reason)

→ _____

7 Busan is where you can see famous movie stars. (the city)

→ _____

8 She needs to know the way she can get along with strangers.
(how)

→ _____

9 Please return the dictionary you borrowed from the library. (that)

→ _____

B 주어진 문장을 한 문장으로 완성하시오.

1 You met Jim last night. It began to snow then.

→ _____ *You met Jim last night, when it began to snow.* _____

2 My brother was running down the street. He saw Kate then.

→ _____

3 We went to the museum. I saw famous statues there.

→ _____

4 Jerry moved here in 2003. His daughter was born that year.

→ _____

5 The professor entered the classroom. He started to give us a
lecture there.

→ _____

Practice More II

A 빈칸에 알맞은 것을 채우시오.

1 Summer is the season _____*when*_____ a lot of people enjoy swimming.

2 The professor explained _____ we could understand this theory.

3 New York is the city _____ I want to go.

4 It was a period _____ people didn't go to work.

5 This is _____ I bought this wooden table.

6 Sora invited Harry to her birthday party _____ he had apologized about his mistake.

7 No matter _____ cheap this product is, it looks useless.

8 It is a country _____ tourists are not in danger.

9 Can you let me know _____ he will return to his hometown?

10 There were many occasions _____ they came late.

B 다음 문장에서 어법상 <u>어색한</u> 것을 찾아 바르게 고치시오.

1 Whenever want you, you can call me.

   ___*want you*___ ➡ ___*you want*___

2 We visited the village what we used to live in.

   _____ ➡ _____

3 I don't understand the way how to make the cake.

   _____ ➡ _____

4 This is where came I every time I felt depressed.

   _____ ➡ _____

5 Amy who sister lives in Japan passed the exam.

   _____ ➡ _____

6　I can't guess when they left so early.

_____ ➡ _____

7　Do you know the year where the woman died?

_____ ➡ _____

8　I recalled the day what he left me.

_____ ➡ _____

9　He showed me which he makes pasta with cream sauce.

_____ ➡ _____

10　No matter what eat you, you should be thankful for it.

_____ ➡ _____

C　괄호 안에서 알맞은 것을 고르시오.

1　I did nothing harmful, so I don't understand ((why) / where) she was angry.

2　This is the box (in which / for which) I used to hide my precious things.

3　I will follow anything (what / that) he suggests.

4　Korea is a country (in which / in that) there are various traditional activities.

5　I remember the day when you (came to / have came) my class for the first time.

6　They found out (the reason / the day) Sam didn't buy anything last night.

7　However (tired he / he tired) may be, he must finish the project.

8　I will tell you the reson (why / in why) Jane lied to her family.

9　Come on and sit (however / wherever) you like.

10　Do not buy a useless thing, (however / whatever) cheap they may be.

Practice More II

Answer Keys p. 49~50

D 주어진 단어를 알맞게 배열하여 문장을 완성하시오.

1 (you, want, you, whenever, leave, may)

→ _____ *You may leave whenever you want.* _____

2 (my parents, a, me, I, mistake, scold, whenever, make)

→ _____

3 (I, the party, know, didn't, to, they, come, don't, why)

→ _____

4 (do, our baby, know, was, you, the day, born, when)

→ _____

5 (Brian, reveal, money, didn't, saved, the way, he)

→ _____

6 (let's, the cookie, bought, the shop, you, go, where, to)

→ _____

7 (this, the problem, is, solve, we, the way, can)

→ _____

8 (the boys, bought, went, where, the store, the soccer ball, to, they)

→ _____

9 (whenever, her, she, my phone call, I, answers, call)

→ _____

10 (the stadium, very, where, small, played, was, soccer, they)

→ _____

내신 최다 출제 유형

01 다음 밑줄 친 부분의 쓰임이 나머지 넷과 다른 것을 고르시오. [출제 예상 90%]

① Do you know <u>what</u> he does now?
② Does she know <u>what</u> she is good at?
③ She is asking Paul <u>what</u> she can do for him.
④ I talked about <u>what</u> I wanted to be in the future.
⑤ <u>What</u> do you want to be when you grow up?

02 다음 빈칸에 공통으로 들어갈 알맞은 말을 고르시오. [출제 예상 85%]

> • What is the thing _____ is most precious to you?
> • He gave her the book _____ he bought yesterday.

① what   ② that   ③ if
④ why   ⑤ when

03 다음 중 빈칸에 들어갈 말이 나머지 넷과 다른 것을 고르시오. [출제 예상 95%]

① Peter forgot to bring the lunchbox _____ you asked.
② Please tell me everything _____ you know about her.
③ Let's drink something _____ isn't too cold.
④ Nothing _____ she heard is true.
⑤ Can you see _____ is written on the board?

04 다음 밑줄 친 부분을 생략할 수 있는 문장을 고르시오. [출제 예상 80%]

① The lady <u>who</u> sits there is my homeroom teacher.
② This is the road <u>which</u> leads to Daegu.
③ Look at the house in <u>which</u> they live.
④ Jane remembered the boy <u>whom</u> she saw at church yesterday.
⑤ I know a girl <u>whose</u> mother is a painter.

05 다음 두 문장을 한 문장으로 연결한 것 중 어법상 틀린 것을 고르시오. [출제 예상 90%]

> The town is not famous. I live in it.

① The town where I live is not famous.
② The town that I live in is not famous.
③ The town in that I live in is not famous.
④ The town which I live in is not famous.
⑤ The town in which I live is not famous.

06 다음 중 어법상 어색한 문장을 고르시오. [출제 예상 90%]

① This moment is when we eat lunch.
② I like the way how you can solve the problem.
③ That's the reason why I learn Chinese.
④ My friends live in the city where I lived before.
⑤ She remembers the day when she broke up with me.

[01~02] 다음 두 문장의 뜻이 같도록 할 때 빈칸에 알맞은 것을 고르시오.

01

> Give it to anyone who you love.
> = Give it to _____ you love.

① whichever
② whomever
③ whatever
④ however
⑤ whenever

02

> No matter where she may be, she must be found.
> = _____ she may be, she must be found.

① Whenever
② Whoever
③ Whatever
④ Wherever
⑤ However

[03~04] 다음 밑줄 친 부분이 어법상 어색한 것을 고르시오.

03
① She has passion for which she composed the poems.
② Do you have something that you can write on?
③ This is the bank in which my father works.
④ This is the arm chair on which my grandma sat.
⑤ There are many English actors of whom I am aware.

04
① Today is the Sunday on which I will go fishing with my friends.
② Will you show me the office in which you work?
③ Can you tell me the reason how you are late for the class?
④ This is the place where my sister works.
⑤ Think about the days when you were a child.

★★★
05 다음 밑줄 친 that의 쓰임이 올바른 것을 고르시오.
① This is that the team won the contest?
② Can you show me the boy that father is a doctor?
③ She spent all the money that her husband earned.
④ Tony grew up in a city in that everything was out-of-date.
⑤ Jerry founded the company, that is now making organic produce.

Note   organic produce 유기농 제품

★★★
06 다음 문장의 밑줄 친 부분을 that으로 바꿔 쓸 수 있는 것을 고르시오.
① This is exactly what I want to buy.
② I use the same books which Jessy used.
③ He had an oven, which was made before 2000.
④ This is the painting of which Sally is very fond.
⑤ Timmy had two sons, who were singers.

07 다음 빈칸에 what이 들어갈 수 <u>없는</u> 것을 고르시오.

① We should know _____ is the most important in our life.

② These steps are _____ I should follow to succeed in life.

③ Can you tell us _____ the picture means?

④ We respect her for _____ she is.

⑤ Those are very helpful tools _____ remove the weeds.

[08~10] 다음 빈칸에 들어갈 알맞은 말을 고르시오.

08

Do you mean money is _____ makes you happy?

① what   ② which   ③ that
④ who   ⑤ how

09

Jacky wants to enter the university, _____ hard it may be.

① whomever   ② whatever
③ whenever   ④ however
⑤ whichever

10

You have to try hard _____ you do.

① whenever   ② whatever
③ whoever   ④ whicheve
⑤ wherever

[11~12] 다음 밑줄 친 부분 중 그 쓰임이 <u>잘못된</u> 것을 고르시오.

★★★
11 ① Next summer is <u>when</u> Brandon plans to go to Greece.

② That is <u>why</u> their music can hardly be recognized.

③ The cat <u>that</u> is sleeping under the sofa is called Nana.

④ I went to the park <u>where</u> is my favorite place.

⑤ A comet has a tail <u>which</u> is made of frozen gases.

★★★
12 ① Mr. Park will show you <u>how</u> this project got started.

② Archeologists study <u>the way how</u> primitive people lived.

③ I studied in Chicago <u>where</u> I made friends with people from all over the world.

④ I'm going to Australia in November <u>when</u> it is not full of tourists.

⑤ She explained to us <u>the way</u> she had lost weight.

13 다음 주어진 문장의 밑줄 친 부분과 쓰임이 같은 것을 고르시오.

> I really respect <u>how</u> he answered when the children asked weird questions.

① They are not much interested in <u>how</u> other people think.

② <u>How</u> did you make her decide it so quickly?

③ <u>How</u> am I supposed to live without him?

④ <u>How</u> does she usually spend her weekends?

⑤ They told me <u>how</u> cute their baby is.

14 다음 빈칸에 공통으로 들어갈 알맞은 말을 고르시오.

> • A police officer looked into the trunk of the car _____ stolen money was found.
> • The area is a desert land _____ few people live.

① which   ② how   ③ what
④ when   ⑤ where

15 다음 두 문장을 한 문장으로 쓸 때 빈칸에 알맞은 것을 고르시오.

> Mrs. Han taught a girl. The girl's mother was a famous actress.
> = Mrs. Han taught a girl _____ mother was a famous actress.

① who   ② that   ③ which
④ whose   ⑤ whom

16 ★★★ 다음 중 어법상 어색한 것을 고르시오.

① This is the watch that I lost.

② I know a girl, that can speak English very well.

③ I saw Mike whose hair is brown.

④ Look at the boy and the dog that are running along the river.

⑤ This is the biggest lake that I have ever seen.

17 다음 밑줄 친 부분 중 생략할 수 <u>없는</u> 것을 고르시오.

① She listens to music <u>which</u> makes her sad.

② He knows the girl <u>whom</u> Sally told me about.

③ I asked him the reason <u>why</u> I should learn English.

④ The restaurant <u>which</u> you recommended was excellent.

⑤ Night is the time <u>when</u> the moon rises.

18 ★★★ 다음 밑줄 친 부분을 <u>잘못</u> 바꿔 쓴 것을 고르시오.

① Have you seen the pictures <u>which</u> Jane drew? (= that)

② <u>No matter who</u> talks to her, she'll never listen. (= Whoever)

③ I can say <u>anything that</u> I want. (= what)

④ This is the place <u>in which</u> they will live. (= where)

⑤ Jeff met Amy, <u>who</u> told him the news. (= and she)

19 다음 주어진 단어들을 바르게 배열한 것을 고르시오.

> (whoever / genius / drew / picture / is / a / this / real)

① Whoever drew this real picture is a genius.
② A real genius is whoever drew this picture.
③ A real genius is whoever this picture drew.
④ Whoever drew this picture is a real genius.
⑤ Whoever drew this a real picture is genius.

★★★
20 다음 밑줄 친 부분 중 어법상 옳은 것을 고르시오.

① The day <u>which</u> we had a picnic was sunny.
② I found the key <u>which</u> he was looking for.
③ The girl <u>who</u> shoes were stolen was upset.
④ I know the girl with <u>that</u> he danced with.
⑤ This is the city <u>which</u> I was born and grew up.

★★★
21 다음 우리말을 영어로 바르게 옮긴 것을 고르시오.

> 이것이 내가 본 것 중 가장 아름다운 산이다.

① This is the most beautiful mountain that I ever saw.
② This is the most beautiful mountain that I have ever.
③ This is the most beautiful mountain that I have ever seen.
④ This is the most beautiful mountain that I had ever seen.
⑤ This is the most beautiful mountain that I was ever seen.

22 다음 중 주어진 문장의 밑줄 친 when과 쓰임이 같은 것을 고르시오.

> Sunday is the day <u>when</u> I get up late in the morning.

① <u>When</u> do you think you can stop by?
② I love winter <u>when</u> I can make snowmen.
③ Do you know <u>when</u> we have a meeting?
④ Minho used to play basketball after school <u>when</u> he was a middle school student.
⑤ She was reading comic books <u>when</u> I visited her last night.

Answer Keys p. 50~51

◇◇◇◇◇◇◇◇ 서술형 평가 ◇◇◇◇◇◇◇◇

[23~24] 다음 문장과 뜻이 같도록 빈칸에 알맞은 단어를 쓰시오.

23

I remember the day when we first went to the park.

➡ I remember the day _____ _____ we first went to the park.

24

This is the town in which Johnny grew up.

➡ This is the town _____ Johnny grew up.

[25~26] 다음 두 문장을 '전치사＋관계대명사'의 형태로 바꿔 쓰시오.

25

These are her plants. She was looking for them.

➡ _____

26

Do you know the woman? Jerry is talking to her.

➡ _____

[27~28] 다음 우리말과 같은 뜻이 되도록 괄호 안의 단어를 바르게 배열하시오.

★★★
27

그녀는 내가 방문할 때마다 책을 읽고 있다.
(she / reading / a / is / whenever / book)

➡ _____ I visit.

★★★
28

나는 그가 내 제안을 거절한 이유가 궁금하다.
(why / suggestion / he / my / refused)

➡ I wonder about _____
_____.

[29~30] 다음 괄호 안의 단어를 배열하여 올바른 문장을 완성하시오.

★★★
29

(whoever / have / it / could / the / wanted / bag)

➡ _____

★★★
30

(I / in / Japanese / a / novel / is / bought / which / written)

➡ _____

13

Chapter
접속사

Point Check I

◆ **접속사:** 단어와 단어, 구와 구, 절과 절을 연결하는 말이다.

◆ **접속사의 종류:** 등위접속사, 상관접속사, 종속접속사, 그리고 접속부사가 있다.

◈ 접속사의 종류 및 의미

<table>
<tr><th colspan="3">접속사의 종류</th><th>의미</th></tr>
<tr><td rowspan="5">등위접속사</td><td colspan="2">and</td><td>~와, 그리고, ~하고나서</td></tr>
<tr><td colspan="2">but</td><td>하지만, 그러나</td></tr>
<tr><td colspan="2">or</td><td>또는, 아니면</td></tr>
<tr><td colspan="2">so</td><td>그래서, 그러므로</td></tr>
<tr><td colspan="2">for</td><td>왜냐하면, ~하기 때문에</td></tr>
<tr><td rowspan="5">상관접속사</td><td colspan="2">both A and B</td><td>A와 B 둘 다</td></tr>
<tr><td colspan="2">either A or B</td><td>A와 B 중 하나는</td></tr>
<tr><td colspan="2">neither A nor B</td><td>A와 B 둘 다 ~아닌</td></tr>
<tr><td colspan="2">not A but B</td><td>A가 아니라 B</td></tr>
<tr><td colspan="2">not only A but (also) B
(= B as well as A)</td><td>A뿐만 아니라 B도</td></tr>
<tr><td rowspan="21">종속
접속사</td><td rowspan="3">명사절을 이끄는
접속사</td><td>that</td><td>~하는 것 (주어, 보어, 목적어 역할)</td></tr>
<tr><td>whether</td><td>~인지 아닌지</td></tr>
<tr><td>if</td><td>~인지 아닌지</td></tr>
<tr><td rowspan="7">시간의 부사절을
이끄는 접속사</td><td>when</td><td>~할 때</td></tr>
<tr><td>while</td><td>~하는 동안, ~하면서</td></tr>
<tr><td>before</td><td>~하기 전에</td></tr>
<tr><td>after</td><td>~한 후에</td></tr>
<tr><td>until</td><td>~할 때까지</td></tr>
<tr><td>as</td><td>~할 때, ~하자마자, ~하면서</td></tr>
<tr><td>since</td><td>~이래로, ~이후로</td></tr>
<tr><td>as soon as</td><td>~하자마자</td></tr>
<tr><td rowspan="2">조건</td><td>if</td><td>만약 ~라면</td></tr>
<tr><td>unless</td><td>만약 ~이 아니라면</td></tr>
<tr><td rowspan="3">이유나 원인</td><td>because
as
since</td><td>~때문에, 왜냐하면</td></tr>
<tr><td rowspan="2">목적</td><td>so that
in order that</td><td>~하기 위해서, ~하려고</td></tr>
<tr><td>결과</td><td>so ~ that...</td><td>너무 ~해서 ...한</td></tr>
<tr><td>양보</td><td>though
although
even though (= even if)</td><td>~에도 불구하고, 비록 ~할지라도</td></tr>
</table>

13-1 and / but / or

- **and / but / or**: 대등한 내용과 형태의 단어와 단어, 구와 구, 절과 절을 이어주는 역할을 한다.
  세 개 이상의 단어가 나열될 경우 마지막 단어 앞에 접속사를 쓴다.
- **명령문, and**: 'and'는 '그러면'이라는 뜻으로 앞의 명령문에 대한 긍정의 결과를 나타낸다.
- **명령문, or**: 'or'는 '그렇지 않으면'이라는 뜻으로 앞의 명령문에 대한 부정의 결과를 나타낸다.

1. 등위접속사 and / but / or

접속사	의미
and ~와, 그리고, ~하고나서	앞뒤 항목이 서로 대등하거나 비슷한 것, 이어지는 행위일 때 사용
but 하지만, 그러나	앞뒤 항목이 서로 반대, 대조될 때 사용
or 또는, 아니면	여러 가지 가능성이나 선택 사항 중 하나를 고를 때 사용

- Miranda cooked some spaghetti **and** mushroom soup.
- Linda bought some souvenirs for her friends, **but** they didn't like them.
- Is Kate a doctor **or** a professor?

2. 명령문 and / or

⑴ 명령문, and: ~해라, 그러면… (= if)

- Focus on your work hard, **and** you'll get a great result.
  = **If** you focus on your work hard, you'll get a great result.

⑵ 명령문, or: ~해라, 그렇지 않으면… (= if not, unless)

- Do your homework well, **or** you'll get punished.
  = **If** you don't do your homework well, you'll get punished.
  = **Unless** you do your homework well, you'll get punished.

Answer Keys p. 52

A 빈칸에 알맞은 것을 채우시오.

1 I'm going to register for courses on baking ___*and*___ singing.

2 I ate an orange, pasta, _____ some snacks for dinner.

3 You can choose the red ball _____ the blue ball.

4 Exercise regularly, _____ you'll feel good about yourself.

5 Are you eating the cake _____ not?

6 He thought the book would be popular _____ he was wrong.

7 Tim, shall we go hiking _____ rest at home?

8 Jane and I wanted to go, _____ Thomas refused to go.

9 I had an ice cream _____ cheese for dessert.

10 We tried hard to save the cat, _____ we failed.

B 두 문장이 같은 뜻이 되도록 빈칸에 and와 or 중 바른 것을 쓰시오.

> 보기
> If you exercise regularly, you will be able to lose weight.
> ➡ Exercise regularly, <u>and</u> you will be able to lose weight.

1 If you visit her house, she will be happy.
   ➡ Visit her house, _____ she will be happy.

2 If you join our team, I can help you to get the ticket.
   ➡ Join our team, _____ I can help you to get the ticket.

3 If you don't keep promises, no one can trust you.
   ➡ Keep promises, _____ no one can trust you.

4 If you are kind to others, people will like you again.
   ➡ Be kind to others, _____ people will like you again.

5 If you don't spend more time on your studies, you won't pass the exam.
   ➡ Spend more time on your studies, _____ you won't pass the exam.

13-2 both A and B

- 'both A and B, either A or B, not A but B'를 상관접속사라고 한다. 상관접속사는
  서로 떨어져 있는 한 쌍의 어구가 두 개의 단어나 구를 이어주면서 강조나 첨가의 의미를 갖는다.

1. 상관접속사

상관접속사		동사의 사용
• both A and B	A와 B 둘 다	항상 복수 동사 사용
• either A or B	A와 B 중 하나는	'B'에 동사를 일치
• neither A nor B	A와 B 둘 다 ~아닌	
• not A but B	A가 아니라 B	
• not only A but (also) B (= B as well as A)	A뿐만 아니라 B도	

➡ 'both A and B'가 <u>주어일 때는 복수 취급을</u> 한다.

➡ 'not only A but (also) B'와 'B as well as A'는 같은 뜻이지만, 'A와 B'의 위치가 바뀐다.

- **Both** <u>Cathy</u> **and** <u>Jane</u> are pediatricians.

- **Either** <u>James</u> **or** <u>Max</u> will get first prize.

- I like **neither** <u>Chinese food</u> **nor** <u>Japanese food</u>.

- It is **not** <u>Larry</u> **but** <u>Jack</u> who didn't bring a pencil.

- Handong likes **not only** <u>computer games</u> **but (also)** <u>chess</u>.
  = Handong likes <u>chess</u> **as well as** <u>computer games</u>.

Answer Keys p. 52

A 빈칸에 알맞은 것을 쓰시오.

1 The novel is ___both___ interesting and moving.

2 Sam is not only kind _____ fun.

3 Sally is now _____ in LA or Seoul.

4 Not you _____ Helen should apologize to me.

5 Neither Mary _____ John knows the correct answer.

6 Not only you but also she _____ going to join our club.

7 The 2002 World Cup was held _____ in Korea
_____ in Japan.

8 Both my father and mother _____ having lunch at an
Italian restaurant.

9 The new technology is _____ complex but effective.

10 _____ the man nor the woman speaks Korean.

B 우리말과 같은 의미가 되도록 빈칸에 알맞은 말을 쓰시오.

1 Jerry뿐만 아니라 그의 여동생도 차를 가지고 있다.
➡ ___Not only___ Jerry ___but also___ his sister has a car.

2 그 학생은 단 한 번이 아니라 여러 번 도둑질을 했다.
➡ The student stole _____ just once _____
several times.

3 Minhyuk이나 James가 공항에서 너를 데려갈 것이다.
➡ _____ Minhyuk _____ James will pick you up
at the airport.

4 나는 내 자신뿐만 아니라 우리 가족을 위해서도 최선을 다하고 있다.
➡ I'm doing my best _____ for myself _____ for
my family.

5 우리는 내일 아니면 오늘 떠나야 한다.
➡ We should leave _____ today _____ tomorrow.

6 그 소녀는 춤뿐만 아니라 노래도 잘 부른다.
➡ The girl is good at singing _____ dancing.

that / whether (if)

· **that / whether (if)** : 종속접속사라고 하며, 이들이 이끄는 절은 명사절이 되어서 문장 안에서
주어, 보어, 목적어로 쓰인다.

1. that / whether (if) : 절 앞에 위치해 명사가 되어 주어, 보어, 목적어로 쓰인다.

that ~라는 것	주어절	· That Jessy made a mistake isn't true. = It isn't true that Jessy made a mistake. ➡ 'that'절이 주어일 경우 가주어 it을 사용하여 주절(that)을 문장 뒷 부분으로 보낼 수 있다.
	보어절	· The point is that Jimmy should do his best.
	목적어절	· I think that people should save water.
	동격절	· I heard the news that new river dolphins were discovered in the Amazon. ➡ 'news, fact, opinion' 등의 명사 다음에는 구체적인 내용을 말하는 동격의 that절을 사용한다.
whether / if ~인지 (아닌지)	주어절	· Whether they speak English or Spanish isn't important.
	보어절	· The point is whether we will study hard (or not).
	목적어절	· I wonder whether (=if) it will be hot tomorrow. · I wonder whether (=if) it will be hot or not tomorrow. ➡ 목적어절의 'whether'는 'if'와 바꿔 쓸 수 있으며, 문장 뒤에 'or not' 이 붙어 '~인지 아닌지'의 뜻으로 사용된다. ➡ 'whether or not'이 함께 쓰이면 'if'와 바꿔 쓸 수 없다. ➡ '명사절'을 이끄는 접속사 'if'는 목적어 역할로만 쓰인다.

➡ whether : 양보의 부사절 '~하든지 상관없이'의 의미로도 사용할 수 있다.

· **Whether** they speak English or Spanish, I will meet them.

Answer Keys p. 52

A 다음 빈칸에 알맞은 것을 쓰시오.

1 The woman's strong point is ___*that*___ she loves her job.

2 Jungmin asked _____ we had seen the musical.

3 The point is _____ we should respect other people.

4 It is important _____ we save our honor.

5 She asked him _____ he left or not.

6 _____ the teacher said no is not surprising at all.

7 _____ he buys the car or not doesn't matter to us.

8 The fact is _____ there were many volcanoes.

9 I'm wondering _____ you agreed with this opinion.

10 He likes the idea _____ we can end the day with music.

B 다음 두 문장을 알맞은 접속사를 이용하여 한 문장으로 바꾸어 쓰시오.

1 It is certain. She will come back next week.
➡ _____*It is certain that she will come back next week.*_____

2 She remembered. She had left her wallet on the table.
➡ _____

3 It is doubtful. Does she really want to quit her job?
➡ _____

4 I couldn't know. Was Sam satisfied with the result or not?
➡ _____

5 We think. Students should follow the school rules.
➡ _____

13-4 when / while

• when / while : 시간이나 때를 나타내는 종속접속사로 부사절의 문장을 만든다.

◈ 시간을 나타내는 접속사

when	～할 때	as	～할 때 ～하자마자 ～하면서
while	～하는 동안 ～하면서		
before	～하기 전에	since	～이래로, ～이후로
after	～한 후에	as soon as	～하자마자
until	～할 때까지	once	～하고 나면

• **When** I ate dinner, my sister came back home.

• Jennifer was listening to music **while** she was doing her homework.

• **Before** you leave, check your backpack one more time.

• **After** I went swimming, I got a cold.

• Every student in the classroom made noise **until** the teacher came in.

• I saw Mr. Jackson **as** I took a walk with my dog.

• He replied to me **as soon as** he got the email.

• **Once** you start to play the game, you can't stop.

• **Since** I was 19 years old, I have earned my spending money by myself.

➡ 'since'는 현재완료 시제에 주로 사용된다.

Answer Keys p. 52

A 괄호 안에서 알맞은 것을 고르시오.

1   They should finish their homework ((before) / once) the teacher comes back to class.

2   My sister danced (as / since) she took a bath.

3   Cindy saw Harry (while / once) she was jogging in the park.

4   They have to brush their teeth (after / since) they eat.

5   (Once / As soon as) you start to talk with him, you can't stop.

6   She has been sick (since / until) she came back from camp.

7   (As soon as / Before) John saw me, he began to cry.

8   We have to plant a tree (after / since) it rains.

9   You will have to clean your room (before / while) your mother comes back.

10   (Since / As) he was an elementary school student, Jerry has been interested in soccer.

B 주어진 단어를 알맞게 배열하여 문장을 완성하시오.

1   A girl named Katie called (while, with, you, mother, talked)
    ➡ A girl named Katie called ___*while you talked with mother*___.

2   He turned on the light (soon, left, as, she, the room, as)
    ➡ He turned on the light _____.

3   The director has made almost twelve movies (he, since, student, was, university, a)
    ➡ The director has made almost twelve movies _____
    _____.

4   The children kept playing baseball (it, too, play, until, to, dark, got)
    ➡ The children kept playing baseball _____.

5   We're sure you'll be surprised (you, when, the news, hear)
    ➡ We're sure you'll be surprised _____.

13-5 because / so ~ that... / so that

- **because / as / since**: '이유'나 '원인'의 부사절을 이끄는 접속사이다.
- **so that / in order that**: '목적'의 부사절을 이끄는 접속사이다.
- **so ~ that...**: '결과'의 부사절을 이끄는 접속사이다.

1. because / as / since: 이유, 원인을 나타낸다.

because + 문장 **= since, as** ~때문에, 왜냐하면	• Because I cut my finger on broken glass, mom was worried about me.
	• You must wear a school uniform since that's the rule at your school.
	• I was so hungry as I didn't have breakfast.
because of + 명사(구) ~때문에	• We couldn't go on a picnic because of the rain.

2. so that / in order that: 목적을 나타낸다.

so that **= in order that** ~하기 위해서	• Jane practices singing a lot so that she sings a solo during the concert.
	• I exercise every day in order that I lose weight.

➡ 'so that (= in order that) + 주어 + 동사'는 'so as to (= in order to) + 동사'와 바꿔 쓸 수 있다.

- We study hard **in order that** we go to a good university.
  = We study hard **so that** we go to a good university.
  = We study hard **in order to** go to a good university.
  = We study hard **so as to** go to a good university.

3. so ~ that...: 결과를 나타낸다.

so ~ that... 너무 ~해서 ...하다	• She is so pretty that she can get first place in the beauty contest. [긍정] = She is pretty enough to get first place in the beauty contest.
	• I am so weak that I can't carry the boxes. [부정] = I am too weak to carry the boxes.

Answer Keys p. 52

A 빈칸에 알맞은 말을 쓰시오.

1 I like Sam __because__ he is gentle and smart.

2 The stew was so salty _____ I needed much water.

3 She looked up at the sky _____ she could see the blue moon.

4 The movie is _____ long _____ Jane doesn't want to watch it.

5 Max was terrified _____ the accident.

6 I work out _____ I lose weight.

7 _____ she has no money, she can't buy the medicine.

8 _____ the letter is written in English, I can't read it.

9 Mary is _____ busy _____ she can't go to the concert with us.

10 _____ the storm, Jane can't hold the party tonight.

B 주어진 말을 사용하여 문장을 완성하시오.

1 She broke her leg, so please give her a chair. (as)
 ➡ Please give her a chair _____ *as she broke her leg* _____.

2 The pasta was too spicy for her to enjoy. (so ~ that)
 ➡ The pasta was _____.

3 He could give useful information to you. He has traveled in many countries. (because)
 ➡ _____, he could give useful information to you.

4 I bought some books in order to complete my report. (in order that)
 ➡ I bought some books _____.

5 My sister saved money so as to buy the luxurious bag. (so that)
 ➡ My sister saved money _____.

if/ though

- if: '조건'의 부사절을 이끄는 접속사이다.
- though/although/even though: '양보'의 부사절을 이끄는 접속사이다.

1. if/unless : 조건을 나타낸다.

if 만약 ~라면	• If you want to go to the beach, I will search for a good place.
unless (= if ~ not) 만약 ~이 아니라면	• Unless it snows heavily tomorrow, we'll go over the mountain. = If it doesn't snow heavily tomorrow, we'll go over the mountain.

2. though/although/even though : 양보를 나타낸다.

though although even though (= even if) 비록 ~일지라도 ~에도 불구하고	• Though (Although) I was so sleepy, I had to keep working.
	• Although (Though) it is sunny, we can't go outside to play.
	• Even though (if) she dosen't have a good idea, her team members may have one.

Grammar Plus +

- 양보의 while

  While she is old, she tries to learn new things.

- **even if (= whether ~or not)** : 주로 불확실한 상황을 가정하는 경우에 사용된다.

  We will go to the amusement park **even if** it rains tomorrow.

  = We will go to the amusement park **whether** it rains **or not**.

A   다음 밑줄 친 부분을 어법상 알맞게 고치시오.

1   If it <u>will snow</u>, she will leave next week.

                                                              snows

2   <u>If</u> you study hard, you will fail the exam.

                                                              _____

3   <u>So</u> my sister is only three year old, she can speak well.

                                                              _____

4   You should do it this way <u>unless</u> you aren't against it.

                                                              _____

5   <u>As</u> I like her paintings, I don't like her personality.

                                                              _____

6   I forgave her <u>so</u> she didn't acknowledge her faults.

                                                              _____

7   I'm going hiking <u>even though</u> it rains or not.

                                                              _____

8   We'll just walk there <u>unless</u> it's not far from here.

                                                              _____

9   If he <u>will come</u> back, we will be happy.

                                                              _____

B   주어진 말을 이용하여 두 문장을 한 문장으로 바꾸어 쓰시오.

1   Jane could not solve the problem. She tried hard. (although)

→   *Although she tried hard, Jane could not solve the problem.*

2   He can't open the door. He can't find us. (if)

→   _____

3   Thomas was elected as class president. He was very
     depressed. (although)

→   _____

4   You might get into trouble. You are careful with it. (unless)

→   _____

5   The students are still young. They know lots of things. (even
     though)

→   _____

13-7 접속부사

• 접속부사: 원래는 부사이지만 접속사처럼 쓰여 앞뒤의 내용을 연결하는 것을 접속부사라고 한다. 접속부사는 앞뒤에 '콤마(,)'를 찍어서 구분한다.

1. 순서, 나열

• first of all 우선	• at first 처음에는	• next 다음으로
• at last (finally) 마침내	• in the end 결국, 마침내	• in conclusion 마지막으로
• first(ly), second(ly)... last(ly) 첫 번째, 두 번째....마지막으로		

2. 예시, 강조

• for example 예를 들면	• for instance 예컨대	• in fact 사실
• actually 사실은	• indeed, as a matter of fact 사실상	
• above all (especially) 특히		

3. 전환, 가정

• by the way 그런데	• instead (of) ~대신에	• otherwise 그렇지 않다면

4. 추가

• moreover 게다가	• besides 게다가	• furthermore 뿐만 아니라
• in addition 덧붙여	• in other words 말하자면	• anyway 게다가, 그건 그렇고
• that is to say 다시 말해서		

5. 반대, 대조

• however 하지만	• on the contrary 반대로
• on the other hand 반면에	• in (by) contrast to (with) ~와 대조적으로

6. 결론, 요약

• therefore 그러므로	• as a result 결과적으로	• in short 요컨대
• in a word 한마디로		

Answer Keys p. 53

A 괄호 안에서 알맞은 것을 고르시오.

1   We discussed it for a long time. (In the end / Instead) we decided to give up.

2   Some countries, (for example / indeed), Korea and Japan use chopsticks.

3   The show was awesome, (however / moreover), the tickets weren't sold out.

4   Let's finish the meeting. (By the way / In short), what time is it?

5   (First of all / Actually), we will decide where to go.

6   There are lots of things to study. (Anyway / For instance), English literature and math.

7   I sent John the letter. (However / Therefore), he hasn't replied yet.

8   Helen answered my question. It was, (in a word / anyway) yes.

9   They didn't look sad. (In other words / On the contrary), they didn't care about the fact.

10   The coach says this is the last chance. (Therefore / Besides), I should do my best.

11   Linda is smart. (On the contrary / Above all), she can't solve the easy question.

12   I have brown hair. (That is to say / On the other hand), my brother has black hair.

13   We hope it will be fine. (Otherwise / In fact), we will have to cancel the festival.

Practice More I

Answer Keys p. 53

A 다음 빈칸에 알맞은 말을 쓰시오.

1 ____As____ time passed, the situation seemed to get better.

2 When she works out, she feels healthy _____ excited.

3 He promised me _____ he would quit wasting time.

4 Sally can't join us _____ she has a very important meeting tonight.

5 _____ you feel tired, you can take a rest for a while.

6 The man will have to choose between his dream _____ success.

7 _____ you have dinner, you will have to do the dishes.

8 It was very cold yesterday, _____ the players didn't stop training.

9 Neither my brother _____ I was interested in reading books.

10 Would you like pasta, rice, _____ something else?

B 다음 문장에서 어법상 어색한 것을 찾아 바르게 고치시오.

1 Neither Jane or Nick has to do it.

   ____Neither____ ➡ ____Either____

2 She said she would call but text me as soon as possible.

   _____ ➡ _____

3 It Max will come to the party or not doesn't matter.

   _____ ➡ _____

4 I'm sorry, and I won't go there.

   _____ ➡ _____

5 Please wait that I complete this project.

   _____ ➡ _____

6 They have played much better after the boy became our member.

   _____ ➡ _____

7 I'm sure you'll like her although you meet her.

   _____ ➡ _____

8   It was terribly cold, or Harry was wearing only a shirt.

_____ ➡ _____

9   My daughter is not a golfer nor a teacher.

_____ ➡ _____

10 Because of I had a headache, I had to rest.

_____ ➡ _____

C 주어진 단어를 이용하여 두 문장을 한 문장으로 바꾸시오.

1   The girls are kind. The girls are also positive. (not only ~ but also)

➡ _____*The girls are not only kind but also positive.*_____

2   He is good at playing chess. He is also good at playing soccer. (both)

➡ _____

3   I have a great interest in the concert. Jane doesn't like it. (however)

➡ _____

4   We are certain. The rumor is wrong. (that)

➡ _____

5   Jim can't decide. He should go or stay. (if)

➡ _____

6   I didn't make a flight reservation. I had to extend my visa. (besides)

➡ _____

7   Her personality has changed a lot. She met John. (since)

➡ _____

8   They heard the news. They began to call their family. (as soon as)

➡ _____

9   Throw the ball softly. She can hit it easily. (so that)

➡ _____

10 It is true. Mary will get married to him. (that)

➡ _____

D 주어진 단어를 알맞게 배열하여 문장을 바르게 완성하시오.

1 (they, that, will, are, next week, sure, snow, it, heavily)

➡ *They are sure that it will snow heavily next week.*

2 (so, a few, terrible, weeks, she, the accident, in the hospital, was, for, had to, that, stay)

➡ _____

3 (I, whether, or not, don't, I, the exam, pass, know, will)

➡ _____

4 (it, natural, the environment, people, is, to, want, enjoy, that)

➡ _____

5 (not only, sweets, to, but also, eat, he, like, I)

➡ _____

6 (until, keep, tell, he, stop, I, should, him, to, running)

➡ _____

7 (it, that, the magician's trick, is, figured out, Helen, surprising)

➡ _____

8 (I'm, excited, this game, sure, they, they'll be, try, once)

➡ _____

9 (the boy, my sister, that, doesn't, know, is, she)

➡ _____

10 (either, the meeting, my brother, attend, or, can, I)

➡ _____

내신 최다 출제 유형

01 다음 밑줄 친 if의 뜻이 나머지 넷과 다른 하나를 고르시오. [출제 예상 85%]

① It will be fun if you go together.
② If you visit there, you can see many kinds of birds.
③ I'm not sure if she will come to the party.
④ What if everyone in the world looked the same?
⑤ If I were a bird, I could fly to you.

02 다음 중 어법상 옳은 문장을 고르시오. [출제 예상 90%]

① I don't know how can I make new friends.
② Do you think who the boy in the blue shorts is?
③ What do you know Jenny means?
④ The teacher didn't understand why was I late.
⑤ Just talk to him and ask him how he studies.

03 다음 주어진 문장의 밑줄 친 as와 의미가 같은 것을 고르시오. [출제 예상 85%]

When in Rome, do as the Romans do.

① Minsu is as tall as his brother.
② He bought a diamond ring as he promised.
③ He saw his daughter as she was entering.
④ As her right arm was broken, she couldn't use it.
⑤ Mr. Smith works as a doctor.

04 다음 중 빈칸에 들어갈 알맞은 것을 고르시오. [출제 예상 80%]

The problem is _____ he never wants to play when we go out.

① if   ② what   ③ that
④ because   ⑤ how

05 다음 중 빈칸에 although를 쓸 수 없는 문장을 고르시오. [출제 예상 85%]

① The animals can run fast _____ they look slow.
② She helps others _____ she is not rich.
③ _____ it is raining, many people play in the outdoor swimming pool.
④ _____ I had nothing to say, I was silent.
⑤ _____ the radio is very old, it works very well.

06 다음 문장을 after 또는 before를 사용하여 바꿔 쓰시오. [출제 예상 80%]

I bought some flowers, and then I met him.

➡ _____

07 다음 주어진 문장을 neither를 사용하여 바꿔 쓰시오. [출제 예상 85%]

I could not laugh. I could not cry, either.

➡ _____

[01~05] 다음 빈칸에 들어갈 말로 알맞은 것을 고르시오.

01

Jade _____ Jennifer are making pancakes for their parents.

① but   ② so   ③ or
④ for   ⑤ and

02

A bad attitude can be harmful to you. _____, have a good attitude.

① Therefore   ② Since
③ While   ④ However
⑤ So that

03

There are so many important things people should do. _____, they should read books, research, and learn new things.

① In addition   ② Therefore
③ However   ④ Otherwise
⑤ For example

04

In the future, you can travel to Europe within three or four hours on a rocket plane. _____, you may be able to travel into space.

① However   ② For example
③ In addition   ④ Otherwise
⑤ On the other hand

05

The parking spots were made not for us, _____ for the disabled.

① and   ② or   ③ as
④ but   ⑤ of

[06~07] 다음 우리말에 맞게 빈칸에 알맞은 단어를 고르시오.

06

네가 규칙적으로 운동을 한다면 건강해질 것이다.
If you _____ regularly, you'll be healthy.

① exercising   ② have exercised
③ exercised   ④ will exercised
⑤ exercise

07

Jack도 Tom도 이번 여름에는 캠핑을 가지 않을 것이다.
_____ Jack nor Tom will go camping this summer.

① Either   ② Neither   ③ Not
④ Both   ⑤ But

[08~09] 다음 중 어법상 어색한 것을 고르시오.

08
① Whenever he visits us, he brings some toys.
② Though she is pretty and tall, many boys love her.
③ We have to leave before it rains.
④ I'm not sure if he will come back early.
⑤ As you didn't get up early, you missed the bus.

09
① Mr. Wang is a Chinese, but he likes Korean food.
② The directions are written in Spanish, so he can't read them.
③ Do you want to take a bus or a taxi?
④ We had so a good time that I will never forget it.
⑤ Either he or she is going to Sam's house.

10 다음 밑줄 친 that의 쓰임이 나머지 넷과 다른 것을 고르시오.
① Remember that you should finish the work by tomorrow.
② Timmy said that he lost his house because of the hurricane.
③ Energy that is not used is stored as fat in the body.
④ The chart shows us that exercise makes the body healthy.
⑤ I know that I should study hard for the exam.

11 ★★★ 다음 주어진 문장의 밑줄 친 as와 용법이 같은 것을 고르시오.

> You can decorate the Christmas tree as you want.

① She wasn't as pretty as her sister.
② I asked you to do that as I explained.
③ It wasn't easy to buy an oven as it was very expensive.
④ As he grew older, he became fatter.
⑤ I saw him running fast as I crossed the street.

12 다음 문장 중 의미하는 것이 나머지 넷과 다른 것을 고르시오.
① Jane is my student and Sam is, too.
② Not only Jane but also Sam is my student.
③ Jane as well as Sam is my student.
④ Both Jane and Sam are my students.
⑤ Either Jane or Sam is my student.

13 다음 문장에 이어질 말로 알맞은 것을 고르시오.

> The art lesson doesn't start.

① Besides, we study art.
② On the other hand, the art lesson is done.
③ In addition, we don't have to wait a little bit more.
④ For example, we will wait a little bit more.
⑤ Therefore, we have to wait a little bit more.

Answer Keys p. 54

14 다음 우리말을 영어로 바르게 옮긴 것을 고르시오.

> 나는 영어와 프랑스어 둘 다 못한다.

① I speak neither English nor French.
② I speak not only English but also French.
③ I speak both English and French.
④ I speak English as well as French.
⑤ I speak either English or French.

★★★
15 다음 중 어법상 어색한 것을 고르시오.

① I couldn't do my homework because I had a fever.
② Both my sister and I likes fried chicken.
③ She lost her cell phone, so she couldn't call anyone.
④ Do your best, and your dreams will come true.
⑤ Tell the truth, or you will lose your friends.

16 다음 문장의 밑줄 친 단어 대신에 쓸 수 있는 것을 고르시오.

> It is hard to know if the soldier tells the truth.

① as   ② unless   ③ whether
④ though   ⑤ that

17 다음 중 어법상 옳은 문장을 고르시오.

① Both Justin and Phillip is smart.
② Parents as well children need protection.
③ Neither they or he is going to the swimming pool.
④ Not only Jude but also Mia was working on the new project.
⑤ Either you or he have to attend the meeting.

★★★
18 다음 밑줄 친 부분의 쓰임이 나머지 넷과 다른 것을 고르시오.

① Sally has lived here since she was young.
② Since Max doesn't help her, she has to do it herself.
③ I did not go out since it was snowing.
④ She wore a coat since it was very cold.
⑤ Since James couldn't find me, he left a message.

19 다음 주어진 문장의 밑줄 친 부분과 쓰임이 같은 것을 모두 고르시오.

> I wonder if my teacher will like my gift.

① Even if I want to give up, I will keep going.
② Ask your elder sister if she likes her job.
③ Ben doesn't know if it will be very cold tomorrow.
④ Eat these snacks if you are hungry.
⑤ We will smile if we win the contest.

20 다음 중 빈칸에 필요한 접속사가 <u>아닌</u> 것을 고르시오.

> ⓐ _____ he is old, he always learns new things.
> ⓑ _____ it rained a lot, the stream flooded.
> ⓒ He arrived _____ I was having dinner.
> ⓓ Yuran knows _____ her English has improved.

① that   ② since   ③ while
④ until   ⑤ although

◇◇◇◇◇◇◇◇◇ 서술형 평가 ◇◇◇◇◇◇◇◇◇

[21~23] 다음 주어진 우리말과 같은 뜻이 되도록 빈칸에 알맞은 말을 쓰시오.

21

> 나는 나뿐만 아니라 내 가족을 위해서도 최선을 다할 것이다.

➡ I will do my best _____ for myself _____ for my family.

22

> 너는 일단 우리나라를 방문해 보면 이곳을 좋아할 것이다.

➡ _____, you will like it.

23 ★★★

> 네가 친절하면 모든 친구들이 너를 좋아할 것이다.
> 반면에, 네가 무례하다면 그들은 너를 떠날 것이다.

➡ If you are kind, all of your friends will like you.
_____, if _____, they will leave you.

[24~26] 다음 주어진 두 문장이 같은 뜻이 되도록 빈칸에 알맞은 말을 쓰시오.

24

> On hearing his joke, she started laughing.
> = _____ _____ _____ she heard his joke, she started laughing.

➡ _____

25

> Let's play soccer if it doesn't rain tomorrow.
> = Let's play soccer _____ _____ _____ tomorrow.

➡ _____

★★★
26

Sarah went to bed early in order not to be late for work the next morning.
= Sarah went to bed early _____ _____ she won't be late for work the next morning.

➡ _____

[27~28] 다음 우리말과 같은 뜻이 되도록 괄호 안의 단어를 바르게 배열하여 쓰시오.

27

Tom은 늦게 일어났기 때문에 학교에 지각을 했다.
(Tom / got / as / up / late)

➡ _____, he was late for school.

★★★
28

아버지나 어머니 두 분 중 한 분은 직장에 다니신다.
(father / mother / or / goes / either)

➡ _____ to work.

[29~30] 다음 우리말을 영어로 바르게 옮겨 쓰시오.

★★★
29

나는 역사와 영어 두 과목을 모두 좋아한다.

➡ _____

★★★
30

그 일이 끝났다. 그러므로 나는 일찍 집으로 갔다.

➡ The project was done. _____, _____.

Note

14

Chapter
전치사

Point Check I

◆ **전치사 :** 명사나 대명사 앞에 위치하여, 시간, 장소, 위치, 방향, 수단 등을 나타낸다.

1. 시간, 때를 나타내는 전치사

at	구체적인 시각, 비교적 짧은 시간(때)을 나타낼 때 사용한다.		
on	날짜, 요일, 특정한 날의 아침, 낮, 저녁을 나타낼 때 사용한다.		
in	연도, 월, 계절의 비교적 긴 시간을 나타낼 때 사용한다.		
before	~의 전에	until (till)	~까지 (진행, 계속)
after	~의 후에	for	~동안 (시간)
from	~부터	during	~동안 (기간)
since	~이후로	in	~뒤에, 후에
by	~까지 (완료)	within	~이내에

2. 장소를 나타내는 전치사

at	특정한 지점을 나타내며 비교적 좁은 장소에 쓰인다.
on	표면에 접촉해 있는 것을 나타낸다.
in	공간 안에 속해 있는 것을 나타내며 비교적 넓은 장소에 쓰인다.

3. 방향, 움직임을 나타내는 전치사

to	~로, ~까지	off	~에서 떨어져
for	~으로(목적지)	across	~을 가로질러
toward(s)	~쪽으로(방향)	along	~을 따라서
up	~위로	through	~을 통하여
down	~아래로	around	~주위에
into	~안으로	out of	~밖으로

4. 위치를 나타내는 전치사

under	~아래에	next to	
over	~위에 (뒤덮듯이)	beside	~옆에
below	~(보다) 아래에	by	
above	~(보다) 위에	near	~가까이에
in front of	~앞에	between	~사이에 (둘)
behind	~뒤에	among	~사이에 (셋 이상)

14-1 시간의 전치사 (1)

- **시간의 전치사**: 명사나 대명사 앞에 위치하여, 시간, 요일, 계절의 정확한 때를 나타낸다.

1. at

시각 ➡ 구체적인 시각 앞에 사용	• at 10 a.m.　　• at 11 p.m.　　• at two o'clock • The second train is going to depart at 8:30.
때 ➡ 비교적 짧은 시간 앞에 사용	• at noon　　　　• at night　　　• at lunchtime • at the moment　• at present　• at Christmas • Jimmy and Mary will arrive late at night. Let's eat first.

2. on

날짜, 요일 ➡ 날짜, 요일 앞에 사용	• on Sunday　　• on Mondays　　• on May 5th • My sister's birthday is on March 2nd.
특정한 날, 요일 ➡ 특정한 날이나 그 날의 아침, 저녁, 낮 시간을 나타내는 데 사용	• on Saturday morning　　　• on Tuesday evenings • on New Year's Day　　　　• on Christmas Eve • My family always goes to church on Sunday mornings.

3. in

연도, 월, 계절 ➡ 비교적 긴 시간 앞에 사용	• in summer　　• in 2005　　• in April • My friends and I go skiing every weekend in the winter.
때 ➡ 비교적 긴 시간 앞에 사용	• in the morning　• in the afternoon　• in the past • in the future　　• in the 1900s　　• in the 21st century • The birth rate of this country decreased rapidly in the 2000s.

4. 'at, on, in'을 사용하지 않는 시간 표현

'every, this, that, last, next' 등이 시간을 나타내는 <u>부사구를 이룰 때는</u> 그 앞에 'at, on, in'은 사용하지 않는다.

- Hyorin's whole family will immigrate to America **next year**.

Answer Keys p. 55

A 괄호 안에서 알맞은 것을 고르시오.

1 I'm going to go to the concert (at / in) noon.

2 My father usually wakes up (at / on) seven thirty.

3 What does Sally usually do (on / in) weekends?

4 People are busy and often work late (at / on) night.

5 (In / On) winter, I like to go skiing with my friends.

6 The soccer match will be held (on / in) August 23rd.

7 Kate wanted to get a lot of presents (on / at) Christmas.

8 The train is going to arrive (at / in) three.

9 James was born (on / at) October 23, 1989.

10 The festival will be held (on / at) Thursday.

11 We enjoy skating and flying kite (in / on) Sundays.

12 I will call Max again (in / at) the evening.

13 I heard that the store is going to open (at / in) July.

14 The bookstore opens (at / in) eleven.

15 The city is famous for its many festivals (in / on) December.

Lesson 14-2 시간의 전치사 (2)

• 시간의 전치사: 명사나 대명사 앞에 위치하여, 시간, 요일, 계절의 정확한 때를 나타낸다.

◈ 시간의 전치사

전치사		예문
before	~의 전에	• Please give it back before noon.
after	~의 후에	• Every child learns to brush teeth after eating a meal.
from	~부터	• Stephanie started to take dance calsses from January.
since	~이후로	• I haven't eaten this one since then.
by	~까지 (완료)	• We will finish the project by the day after tomorrow.
until (till)	~까지 (진행, 계속)	• Paul is going to wait here until this weekend.
for	~동안 (시간)	• I have worked for this company for five years.
during	~동안 (기간)	• Thomas has taught English here during the summer.
in	~뒤에, 후에	• My father will arrive here in ten minutes.
within	~이내에	• Hurry up. We have to clean all the rooms within two hours.

☆Check up!

Answer Keys p. 55

A 주어진 우리말과 뜻이 같도록 빈칸에 알맞은 말을 쓰시오.

1 Finish your homework ___before___ lunch. (점심식사 전에)

2 They have been waiting for you _____ eight.
(8시 이후로)

3 Mr. Lee has taught science in this school _____ six years. (6년 동안)

4 Every student has to turn in the paper _____ next week.
(다음 주 까지)

5 Minji will go to America _____ summer vacation.
(여름방학 동안)

6 We have to arrive there _____ three minutes. (3분 이내에)

14. 전치사 **411**

7   The final test will start _____ an hour. (1시간 뒤에)

8   Everyone should go to bed _____ ten. (10시 후에)

9   We will work on the project _____ midnight. (자정까지)

10   The girl started taking baking classes _____ March.
     (3월부터)

B   괄호 안에 알맞은 것을 고르시오.

1   We should finish the report ((before) / until) five.

2   What else did you do (during / for) the holidays?

3   I'll be waiting here for you (for / since) thirty minutes.

4   I'm looking forward to the show. It's coming out (in / since)
     a few days.

5   The woman works (since / from) nine to seven.

6   Jennifer has been studying German (from / since) last year.

7   Harrison and Jessy decided to volunteer at a nursing home
     (in / on) Christmas Eve.

8   A lot of buildings were destroyed (for / during) World War II.

9   Make sure you've packed your stationery (after / before) you
     leave.

10   The gallery will be closed (from / since) February to April
     for repairs.

14-3 장소의 전치사

• **장소를 나타내는 전치사**: 명사나 대명사 앞에서 사람이나 물건이 있는 장소를 정확하게 말해준다.

1. at : ∼에

특정한 지점을 나타내거나 비교적 좁은 장소에 쓰인다.		
• at home	• at the corner	• at the bus stop
• at the top	• at school	• at work
• at a garage sale	• at a contest	• at Maple Street

• We saw famous singers **at the school festival**.

• The air **at the top** of the mountain made me feel refreshed.

2. on : ∼(위)에

표면에 접촉해 있는 것을 나타낸다.		
• on the sea	• on land	• on the road
• on the desk	• on the wall	• on a train
• on a plane	• on a farm	• on the Internet

• Judy decided to take a nap **on the blanket** under the tree.

• Last summer and winter, I helped my uncle **on his farm**.

3. in : ∼(안)에

공간 안에 속해 있는 것을 나타내며 비교적 넓은 장소에 쓰인다.		
• in bed	• in prison	• in church
• in town	• in taxi	• in the sky
• in the world	• in a mirror	• in a book

• I saw that he was hiding something **in his pocket**.

• When I see new words, I look them up **in a dictionary**.

Answer Keys p. 55

A   다음 빈칸에 at, on, in 중 알맞은 것을 쓰시오.

1   There are several students _____*at*_____ the subway station.

2   The little dog was sitting _____ my father's lap.

3   A lot of people stood _____ line to buy the ticket.

4   There were some stars _____ the sky.

5   The man asked us, "Is your sister _____ home?"

6   Sam wrote his address _____ the note.

7   There were a lot of coins _____ the bottom of the sofa.

8   It is difficult to get a seat _____ the bus in the morning.

9   She read about the accident _____ a newspaper.

10 I think you can find interesting things _____ a garage sale.

11 Andy hung the picture _____ the wall.

12 All the boats _____ sea had to return to the port because of the storm.

13 Why don't you look up the word _____ the dictionary?

14 I didn't know that there was garbage _____ the floor.

15 We saw some strange fish _____ the river.

14-4 방향의 전치사

• 방향을 나타내는 전치사: 명사나 대명사 앞에서 사람이나 물건이 있는 방향을 정확하게 말해준다.

1. 방향을 나타내는 전치사

to ~로, ~까지	go, come, return, send, bring, walk 등과 쓰인다.

• Judy and I went to the art gallery to get some information about Renaissance art.

for ~으로(목적지)	가려는 목적지를 나타내며, start, leave 등과 쓰인다.

• Seon left for the airport in a hurry without saying anything.

toward(s) ~쪽으로(방향)	목적지 쪽으로의 방향을 나타내고, walk, come, run, drive, turn, rush 등과 함께 쓰인다.

• Finally, we saw a big ship coming toward the island.

2. 움직임을 나타내는 전치사

up	~위로		off	~에서 떨어져	
down	~아래로		across	~을 가로질러	
into	~안으로		along	~을 따라서	
out of	~밖으로		through	~을 통하여	
onto	~위로		around	~주위에	

 Answer Keys p. 55

A 보기 에서 알맞은 말을 골라 빈칸에 쓰시오.

> 보기
>
> | off | out of | onto | around | from |
> | through | up | for | toward | down |

1 Lily was climbing _____up_____ the ladder to reach the ball.

2 Sam pinned a memo _____ the board.

3 They got _____ the room after three hours.

4 He said that they fell _____ the top of the hill.

5 You can find the hospital _____ the corner.

6 Did you see the man who passed _____ the forest?

7 Children should be careful when they are sliding _____ a slide.

8 We drove the car _____ the shopping mall to park.

9 It's about ten kilometers _____ my home to your school.

10 This flight will leave _____ Tokyo shortly.

14-5 위치의 전치사

· 위치를 나타내는 전치사: 명사나 대명사 앞에서 사람이나 물건이 있는 위치를 정확하게 말해준다.

◈ 위치를 나타내는 전치사

전치사		예시
under	~아래에	· A pair of my earrings was under the bed.
over	~위에 (뒤덮듯이)	· Some sparrows fly over the wall.
below	~ (보다) 아래에	· There is a table below the picture.
above	~(보다) 위에(로)	· The eagle flies above the clouds.
in front of	~앞에	· Tom stood in front of me.
behind	~뒤에	· The little boy hides behind his mom.
next to	~옆에	· The bookstore is next to the school.
beside		· Jim is waiting for me beside the church
by		· A big tree is by my house.
near	~가까이에	· Mr. Parker's house is near the flower shop.
between	~사이에 (둘)	· There are some vegetables between two buns.
among	~사이에 (셋 이상)	· The singer is among her many fans.

Answer Keys p. 55

A 괄호 안에서 알맞은 것을 고르시오.

1   The moon is coming up ((over) / among) the mountain.

2   Mary stood (between / among) Tim and Sally.

3   There is a large park (beside / next) to my house.

4   She hung a painting (above / next) the table.

5   The leader was sitting (around / among) his club members.

6   Put the box in the drawer (near / next) my bed.

7   I know the girl who is dancing (in front of / below) the audience.

8   She finally found a very rare book (among / behind) the desk.

9   The little boy is wearing a shirt (under / by) his coat.

10   There will be a big parade (around / between) the stadium.

11   The game took place (to / in) front of many people.

12   A group of students were standing (from / near) the entrance.

13   There is a fence (between / among) the two buildings.

14   Turn left at the corner, and the hotel is (next / beside) to the hospital.

15   Everyone knows the earth goes (around / below) the sun.

Practice More I

Answer Keys p. 55~56

A   괄호 안에서 알맞은 것을 고르시오.

1   The conference is scheduled to begin ((at) / in) eleven.

2   The famous festival is held (in / on) November.

3   Let's walk (up / by) the hill.

4   The boy raised his hat (above / by) his head.

5   I am going to keep a diary (in / of) English.

6   Mom told me that I should wear a shirt (above / under) the jacket.

7   There are still some students (at / on) the bus stop.

8   I should read this book (until / to) dinner time.

9   Jane and I saw some strange fish (in / on) the river.

10 Cheer up. We only have three more classes (from / before) going home.

B   빈칸에 알맞은 전치사를 쓰시오.

1   I think they are workaholic because they work _____*from*_____ morning to midnight.

2   You should remember the ticket is valid _____ next weekend.

3   This morning, a bike hit a man _____ the crosswalk.

4   I slept _____ the lecture. I didn't hear what the professor said.

5   Don't forget to put the salt _____ the bowl.

6   The boy can't go abroad _____ the holidays.

7   What's the most popular sport _____ your country?

8   We haven't seen the boy _____ last week.

9   I saw the sun disappear _____ the horizon.

10 The hungry dog was lying _____ the sofa.

Practice More I

C 다음 문장에서 어법상 <u>어색한</u> 것을 찾아 바르게 고치시오.

1 My mother was sitting on the table.

                      on ➡ *at*

2 There are big trees into the hill.

                      _____ ➡ _____

3 They have prepared for the party for six o'clock.

                      _____ ➡ _____

4 Where did you live after moving into this city?

                      _____ ➡ _____

5 I met him in Monday.

                      _____ ➡ _____

6 Please call me on noon.

                      _____ ➡ _____

7 People usually go to the sea on summer.

                      _____ ➡ _____

8 Liah usually doesn't eat breakfast at the morning.

                      _____ ➡ _____

9 They knew each other during five years.

                      _____ ➡ _____

10 There are many stars on the sky.

                      _____ ➡ _____

D 우리말 해석에 맞게 단어를 바르게 배열하여 문장을 완성하시오.

1 그 탐험가는 동굴 안으로 이동했다.

(the, the cave, moved, explorer, into)

➡ _____ *The explorer moved into the cave.* _____

2 많은 유물들이 전쟁 중에 도난 당했다.

(many, the war, were, during, relics, stolen)

➡ _____

3 탁자 위에는 두개의 작은 램프와 책 한 권이 있다.

(there, the table, two small lamps, a book, are, and, on)

➡ _____

4 낡은 등대가 언덕 위에 있었다.

(an old, there, hill, the, on, was, lighthouse)

➡ _____

5 그 소설가는 1989년 3월 13일에 태어났다.

(the writer, 1989, was, on March 13, born)

➡ _____

6 그들은 7월부터 봉사 활동을 하기 시작했다.

(they, July, do, from, began, to, work, volunteer)

➡ _____

7 우리는 13시간 이내에 한국으로 돌아가야 한다.

(we, Korea, hours, return, within, should, thirteen, to)

➡ _____

8 Jane은 책들 사이에서 일기장을 찾았다.

(Jane, the books, found, among, a diary)

➡ _____

9 소녀와 그녀의 강아지는 강가를 따라 뛰고 있었다.

(the girl, the river, her dog, running, and, along, were)

➡ _____

10 자동차들이 바다를 가기 위해서 숲을 통과해 달리고 있다.

(Cars, to, driving, to the sea, are, the forest, through, go)

➡ _____

Point Check Ⅱ

◆ **전치사** : 명사나 대명사 앞에 위치하여, 시간, 장소, 위치 방향, 수단 등을 나타낸다.

1. 도구, 수단을 나타내는 전치사

• by + 교통, 통신수단, 방법	• with + 동작의 도구, 수단	• in + 표현의 도구, 수단

2. 여러 의미의 전치사

with	~와 함께, ~에 찬성하여	as	~로서
by	~에 의해	except	~외에는
in	~을 입고 있는	due to	~때문에
without	~없이, ~하지 않고	according to	~에 따르면, ~에 따라
for	~을 위해, ~에 찬성하는	instead of	~대신에
against	~에 반대하는	like	~처럼, ~와 같은

3. 형용사와 함께 쓰는 전치사

• be absent from	~에 결석하다	• be ashamed of	~을 부끄러워하다 수치스럽게 여기다
• be different from	~와 다르다	• be based on	~에 근거하다
• be afraid of	~을 두려워하다	• be busy with	~으로 바쁘다
• be proud of	~을 자랑스러워하다	• be capable of	~을 할 수 있다
• be full of	~으로 가득 차다	• be crazy about	~에 열광적이다 ~을 매우 좋아하다
• be tired of	~에 싫증 나다	• be crowded with	~으로 가득 하다
• be interested in	~에 관심이 있다	• be familiar with	~에 익숙하다, 친숙하다

4. 동사와 함께 쓰는 전치사

• agree to	(제안을) 받아들이다	• break up with	~와 절교하다
• agree with	(사람에) 동의하다	• catch up with	~을 따라잡다
• apologize for	~대해 사과하다	• come up with	~을 찾아내다, 제시하다
• apply for	~에 지원하다	• cut down on	~을 줄이다
• ask for	~을 요구하다	• go out with	~와 사귀다

Lesson 14-6 여러 의미의 전치사 (1)

- 도구, 수단을 나타내는 전치사: 'with'는 도구와 함께 쓰여 '~을 가지고'의 뜻을 가지며, 'by'는 교통수단과 함께 쓰여 '~을 타고'의 뜻을 가진다.
- 전치사의 여러 의미: 명사나 대명사 앞에서 찬반, 동의 등의 의미를 가진 전치사들도 있다.

1. 도구, 수단, 재료를 나타내는 전치사

by + 교통, 통신수단, 방법	• by bike (subway, bus, car, boat) • by land (ship, sea) • by plane (air) • by mail, fax • I went to my grandmother's house by bus.
with + 동작의 도구, 수단	• with a knife (hammer, spoon) • with the key • with a phone (camera) • He broke the stone with a hammer.
in + 표현의 도구, 수단	• in Korean (Chinese, a low voice) • in a modern style • in ink (pencil, watercolor) • Lina always draws pictures in red pencil.

2. 여러 의미의 전치사

전치사		예시
with	~와 함께	• It was a good experience to work with you.
	~와 ~에 찬성하여	• Molly always agrees with Jerry's opinion.
	~에 대하여	• She fixed the problem with the information I gave her.
	~을 가지고 있는	• The woman with long blond hair is my aunt.
	~의 몸에 지니고 있는	• We don't have any money with us now.
	~을 사용하여 ~으로	• Korean people eat rice with chopsticks and spoons.
without	~없이 ~하지 않고	• These days, we can't imagine the world without cell phones.
for	~을 위해 ~에 찬성하는	• We're for the new rule of not wearing school uniforms.
against	~에 반대하는	• Is there anyone else against this plan?

A   빈칸에 by, with, in 중 알맞은 전치사를 쓰시오.

1   It will be faster to go there _____*by*_____ bus.

2   Tina broke the window _____ a big hammer.

3   John began his speech _____ bowing to the audience.

4   I may be able to decorate the box _____ fancy wrappers.

5   People kept on talking _____ sign language.

6   I bought some books and sent them to Mina _____ post.

7   She took some wonderful pictures _____ the camera.

8   Please send your document to me _____ fax.

9   I could open the room _____ the key.

10   We are going to take a trip _____ train.

B   괄호 안에서 알맞은 것을 고르시오.

1   She was chopping the carrots (by / (with)) a knife.

2   It looks strange. Do you have another shirt (with / in) blue?

3   Let's go to school (on / to) foot. We have enough time to go.

4   I met him, and we talked to each other (in / with) English.

5   My family will go to Busan (in / with) Tim's car.

여러 의미의 전치사 (2)

• 전치사의 여러 의미 : 명사나 대명사 앞에서 원인, 이유, 주제를 나타내는 전치사들도 있다.

◆ 여러 의미의 전치사

전치사		예시
like	~처럼 ~와 같은	• In the movie, he flew like a bat.
by	~에 의해	• She recommended a book written by Emily Bronte.
	~함으로써	• Douglas got a lot of toy cars by collecting them one by one.
	(정도) ~로 ~만큼	• The water of this city has decreased by 20% since last year.
in	~을 입고 있는	• The girl in a yellow raincoat is my niece, Julie.
	(방법, 크기, 도구) ~로	• He couldn't erase it because he wrote it in pen.
as	~로서	• Cherry tomatoes are well known as a low-caloric food.
except	~외에는	• Bobby didn't tell anyone except his wife about the news.
due to	~때문에	• All of the subways are delayed due to the weather conditions.
according to	~에 따르면 ~에 따라	• According to the news, two students in Gwangju will enter Harvard University.
instead of	~대신에	• If you want to lose weight, just walk instead of driving the car.

A 괄호 안에서 알맞은 것을 고르시오.

1 The classroom was used (like / (as)) a meeting room during the discussion.

2 I like the music composed (by / to) him.

3 We had better cut the pie (in / as) eight pieces to share it with everyone.

4 My little sister dressed up (like / in) Catwoman at last nights' party.

5 We had to use this box (as / like) a chair while we were waiting for him.

6 The store is open everyday (except / for) Saturday.

7 There are many galleries in Seoul (like / by) Kim's gallery.

8 I have a problem (with / without) the new computer program.

9 Helen tends to judge people (like / by) their appearances.

10 (Instead of / Due to) helping his parents, he went out with his friends.

11 Everyone arrived on time (except / without) Brian. Our teacher was so angry.

12 She recommends vegetarianism (as / with) an easy way to eat healthy.

13 All of the cars stopped (due to / instead of) the accident.

14 The project was proceeding (according to / in) his plan.

15 Minhyuk did a fine job (as / by) the class president this semester.

14-8 형용사와 함께 쓰는 전치사

• 형용사와 함께 쓰는 전치사: 'be동사 + 형용사 + 전치사'의 형태를 가지고 있으며, 일상생활에서 자주 쓰이는 표현들이 많으므로 외워두자.

◈ 형용사와 함께 쓰는 전치사

• be absent from	~에 결석하다	• be ashamed of	~을 부끄러워하다 수치스럽게 여기다
• be different from	~와 다르다	• be based on	~에 근거하다
• be afraid of	~을 두려워하다	• be busy with	~으로 바쁘다
• be proud of	~을 자랑스러워하다	• be capable of	~을 할 수 있다
• be full of	~으로 가득 차다	• be crazy about	~에 열광적이다 ~을 매우 좋아하다
• be tired of	~에 싫증 나다	• be crowded with	~으로 붐비다
• be interested in	~에 관심이 있다	• be familiar with	~에 익숙하다, 친숙하다
• be curious about	~에 호기심이 있다	• be frightened at	~에 놀라다
• be good at	~을 잘하다	• be late for	~에 지각하다
• be sorry for (about)	~을 미안해하다	• be ready for	~을 위한 준비가 되다
• be famous for	~으로 유명하다	• be responsible for	~에 책임이 있다

 Check up!

Answer Keys p. 56

A 빈칸에 알맞은 전치사를 쓰시오.

1 Nick is good ____at____ playing soccer and baseball.

2 We have been interested _____ gardening.

3 Lisa was frightened _____ the sudden noise.

4 There is a room full _____ balloons and flowers.

5 She was famous _____ bad acting.

6 I was really surprised because the streets were crowded _____ many people.

7 Don't be late _____ the meeting.

8 Harry got married _____ Jane last year.

9 John is tired _____ preparing for the party alone.

10 I was curious _____ how to fix cars.

Lesson 14-9 동사와 함께 쓰는 전치사

- 동사와 함께 쓰는 전치사: '동사 + 전치사', '동사 + 부사 + 전치사'의 형태로, 동사와 전치사를 분리할 수 없으며 뒤에 목적어를 취한다.

1. '동사 + 전치사'

• agree to	(제안을) 받아들이다	• concentrate on	~에 집중하다
• agree with	(사람에) 동의하다	• depend (rely) on	~에 의존하다
• apologize for	~에 대해 사과하다	• die of (from)	~으로 사망하다
• apply for	~에 지원하다	• get over	~을 극복하다, 회복하다
• ask for	~을 요구하다	• hear about	~에 관해 듣다
• believe in	~을 믿다	• hear from	~으로부터 소식을 듣다
• belong to	~에 속하다	• look into	~을 조사하다
• care about	~을 신경 쓰다	• pay for	~에 대가를 지불하다
• care for	~을 좋아하다, 돌보다	• suffer from	~으로 고통 받다
• consist of	~으로 구성되다	• wait for	~을 기다리다

2. '동사 + 부사 + 전치사'

• break up with	~와 절교하다	• go out with	~와 사귀다
• catch up with	~을 따라잡다	• keep up with	~와 보조를 맞추다 연락하다
• come up with	~을 찾아내다, 제시하다	• put up with	~을 참다
• cut down on	~을 줄이다	• run out of	~을 다 소비하다

 **Check up!**

Answer Keys p. 56

A 다음 문장의 빈칸에 맞는 전치사를 쓰시오.

1 Paul didn't break up ____with____ John although John made a big mistake.

2 I tried to concentrate _____ listening to music.

3 Some people care _____ other people's opinions too much.

4 She applied _____ the job, but she was turned down.

5 I think Suzie should apologize _____ yelling at her teacher. It was rude.

6 The result depends _____ how hard we work.

7 The doctor told me that I should cut down _____ snacks.

8 After sending the letter to Katie, I waited _____ her reply.

9 They suddenly laughed _____ me.

10 He said he looked forward _____ my quick reply.

B 다음 우리말 해석에 맞게 빈칸에 알맞은 말을 쓰시오.

1 그는 회의 내내 많은 아이디어를 제공했다.
   ➡ He _____came up with_____ many ideas during the meeting.

2 그들은 육상 대회를 준비하면서 모든 에너지를 소비했다.
   ➡ They _____ by preparing for a track meet.

3 Mr. Brown은 어젯밤 심장마비로 사망했다.
   ➡ Mr. Brown _____ last night.

4 나는 그 두통 때문에 밤새 고통 받았다.
   ➡ I _____ a headache all night long.

5 그녀는 그와 결국 사귀기로 결정했다.
   ➡ She finally decided to _____.

Practice More II

A 빈칸에 알맞은 전치사를 쓰시오.

1 I'm sorry _____*for*_____ the mistake.

2 This movie is based _____ a true story. So, I'm really moved.

3 Billy didn't tell anyone _____ me about his secret.

4 Fortunately, I can correct the answer because I wrote it _____ pencil.

5 When he arrived there, he ran up the hill _____ a horse.

6 Although I would like to vote _____ the policy, I'm too young to vote.

7 He agreed _____ my opinion. He thought it would be useful.

8 According _____ the professor, there will be a pop quiz next week.

9 _____ his smoking habit, my uncle got lung cancer.

10 My parents are proud _____ me. That makes me happy.

B 괄호 안에서 알맞은 것을 고르시오.

1 Andy is so crazy (about / on) playing soccer. He plays soccer everyday.

2 It can live for weeks (without / against) eating anything.

3 I'd like to have a bottle of milk (instead of / due to) orange juice, please.

4 Do you happen to know why Thomas was mad (at / to) her?

5 When I was young, I dreamed (about / in) becoming a nurse.

6 She was really shocked because everyone laughed (for / at) her.

7 (According to / Due to) the weather forecast, there will be a heavy storm next week.

8 They apologized (of / for) insulting me, so I could forgive them.

9 My baby dressed up (by / like) a spider for the Halloween party.

10 I could watch my best friend (on / in) TV.

C 다음 문장에서 어법상 어색한 것을 찾아 바르게 고치시오.

1 She was interested of English literature.

_____of_____ ➡ _____in_____

2 Minsu isn't familiar by this situation.

_____ ➡ _____

3 Teenagers usually depend with their parents when they are in trouble.

_____ ➡ _____

4 I apologized to being so late.

_____ ➡ _____

5 My sister doesn't care for other people's opinions.

_____ ➡ _____

6 They were jealous to Mina because she got first prize in the contest.

_____ ➡ _____

7 This is my first time to travel with plane.

_____ ➡ _____

8 I can't imagine the world without he.

_____ ➡ _____

9 She has been married with James for a year.

_____ ➡ _____

10 We are responsible to the accident.

_____ ➡ _____

Practice More Ⅱ

Answer Keys p. 56~57

D 주어진 우리말 해석에 맞게 단어를 알맞게 배열하시오.

1 축제 동안 모든 거리들이 사람들로 가득했다.

(all the streets, the festival, crowded, during, people, were, with)

➡ *All the streets were crowded with people during the festival.*

2 엄마는 채소로 가득한 바구니를 들고 있었다.

(mom, of, holding, was, full, the basket, vegetables)

➡ _____

3 오늘 뉴스에 따르면 다음 주부터 장마가 시작될 것이다.

(According to, next week, start, the monsoon, today's news, will)

➡ _____

4 Emma는 어제 일어난 교통사고에 놀랐다.

(Emma, yesterday, was, that, at, happened, frightened, the accident)

➡ _____

5 나는 그들을 다시 한 번 미국에서 볼 것을 고대하고 있다.

(I'm, America, to, them, in, seeing, forward, again, looking)

➡ _____

6 그들은 그의 죽음에 관한 소문을 믿고 있었다.

(They, his death, believed, about, the rumor)

➡ _____

7 그녀는 일 때문에 바빠서 저녁식사를 준비할 수 없었다.

(She, work, was, prepare, busy, couldn't, with, so, dinner, she)

➡ _____

8 나는 전적으로 혼자 그 프로젝트를 맡을 수 있었다.

(I, myself, was, the project, all, capable, by, of, doing)

➡ _____

9 Sam은 지구 온난화와 관련된 책을 찾는 중이다.

(Sam, global warming, is, related, looking, books, for, to)

➡ _____

Answer Keys p. 57

내신 최다 출제 유형

01 다음 빈칸에 들어갈 말로 알맞은 것을 고르시오. [출제 예상 85%]

> I had to stay in the cabin _____ heavy rain.

① because   ② of   ③ as
④ because of   ⑤ as

02 다음 주어진 문장의 밑줄 친 부분과 쓰임이 다른 것을 고르시오. [출제 예상 90%]

> Jinny hopes to be a good dancer like Hyoyeon.

① He walked like a bear.
② It looks like a real flower.
③ I hope you like what I like.
④ She must be outgoing like me.
⑤ Jimmy ran like a cheetah.

03 다음 중 어법상 어색한 것을 고르시오. [출제 예상 85%]

① She has a nice house near the beach.
② Why don't you look it up at the dictionary?
③ Sammy advised me to study hard at school.
④ I learned many things after my adventures at sea.
⑤ I always tell her to do her best at work.

04 다음 중 어법상 옳은 것을 고르시오. [출제 예상 80%]

① Yesterday I read the article in the newspaper.
② He went to his uncle's house in foot.
③ She guesses Tim saw them in TV.
④ Jennifer heard me make a noise at the subway.
⑤ At last, Ian managed to be at land.

05 다음 빈칸에 공통으로 들어갈 알맞은 것을 고르시오. [출제 예상 90%]

> • Most people go to work _____ bus or subway.
> • I think you should start _____ doing small things.

① through   ② on   ③ in
④ from   ⑤ by

06 다음의 우리말과 같은 뜻이 되도록 빈칸에 알맞은 말을 고르시오. [출제 예상 85%]

> 그것들은 한 세대에서 다른 세대로 전해진다.
> = They are passed on _____ one generation _____ another.

① from – in   ② to – on   ③ by – to
④ from – to   ⑤ to – to

07 다음 문장에서 어법상 틀린 곳을 찾아 바르게 고치시오. [출제 예상 80%]

> Have you noticed any differences among London and Chicago?

_____ ➡ _____

[01~05] 다음 빈칸에 알맞은 말을 고르시오.

01

> Stephanie gets up _____ 6 a.m. and jogs for an hour.

① in   ② to   ③ at
④ for   ⑤ by

02

> _____ the past, people didn't know to generate electricity.

① At   ② On   ③ By
④ In   ⑤ To

03

> My father wants the whole family to have dinner together _____ the weekends.

① in   ② on   ③ at
④ to   ⑤ by

04

> Richard Ⅲ was named _____ Richard Ⅰ who the campaign and won many victories during the third Crusade.

① before   ② to   ③ with
④ toward   ⑤ after

05

> I had no clothes to wear _____ one in small sizes.

① except   ② because   ③ instead of
④ without   ⑤ of

★★★
06 다음 중 어법상 <u>어색한</u> 것을 <u>모두</u> 고르시오.

① What was the greatest invention in the 19th century?
② What changes do young people want in the future?
③ She will have so many things to do in this year.
④ In the morning, I dressed up in my finest clothes.
⑤ In last Monday, a parcel arrived at Jenny's house.

[07~10] 다음 빈칸에 공통으로 들어갈 알맞은 말을 고르시오.

07

> • It was last winter when my sister came back _____ London.
> • Where are Jack and Mary _____?

① to   ② around   ③ from
④ for   ⑤ over

08
- A man _____ green eyes and gray hair wants to meet you.
- My son was very pleased _____ the toy robots.

① by   ② with   ③ for
④ to   ⑤ of

★★★
09
- It has been a very long time _____ she left.
- John and Douglas have been best friends _____ they were young.

① of   ② by   ③ for
④ from   ⑤ since

10
- One sunny day _____ spring, I was taking a walk along the river.
- Billy was born _____ California.

① at   ② on   ③ of
④ in   ⑤ with

[11~15] 다음 빈칸에 들어갈 말이 알맞게 짝지어진 것을 고르시오.

11
- My dream is to travel _____ the world.
- Luna has to do lots of work to prepare _____ their trip.

① around – to   ② around – in
③ around – for   ④ over – to
⑤ over – of

12
- She was headed _____ the library when I ran into her.
- I have planned to study French on Thursday _____ five and seven o'clock.

① for – between   ② from – between
③ to – among   ④ of – among
⑤ of – between

★★★
13
- The natural history museum is filled _____ students.
- His university is famous _____ its long history.

① with – for   ② for – with
③ to – for   ④ with – to
⑤ of – for

14
- John and I are crazy _____ rock music festivals.
- The books in the old library were covered _____ dust.

① about – for   ② for – with
③ about – with   ④ with – for
⑤ to – of

15
> • Bill asked her to show him how to fix the car _____ Monday and Tuesday.
> • You should draw a picture _____ pen first.

① on – to ② on – in ③ in – at
④ by – on ⑤ to – in

16 다음 중 어법상 어색한 것을 고르시오.

① How much does Helen care about her beauty?
② I just have to wait for someone to find me.
③ I cannot concentrate with my studies because I am sick.
④ Though they are different from one another, they belong on the same team.
⑤ Grace doesn't laugh at him even when he makes funny faces.

★★★
17 다음 중 어법상 옳은 문장을 모두 고르시오.

① Joanne can speak in least two languages because of her Korean mom.
② The library was full of many girls and boys.
③ I got out of my car to look closer at the scene.
④ I believe on my parents. They'll always support me.
⑤ The girl was please with the new shoes.

[18~20] 다음 우리말과 같은 뜻이 되도록 빈칸에 알맞은 말을 고르시오.

18
> 우리 가족은 에너지를 절약하는 데 매우 능숙하다.
> = My family is very good _____ saving energy.

① for ② to ③ of
④ in ⑤ at

19
> 우리는 지구상의 다른 모든 것들과 사람들이 잘 살기 위해서 서로 의존해야 한다는 것을 잊지 말아야 한다.
> = We should not forget that people and the other living things in the earth depend _____ each other to live well.

① in ② on ③ to
④ to ⑤ by

20
> 큰 벌 한 마리가 Jeff의 얼굴을 쏘았다.
> = A big bee stung Jeff _____ his face.

① in ② to ③ for
④ on ⑤ with

◇◇◇◇◇◇◇◇◇ 서술형 평가 ◇◇◇◇◇◇◇◇◇

[21~23] 다음 글에서 어법상 틀린 부분을 찾아 고쳐 쓰시오.

21

Peter broke the little cookie to small pieces for the birds.

_____ ➡ _____

22

Dangerous gases were coming out off the box which was delivered.

_____ ➡ _____

23

Sam and Lian will come back home until 5 o'clock this afternoon.

_____ ➡ _____

[24~26] 다음 우리말과 같은 뜻이 되도록 빈칸에 알맞은 말을 쓰시오.

24

너는 저기 노란색 우비를 입은 소녀를 아니?

➡ Do you know the girl who is _____ _____ _____ _____ ?

25

그들은 큰 희망과 꿈을 가지고 육지에 발을 들였다.

➡ They _____ _____ _____ _____ _____ great hopes and dreams.

26

Rachel은 관중들 앞에서 피아노를 연주하는 것이 두렵다.

➡ Rachel _____ _____ _____ playing the piano _____ _____ _____ the audience.

[27~28] 다음 괄호 안의 단어를 배열하여 올바른 문장을 만드시오.

★★★
27

(Jay / music / dance / has been / and / in / interested)

➡ _____

★★★
28

(they / concentrate / couldn't / on / was / saying / the / teacher / what)

➡ _____

Note

15

Chapter
일치와 화법

Point Check I

◆ **수의 일치:** 주어의 단/복수에 따라 동사도 역시 단/복수를 사용하는 것을 말한다.

◆ **시제의 일치:** 두 개 이상의 절을 하나로 합쳤을 때 주절의 동사와 종속절의 동사의 시제를 맞추는 것을 말한다.

◆ **화법:** 다른 사람의 말을 전달하는 방법을 말한다.

1. 수의 일치

• both A and B	복수 취급	• a number of + 복수명사	복수 취급 (주어: 복수명사)
• all, some, most, half of + 명사구	명사에 일치	• the number of + 복수명사	단수 취급 (주어: the number)
• every, each, -one (body), -thing	단수 취급	• not A but B • either A or B • neither A nor B	B에 일치

2. 시제의 일치

주절의 동사가 현재형	종속절의 시제는 과거, 현재, 현재완료, 미래형이 올 수 있다.	
주절의 동사가 현재형이 아닐 경우	(1) 종속절의 현재 ➡ 과거	(3) 종속절의 과거 ➡ 과거완료
	(2) 종속절의 조동사 ➡ 조동사의 과거형	(4) 종속절의 현재완료 ➡ 과거완료
시제 일치의 예외	**진리, 사실, 습관:** 항상 현재형 사용 **역사적 사실:** 항상 과거형 사용 **가정법:** 'wish'의 시제가 바뀌더라도 가정법의 시제(were)는 바뀌지 않는다.	

3. 화법 전환

공통	① 콤마(,)와 따옴표(" ") 삭제 ② 지시대명사나 부사(구)는 전달하는 사람의 입장으로 바꾼다. ③ 주절과 종속절의 시제는 일치시킨다. 단, 주절의 시제가 과거일 때 종속절의 시제는 과거 또는 과거완료
평서문	① 'say → say', 'say to → tell' ② 콤마(,)와 따옴표(" ") 대신 'that' 사용 (that 생략 가능)
의문문	① say, say to → ask ② • 콤마(,), 따옴표(" "), 물음표(?) 없애고 'if' 또는 'whether'를 사용 (의문사가 없는 경우) • 콤마(,), 따옴표(" "), 물음표(?) 없애고 의문사로 두 문장을 연결 (의문사가 있는 경우) ③ '주어+동사'의 어순
명령문	① 전달 동사는 말투에 구분해서 사용 [명령: tell], [충고: advise], [부탁: ask, beg] ② 명령문의 동사를 'to부정사'로 바꾸고, 부정문일 경우 'to'앞에 'not'을 붙여준다.

15-1 수의 일치

- **수의 일치:** 주어의 단/복수에 따라 동사도 단/복수를 사용하는 것을 말한다. 하지만 때에 따라 주어가 복수의 형태나 의미를 가지고 있어도 동사는 단수가 되거나 그 반대의 경우도 있다.

1. 수의 일치

• both A and B	복수 취급	• a number of + 복수명사	복수 취급 (주어: 복수명사)
• all, some, most, half of + 명사구	명사에 일치	• the number of + 복수명사	단수 취급 (주어: the number)
• every, each, -one (body), -thing, • 시간, 금액, 거리, 중량의 명사구	단수 취급	• not A but B • either A or B • neither A nor B • not only A but also B	B에 일치

- **Both** Gina **and** Sally **are** the best students this year.
- **Every** student **has** his or her own dream.
- **Two months is** sufficient time to prepare for the exam.
- **Not** my sister **but** I **want** to join a reading club.
- **Neither** Greg **nor** Mickey **likes** soap operas.
- **Most of the** students **want** to take a field trip tomorrow.
- **A number of** fans **go** to the airport to see the famous actor.
- **The number of** boxes in the container **is** about 100.

* his or her: 그들의
(그의 또는 그녀의 – 단수로 모두의 뜻을 가질 경우 특정한 성별이 정해져 있지 않을 때 사용한다.)

Answer Keys p. 58

A 괄호 안에서 알맞은 것을 고르시오.

1 Each boy in the class (have / has) to make a summer vacation plan.

2 Five kilometers (is / are) not a long distance to run.

3 A number of people (gathers / gather) to see John.

4 Both Jim and Kate (are / is) going to visit the gallery next Tuesday.

5 Not my brother but I (buy / buys) the new computer.

6 The number of the girls (was / were) about fifty.

7 Everyone who knows about the issue (has / have) to write the report.

15. 일치와 화법 **441**

시제의 일치

> • **시제의 일치:** 두 개 이상의 절을 하나로 합쳤을 때 앞 절의 동사와 뒷 절의 동사의 시제를 맞추는 것을 뜻한다. '주어 + 동사'의 형태를 주절이라고 하고, '접속사 + 주어 + 동사 ～'처럼 접속사가 있는 절을 종속절이라고 한다.

1. 주절의 동사가 현재형일 경우: 종속절의 시제는 과거, 현재, 현재완료, 미래형이 올 수 있다.

- I **think** that the movie, The Avengers: Age of Ultron **was (is, will be)** funny.

2. 주절의 동사가 현재형이 아닐 경우

(1) 종속절의 현재 ➡ 과거

- We **think** that Brandon **sings** pretty well.
  = We **thought** that Brandon **sang** pretty well.

(2) 종속절의 조동사 ➡ 조동사의 과거형

- William **says** that he **will marry** Julia.
  = William **said** that he **would marry** Julia.

(3) 종속절의 과거 ➡ 과거완료

- Everyone **thinks** that Tonny **broke** the window.
  = Everyone **thought** that Tonny **had broken** the window.

(4) 종속절의 현재완료 ➡ 과거완료

- Jinny **knows** that they **have done** their best.
  = Jinny **knew** that they **had done** their best.

3. 시제 일치의 예외

(1) 진리, 사실, 습관: 항상 현재형 사용

- We say that the earth **is** round. [진리]

- Mrs. Parker said that the class **starts** at nine tomorrow. [사실]

- He told me that he **gets** up at 6:30 every morning. [습관]

(2) 역사적 사실: 항상 과거형 사용

- Our history teacher said that World War II **started** in 1939.

(3) 가정법: 'wish'의 시제가 바뀌더라도 가정법의 시제(were)는 바뀌지 않는다.

- I wish that my teddy bear **were** with me.
  = I wished that my teddy bear **were** with me.

A   괄호 안에서 알맞은 것을 고르시오.

1   We know that everyone (needs / needed) to be protected by the government.

2   Jane said that she (would / will) go to the stadium to watch the game.

3   She believes that her sister (came / will come) here next week.

4   I thought that the professor (isn't / wasn't) angry.

5   They told me that I (was / will be) the only person for the position.

6   Many students believed that they (could / can) pass the final exam.

7   She knew that I (am / was) interested in dancing.

8   The girl thought that her mother (had made / makes) the cake before she came back.

9   Leo told us that he (was / is) going to leave town.

10   Kevin thinks that his friends (bought / will buy) his gift last night.

B   주어진 문장의 시제를 과거로 바꾸어 다시 쓰시오.

1   Max says that his sister is busy now.

   ➡ _____*Max said that his sister was busy then.*_____

2   I think that Alex is not ready to resign.

   ➡ _____

3   The woman says that she has been waiting for the bus.

   ➡ _____

4   We understand that the girl didn't do anything for us.

   ➡ _____

5   John says that he has never tasted such a delicious pizza.

   ➡ _____

15-3 평서문의 화법 전환

- **직접화법**: 누군가의 말을 따옴표 (" ")를 사용해 직접적으로 전달하는 방법이다.
- **간접화법**: 누군가의 말을 전달하는 사람의 입장으로 바꿔서 간접적으로 전달하는 방법이다.

1. 직접화법에서 간접화법으로 전환하기

직접화법	• Jen said, "I want to go on a vacation."
간접화법	• Jen said that she wanted to go on a vacation.

① 직접화법의 동사 변환: 'say → say', 'say to → tell'

② 콤마(,)와 따옴표 (" ") 대신 'that' 사용 (that 생략 가능)

③ 지시대명사나 부사(구)는 전달하는 사람의 입장으로 바꾼다.

④ 주절과 종속절의 시제는 일치시킨다. 단, 주절의 시제가 과거일 때 종속절의 시제는 과거 또는 과거완료로 고친다.

2. 간접화법으로 전환할 때의 지시대명사와 부사구

직접화법	간접화법	직접화법	간접화법
this / these	that/those	here	there
ago	before	now	then
yesterday	the previous day (the day before)	today	that day
next week	the following week	tonight	that night
tomorrow	the next day (the following day)	last night	the previous night (the night before)

- Nabin said, "I'll break up with Peter **tomorrow**."
  = Nabin said that she **would** break up with Peter **the next day**.

- Remi said to me, "I **wanted** to go shopping yesterday."
  = Remi told me that she **had wanted** to go shopping <u>the previous day</u>.

  (= the day before)

Answer Keys p. 58

A 다음의 직접화법을 간접화법으로 바르게 바꿔 쓰시오.

1 He said, "I'm going to leave here."

➡ *He said that he was going to leave there.*

2 Mina says, "My teacher helps me finish my homework."

➡ _____

3 Nick says to me, "I love you so much."

➡ _____

4 They said, "He has practiced playing the piano for a month."

➡ _____

5 She says, "I jog two miles every evening."

➡ _____

6 Helen usually says to us, "You have to study hard."

➡ _____

7 John said to me, "I want to eat something delicious."

➡ _____

8 The girls said to me, "We saw the movie last week."

➡ _____

9 Kate says, "My parents are going to visit our school today."

➡ _____

B 다음 간접화법을 직접화법으로 바르게 바꿔 쓰시오.

1 Lily tells us that she wants to buy the house to live in with her family.

➡ *Lily says to us, "I want to buy the house to live in with my family."*

2 Tom said that he would not participate in the contest.

➡ _____

3 My father told me that he had bought something for me.

➡ _____

4 She told her mother that she could pass the final exam.

➡ _____

5 They told Joe that they didn't like to go hiking with him.

➡ _____

15-4 의문문의 화법 전환

- **의문문의 화법 전환**: 직접화법에서의 전달동사 'say (to)'를 'ask'로 바꿔준다.

1. 의문사가 없는 의문문의 화법 전환

직접화법	• Toby **said**, "Are you going camping tomorrow?"
간접화법	• Toby **asked** if (whether) I was going camping the next day.

① 직접화법의 동사 변환: 'say/say to → ask'로 바꾼다.
② 콤마(,)와 따옴표 (" ") 대신 'if 또는 whether'을 사용하고, '주어＋동사~'의 어순으로 한다.
③ 지시대명사나 부사(구)는 전달하는 사람의 입장으로 바꾼다.

2. 의문사가 있는 의문문의 화법 전환

직접화법	• Dahee **said to me**, "Where are you going this winter?"
간접화법	• Dahee **asked me** where I was going that winter.

① 직접화법의 동사 변환: 'say/say to → ask'로 바꾼다.
② 콤마(,)와 따옴표 (" ") 대신 '의문사'를 사용한다.
③ 간접의문문의 어순인 '의문사＋주어＋동사'로 바꾼다.
   단, 의문사가 주어로 사용되었을 경우 '의문사＋동사'의 어순으로 한다.
④ 지시대명사나 부사(구)는 전달하는 사람의 입장으로 바꾼다.

- 의문사가 주어일 경우
- Brenda **said to** me, "**Who** gave you the tie?"

  = Brenda asked me **who** had given me the tie.

A 괄호 안에서 알맞은 것을 고르시오.

1 The girl (told /(asked)) if I could solve the problem.

2 Tim asked her if she (can buy / could buy) some kimchi for him.

3 Joe asked us whether we (has been / had been) to Paris before.

4 The woman asked the boy (why / that) he was crying on the street.

5 Mr. Han asked the students (which / how) he should go to the station.

6 People asked me (where / when) I was going to leave town.

7 The woman asked him if he (seen / had seen) the dog before.

8 She asked us where (she could / could she) find the bus stop.

9 Sally asked me if she (could attend / attended) the meeting.

10 My teacher asked if (we knew / we have known) the girl's address.

B 화법을 바꿀 때 빈칸에 알맞은 말을 쓰시오.

1 He said, "Do they want to buy this dress?"
  ➡ He _____ *asked if they wanted to buy that dress.* _____

2 She said to me, " What kind of scarf do you like most?"
  ➡ She _____

3 John said to Jane, "Are you going to go abroad to study?"
  ➡ John _____

4 They said to me, "What time did you finish your homework?"
  ➡ They _____

5 I said to her, "Would you like to have something to drink?"
  ➡ I asked _____

명령문의 화법 전환

• **명령문의 화법 전환**: 간접화법으로 전환할 때 두 절을 연결해 주는 말로 'to'를 사용한다.

1. 명령문의 화법 전환

직접화법	• Our teacher **said to us**, "Listen carefully."
간접화법	• Our teacher **told us** to listen carefully.

① 직접화법의 동사 변환: 'say/say to'는 의미에 따라 'tell, order, instruct, ask, beg, request, advise'로 바꾼다.
② 콤마(,)와 따옴표(" ") 대신 'to'를 사용한다. (→ to부정사이므로 동사는 항상 원형이며 시제 변화는 없다.)
③ 부정대명사일 경우 'not to부정사'의 형태로 바꾼다.
④ 지시대명사나 부사(구)는 전달하는 사람의 입장으로 바꾼다.

2. 간접화법으로 전환할 때의 전달 동사

명령	tell, order, command, instruct
충고	advise
부탁 (주로 **please**가 있는 문장)	ask, beg, request

✰Check up!

Answer Keys p. 58

A 괄호 안의 말을 사용하여 주어진 문장을 간접화법으로 바꾸시오.

1 The doctor said to her, "Exercise regularly and stay healthy." (advise)
➡ The doctor _advised her to exercise regularly and eat healthy._

2 Joe said to her, "Do not run here." (tell)
➡ Joe _____

3 The rich man said to the prince, "Help the poor." (advise)
➡ The rich man _____

4 The man said to his son, "Do not study all night." (tell)
➡ The man _____

5 Mr. Park said to us, "Do not be late for the meeting." (order)
➡ Mr. Park _____

Practice More I

Answer Keys p. 59

A 괄호 안에서 알맞은 것을 고르시오.

1 Every number (has / have) a meaning.

2 Six pounds of meat (is / are) being baked for the party.

3 What all of the students do (are / is) cheering for him.

4 Not your sister but you (has / have) to help your parents.

5 A number of people (was / were) injured in the accident.

6 Either my dog or your cat (dislikes / dislike) to walk along the river.

7 She said that Jane (had seen / has seen) the film three years before.

8 Some of the money (was / were) sent to my account.

9 The students knew that France (invaded / has invaded) Joseon that year.

10 Half of the money (was / were) donated to charity.

B 주어진 문장의 시제를 과거로 바꿀 때 빈칸에 알맞은 말을 쓰시오.

1 The girl says that he has to finish the project by six.
→ The girl said that _____he had to finish the project by six._____

2 Max says that he wants to go to the amusement park.
→ Max said that _____

3 The experts expect that the economy will improve.
→ The experts expected that _____

4 Mary knows that the sun rises in the east.
→ Mary knew that _____

5 Mr. Han says that he has already bought the shoes.
→ Mr. Han said that _____

6 The students believe that their team will be able to win the game.
→ The students believed that _____

7 Mike says that he has to help his father to repair the roof.
→ Mike said that _____

Practice More Ⅰ

8 The police believe that she has hidden the box somewhere in the house.
   ➡ The police believed that _____

9 We say that we can solve the problem without any hints.
   ➡ We said that _____

10 I think that she will come back soon.
   ➡ I thought that _____

C 주어진 문장과 의미가 같도록 문장을 완성하시오.

1 Mary says, "I always eat breakfast in the morning."
   ➡ Mary says that *she always eats breakfast in the morning.*

2 He said to her, "Can you pick me up when I come back to Korea?"
   ➡ He asked her _____

3 The teacher said to me, "Don't forget to bring your homework next week."
   ➡ The teacher told me _____

4 John said to us, "What did you see in the museum?"
   ➡ John asked us _____

5 I said to mom, "How did you make the stew?"
   ➡ I asked mom _____

6 Brian said, "I enjoy watching movies every weekend."
   ➡ Brian said that _____

7 Mina said, "Do you want to go to the party?"
   ➡ Mina asked _____

8 Mina said to Jim, "I don't think I can pass the exam."
   ➡ Mina told Jim that _____

9 Billy said to the man, "Why did you repair your old car?"
   ➡ Billy asked the man _____

10 Ann says to me, "I'll always be with you."
   ➡ Ann told me that _____

D 주어진 문장을 간접화법 또는 직접화법으로 바꾸시오.

1 He told me that I had to buy that shirt for the party.

➡ He _____ *said to me, "You have to buy this shirt for the party."* _____

2 The woman asked where she could find the nearest subway station.

➡ The woman _____

3 People said to her, "Stop studying and take a rest."

➡ People _____

4 Mary told me not to eat too many sweets.

➡ Mary _____

5 Smith said that he had forgotten the location of that day's meeting.

➡ Smith _____

6 Mrs. Brown said to us, "I've never allowed you to use my kitchen."

➡ Mrs. Brown _____

7 I said to the guide, "When was the long bridge built?"

➡ I _____

8 Max asked whether he had to wait for Helen.

➡ Max _____

9 Linda said to me, "Drink lots of water and exercise regularly."

➡ Linda _____

10 The experts told us that there would be an economic crisis in a year.

➡ The experts _____

중간 기말고사 예상문제

내신 최다 출제 유형

01 다음 중 어법상 올바른 것을 고르시오. [출제 예상 85%]

① There is all the members of the band.

② All the money was gone.

③ All the children seems joyful.

④ All the girls in my class was playing soccer.

⑤ Where has all the monkeys gone?

02 다음 밑줄 친 부분이 어법상 옳은 것을 고르시오.
[출제 예상 90%]

① Either you or I are right.

② One of the boys speaks English very well.

③ Both of the girls doesn't wear glasses.

④ Each of us have pictures of the actress.

⑤ Some of the oranges looks fresh.

03 다음 우리말을 시제에 맞게 영어로 바르게 고친 것을 고르시오. [출제 예상 85%]

> 그녀는 Jeff가 올 것이라고 생각했다.

① She thought that Jeff will come.

② She thought that Jeff could come.

③ She thought that Jeff might come.

④ She thought that Jeff should come.

⑤ She thought that Jeff would come.

04 다음 빈칸에 들어갈 알맞은 말을 고르시오.
[출제 예상 80%]

> Neither Mary nor her parents _____ at home.

① is   ② was   ③ are

④ is not   ⑤ do

05 다음 중 어법상 어색한 것을 고르시오. [출제 예상 90%]

① He wanted to make sure that everyone was safe.

② I believed that it would snow.

③ She said that she wanted to have a steak.

④ He thought he will win the game.

⑤ Helen told me that she was going to be a singer.

06 다음 밑줄 친 부분을 알맞게 고친 것을 고르시오.
[출제 예상 90%]

> When I finished doing the dishes,
> I found that somebody has taken the ring.

① takes   ② had taken

③ would take   ④ was taken

⑤ had been taken

07 다음 빈칸에 들어갈 말로 알맞지 않은 것을 고르시오.
[출제 예상 85%]

> Mrs. Brown asked me _____.

① when they left

② who made that thing

③ what he should do to become a tennis player.

④ what I wanted to be in the future

⑤ where I found it

[01~03] 다음 문장을 간접화법으로 바꿀 때 빈칸에 들어갈 알맞은 말을 고르시오.

01

He said, "I have to buy some books."
= He said that he _____ to buy some books.

① had   ② have   ③ has
④ having   ⑤ must

02

She said, "I can finish it tomorrow."
She said that _____.

① she can finish it the following day.
② she couldn't finish it the following day.
③ she could finish it the following day.
④ she could finish it tomorrow.
⑤ she could finish it the day.

03

He said to me, "Are they going to help her?"
= He asked me _____ they were going to help her.

① unless   ② that   ③ if
④ whenever   ⑤ how

[04~05] 다음 중 어법상 어색한 것을 고르시오.

04

① Fifteen miles is a good distance for you to run in a day.
② Thirty dollars are too expensive for the pen.
③ Social studies is Jenny's favorite subject.
④ Twenty kilograms is heavy for us to carry.
⑤ Ten years have passed since he came.

05 ★★★

① Benny studies much harder this year than he did last year.
② Both her health and money are very important to her.
③ She as well as you is my good friend.
④ Not you but he are the person who I want to be with.
⑤ Vietnam is located in Southeast Asia.

[06~07] 다음 문장을 간접화법으로 바르게 바꾼 것을 고르시오.

06

She said to me, "You are so smart."

① She told to me that I was so smart.
② She said me that I was so smart.
③ She said to me that I was so smart.
④ She told me that I am so smart.
⑤ She told me that I was so smart.

★★★
07

He said to me, "Why are you so sad?"

① He asked to me why I was so sad.
② He asked me why I am so sad.
③ He asked me why am I so sad.
④ He asked me why was I so sad.
⑤ He asked me why I was so sad.

[08~10] 다음 빈칸에 알맞은 말을 고르시오.

08

People asked him _____ he liked going to football games.

① which   ② whether   ③ how
④ what   ⑤ as

09

Mom told us _____ careful.

① is   ② are   ③ be
④ to be   ⑤ being

10

The clerk told the children _____ in the library.

① to be run   ② not run   ③ not to run
④ to not run   ⑤ not be running

[11~12] 다음 문장을 직접화법으로 바르게 바꾼 것을 고르시오.

11

James said that he would do his best.

① James said, "I will do my best."
② James said, "I would do my best."
③ James said, "He will do his best."
④ James says, "I will do my best."
⑤ James said to, "I will do my best."

★★★
12

The doctor advised me not to drink much coffee.

① The doctor said to me, "Do not drink much coffee."
② The doctor said me, "Do not drink much coffee."
③ The doctor said, "Do not drink much coffee."
④ The doctor says to me, "Do not drink much coffee."
⑤ The doctor say, "Do not drink much coffee."

★★★
13 다음 중 어법상 옳은 것을 <u>모두</u> 고르시오.

① Every books in my classroom has been read.
② All of the land belongs to my father.
③ All of the passengers were saved from the accident.
④ The water in the well were polluted.
⑤ Most of his paintings was about flowers.

14 다음 중 어법상 어색한 것을 모두 고르시오.

① Some of muffins are for you.
② The teacher and poet is my aunt.
③ I know that her family is all kind and nice.
④ The people often visits the famous area.
⑤ Tommy and I am good students.

15 다음 문장을 간접화법으로 바꿀 때 빈칸에 알맞은 말을 고르시오.

> I said to her, "Can I help you?"
> = I asked her _____

① I could help her
② if I can help she
③ if I could help you
④ if I could help her
⑤ if I can help her

★★★
16 다음 중 화법 전환이 잘못된 것을 고르시오.

① She always said to us, "Study hard."
 → She always told us to study hard.

② I said to Jerry, " You have to drive a car carefully."
 → I told Jerry that he had to drive a car carefully.

③ Mr. Smith said to Mark, "Don't make a noise."
 → Mr. Smith told Mark don't make a noise.

④ He said to me, "Where do you want to go?"
 → He asked me where I wanted to go.

⑤ Linda said to him, "I'll tell you the truth."
 → Linda told him that she would tell him the truth.

[17~18] 다음 대화의 빈칸에 알맞은 말을 고르시오.

17
> A What did the doctor say to you?
> B He advised _____ at least twice a week.

① to me to exercise
② me to exercise
③ to me exercising
④ me exercise
⑤ to me exercise

18

A Who knows the truth?
B Maybe both Mary and Judy
_____ it.

① done   ② known   ③ knew
④ knows   ⑤ know

[19~20] 다음 빈칸에 들어갈 말이 바르게 짝지어진 것을
고르시오.

19

• A number of students _____
abroad.
• Half of the apple _____ yours.

① studying − is   ② studies − is
③ study − is   ④ study − are
⑤ studies − are

20

• Wendy wonders _____ the
music is nice.
• Can you tell us _____ she likes
to play soccer?

① what   ② that   ③ to
④ whether   ⑤ who

[21~22] 다음 밑줄 친 부분 중 어법상 어색한 곳을
고르시오.

21

① A number of ② student are ③ present
at the concert. ④ Some of ⑤ them are
my classmates.

22

The boy ① said ② that he ③ know acid
rain ④ harms ⑤ wildlife.

★★★
23 다음 짝지어진 문장들 중 직접화법으로 바르게
바꾼 것을 고르시오.

① Emily said that she had lost her earrings
the day before.
→ Emily said, "I lost my earrings
yesterday."

② Kelly told me that she would leave the
next day.
→ Kelly said to me, "I will leave the
next day."

③ She asked me if I knew the history of
this tower.
→ She said to me, "Did you know the
history of this tower?"

④ He asked Amy not to park there.
→ He said to Amy, "No park here."

⑤ Jennifer told Justin that she was taking
a walk.
→ Jennifer said to Justin, "I was taking
a walk."

★★★
24 다음 두 문장을 간접의문문으로 쓸 때 <u>어색한</u> 것을 <u>고르시오.</u>

① I want to know. + Who solved the problem?
→ I want to know who solved the problem.

② Can you tell me? + What time does the train arrive?
→ Can you tell me what time the train arrives?

③ I wonder. + Was she at home?
→ I wonder whether she was at home.

④ Do you remember? + Does he live in Busan?
→ Do you remember if he lives in Busan?

⑤ Do you think? + Will he get first prize?
→ Do you think will he get first prize?

◇◇◇◇◇◇◇◇◇ 서술형 평가 ◇◇◇◇◇◇◇◇◇

[25~27] 다음 문장을 간접화법으로 바꿀 때 빈칸에 알맞은 말을 쓰시오.

25
> Brandon said to me, "I will help you."

➡ Brandon _____ me _____ he _____ help me.

26
> Sammy said, "Can you play baseball with us?"

➡ Sammy _____ _____ I _____ play baseball with them.

27
> The foreigner said to me, "Can you speak Spanish?"

➡ The foreigner _____ me _____ I _____ speak Spanish.

[28~30] 다음 주어진 직접화법의 우리말을 간접화법으로 바꿀 때 빈칸에 알맞은 단어를 쓰시오.

28
> 그녀는 상사에게 "오늘 밤에 이 보고서를 끝낼게요."라고 말했다.

➡ She _____ her boss _____ she _____ _____ that report _____ _____.

29
> 그는 내게 "내일 한가하니?"라고 물었다.

➡ He _____ me _____ _____ _____ _____ the _____ day?

Answer Keys p. 59~60

30

> 그녀는 내게 "창문을 닫아라."라고 말했다.

➡ She _____ me _____ _____ the window.

[31~33] 다음 직접화법을 간접화법으로 바꿔 쓰시오.

★★★
31

> He said, "I can fix the bike today."

➡ _____

32

> The professor said to the students, "Turn in your reports."

➡ _____

★★★
33

> Steven said to her, "Where did you put the books?"

➡ _____

[34~35] 다음 괄호 안의 단어를 바르게 배열하여 문장을 완성하여 쓰시오.

★★★
34

> (you / me / if / could / took / tell / she / trip / a)

➡ _____

★★★
35

> (who / think / you / her / made / do / sad)

➡ _____

16 Chapter

특수구문

Point Check I

◆ **강조구문**: 강조하고 싶은 말을 'It'과 'that' 사이에 넣어 그 의미를 강조하는 문장을 말한다.

◆ **도치**: '주어＋동사'의 어순이 바뀌어 사용될 때를 말한다.

◆ **생략**: 앞서 나온 말이 뒤에 다시 나오는 경우 그 말을 생략할 수 있다.

◆ **동격**: 문장에서 주어, 목적어, 보어를 다시 한 번 설명해 주는 말이다.

1. 강조구문

It＋be동사＋강조어구＋that...	• It was at the used bookstore that I bought a book.
의문사＋be동사＋it that ～?	• Who was it that broke the vase?

2. 도치

There/Here＋동사＋주어	• There is some juice on the table.
So+동사+주어 Neither (Nor)＋동사＋주어	• **A** Ann didn't like Jack. **B** Neither (Nor) did I. • **A** Jen is so smart. **B** So is Sam.
부정어＋조동사＋주어＋동사	• Never does Tim have any paper.

3. 생략

반복되는 말	• Kate went shopping and (she) bought two dresses.
주어＋be동사	• Ben was annoyed when (he was) asked unexpected questions a lot.
관계대명사	• I know him (who is) smiling at me. [주격 관계대명사＋be동사]

4. 동격

명사＋명사	• My best friend, Lucy plays the piano well.
명사＋of＋동명사(구)	• Her hope of dancing on the stage will come true.
명사＋to부정사	• His plan to travel around the world alone is impossible.
명사＋that절	• Everyone knows the fact that Sammy will move to Canada.

Lesson 16-1 It... that 강조구문

- **강조구문**: 강조하고 싶은 말을 'It'과 'that' 사이에 넣어 문장의 주어, 목적어, 부사어의 의미를 강조하는 문장을 말한다.

1. It＋be동사＋강조어구＋that...: 주어, 목적어, 부사구(장소, 시간)가 주로 강조됨

- Gina found a good restaurant on Rodeo Street last week.

  ➡ **It was Gina that** found a good restaurant on Rodeo Street last week. [주어 강조]

  ➡ **It was a good restaurant that** Gina found on Rodeo Street last week. [목적어 강조]

  ➡ **It was on Rodeo Street that** Gina found a good restaurant last week. [장소 부사구 강조]

  ➡ **It was last week that** Gina found a good restaurant on Rodeo Street. [시간 부사구 강조]

2. 의문사＋be동사＋it that ～?

- What do they want to buy in this shop?

  ＝ **What is it that** they want to buy in this shop?

- Who took care of your nephew?

  ＝ **Who was it that** took care of your nephew?

Answer Keys p. 61

A 밑줄 친 부분을 강조하는 문장을 쓰시오.

1 The pasta you made tastes really delicious.
  ➡   *It is the pasta you made that tastes really delicious.*

2 Lily found a piece of cake in the box.
  ➡

3 I called her three times last night.
  ➡

4 We met the professor in the shop.
  ➡

5 Who wants to go to the grocery store to buy some carrots?
  ➡

6 John sent me the letter on August 15th.
  ➡

7 My mom made me the beautiful dress for the party.
  ➡

16-2 강조어구

> • **강조어구**: 명사를 강조할 때는 'the very'를, 형용사, 부사를 강조할 때는 'very, this, that'을, 동사를 강조할 때는 '조동사 do'를 사용한다.

1. 동사 강조_조동사 do: 동사 앞에 사용되어 동사의 의미를 강조한다.

- Iris and Leo **do** sing very well. (Iris and Leo sing very well.)
- Ian **does** love cheese pizza. (Ian loves cheese pizza.)
- I **did** finish my homework. (I finished my homework.)

2. 재귀대명사의 주어, 목적어 강조

(1) 주어 강조: 주어나 문장 뒤에 쓴다.

- My little sister **herself** cooked spaghetti.

  = My little sister cooked spaghetti **herself**.

(2) 목적어 강조: 목적어 뒤에 쓴다.

- They met the chairman **himself** in his office.

3. 비교급의 강조

(1) 비교급 강조: much, even, still, far, a lot

- Brad is **much** more handsome than Leo.

(2) 형용사/부사 강조

- Emily has drunk **this (that)** much.

4. 명사의 강조: the very (바로 그)

- This is **the very** smartphone that I'd love to buy.

5. 부정문, 의문문의 강조: at all (전혀, 조금이라도)

- We didn't know anything **at all** about the rumor.

Answer Keys p. 61

A 밑줄 친 부분을 강조하는 문장을 쓰시오.

1 My little brother <u>likes</u> playing soccer.

➡ *My little brother does like playing soccer.*

2 I <u>love</u> eating something sweet.

➡ _____

3 People <u>insisted</u> that they should be protected by us.

➡ _____

4 I <u>went</u> apple picking at Billy's house last month.

➡ _____

5 It is <u>hotter</u> today than last week.

➡ _____

6 We <u>finished</u> all our summer vacation homework.

➡ _____

7 John <u>didn't</u> show up for the meeting.

➡ _____

8 This is the <u>place</u> where they bought the ring.

➡ _____

9 The phone <u>rang</u>, but I couldn't answer it.

➡ _____

10 That's the <u>movie</u> I've been looking for.

➡ _____

B 주어진 강조어구를 알맞은 위치에 넣어 문장을 완성하시오.

1 Your summer plan sounds boring. (does)

➡ *Your summer plan does sound boring.*

2 Things are better than before. (even)

➡ _____

3 We have never been far away from our base camp. (this)

➡ _____

4 Did she find out anything? (at all)

➡ _____

5 We met our favorite actor at the airport. (did)

➡ _____

• **도치**: '주어 + 동사'의 어순이 바뀌는 것을 말한다. 강조하고 싶은 말을 문장의 맨 앞에 두고
  '주어 + 동사'의 어순을 바꾸어 사용한다.

1. There / Here + 동사 + 주어

- **There was something strange** between apples and oranges.

- **Here is some water** you can drink.

※ 주어가 대명사인 경우 도치를 하지 않는다.
  - There **it** flies.
    → There **flies** the bird.

2. So + 동사 + 주어 / Neither(Nor) + 동사 + 주어

- **A** Jessy goes to buy some comic books.

  B So do I.

- **A** Anna didn't like to eat tomatoes.

  B Neither (Nor) did Tom.

➡ 사용하는 동사와 시제에 따라 'do' 외에도 'be동사, 조동사', '현재형, 과거형'을 모두 사용할 수 있다.

➡ 'so + 동사 + 주어' = '주어 + 동사, too' ~도 또한...이다

➡ 'Neither (Nor) + 동사 + 주어' = '주어 + 동사 + not, either' ~도 또한 ...이 아니다

3. 부정어의 도치: little, never, hardly, not until

(1) 부정어 + 조동사 + 주어 + 동사

- Mike never broke a promise to me.

  = **Never did Mike break** a promise to me.

(2) not until ~ 조동사 + 주어 + 동사

- **Not until** last month **did I get** the money.

Grammar Plus +

- **hardly A before B = no sooner A than B** (A가 하자마자 B하다)
  → A에는 과거완료를, B에는 과거형의 동사를 쓴다.
  ex) **No sooner** had he left the party **than** the magic show started.

4. 장소, 방향의 부사구 + 동사 + 주어

- Three girls sat **under the big tree**.

  = **Under the big tree sat three girls.**

Answer Keys p. 61

A 괄호 안에서 알맞은 것을 고르시오.

1 On the hill (is / are⃝) some horses.

2 In the dining room (was / were) many people standing.

3 Never (do / does) my sister have lunch at home.

4 Under the old bridge (stands / stood) two boys.

5 Hardly (he had / had he) come back to Korea when she started complaining.

6 No sooner had I come home than I (turn / turned) on TV.

7 She said she couldn't agree with your opinion.
   Neither (could I / I could).

8 Here (he comes / comes he).

9 He said he loved me. So (I did / did I).

10 Little (did we / we did) know, the team would win.

B 보기 와 같이 문장을 주어진 표현으로 바꾸어 쓰시오.

> 보기
>
> The dogs were on the sofa.
>
> ➡ On the sofa <u>were the dogs</u>.

1 The storm came down and destroyed everything.
   ➡ _____ and destroyed everything.

2 She has never read such a horrible story.
   ➡ Never _____

3 Helen had no sooner entered the meeting room than the light was turned on.
   ➡ No sooner _____

4 A pine tree stood on the top of the hill.
   ➡ On the top of the hill _____

5 Minhyuk had hardly woken up when the phone rang.
   ➡ Hardly _____

• **생략**: 앞서 나온 말이 다시 나오는 경우 그 말을 생략할 수 있다.
접속사가 이끄는 절에서 '주어 + be동사'가 없어도 의미 파악이 되면 생략이 가능하며,
관계대명사 절에서 '주격 관계대명사 + be동사' 또는 '목적격 관계대명사'를 생략할 수 있다.

1. 반복되는 말의 생략

• Jane visited her grandmother's and **(she)** helped her water the garden.

• Some were for the new system, some **(were)** against it.

• You can do the puzzle if you want to **(do it)**.

2. '주어 + be동사'의 생략

(1) 부사절에서 '주어 + be동사'가 주절의 주어와 같을 경우 생략 가능

• Maria was nervous when **(she was)** elected as team leader.

• Tom looks much better than **(he was)** last week.

(2) 감탄문에서의 생략

• What a beautiful girl **(she is)**!

• How great **(it is)**!

3. 관계대명사의 생략

(1) 주격 관계대명사 + be동사

• Look at the woman **(who is)** taking pictures over there.

(2) 목적격 관계대명사

• The man **(whom)** I liked was called 'Pooh Bear.'

4. 대용어구

• **A** Do you think she will come back later?

  B I think **so**. (= I think that she will come back later.)

  I think **not**. (= I don't think that she will come back later.)

  → 실제 표현에서는 'I don't think so.'의 표현을 더 많이 사용한다.

◈ so, not과 함께 쓰이는 동사(구)

• think	• hope	• believe	• expect	• guess	• suppose	• be afraid

Answer Keys p. 61

A 주어진 말은 생략된 말이다. 알맞은 위치에 넣어 문장을 다시 쓰시오.

1 He played the violin and danced to the music. (he)

➡ *He played the violin and he danced to the music.*

2 Catch me if you can. (catch me)

➡ _____

3 You can try the contest if you would like to. (try it)

➡ _____

4 She ate seven pieces of pizza. So, only one left. (piece is)

➡ _____

5 My cat is bigger than yours. (cat)

➡ _____

6 I'll go and meet her if necessary. (it is)

➡ _____

7 The woman welcomed us kindly, though sick. (she was)

➡ _____

B 보기 와 같이 질문에 대한 답이 뜻하는 것을 완전한 문장으로 다시 쓰시오.

> **보기**
>
> **A** Do you think John can pass the exam?
>
> **B** I think so. ➡ I think that he can pass the exam.
>
> I think not. ➡ I don't think that he can pass the exam.

1 **A** Has Sam turned in his report?

   B I think not. ➡ _____

2 **A** Will the boys come to the party?

   B I believe so. ➡ _____

3 **A** Do you think he won't come back to our town?

   B I'm afraid so. ➡ _____

4 **A** Do they think the rumor is true?

   B They believe not. ➡ _____

5 **A** The girls did the wrong thing. What do you think?

   B I think not. ➡ _____

- **동격**: 주어, 목적어, 보어를 다시 한 번 설명해 주는 것이며, 동격의 자리에는 단어, 구, that이 이끄는 절이 올 수 있다.
- **무생물이 주어일 때**: 무생물이 주어로 쓰인 경우 사람을 주어로 하여 같은 뜻으로 바꿀 수 있다.

1. 동격

(1) '명사 + 명사'의 동격

- She was helped by **Mary, her eldest sister.**
  (Mary is her eldest sister.)

(2) '명사 + of + 동명사구'의 동격

- **My dream of singing solo on stage** came true.
  (My dream was singing solo on stage.)

(3) '명사 + to부정사'의 동격

- **Her plan to be a famous hair stylist** came true.
  (Her plan was to be a famous hair stylist.)

(4) '명사 + that절'의 동격

- Nobody knows **the fact that the man is a liar.**
  (The fact is that the man is a liar.)

2. 무생물이 주어일 때

(1) 무생물 + make + 목적어 + 목적격보어: ~하게 만들다

- **What** makes you guess so?

  ➡ **Why** do you guess so?

(2) 무생물 + prevent/ stop/ keep + 목적어 + from -ing: ~하지 못하게 하다

- The rain **stopped** us **from going** camping.

(3) 무생물 + enable + 목적어 + to부정사: ~할 수 있게 하다

- The machine **enables** them **to buy** caramels easily.

Answer Keys p. 62

A 보기와 같이 두 문장을 한 문장으로 바꿔 쓰시오

> 보기
>
> Inho is very gentle. He is a writer.
>
> ➡ Inho, a writer, is very gentle.

1 Let me introduce my daughter. She is Linda.

➡ _____

2 Everyone knows the fact. The fact is that the boy stole the bike.

➡ _____

3 His dream will come true. His dream is to become a famous actor.

➡ _____

4 They gave up the idea. The idea is selling some snacks at the festival.

➡ _____

5 My plan is to make a new dress for Sally. I think this plan is possible.

➡ _____

B 주어진 해석에 맞게 빈칸에 알맞은 말을 쓰시오.

1 태풍 때문에 그들은 축제를 즐길 수 없었다.

➡ The storm prevented ___them from enjoying___ the festival.

2 무엇이 네가 그렇게 행동하도록 만드니?

➡ _____ makes you behave so?

3 그가 우리에게 준 정보 덕분에 숙제를 마칠 수 있었다.

➡ The information that he gave us enabled us _____ our homework.

4 나는 영어 시험 결과 때문에 잠을 잘 수 없다.

➡ The result of the English test _____ me from _____.

5 그 말은 Ann이 마을을 떠나지 못하게 했다.

➡ The word kept Ann _____ the town.

Practice More **I**

A 주어진 문장을 강조구문으로 바꿀 때 빈칸을 채우시오.

1 Amy turned in the report this afternoon.
➡ It was the report _____*that Amy turned in this afternoon*_____ .

2 The black car hit the old woman.
➡ It _____ that the black car hit.

3 I lost my bag in the Italian restaurant.
➡ It was in the Italian restaurant _____ .

4 The boy hid his car key in the basket.
➡ It was the boy _____ .

5 What made you sad over the weekend?
➡ What _____

6 The boy wanted to play the piano well.
➡ It was to play the piano well _____ .

7 Who do you want to invite to your wedding?
➡ Who _____

8 Two girls stood in front of my house.
➡ In front of my house _____ .

9 The police officer arrested the thieves.
➡ The police officer _____ arrested the thieves.

10 We never have anything to eat before bedtime.
➡ Never _____ anything to eat before bedtime.

B 괄호 안에서 알맞은 것을 고르시오.

1 In fact, my brother does (likes /(like)) playing baseball.

2 That's okay. She (does / did) her best when she participated in the contest.

3 The black shirts look (very / far) better than the others.

4 Next to the houses (are / is) the famous hospital.

5 Little (did / is) she know, the real problem was her attitude.

6 She said she was tired and sleepy. (So was / Was so) I.

7 Here (comes the bus / the bus comes).

8 Scarcely (have / had) I closed the window when rain started to come down.

9 Not until tonight (was / could) she finish her project.

10 Mr. Park wanted to give Helen her present (him / herself).

C 다음 밑줄 친 부분에서 생략 가능한 부분을 제외하고 다시 쓰시오.

1 The boys had dinner and they started to discuss the issue.
➡ _____ started to discuss the issue _____

2 He said we can use his computer if we want to use it.
➡ _____

3 The social issue would be interesting, if it was true.
➡ _____

4 This is the car that was bought by my father three years ago.
➡ _____

5 Though it was big, the boy could eat it all.
➡ _____

6 The novel which she wrote was sold out.
➡ _____

7 When she was a little girl, Kelly couldn't go to school.
➡ _____

8 The prices are lower this month than they were last month.
➡ _____

9 Though he is fat, he is good at every sport.
➡ _____

10 The girl whom Jungmin loves is my sister.
➡ _____

Practice More I

D 주어진 문장과 같은 뜻의 문장이 되도록 빈칸을 채우시오.

1 I couldn't enjoy the trip because of the bad weather.
➡ The bad weather stopped us ___*from enjoying*___ the trip.

2 I'm happy because I got Paul's concert ticket.
➡ Paul's concert ticket _____ me _____.

3 People can find information because of the search engine.
➡ The search engine _____ people _____ information.

4 Tim has a dream. His dream is to build a big house to live in with his family.
➡ Tim has a dream _____

5 Our plan is to go abroad to study English. It is helpful to us.
➡ Our plan _____ is helpful to us.

6 She stayed up late last night because she had a lot of work to do.
➡ A lot of work to do _____ last night.

7 The news shocked me. They say the bus fell off the cliff.
➡ The news _____ made me shocked.

8 Everybody didn't believe the fact. The fact is that she was not a thief.
➡ Everybody didn't believe the fact _____.

9 Tim couldn't answer the phone because of his crying baby.
➡ His crying baby prevented Tim _____ the phone.

10 People live longer than before because of medicine.
➡ Medicine _____ people _____ longer than before.

내신 최다 출제 유형

01 다음 중 강조 표현이 바르지 <u>못한</u> 것을 고르시오.
[출제 예상 85%]

① It was for her husband that Nancy bought a tie.
② It is her friend that will help her when she is in need.
③ It is today that I have a meeting in my office.
④ It was the bus that she met him last night on.
⑤ It was Julie that was crying under the tree.

02 다음 중 어법상 틀린 것을 고르시오.
[출제 예상 90%]

① She didn't pass the exam, and neither did you.
② Not a world did Tim say all day long.
③ Never I have seen such a beautiful sight.
④ Here they come.
⑤ On the bench sat the woman.

03 다음 중 밑줄 친 부분의 쓰임이 나머지 넷과 <u>다른</u> 것을 고르시오.
[출제 예상 85%]

① <u>It is</u> sad <u>that</u> a lot of koalas are dying.
② <u>It is</u> true <u>that</u> Mina is going to move to the country.
③ <u>It is</u> funny <u>that</u> we can see the magic show.
④ <u>It is</u> Hong Myeong-Bo <u>that</u> scored a goal for Korea.
⑤ <u>It is</u> amazing <u>that</u> you can dance that well.

04 다음 주어진 문장의 밑줄 친 부분과 용법이 <u>다른</u> 것을 고르시오.
[출제 예상 80%]

> She <u>does</u> love her daughter and son.

① I <u>did</u> meet him at the park.
② He <u>did</u> do his best.
③ Dad and I <u>did</u> the dishes after dinner.
④ Boys <u>do</u> like to play baseball.
⑤ Girls <u>do</u> like to wear pretty dresses.

05 다음 밑줄 친 우리말을 영어로 바르게 옮긴 것을 고르시오.
[출제 예상 95%]

> I can't swim. <u>또한 나는 자전거도 못 탄다.</u>

① Nor I can ride a bike.
② No can I ride a bike.
③ No I can ride a bike.
④ And I can't ride a bike.
⑤ Nor can I ride a bike.

06 다음 중 어법상 옳은 것을 고르시오.
[출제 예상 90%]

① Not a word I said all day long.
② Only then she came to feel at ease.
③ Never did I see him again.
④ Never he has seen such a pretty woman.
⑤ Here and there a lot of flowers stood.

[01~03] 다음 두 문장이 같은 뜻이 되도록 빈칸에 들어
갈 알맞은 말을 고르시오.

01

When a boy, I would sometimes go
fishing with my dad.
= When _____ _____ a boy,
  I would sometimes go fishing with
  my dad.

① he was   ② was he   ③ he is
④ I was   ⑤ was I

02

It is still slower to ride a bike than to
drive a car.
= It is _____ slower to ride a bike
  than to drive a car.

① many   ② very   ③ much
④ so   ⑤ pretty

03

Kelly won't agree with you. I won't
agree with you, either.
= Kelly won't agree with you.
  _____

① Neither won't I.   ② Neither will I.
③ Either will I.   ④ Neither I will.
⑤ Either I will.

04 다음 밑줄 친 부분의 쓰임이 잘못된 것을 고르시오.

① I did put them in the refrigerator.
② Wendy did see me in front of City Hall.
③ The cakes do look very delicious.
④ We do think Bobby wasn't wrong.
⑤ Mrs. White did taught math two years ago.

05 다음 중 밑줄 친 부분의 용법이 나머지 넷과 다른
것을 고르시오.

① It was the camera that I lost yesterday.
② It is Tom that I will work with.
③ It is certain that the armchair is
   comfortable.
④ It was in the food court that I looked for
   the man.
⑤ It was they that thought of the machine
   at first.

06 다음 문장의 밑줄 친 부분 중 어법상 잘못된 것을
고르시오.

① Never ② Amy has dreamed ③ that
she would ④ become ⑤ such a good
wife.

07 다음 문장을 의문사를 강조하는 문장으로 바꿀 때 빈칸에 들어갈 알맞은 말을 고르시오.

> Who broke her glasses?
> = Who _____ broke her glasses?

① it was that
② was it that
③ it that was
④ was that it
⑤ that it was

08 다음 중 밑줄 친 much의 의미가 나머지 넷과 다른 것을 고르시오.

① How <u>much</u> do you know about him?
② The town is <u>much</u> nicer than yours.
③ Eating too <u>much</u> is not good for you.
④ They have missed me so <u>much</u> for 10 years.
⑤ He could not understand <u>much</u> about her school.

09 다음 빈칸에 알맞은 말을 고르시오.

> _____ promise her you won't cry.

① Have
② Be
③ Not
④ Do
⑤ Has

10 다음 밑줄 친 부분 중 생략할 수 있는 것을 고르시오.

① I liked his father <u>who is</u> nice and kind.
② Do you know the boy <u>who is</u> standing over there?
③ She has a son <u>who is</u> 15 years old.
④ Those <u>who are</u> very sick need much care.
⑤ <u>Who is</u> your new English teacher?

11 다음 중 강조를 나타내는 문장이 <u>아닌</u> 것을 고르시오.

① It was this bike that I bought here.
② He himself cleaned the house.
③ Amy did her homework after dinner.
④ This is the very book I have read several times.
⑤ Brandon didn't say a word at all.

12 다음 빈칸에 공통으로 들어갈 알맞은 말을 고르시오.

> • Thomas fell in love with the _____ woman.
> • You will get better _____ soon.

① much
② very
③ quite
④ just
⑤ far

[13~14] 다음 우리말을 바르게 영작한 것을 고르시오.

★★★
13

> 우리 중에 아무도 독일에 가본 적이 없다.

① Neither of us has been to Germany.

② Not all of us have been to Germany.

③ None of us went to Germany.

④ None of us has been to Germany.

⑤ None of us have been to Germany.

★★★
14

> 나는 저런 음악을 들어본 적이 없다.

① Never hear I such that music.

② Never I hear such that music.

③ Never I had heard such that music.

④ Never have I heard such that music.

⑤ Never I have heard such that music.

15 다음 밑줄 친 it의 쓰임이 나머지 넷과 다른 것을 고르시오.

① It was yesterday that Jeff and Catherine arrived.

② It is hard for me to decide what to do.

③ It was surprising that he drove fast.

④ It is important that you keep a diary.

⑤ It is necessary that you have a good attitude.

16 다음 글의 밑줄 친 부분 중 생략할 수 있는 것을 고르시오.

> ① Larry can ② play baseball today but ③ James ④ can't ⑤ play baseball today.

17 다음 중 어법상 어색한 것을 고르시오.

① Jen is a dentist and so is Tom.

② Here two oranges and three bananas are.

③ She is not in the least worried about the result.

④ It was James who solved the hardest math problem.

⑤ Kelly herself didn't do the project.

Note　not in the least (=not at all) 전혀, 조금도

18 다음 밑줄 친 부분을 바르게 고친 것을 고르시오.

> Never I realized that I had lost my wallet.

① realized I　　　② did I realized

③ did I realize　　④ I do realized

⑤ I did realize

★★★

19 다음 두 문장의 의미가 <u>다른</u> 것을 고르시오.

① My sister stood at the bus stop.
  = At the bus stop stood my sister.

② The rich are not always happy.
  = Rich people are never happy.

③ I really hope he'll be happy.
  = I do hope he'll be happy.

④ James is handsome and Jack is, too.
  = James is handsome and so is Jack.

⑤ Steven is the very person that I was looking for.
  = It is Steven that I was looking for.

20 다음 대화의 빈칸에 들어갈 말이 바르게 짝지어진 것을 고르시오.

| A _____ is Joy whom I wanted to invite to my party. |
| B Look outside. There _____ comes! |

① He – he
② It – it
③ He – Tim
④ This – Tim
⑤ It – he

◇◇◇◇◇◇◇◇◇ 서술형 평가 ◇◇◇◇◇◇◇◇◇

[21~22] 다음 문장에서 생략할 수 있는 부분을 찾아 쓰시오.

21

| When they are asked for it, most people will act like we did. |

➡ _____

22

| The season of this picture was estimated to be fall when it was painted. |

➡ _____

[23~25] 다음 두 문장이 같은 뜻이 되도록 빈칸에 알맞은 말을 쓰시오.

23

| Jamal is faster today than yesterday.
= Jamal is faster today than ____ _____ yesterday. |

➡ _____

24

| I never told her what happened to me last week.
= Never _____ _____ _____ her what happened to me last week. |

➡ _____

25

She will go to the top of the mountain covered with snow.

= She will go to the top of the mountain _____ _____ covered with snow.

➡ _____

28

그들 중 아무도 전에 이탈리아에 간 적이 없다.
(none / have / been / them / of)

➡ _____

to Italy before.

[26~28] 다음 우리말과 같은 뜻이 되도록 괄호 안의 단어를 바르게 배열하시오.

★★★
26

산의 여행에 대한 기록을 쓰면서 나는 바로 자연의 본질을 표현할 수 있었다.
(I / nature / of / express / could / the / essence / very)

➡ _____

by writing a journal about the journey of mountains.

(Note) essence 본질

★★★
29 다음 밑줄 친 부분을 강조의 조동사 do를 사용하여 문장을 다시 쓰시오.

I <u>really hoped</u> that he would come back safe.

➡ _____

27

Jane은 방학 동안에 운동을 전혀 하지 않아서 살이 좀 쪘다.
(Jane / at / didn't / all / exercise)

➡ _____

and gained some weight over the vacation.

★★★
30 다음 문장을 주어진 단어로 시작하여 다시 쓰시오.

I hardly visited Canada after I had returned to my hometown.

➡ Hardly _____

_____

Note

Grammar Master Level 3

펴낸이	임 병 업
펴낸곳	(주)월드컴 에듀
디자인	임예슬 · 김지현
저자	신은진
편집	김채원
감수	Amy Smith
등록	2015년 10월 15일
주소	서울특별시 강남구 도곡동 411-2
	차우빌딩, 5층
전화	02)3273-4300 (대표)
팩스	02)3273-4303
홈페이지	www.wcbooks.co.kr
이메일	wc4300@wcbooks.co.kr

GRAMMAR

③

정답 및 해설

WorldCom Edu

Chapter 01 문장의 형식

Lesson 1-1 부가의문문

p. 012

A
1	isn't he?	2	will it?
3	has she?	4	didn't he(she)?
5	will you?	6	arent' I?
7	can't she?	8	isn't it?
9	do we?	10	hasn't she?
11	shall we?	12	can't you?
13	didn't they?	14	was there?
15	does she?	16	will you?
17	aren't you?	18	aren't I?
19	do you?	20	shall we?

Lesson 1-2 간접의문문

p. 013~014

A
1 where the nearest French restaurant is?
2 what made you so sad?
3 if(whether) he has an appointment today.
4 how far it is from here to your house?
5 when the car accident happened?
6 who will look after Tom while his mother is cooking.
7 if(whether) she got married to the Korean man?
8 if(whether) she has any children.
9 if(whether) your dream will come true.
10 if(whether) you can finish it by tomorrow.

B
1 Why do you think she started exercising?
2 Where do you think she is from?
3 I know where you went after school last Friday.
4 When do you believe you can buy this car?
5 Please tell me if(whether) you are Tim's father.
6 Why do you think they broke up?
7 Who do you suppose will be the team leader?

Lesson 1-3 문장의 형식_1형식과 2형식

p. 016

A
1	There are	2	fast
3	happy	4	dangerous
5	lovely	6	useful
7	rough	8	disappointed
9	angry	10	sweet
11	delicious	12	good
13	tired	14	looks like
15	tasteless		

B
1 a lot of wild flowers on the field. (1형식)
2 smell disgusting. (2형식)
3 danced on a big stage. (1형식)
4 sounds ecstatic. (2형식)
5 became a big monster. (2형식)

Lesson 1-4 문장의 형식_3형식과 4형식

p. 018

A
1	to become	2	opening
3	writing	4	going
5	to get	6	to attend
7	writing		
8	practicing/to practice		
9	taking		
10	to quit		

B
1	to	2	for
3	to	4	of
5	for	6	to
7	of	8	for
9	to	10	for

Lesson 1-5 문장의 형식_5형식

p. 019

A
1	to pick me up	2	interesting
3	clean	4	class president
5	play (playing)	6	a baby
7	to buy	8	cut
9	fantastic	10	to take part in

A 1 would he?
  2 hasn't she?
  3 shall we?
  4 don't they?
  5 will you?
  6 shouldn't they?
  7 will you?
  8 shall we?
  9 aren't I?

B 1 the girl is
  2 Who do you
  3 who can
  4 if(whether)
  5 do you
  6 will you
  7 aren't they
  8 do you
  9 what made

C 1 didn't
  2 happy
  3 fix
  4 to go
  5 for his son
  6 of her students
  7 boring
  8 to make

D 1 They elected Amy leader of English speaking team.
  2 The news made me study harder.
  3 Grandmother cooked a delicious breakfast for us.
  4 They approached the building.
  5 Helen didn't allow her children to run in the house.
  6 I wonder if his dream came true.
  7 Please tell me who will get an A on the English test.

중간 기말고사 예상문제

내신 최다 출제 유형

p. 022

01 ② 02 ④ 03 ③ 04 ⑤ 05 ②
06 ③

해설

01 감각동사 뒤에 형용사가 보어로 온다. well → good
02 ① knowing → know, ② to feel → feel, ③ to play → play,
   ⑤ cleaned → clean
   → 사역동사의 목적격보어로는 원형부정사가 온다.
03 5형식: 주어＋동사＋목적어＋목적격보어
   → 지각동사의 목적격보어는 원형부정사가 온다.
04 첫 번째 문장: 지각동사 'see'의 목적격 보어 자리에는 원형부정사가 온다.
   두 번째 문장: 주격보어 자리에 동명사가 온다.
05 'make'는 간접목적어 앞에 전치사 'for'와 함께 쓰인다.
06 ⓑ badly → bad, ⓓ terribly → terrible

p. 023~027

01 ② 02 ⑤ 03 ② 04 ④ 05 ③
06 ② 07 ⑤ 08 ① 09 ③ 10 ⑤
11 ①,② 12 ③,④ 13 ⑤ 14 ② 15 ②
16 ④ 17 ① 18 ⑤ 19 ① 20 ①④⑤

〈서술형 평가〉

21 sounded
22 didn't you
23 keep(prevent), from
24 to → for
25 Does he where → Where does he
26 Where did you think they went last weekend?
27 My father cooked some food for us.
28 Robert shows us something funny everyday.
29 It provides the participants with a chance to learn how to exercise correctly.
30 I prefer reading books in the library to going shopping.

해설

01 buy＋직접목적어＋for＋간접목적어_3형식 문장
02 ask＋직접목적어＋of＋간접목적어_3형식 문장
03 〈보기, ②〉 5형식 문장
04 〈보기, ④〉 5형식
05 〈보기, ③〉 3형식
06 의문사가 없는 의문문을 간접의문문으로 전환 할 때 'if(whether)'를 사용하여 문장을 연결한다.

07 'think'처럼 생각이나 추측을 나타내는 동사가 올 때는 의문사가 문장의 제일 앞에 위치한다.

08 의문사가 직접의문문의 주어로 쓰였을 경우, 간접의문문으로 전환할 때 직접의문문의 어순을 그대로 적용한다.

09 사역동사 'let'의 목적격보어로는 동사원형이 와야 한다.
disturbs → disturb

10 ⑤ richly → rich

11 ③ understand → to understand,
④ to start → start(starting), ⑤ see → to see

12 ① finish → to finish, ② to encourage → encourage,
⑤ take → to take
* 'help'는 준사역동사로서 목적격 보어로 동사원형 또는
to부정사 모두 올 수 있다.

13 주절이 긍정이므로 부가의문문은 부정이 되어야 하며,
'동사+not'은 줄임말 형태가 되어야 한다.

14 'Let's~' 명령문의 부가의문문은 긍정, 부정에 상관없이 'shall
we'를 사용한다.

15 명령문의 부가의문문은 긍정, 부정에 상관없이 'will you'를
사용한다.

16 'got'의 목적격보어로 to부정사가 온다.

17 'tell'의 목적격 보어로 to부정사가 오며, to부정사의 부정형은
'not+to부정사'이다.

18 'Mary didn't know.+What did it mean?'을 하나의 문장으
로 만든 간접의문문이다.
의문사가 있는 경우 '의문사+주어+동사'의 어순을 사용한다.

19 'allow'의 목적격보어는 to부정사이다.

20 ① truly → true, ④ sillier → silly ⑤ friend → friendly

〈서술형 평가〉

21 'sound' ~하게 들리다

22 주절이 긍정이면 부가의문문은 부정이다. 시제가 일반동사 과거
형이기 때문에 부가의문문의 동사 역시 과거형으로 한다.

23 'keep(prevent) ~from 동사-ing'
~이 ...(동사-ing)하는 것을 막다

24 'find'의 간접목적어는 'for+목적격'이다.

25 'suppose'와 같이 생각이나 추측을 나타내는 동사가 나올 경우
의문사는 문장의 맨 앞에 위치한다.

26 'think'처럼 생각이나 추측을 나타내는 동사가 올 때는 의문사가
문장의 맨 앞에 위치하게 된다.

27 'cook'의 간접목적어의 형태는 'for+목적격'이다.
→ 3형식 전환 문장: 주어+동사+목적어+전치사+목적격

28 'to+목적격'에서 'to'를 삭제하고 목적어를 동사 뒤로 보낸다.
→ 4형식: 주어+동사+간접목적어+직접목적어

29 'provide A with B' A에게 B를 제공하다

30 'prefer A to B' B보다 A를 더 좋아하다

Chapter
02 동사의 시제

Lesson 2-1 be동사, 일반동사 현재형

★Check up!

p. 032

A
1 drives
2 studies
3 does not want
4 are
5 boils
6 drinks/feels
7 enjoy
8 is
9 live
10 is
11 gathers
12 gets
13 do not buy
14 mixes
15 cries

Lesson 2-2 be동사, 일반동사 과거형

★Check up!

p. 034

A
1 cooked
2 helped
3 played
4 borrowed
5 changed
6 worried
7 tried
8 hugged
9 planned
10 loved

B
1 was
2 helped
3 replied
4 had
5 washed
6 Were
7 moved
8 welcomed
9 Were
10 begged

Lesson 2-3 일반동사의 과거형_불규칙변화

★Check up!

p. 036~37

A
1 swept – swept
2 threw – thrown
3 got – gotten
4 stood – stood
5 arose – arisen
6 saw – seen
7 shook – shaken
8 ate – eaten
9 strove – striven
10 wove – woven

---

11 sank – sunk
12 thought – thought
13 flew – flown
14 sowed – sown(sowed)
15 stole – stolen
16 forgave – forgiven
17 lay – lain
18 heard – heard

B
1 left
2 sent
3 drove
4 brought
5 threw
6 jogged
7 broke
8 prayed
9 taught
10 married

Lesson 2-4 진행형

★Check up!

p. 039

A
1 is snowing
2 is speaking
3 was making
4 is wearing
5 was dancing
6 aren't talking
7 wasn't having
8 Are/preparing

B
1 was belonging → belonged
2 is freezing → freezes
3 is having → has
4 am wanting → want
5 runs → is running
6 made → was making
7 was seeing → saw
8 studied → were studying

Lesson 2-5 미래형

★Check up!

p. 040

A
1 will buy
2 are going to have
3 will write in a diary
4 Is, going to go
5 will catch
6 aren't(are not) going to go
7 will leave
8 will not(won't) come
9 Are/going to take

Practice More Ⅰ

p. 041~43

A
1	felt	2	snows
3	bought	4	were
5	forgot	6	moved
7	blossom	8	rose
9	started	10	gave

B
1	(T)	2	(F)
3	(F)	4	(T)
5	(F)	6	(T)
7	(F)	8	(T)
9	(T)		

C
1	are taking	2	got
3	knows	4	was cooking
5	will be	6	finishes
7	doing	8	was playing
9	are reading	10	am going to have

D
1 She is doing the dishes in the kitchen.
2 What are you going to do this weekend?
3 He was cleaning his room when I entered the room. (= When I entered the room, he was cleaning his room.)
4 He is drinking the cherry juice that his mom made.
5 When I stopped dancing, the audience gave me a big hand. (= The audience gave me a big hand when I stopped dancing.)
6 When John came back, the baby was sleeping. (= The baby was sleeping when John came back.)
7 I am looking forward to watching director Park's next movie.
8 Tommy broke his leg while he was riding a bike.
9 He was worried because the homework was too hard.
10 I forgot to turn off the light in the room, so I had to go back home.

Lesson 2-6 현재완료

Check up!

p. 046

A
1 has/finished [완료]
2 has been sick [계속]
3 Have/eaten [경험]

4 has cleaned [완료]
5 have been [경험]
6 have/arrived [완료]
7 have gone [결과]
8 has/driven [경험]
9 has broken [결과]
10 have known [계속]

B
1	for	2	since
3	for	4	since
5	for	6	for
7	since		

Lesson 2-7 현재완료와 과거형

Check up!

p. 047

A
1	has been	2	has studied
3	Have you ever eaten	4	have you been
5	has lost	6	didn't snow
7	knew	8	go
9	has lived	10	made

Lesson 2-8 현재완료 진행형

Check up!

p. 049

A
1 has been making
2 have been studying
3 has been reading
4 have been looking for
5 have been playing
6 have been preparing
7 has/been doing
8 Has/been playing
9 has not been listening

B
1 have known
2 has been fixing
3 seems
4 has been studying
5 has been having
6 have wanted
7 has not been
8 Have they been
9 have been

Lesson 2-9 과거완료

Check up! p. 051

A 1 had/left 2 became
3 had met 4 had forgotten
5 lost 6 had finished
7 had ended 8 had been sad
9 had/had 10 had fallen

B 1 had been thinking
2 had not been studying
3 Had/been waiting
4 had been discussing
5 had been working
6 Had/been enjoying
7 had not been paying
8 had been living
9 had not been working
10 had been running

Lesson 2-10 미래완료

Check up! p. 052

A 1 will have fixed
2 will have comeback
3 Will/have been studying
4 will have watched
5 will not have arrived

Practice More Ⅱ p. 053~055

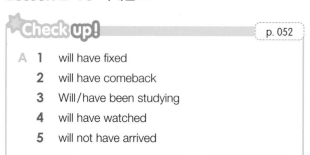

A 1 done 2 talked
3 for 4 have met
5 have been working 6 have seen
7 broken 8 arrived
9 had fallen asleep 10 been

B 1 Alex had started to learn how to bake bread.
2 They haven't stayed in the hotel.
3 She had been weak until the age of fifteen.
4 The boy will have woken up at seven.
5 I have known Helen since I was young.
6 He had left the house before she called him.
7 It has been snowing since last week.

8 He had studied for an hour before he came.
9 We had joined the soccer club.

C 1 leaves
2 painting
3 had finished
4 had given
5 met
6 will/am going to
7 has played
8 read
9 had seen
10 took

D 1 Joy lost the watch which I had given to her.
2 I've decided to learn Spanish one month ago.
3 My father had been studying in Japan for seven years
4 Minsu moved to Daejeon three years ago and he has lived there since.
5 I have used this room since my sister moved out.
6 They have been studying for tomorrow's final exam since ten o'clock.
7 It has been raining for four hours.
8 John has talked to my daughter on the phone several times.
9 I have been waiting for him for three hours.
10 Linda gave her mom a dress that she had bought two weeks before.

중간 기말고사 예상문제

내신 최다 출제 유형 p. 056

01 ①   02 ②   03 ③   04 ①
05 He has been playing the drums for three hours.
06 arrived at the airport, the airplane had already taken off

해설

01 'since I was a kid' 어렸을 때부터~ 의 구문으로 과거의 특정 시점부터 현재까지 계속되는 현상을 표현하는 현재완료 사용
02 〈보기, ②〉 현재완료-계속, ① 완료, ③,④,⑤ 경험
03 ① had → has, ② has studied → studied, ④ have → had, ⑤ for → since

04 과거에서부터 현재까지 계속 진행되는 것을 의미하고 있으므로 현재완료 진행형을 써야 한다.

05 과거에서부터 현재까지 계속 진행되는 것을 의미하고 있으므로 현재완료 진행형을 써야 한다.

06 부사절은 과거, 그 뒤의 문장은 더 과거이기 때문에 과거완료를 써준다.

p. 057~062

01 ④	02 ⑤	03 ②	04 ③	05 ②
06 ③	07 ④	08 ②	09 ④	10 ②
11 ⑤	12 ①	13 ③	14 ④	15 ③
16 ③	17 ②	18 ⑤	19 ④	20 ②
21 ①,③	22 ③,⑤	23 ④,⑤	24 ②,③	25 ④
26 ③	27 ⑤			

〈서술형 평가〉

28 has been reading

29 have been interested

30 have been cleaning

31 has taken care of → took care of

32 since → for

33 Susie took a shower / she had eaten breakfast.

34 I have been waiting for a taxi for twenty minutes.

35 Alie lost the glove that his father had given to him.

36 remembered / had given

37 arrived / had / left

38 My grandmother will be watering the garden.

39 Tom has just started his homework.

40 Elly had not started yet when

해설

01 write – wrote – written

02 think – thought – thought

03 과거보다 더 이전에 벌어진 일이므로 과거완료가 와야 한다.

04 과거보다 더 이전에 벌어진 일 이므로 과거완료가 와야 한다.

05 〈보기, ②〉 현재완료 – 경험, ① 결과, ③,④ 완료, ⑤ 계속

06 〈보기, ③〉 현재완료 – 경험 ① 계속, ②,⑤ 결과, ④ 완료

07 과거보다 더 과거인 과거완료형을 써 주는 것이 알맞다.

08 완료를 묻는 의문문에는 'yet'을, 긍정의 대답에는 'already'를 사용한다.

09 현재완료의 '결과'를 나타내는 표현이다.

10 과거보다 더 이전에 일어난 일이므로 과거완료를 사용한다.

11 현재완료의 계속적 용법이다. 'since' ~한 이후로

12 현재완료의 계속적 용법이다. 'for' ~하는 동안

13 현재진행형은 미래를 나타내는 부사와 함께 쓰여 미래를 표현하기도 한다.

14 과거보다 더 이전에 일어난 일이기 때문에 과거완료를 사용한다.

15 과거보다 더 이전에 일어난 일이기 때문에 과거완료를 사용한다.

16 had seen → will have seen

17 'Robby and Jenny'는 복수형 주어이다.
    is not going to study → are not going to study

18 명사절의 'if~'에서 미래의 의미는 그대로 미래형으로 나타낸다.

19 경험을 나타내는 현재완료의 의문문이다.

20 'be planning to' ~할 계획이다 – 미래형의 대답으로 보아 질문도 미래의 의미를 담는 것이 알맞다.

21 ② forbade → forbidden,
    ④ lied → laid (놓다: lay – laid – laid), ⑤ rose → risen

22 '① an hour ago, ② last year, ④ last night'들은 특정한 과거 시점을 나타내기 때문에 현재완료와 함께 사용할 수 없다.

23 have been → has been, ⑤ has been froze → frozen

24 ① were → been (How have you been? 안부를 물어보는 인사), ④ has asked → had asked, ⑤ see → seen

25 ④ 주절은 미래진행형으로, 부사절은 현재형으로 미래를 나타낸다.

26 ③ 미래를 뜻하는 부사와 함께 쓰여 가까운 미래를 의미 ①,②,④,⑤ 현재진행형

27 첫 번째 문장: 'but'의 의미를 생각했을 때 앞의 말에 대한 반대의 뜻을 가진 'won't'가 알맞다.
    두 번째 문장: 미래를 뜻하는 'will be windy'가 알맞다.
    (windy는 형용사이기 때문에 'be'가 앞에 나와야 한다.)

〈서술형 평가〉

28 과거에 시작한 동작이 현재까지 진행되고 있으므로 현재완료 진행형을 써준다.

29 'since'는 현재완료의 계속적 용법과 함께 사용하는 부사이다.

30 과거에 시작한 동작이 현재까지 진행되고 있으므로 현재완료 진행형을 써준다.

31 'when'은 과거의 특정한 시점을 말 할 때 쓰기 때문에 현재완료와 함께 사용할 수 없다.

32 'for' 사건이 일어난 시간의 길이를 나타낼 때 사용한다.

33 'after' 뒤에 더 이전의 과거가 나온다.(아침을 먹고 난 후 샤워를 했다)

34 과거에 시작한 동작이 현재까지 이어지고 있기 때문에 현재완료 진행형을 쓴다.

35 글러브를 준 것이 먼저 일어난 일이므로 대과거를 사용한다.

36 기억하다 remember, 선물을 주었던 것이 더 과거이므로 과거완료 had given을 사용한다.

37 도착했다 (arrived)보다 떠난 것이 더 과거이므로 과거완료 had left를 사용한다.

38 미래진행형 'will be+동사-ing'

39 현재완료형 'has just+과거분사'

40 과거완료형 'had+과거분사'

Chapter

03 조동사

Lesson 3-1 do

p. 065~066

A
1	didn't meet	2	do like
3	do not teach	4	do
5	does love	6	does make
7	did laugh	8	didn't like
9	could	10	does like

B
1	does(did)	2	does(did)
3	Do(did)	4	do(did)
5	did	6	do(did)
7	does	8	does

Lesson 3-2 can (could)

p. 068

A 1 is able to dance
2 can stop
3 wasn't able to catch
4 were able to win
5 Could / drive

B 1 Emily will be able to pass the exam next time.
2 I couldn't ride a bike when I was young.
(When I was young, I couldn't ride a bike.)
3 He can't be a leader in our group.
4 Can you help me before doing your
homework? (Before doing homework,
can you help me?)
5 Can he explain what happened to her?

Lesson 3-3 may (might)

p. 069

A 1 goes − go
2 eats − eat
3 doesn't may − may not
4 Do may − May
5 are may − may
6 not might − might not
7 arrives − arrive
8 studied − study

Lesson 3-4 must / have to

p. 071

A 1 must(have to) wear
2 have to wait
3 have to take
4 must(have to) go
5 must(have to) be

B 1 He must be hungry now.
2 Some students don't have to wear uniforms.
3 We must not play on the grass.
4 Harry and Maria must be a couple.
5 The doctor says that I have to exercise for my
health.
6 He has to go to church every Sunday morning.
(=Every Sunday morning, he has to go to
church.)
7 He need not have a test.
8 She must feed the dogs every day.

Practice More I

p. 072~74

A
1. May
2. must
3. can
4. wasn't able to
5. was able to
6. doesn't need to / need not
7. must
8. don't need to / need not
9. am not able to

B
1. being → be
2. copies → copy
3. will must → must (will have to)
4. could → can
5. had to → have to
6. not needs → need not / doesn't need to
7. will must → must (will have to)
8. tells → tell
9. did → do

C
1. does love to act
2. have to wait in line.
3. must not play
4. can walk twenty miles
5. may not repair the radio.
6. did encourage his students to practice
7. be able to buy
8. couldn't find the difference.
9. must not exercise
10. don't have to buy

D
1. have to
2. must not change
3. may(can) stay
4. must be tired
5. Can(May) / borrow
6. may break
7. had to take
8. will be able to speak
9. cannot be
10. doesn't have(need) to

Lesson 3-5 will (would)

Check up!

p. 077

A
1. would rather
2. would like to
3. be able to
4. Would
5. would rather
6. would like

B
1. would rather exercise than sleep.
2. Would you press
3. will go to Russia
4. would rather take a bus than walk.
5. would like to eat the most delicious food

Lesson 3-6 should / ought to / had better

Check up!

p. 078

A
1. should(ought to) listen
2. should(ought to) apologize
3. should(ought to) be
4. should(ought to) give
5. should(ought to) reply

Lesson 3-7 would / used to

Check up!

p. 079

A
1. used to(would) get
2. used to(would) spend
3. used to be
4. used to(would) hide
5. used to(would) like
6. used to be
7. used to(would) take
8. used to live
9. used to have

Lesson 3-8 조동사＋have＋과거분사

Check up! p. 080

A 1 shouldn't have used
  2 cannot(can't) have been
  3 must have been
  4 should have thought
  5 should have hurried up

Practice More Ⅱ p. 081~82

A 1 Can   2 be able to
  3 may decide   4 might study
  5 must not be   6 doesn't have to
  7 would rather   8 should not
  9 used to (would)   10 used to (would)

B 1 will can → can   2 must → had to
  3 to not → not to   4 may → might
  5 had better → would rather
  6 did → done

C 1 would rather exercise
  2 will be able to
  3 must have suffered
  4 should have arrived
  5 Would you pass
  6 should have thought

D 1 She had better leave now.
  2 You won't be able to repair the car.
  3 He used to teach science at school.
  4 Sometimes I would drink coffee here.
  5 I would rather go swimming than go fishing.
  6 Can you design the model?

중간 기말고사 예상문제

내신 최다 출제 유형 p. 083

01 ③   02 ④   03 ⑤   04 ③   05 ①
06 should have told her the truth

해설

01 'don't have to'는 don't 'need to', 'need not'으로 바꿔 쓸 수 있다.
02 과거에 대한 강한 추측은 'must have＋과거분사'로 한다.
03 시험공부를 하지 않았음에도 만점을 받았으므로, 다음 문장은 '쉬웠던 것이 틀림없다'의 표현이 나와야 한다.
04 'would rather'의 부정형은 'would rather not'이다.
05 ① ～해야한다(의무), ②,③,④,⑤ ～임에 틀림없다(추측)
06 후회를 나타내는 표현 'should have＋과거분사' ～했어야 했다

p. 084~088

01 ③   02 ②   03 ⑤   04 ②   05 ④
06 ③   07 ①   08 ②   09 ③   10 ⑤
11 ②   12 ①   13 ④   14 ③   15 ⑤
16 ②   17 ④   18 ②   19 ③   20 ⑤
21 ①   22 ③,④   23 ④   24 ②   25 ③
26 ②

〈서술형 평가〉

27 I used to(would) write in my diary in English.
28 Jessy used to(would) dance at a dancing club.
29 So do I.
30 Neither could I.
31 He must have eaten all the oranges in the refrigerator.
32 Nancy used to be the best student in the class.
33 We should have brought a map.

해설

01 'would like to＋동사원형' ～을 하고 싶다
02 'had better'～하는 것이 낫다
03 'would' ～하곤 했다 – 과거의 습관을 나타낼 때 사용한다.
04 ② 'can' ～할 수 있다
05 'ought to'의 부정형은 'ought not to'이다.
06 ③ 추측, ①,②,④,⑤ 의무
07 ① ～해도 좋다(허락), ②,③,④,⑤ ～일지도 모른다(추측)
08 ② start → starting
09 ③ 조동사와 조동사는 함께 사용될 수 없다.
10 〈보기, ⑤〉 강조를 뜻하는 do
11 강조를 위한 'do 동사'는 아무런 뜻이 없으므로 생략이 가능하다.

12 'may'와 'could'는 허락을 나타내는 조동사로 쓸 수 있다.

13 'may have+과거분사' ~했을지도 모른다

14 'cannot have+과거분사' ~했을 리가 없다

15 'must' ~인 것이 틀림없다

16 ②'~하다'의 일반동사, ①,③,④,⑤ 강조를 뜻하는 조동사

17 금지의 표현이 들어가야 하는데 ④번은 미래의 부정형이다.

18 'can' ~할 수 있나요?, 과연~일까?, ~해도 되나요?

19 'would like+명사' ~하고 싶다

20 'give up' 포기하다

21 ought → ought to ~해야 한다

22 ③,④ 'doesn't need to = doesn't have to = need not' ~할 필요가 없다

23 'must have+과거분사' ~였던 것이 틀림없다

24 'be able to' ~할 수 있다

25 'should' ~해야 한다, 'should have+과거분사' ~했어야 한다.

26 'may' 허락, 추측의 의미를 가지고 있다.

〈서술형 평가〉

27 'used to(would)' ~하곤 했었다 – 과거의 습관을 나타냄

28 'used to(would)' ~하곤 했다 – 과거의 습관을 나타냄

29 긍정의 대답에 'so do I' 사용– 동사 'do' 대신 질문자의 동사와 일치시켜 준다.

30 부정의 대답에 'neither do I' 사용 – 동사 'do' 대신 질문자의 동사와 일치시켜 준다.

31 'must have+과거분사' ~했던 것이 틀림없다

32 'used to' ~하곤 했다

33 'should have+과거분사' ~했어야 했다

Chapter

04 명사, 관사와 대명사

Lesson 4-1 명사의 종류

★Check up! p. 092

A
1	Dogs	2	The family
3	families	4	house
5	students	6	information
7	eat	8	life
9	bees	10	police
11	equipment	12	water/food
13	salt/oil	14	ceremony
15	A worker		

Lesson 4-2 셀 수 있는 명사의 복수형

★Check up! p. 094

A
1	geese	2	houses
3	rivers	4	thieves
5	mice	6	beliefs
7	aisles	8	children
9	leaves	10	deer
11	knives	12	knees
13	teeth	14	giraffes
15	superheroes	16	buses
17	hairbrushes	18	axes
19	volcanoes	20	challenges
21	diaries	22	jewels
23	churches	24	eyelashes

B
1	parties	2	wolves
3	babies	4	exhibitions
5	hats	6	forms
7	axes	8	potatoes
9	giraffes	10	ankles/ankle

Lesson 4-3 셀 수 없는 명사의 복수형

★Check up! p. 096

A
1 loaves of bread
2 slice(piece) of pizza
3 cups of coffee.
4 cartons(glasses, bottles) of milk
5 piece of furniture?
6 bunches of bananas
7 glasses(bottles) of cold water
8 bag of flour
9 bag of snacks.
10 piece of advice.
11 pieces of chocolate cake
12 bowl of soup./bottles(glasses) of juice
/pounds(loaves) of meat.
13 bowl of/carton of
14 sheets of paper
15 spoonfuls(teaspoonfuls) of salt

Lesson 4-4 추상명사의 관용적 표현

★Check up! p. 097~98

A
1	purposely	2	courageous
3	useless	4	perfectly
5	of importance	6	of use
7	hastily	8	mistakenly
9	Occasionally	10	valuable
11	wise	12	with ease
13	with kindness	14	purposely
15	useless		

Lesson 4-5 명사의 소유격

★Check up! p. 100

A
1 Helen's leg
2 boy's
3 The color of his jacket
4 parents' car
5 women's university
6 today's newspaper

7 aunt's dress

8 business of yours

9 father's

B **1** Tomas's hobby **2** a girls' high school.

3 A friend of mine **4** Helen's mother.

5 The children's clothes

6 The legs of the table

7 my brother's photo.

8 My mother−in−law's pasta

9 The music of Beethoven

10 Any/of his/of mine

Lesson 4-6 부정관사 a / an

Check up!

A **1** a **2** a

3 an **4** an

5 a **6** a

7 a **8** a

9 a **10** a

11 an **12** an

Lesson 4-7 정관사 the

Check up! p. 103

A **1** the **2** a/The

3 the **4** a

5 The **6** the

7 the **8** a/the

9 the **10** the

B **1** X **2** the

3 the **4** the

5 a **6** The

7 X **8** X

9 X **10** X

Practice More I

A **1** knives **2** kinds

3 messages **4** crowd

5 say **6** cattle

7 fish **8** were

9 money **10** candles

B **1** There are four boys on the sofa.

2 We have a few special holidays this year.

3 I have many exciting hobbies.

4 There are some old tables in my grandmother's room.

5 There are two women dancing in the park.

6 He has three important pieces of evidence related to this accident.

7 I ate two pieces of pizza for lunch.

8 He bought four bottles of juice.

9 The English teacher used many pieces of chalk.

10 I bought two boxes of apples.

C **1** John → John's

2 the → a

3 sheet → sheets

4 The mom → My mom

5 review a → review the

6 A → The

7 a → the

8 the air → air

9 the soccer → soccer

10 The Mr. Kim → Mr. Kim

D **1** There were some pieces of broken glass on the desk.

2 Has Helen ever traveled by sea?

3 The students have been waiting for their teacher for two hours.

4 This is the second longest river in the world.

5 The boy's grade was higher than my daughter's.

6 I bought three pieces of pizza and two cartons of milk.

7 Her uncle's house has a good view at night.

8 My daughter will be better in a day or two.

9 What a wonderful day! Let's go to the picnic.

10 They made a fire when they were in danger.

정답 및 해설 **13**

Lesson 4-8 재귀대명사

p. 108~109

A 1 by
  2 yourself
  3 herself
  4 myself
  5 them
  6 herself
  7 you
  8 yourself
  9 myself
  10 myself

B 1 by herself
  2 Make yourself at home
  3 Help yourself!
  4 talks (says) to herself.
  5 finished

Lesson 4-9 'it'의 용법

p. 111~112

A 1 ⑤   2 ④
  3 ①   4 ③
  5 ②   6 ①
  7 ⑤   8 ④
  9 ③   10 ⑤

B 1 It is important
  2 It was very difficult
  3 it impossible
  4 it is a good idea to ask
  5 It was my husband
  6 It is necessary
  7 It was the book that he found
  8 It was nice talking
  9 It was the thief
  10 It / stay up

Lesson 4-10 부정대명사_one / another / other (1)

p. 113~114

A 1 one   2 it
  3 another   4 One
  5 others   6 one another
  7 one   8 others
  9 others   10 another

B 1 it   2 other
  3 one   4 another
  5 others (the others)   6 another
  7 the others   8 others
  9 one   10 another

Lesson 4-11 부정대명사_one / another / other (2)

p. 115~116

A 1 the other   2 Some
  3 the others   4 another / the other
  5 the other   6 other
  7 others   8 others
  9 the others

B 1 One / the other   2 another / the other
  3 others   4 Some / others
  5 Some / the others

Lesson 4-12 부정대명사 _all / both

p. 117

A 1 was   2 have
  3 They all   4 was
  5 They both   6 are
  7 shirts   8 have

Lesson 4-13 부정대명사_each / every

★Check up! p. 118

A 1 students   2 road
  3 word   4 was (is)
  5 weeks   6 child

Lesson 4-14 부정대명사_some / any / no

★Check up! p. 119~120

A 1 Somebody
  2 something
  3 Anybody
  4 anything
  5 anybody
  6 anybody
  7 something
  8 anybody
  9 something
  10 anything

B 1 some sugar   2 any good books
  3 any money   4 nothing
  5 some water   6 don't/any

Lesson 4-15 부정대명사_either / neither

★Check up! p. 121~122

A 1 either/you   2 Either
  3 neither/them   4 either/or
  5 Neither   6 Either/or
  7 either   8 neither/nor
  9 neither   10 Neither

Lesson 4-16 전체부정과 부분부정

★Check up! p. 123

A 1 None/like
  2 Not all
  3 not always
  4 not/anybody (anyone)
  5 not/both

Practice More Ⅱ p. 124~126

A 1 this   2 These
  3 that   4 that
  5 this/that   6 those
  7 It   8 that
  9 those   10 that

B 1 Some/the others
  2 One/another/the other
  3 One/the other
  4 Some/the others
  5 One/another/the other

C 1 nobody
  2 has
  3 other
  4 likes
  5 all
  6 any
  7 not always
  8 nor
  9 student
  10 each
  11 boys
  12 all
  13 one
  14 anything/everything
  15 wants

D 1 Both my mom and dad speak English fluently.
  2 I didn't receive anything from my brother on my birthday.
  3 Only one of ten people accepted the proposal and the others refused it.
  4 Any of the students could fail the exam.
  5 Because I'm very busy, I can hardly buy anything. (= I can hardly buy anything because I'm very busy.)
  6 Sadly, none of the birds were left in the cage.
  7 It is important to exercise everyday.
  8 There were not any books in the bag.
  9 and the other is reading books.

중간 기말고사 **예상문제**

내신 **최다 출제** 유형　　　　　　　p. 127

01 ②　　02 ⑤　　03 ②　　04 ②　　05 ④

06 ③　　07 ②

해설

01 ① broke → broken, ③ eat → eating
④ sadness → sad, ⑤ is → are

02 ①,②,③,④ 비인칭 주어 it, ⑤ 가주어 it

03 ② one of them은 단수이므로 'himself' 또는 'herself'가 와야
한다.

04 of wise → of wisdom (현명한)

05 주어가 'they'이므로 'themselves'가 와야 한다.

06 one~, the other... 하나는~, 나머지 하나는...
one~, another..., the others- 하나는~, 다른 하나는..., 나머지는...

07 〈보기, ②〉 가주어 it, ①,③ 대명사 it, ④,⑤ 비인칭 주어 it

p. 128~134

01 ③	02 ①	03 ③	04 ⑤	05 ④
06 ②	07 ③	08 ①,③	09 ②	10 ⑤
11 ③	12 ④	13 ②	14 ③	15 ⑤
16 ②	17 ③	18 ②	19 ②	20 ①
21 ④	22 ④	23 ④	24 ②	25 ③
26 ②	27 ⑤	28 ③	29 ①	30 ④
31 ②,③	32 ⑤	33 ③	34 ③,④	35 ①,⑤

〈서술형 평가〉

36 your brother's a notebook → your brother's
notebook

37 applications forms → application forms

38 others → other

39 by　　　　　40 It is

41 It seems　　42 of use

43 another, other

44 Lily feels tired easily because of a new task.

45 Some of the test questions were easy, but the
others were difficult.

해설

01 ① sheep – sheep, ② ox – oxen,
④ branch – branches, ⑤ woman – women

02 ② deer – deer, ③ souvenir – souvenirs, ④ fly – flies,
⑤ goose – geese

03 bush – bushes

04 belief – beliefs

05 'by oneself' 혼자서

06 'one~, the other~' 하나는 ~이고, 다른 하나는~

07 'one~, another..., the other –' 하나는 ~이고,
다른 하나는 ...이고, 나머지 하나는 –

08 ② is → are, ④ tooth → teeth, ⑤ ways → way

09 ② 강조용법의 재귀대명사는 생략이 가능하다.
①,③,④,⑤ 재귀적 용법

10 ① 비인칭 주어, ② seems that~의 주어, ③ It~that 강조구문,
④ 사물을 가리키는 it

11 '그 자체로서'의 뜻으로, 전치사 in의 목적어

12 ① a hour → an hour, ② Korean's → Korea's,
③ a old lady → an old lady,
⑤ an university → a university

13 ① waters → water, ③ a few → a little, ④ many → much,
⑤ health → healthy

14 ③ ~당 ~마다, ①,②,④,⑤ 하나의

15 ①,②,③,④ 관사를 쓰지 않는다.

16 부정문에서는 'anyone'을 사용한다.

17 ③ 'that'이 들어가야 한다. ①,②,④,⑤ it

18 〈보기, ②〉 일반적인 사람을 가리키는 대명사, ①,③ 앞의 나온
명사의 반복을 피하기 위한 대명사, ④ 한 사람, ⑤ 하나의

19 ② are → is : 'each of + 복수명사 + 단수동사'의 형태이다.

20 긍정문에서는 'someone'을 사용한다.

21 〈보기, ④〉 강조용법 it, ①,② 가주어 it, ③,⑤ 가목적어 it

22 〈보기, ④〉 가주어 it, ①,②,③,⑤ 비인칭 주어 it

23 그녀는 모두를 초대하는 것을 좋아한다.

24 All we → We all

25 one – 앞의 반복된 명사가 단수이다.
He – Jinsu를 가리킨다
it – 앞의 명사와 같으므로 it을 쓴다.
other – 뒤에 복수 명사가 나오므로 'other'가 맞다.

26 'Both' 둘 다

27 ① piano → the piano, ② third → the third,
③ the dinner → dinner, ④ the basketball → basketball

28 ① many → much, ② going → going to, ④ have → has,
⑤ going → go

29 is → are

30 few → little

31 ① thief – thieves, ④ cry – cries, ⑤ child – children

32 'It is ~ that' 구문에서 동사는 강조할 수 없다.

33 a loaf of milk → a glass(bottle) of milk

34 ① Only → The only, ② an → a, ⑤ a → an

35 ① others's → others', ⑤ the day → a day

〈서술형 평가〉

36 소유격은 관사, 부정대명사와 나란히 쓸 수 없다.

37 '명사+명사'에서 첫 번째 명사는 단수형으로 한다.

38 'other+복수명사'

39 'on a 교통수단' = 'by 교통수단' ~을 타고

40 to부정사를 진주어로 하는 가주어 it

41 '주어+seem+to부정사' = 'It seems that~'

42 'of use' = 'useful' 유용한, 쓸모 있는

43 'another+단수명사' 또 다른, 'other+복수명사'

44 'with ease' = 'easily' 쉽게

45 'some of+복수명사' ~중의, 'the others' 나머지들

Chapter 05 수동태

Lesson 5-1 일반적인 수동태

p. 137~138

A
1 is cleaned   2 was found
3 was loved   4 was seen
5 will be opened   6 was fixed
7 is used   8 was bought
9 was stolen   10 was built

B
1 Another interesting detective novel was written by the author.
2 This proposal was refused to accept by the manager.
3 Some people are attracted by her beautiful smile.
4 A live concert will be performed by the band this evening.
5 Some cookies will be brought for the party (by them).
6 The kite was made by Jim and Tim yesterday.

Lesson 5-2 수동태의 부정문과 의문문

p. 140

A
1 What was found by her in the room?
2 Is the graduation test taken by many students?
3 Which pen is used by Hana every day?
4 Were the windows broken by Tom?
5 The table was not made by Harry and his son.
6 Is the iguana kept by Lina in her room?
7 What kind of movie will be watched by them tonight?
8 Were any pictures on the wall drawn by Sam?
9 Who was invited to the big party by Max?
10 She will not be picked up by Thomas because he is so busy.
11 Where was the minicar model made by Suho?
12 Are many abandoned dogs helped by the organization?
13 When was the hole dug by him?
14 The flower shop was not run by them.
15 Why was the conference canceled by the community?

Lesson 5-3 진행형 수동태

p. 141~142

A
1 are being shown?
2 being repaired
3 being televised
4 being discussed
5 being played
6 being washed
7 being cooked
8 are being recommended
9 is being done
10 is/being built
11 are being placed
12 is being read
13 is being fixed
14 is being treated
15 being criticized

Lesson 5-4 완료형 수동태

p. 143~144

A
1 has not been revealed
2 Has/been solved
3 Have/been paid
4 have not (haven't) been set
5 have been invited
6 has not (hasn't) been released
7 have been drawn

B
1 has been used
2 have been helped
3 has been painted
4 has been postponed
5 has been invented
6 has been used
7 has been celebrated
8 have already been returned
9 Have/been recycled
10 has been prepared

Lesson 5-5 조동사의 수동태

Check up!

p. 145~146

A
1 will be bought
2 will be improved
3 may not be scolded
4 will be brought
5 must be kept
6 will be planted
7 must not be copied
8 Should / be finished
9 can / be started
10 can be scored

B
1 may be accepted
2 be taken
3 will be brought
4 can be done
5 have to be taken care of
6 be repaired
7 have been rescued

Practice More I

p. 147~149

A
1 is (was) directed
2 is (was)
3 are (were) caused
4 are (were) sold
5 were (being) roasted
6 is (was) defeated
7 been treated
8 announced
9 been written
10 been protected

B
1 The pizza was delivered to me by him.
2 The riddle has already been solved by the students.
3 The deadline for the reports should not be forgotten by you.
4 The box isn't being moved by the robot.
5 All the hotel rooms ought to be cleaned by the lady.
6 My heart was broken by Sam's words.
7 The rules are not followed by the factory.

8 When was this file found by her?
9 This special chocolate was not produced by the company.
10 Is the final game held in the stadium by them?

C
1 read → been read
2 used → using
3 seeing → seen
4 explored → been explored
5 recycling → recycled
6 be used → being used
7 be not → not be
8 learning → learned
9 being → be
10 being → been

D
1 The broken printer is being fixed by the repairman.
2 The container is being moved by the large helicopter.
3 The walls of the Ann's house were being painted by volunteers.
4 A new business is being developed by James.
5 He was asked such a stupid question.
6 A wooden hut will be made for Harry by his father.
7 Cheating has never been accepted by the teacher.
8 A delicious dinner was being prepared for Minji.
9 The used cars on the street were being sold.
10 The old washing machine is being fixed by Tom.

Lesson 5-6 4형식 문장의 수동태

Check up!

p. 151~152

A
1	to	2	to
3	for	4	of
5	to	6	for
7	to	8	to
9	for	10	for

B
1 will be given a pink hat / will be given to James
2 wasn't shown my report card / wasn't shown to my mom

3 were given valuable lessons / were given to us

4 was asked some stupid questions
/ were asked of him

5 were told interesting news / was told to her students

C **1** A birthday present was bought for us

2 The poor will be helped

3 Two raincoats will be brought to us

4 English grammar was taught to me

5 The rooms were rented to those visitors

Lesson 5-7 5형식 문장의 수동태

Check up!

p. 153~154

A **1** My dog was named Alex by me.

2 She was elected leader by them.

3 This room should be kept clean by us.

4 She was heard singing some sad songs by him.

5 The new plane will be called Last Glory by us.

6 The students were asked to keep quiet by me.

7 The dog has been left alone in the garden by us.

8 Some girls were seen dancing on the stage by me.

9 I'm called little princess by my father.

10 We were usually told to do our best by the coach.

B **1** seen **2** made

3 to join **4** learn

5 to go **6** singing

7 to bring

Lesson 5-8 기타 수동태 (1)

Check up!

p. 155

A **1** being talked

2 to be done

3 was

4 Being left (To be left)

5 to be invited

6 being disturbed (to be disturbed)

Lesson 5-9 기타 수동태 (2)

Check up!

p. 156~157

A **1** was laughed at

2 were taken care of

3 should be put off

4 are looked down on

5 is made use of

6 was turned off

7 couldn't be caught up with

8 The sick baby was looked after

9 was thrown away

10 was talked about

Lesson 5-10 by이외의 전치사를 사용하는 수동태

Check up!

p. 158~159

A **1** were surprised at

2 be crowded with

3 were involved in

4 tired of

5 was so pleased with

6 was known for

7 was filled with

8 were satisfied with

9 was disappointed at

10 was interested in

B **1** The road was covered with a lot of dust.

2 My parents were disappointed at my test result.

3 I heard that the doll was made out of chocolate (by people).

4 I am worried about tomorrow's math test.

5 People were excited at the game.

Practice More II

p. 160~162

A **1** given **2** to

3 told to leave **4** made happy

5 to play **6** was told

7 were shown **8** written

9 be chosen **10** be treated

B
1　was brought to their mom
2　were told to me
3　was asked the same question
4　A robot will be made for John
5　was turned on by him
6　were surprised at
7　am worried about
8　was seen to play the drums
9　was seen to enter
10　was seen to knock

C
1　in → with　　2　for → of
3　keep → to keep　　4　for → of
5　was → were　　6　for → at
7　to → with
8　said → is said (was said)
9　calling → called
10　been advised → advised

D
1　The old roof has been painted green.
2　Her ring is made of pearls and diamonds.
3　A moving story is read to us by our mom.
4　A birthday card will be given to me by Jane.
5　The players are expected to choose their leader for the game.
6　My son has been named John by my mother.
7　The game was called off because of the rain.
8　He was bored to death with the drama.
9　Lily was dressed in a red dress.
10　A doghouse is being made for my mother.

중간 기말고사 예상문제

p. 163

내신 최다 출제 유형

01 ②　　02 ②　　03 ③　　04 ②

해설

01　'조동사+be+과거분사' – ① should be turned,
③ should be returned, ④ should not be eaten,
⑤ must be done
02　'that'절을 목적어로 하는 문장의 수동태는 that절의 주어를 문장의 주어로 쓸 경우 'that절의 주어+be동사+과거분사+to+동사원형'의 형태가 된다.
03　조동사가 있는 수동태는 '조동사+be+과거분사'의 형태를 가진다.
04　직접목적어가 주어로 쓰인 동사 buy의 수동태 문장은 간접목적어 앞에 전치사 for를 넣어준다.

p. 164~169

01 ①	02 ⑤	03 ③	04 ②	05 ⑤
06 ②	07 ④,⑤	08 ①,②	09 ①	10 ③
11 ④	12 ③	13 ⑤	14 ②	15 ⑤
16 ①	17 ②	18 ②,③	19 ③	20 ④
21 ②	22 ⑤	23 ③	24 ①④⑤	25 ①
26 ②	27 ④	28 ③	29 ①②④	30 ①

〈서술형 평가〉

31　will be practiced
32　is being tried
33　have been baked by me
34　was told / by Mary / were told to me by Mary
35　was asked / by a pretty woman. / was asked of Jim by a pretty woman.
36　The man was laughed at by most people.
37　The deadline has been put off by Jimmy for a long time.
38　It is said that the musician / is said to be a genius
39　I was allowed to leave by them comfortably.
40　Where was the piano played by him?

해설

01　teach – to / make – for
02　'be covered with' ～로 덮여 있다,
'be worried about' ～대해 걱정하다
03　must had praised → must have praised
04　are not considering → are not considered
05　①,②,③,④ to, ⑤ for
06　① for → to, ③ for → to, ④ to → for, ⑤ to → for
07　① has been → have been, ② have been → has been, ③ will train → will be trained
08　③,④,⑤ 동사, 'cook, buy, choose'는 직접목적어만을 수동태의 주어로 쓴다.
09　능동태의 지각동사의 목적격보어로 원형부정사가 올 경우, 수동태에서는 to부정사를 사용한다.
10　능동태 문장에서는 사역동사 'help'의 목적격보어로 원형부정사 또는 'to부정사'를, 수동태에서는 'to부정사'를 사용한다.
11　'have'는 수동태로 사용할 수 없는 사역동사이다.
12　'resemble'은 수동태로 사용할 수 없다.
13　'ought to+be+과거분사'
14　'may not be+과거분사'
15　'be filled with' ～로 가득차다
16　for his father → by his father
17　by: 'be interrupted by ～에게 방해받다' ①,③,④,⑤ in

18 ②, ③ 'publish 출판하다'의 뜻으로 장소와 시간 모두
물어볼 수 있다.

19 'let'의 수동태는 'be allowed to'를 사용한다. 부정문은
'be not allowed to'로 만든다.

20 'Do(es)+주어+have to be+과거분사'

21 'what'은 단수 취급한다.

22 의문사가 없는 의문문의 수동태: 'be동사+주어+과거분사~?'

23 cooked to me → cooked for me

24 ② satisfying → satisfied, ③ is filled of → is filled with
⑤ was disappointed of → was disappointed at

25 현재완료 수동태: 'have not been+과거분사'

26 5형식 문장의 수동태로 'ask'의 목적어로 'to부정사'가 쓰인다.

27 'to부정사'의 수동태이다.

28 '동명사'의 수동태이다.

29 ① was build → was built, ② 'weigh'가 상태를 나타내므로
수동태로 사용할 수 없다. ④ will be bake → will be baked

30 wrote → written

〈서술형 평가〉

31 조동사가 있는 수동태는 '조동사+be+과거분사'의 형태를 갖는다.

32 진행형의 수동태: 'be동사+being+과거분사'

33 완료형의 수동태: 'have(has) been+과거분사'

34 직접목적어가 수동태의 주어가 되는 경우 간접목적어 앞의
전치사는 'tell – to'가 된다.

35 직접목적어가 수동태의 주어가 되는 경우 간접목적어 앞의 전치사는
'ask – of'가 된다.

36 동사구의 수동태: 두 개 이상의 단어가 구로 묶여 동사 역할을
하므로 떨어뜨리지 않는다.

37 동사구의 수동태: 두 개 이상의 단어가 구로 묶여 동사 역할을
하므로 떨어뜨리지 않는다.

38 'that'절을 포함한 문장의 수동태는 'It is~ that' 구문으로
바꾼다.

39 '5형식 문장: They let me leave comfortably.'의 수동태
문장이다.

40 의문사가 있는 의문문의 수동태: '의문사+be 동사+주어+과거
분사~?'
능동태 문장: Where did he play the piano?

Chapter 06 부정사

Lesson 6-1 부정사의 형태

p. 173

A 1 not to fail the exam.
2 to be enjoying
3 to be done
4 to watch
5 not to lose
6 not to be late
7 never to take
8 to be painting
9 to be fixed
10 to have

Lesson 6-2 부정사의 명사적용법

p. 174~175

A 1 주어   2 주격보어
3 주어   4 목적격 보어
5 목적어

B 1 It is my dream to live a happy life.
2 It is important to exercise regularly.
3 It is my special goal to travel around the world.
4 It is not easy to know yourself.
5 It is really hard to get an A on the science test.

C 1 to return these books by six.
2 to quit this project.
3 to write interesting novels.
4 to take a swimming class.
5 to take a nap for a while.
6 to confess why he stole Hana's ring.
7 to prepare for a party alone.
8 to show me the answer sheet.
9 to become a world-famous model.
10 to get a scholarship and make her parents happy.

Lesson 6-3 의문사 + to부정사

p. 176

A 1 where to go
2 when to leave.
3 which pants to wear
4 how to open
5 what he should say
6 what to eat
7 how they should play
8 how to save
9 what he should do

Lesson 6-4 부정사의 형용사적 용법

p. 177~178

A 1 a lot of books to read.
2 many toys to play with.
3 some juice to drink.
4 some noodles to cook for dinner.
5 exercising to lose weight?
6 anybody to help her move the boxes?
7 to make rules to protect animals.
8 a nice person to teach the students.
9 a desk to put these things on.
10 a friend to talk to.

B 1 Jane and I are to go hiking this weekend.
2 you are not to make any noise in this place.
3 The wine festival is to be held next week.
4 if you are to achieve your goal.
5 We are to meet tomorrow morning
6 He was to die in World War I.
7 You are to hand in the report
8 was not to be eaten.
9 Harry is to come back

Lesson 6-5 부정사의 부사적 용법

A 1 He went to the subway station in order to pick her up.

2 They went out so as to do volunteer work.

3 Tim turned off the light so that he could go to bed.

4 I opened the window so as to ventilate the room.

5 I checked out some reports for my graduation thesis.

6 I dropped by his house so that I could give him a birthday present.

7 She will call Mary in order to let her know the facts.

8 Mr. Kim sent me an email so as to remind me of the proposal.

9 for milk and cheese.

B 1 disappointed to see his test result.

2 sorry to make the same mistake.

3 a genius to solve the problem without hints.

4 grew up to be a fashion designer.

5 honest to act like that.

Practice More I

A 1 to volunteer   2 to save

3 what   4 to go

5 tell   6 like her

7 what   8 to fix

9 to correct   10 be

B 1 Sam asked what he should buy for his daughter's graduation present.

2 Let's discuss where we should go this holiday.

3 The boys have learned how they should direct a movie.

4 Tell me which cup I should choose among these.

5 I didn't know where I should visit first during the trip.

6 Sorry, I can't remember when I should turn left or right.

7 Helen asked the waiter where she should borrow an umbrella.

8 Please tell me which phone I should buy.

9 The students wanted to learn how they should play that computer game.

10 Bill showed me how I should solve the riddle.

C 1 found → to find

2 having → have

3 as so → so as

4 not be → be

5 sit → sit on

6 be read → read

7 going → to go

8 studied → to study

9 got → get

10 using → to use

D 1 I was sad to watch the documentary.

2 She said that to see is to believe.

3 Let's find a hotel to stay in.

4 The princess was to marry him at seventeen.

5 They agreed to join our community next semester.

6 Lily will not ask you to help her before she tries it.

7 Her job is to hand out some samples on the street.

8 If somebody is to join our dance team, they must audition.

9 I want you to succeed in everything you do.

10 James started exercising regularly so that he could run a marathon.

Lesson 6-6 to부정사의 시제

A 1 seems to be

2 is likely to be postponed.

3 to have made a big mistake.

4 to go to America to study English

5 to have eaten up all the cakes

6 to have met each other.

Lesson 6-7 원형부정사와 대부정사

p. 187

A
1 show
2 dance(dancing)
3 plant(planting)
4 call(calling)
5 play(playing)
6 lie(lying)
7 solve(to solve)
8 clean
9 fix
10 find
11 change
12 following(follow)
13 remodel
14 memorize
15 crying(cry)

Lesson 6-8 부정사의 의미상의 주어

p. 188

A
1 for
2 of
3 for
4 of
5 of
6 for
7 for
8 of
9 of

Lesson 6-9 자주 쓰이는 부정사 표현

p. 189

A
1 Brian is tall enough to reach the shelf.
2 Kate is too tired to go hiking
3 Jane is smart enough to solve any problems.
4 Emily is too lazy to clean her room
5 The statue is too heavy to move.

Practice More II

p. 190~192

A
1 for
2 important
3 of
4 of
5 for
6 dangerous
7 play(playing)
8 find(to find)
9 not to

B
1 add
2 crying(cry)
3 use
4 couldn't
5 to be
6 to watch
7 of him
8 not to put off
9 for us
10 to be repaired

C
1 Jack is too busy to go with us.
2 Sara is smart enough to teach us how to solve the problem.
3 My laptop is too old-fashioned to run the application.
4 Linda was too nervous to sit still.
5 Our team is strong enough to win this game.
6 I was too sick to exercise.
7 Kate is too ambitious to be satisfied with the result.
8 Adam is too young to travel alone.
9 It was too cloudy for us to see stars.
10 The book was interesting enough to read overnight.

D
1 The knot is easy to untie.
2 The cookie is hard for me to bite.
3 She refused to answer my question.
4 It was brave of her to save the dog in the fire.
5 It was easy for us to remember her name.
6 The children appeared to have found the wrong answer.
7 The teacher told his students never to open the box.
8 My brother is smart enough to get first prize in the olympiad.
9 Mr. Park had the workers build that tower.
10 Your pizza is so delicious that it sold out.

중간 기말고사 예상문제

내신 **최다 출제** 유형

p. 193

01 ③   02 ②   03 ①   04 ⑤   05 ③
06 ④   07 to clean → clean(cleaning)

해설

01 'to부정사'의 주어는 뒤로 넘기고, '가주어 it'이 앞으로 왔다.

02 '의문사+to부정사' 구문이며, '언제 ~할지'는 'when+to부정사'로 표현한다.

03 ① of+목적격, ②,③,④,⑤ for+목적격

04 첫 번째 문장: 읽을 ~(형용사적 용법),
두 번째 문장: 읽는 것(명사적 용법)

05 to sing → sing(singing)

06 ① answer → to answer, ② fix → to fix,
③ touched → touch(touching), ⑤ to watch → watch
(watching)

07 watch의 목적격보어로는 원형부정사 또는 현재분사가
와야 한다.

p. 194~200

01 ⑤	**02** ②	**03** ④	**04** ②	**05** ⑤
06 ⑤	**07** ②	**08** ④	**09** ③	**10** ②
11 ④	**12** ②	**13** ①	**14** ⑤	**15** ②
16 ④	**17** ③	**18** ②	**19** ①	**20** ②
21 ⑤	**22** ④	**23** ③	**24** ②,⑤	**25** ③
26 ②	**27** ⑤	**28** ①	**29** ②	**30** ③

〈서술형 평가〉

31 difficult too → too difficult

32 seemed be → seemed to be

33 booked → book(to book)

34 too, to

35 how to

36 in order to

37 to invite

38 to keep

39 I'm too busy to think about anything else.

40 smart enough to decide what she wants to be

41 Kevin and Hatty seem to be surprised

42 It is not easy for someone to make their own
decisions.

43 It took five hours for them to get here.

해설

01 'want to+동사원형'

02 to부정사의 부정형은 'not to+동사원형'이다.

03 'what to+동사원형' 무엇을 ~할지

04 부정사의 의미상의 주어는 'for+목적격'이다.

05 사역동사의 목적격보어는 원형부정사 이다.

06 'tell'의 목적격보어로 'to부정사'가 온다.

07 'so that 주어+can't'=too~to... 너무 ~해서 ...할 수 없다

08 ④ 예정, ①,②,③,⑤ 의무

09 to tickle → tickle(tickling)

10 think → to think

11 ④ 명사적 용법, ①,②,③,⑤ 부사적 용법

12 ② 형용사적 용법, ①,③,④,⑤ 부사적 용법

13 ② forming → to form, ③ do → to do, ④ see → to see,
⑤ find → to find

14 사역동사의 목적격보어는 원형부정사이다. 'ask'의 목적격보어
는 'to부정사' 이다.

15 'enough' 충분한, '형용사+enough+to 부정사'
~할 정도로 충분한

16 ①,②,③,⑤ 명사적 용법, ④ 부사적 용법

17 '예정'을 나타내는 'be to' 용법
– 'be supposed to'~할 예정이다

18. 'enough to 부정사' ~할 정도로 충분한, '종이 위에 쓸 ~'
의 뜻을 가진 전치사 'on'이 필요하다.

19 'ask'는 목적격보어로 to부정사를 취한다.

20 〈보기, ②〉 부사적 용법, ①,③,④,⑤ 명사적 용법

21 〈보기, ⑤〉 형용사적 용법, ①,② 형용사를 꾸며주는 부사적
용법, ③,④ 명사적 용법

22 'interest → interesting' to부정사 앞에 형용사가 오는 것이 맞다.

23 'learning → to learn(또는 learn)' 'help'의 목적격보어로는 to
부정사 또는 원형부정사가 와야 한다.

24 ① of you → for you, ③ for you → of you,
④ of me → for me

25 '형용사+enough+to부정사' ~할 정도로 충분히 ...한

26 'It is time for+목적격+to부정사' ~가 ...할 시간이다

27 ⑤ 'so~that... ~해서 ..했다'의 구문으로 결과를 나타낸다.
①,②,③,④ 목적을 의미한다.

28 to sit with → to sit on

29 'careless'의 의미상의 주어는 'of+목적격'이다.

30 so that can't = too~to와 바꿔쓸 수 있다
– 너무 ~해서 ...할 수 없는

〈서술형 평가〉

31 'too+형용사+to부정사' 너무 ~해서 ...할 수 없는

32 'seem to부정사' ~처럼 보이다

33 준사역동사 help의 목적격보어는 원형부정사 또는 to부정사가
올 수 있다.

34 'so 형용사 that 주어 can't'
= 'too~to...' 너무 ~해서 ...할 수 없는

35 '의문사+주어+should+동사원형'='의문사+to부정사'

36 'in order to' ~하기 위해서

37 '의문사+to부정사'

38 'enable'의 목적격보어는 to부정사가 온다.

39 'so 형용사 that 주어 can't'=' too+형용사+to부정사'

40 'so 형용사 that 주어 can'='형용사+enough+to부정사'

41 'It seems that~' = '주어+seem(s)+to부정사'

42 'It~ to' 구문 안에 의미상의 주어 'for+목적격'이 들어 있다.

43 'It take~ to부정사...' ...하는 데 ~이 걸리다

Chapter 07 동명사

Lesson 7-1 동명사의 형태와 역할

☆Check up!   p. 204

A
1	Being	2	making
3	passing	4	Learning
5	coming	6	watching
7	talking	8	Traveling
9	wearing	10	Correcting
11	Getting	12	Drinking
13	overeating	14	running
15	selling		

Lesson 7-2 동명사를 목적어로 하는 동사

☆Check up!   p. 205

A
1	hiding	2	accepting
3	going	4	closing
5	staying	6	doing
7	discussing	8	buying
9	living	10	planning
11	learning	12	holding
13	singing		

Lesson 7-3 동명사와 to부정사를 목적어로 쓰는 동사

☆Check up!   p. 207

A
1	meeting	2	to go
3	posing	4	to plan / planning
5	eating / to eat	6	dancing / to dance
7	writing	8	making / to make
9	fighting / to fight	10	moving

B
1	watching	2	to lock
3	complaining	4	to get
5	joining	6	to check
7	seeing	8	to say
9	buying	10	to turn in

Lesson 7-4 동명사와 현재분사

☆Check up!   p. 208

A
1	현재분사	2	현재분사
3	동명사	4	현재분사
5	동명사	6	현재분사
7	동명사	8	현재분사
9	동명사	10	현재분사

Practice More I

p. 209~211

A
1	helping	2	Persuading
3	bothering	4	watching
5	Being	6	repairing
7	Giving	8	turning off
9	having	10	buying

B
1	having seen
2	to lock
3	living
4	eating as much
5	is
6	going
7	discussing
8	giving
9	working out
10	running

C
1 They began moving the box on the table.
2 I hate putting off my promise.
3 John likes doing homework at night.
4 Sorry, we didn't intend making him cry.
5 My sister prefers watching movies on weekends.
6 Have you finished cleaning your classroom?
7 I couldn't imagine meeting him here.
8 We intend visiting a nursing home.
9 Her hobby is playing the drums.
10 He enjoys reading detective novels.

D
1 Don't forget to wear your uniform next Monday.
2 They would like to buy a sleeping bag.
3 My father is considering buying a new house for our family.
4 I really regret leaving the party so early.

5 Then try to find something interesting.

6 You should stop swimming here.

7 We have to avoid making the same mistake.

8 The rain continued falling whole weekend.

9 His father enjoys watching comedy shows.

10 Let's go on singing together.

Lesson 7-5 동명사의 의미상의 주어

p. 213~214

A **1** my sister's using my laptop.

   2 his telling some information

   3 his being late for the meeting.

   4 Minho's losing the game.

B **1** I don't like his going to such a dangerous place.

   2 Do you mind (my) borrowing your car?

   3 I am sure of his being James.

   4 He is certain of Cindy's coming back home soon.

   5 Everybody remembers her winning the game.

   6 The teacher suggests Peter's participating in the competition.

   7 They are disappointed Yuna's breaking the rule.

   8 I want Mr. Lee's being the coach of our team.

   9 Sam is certain of the movie's being famous.

   10 She is proud of her son's having a doctorate.

Lesson 7-6 동명사의 시제

p. 215

A **1** Thomas admits being guilty.

   2 Jieun suggests inviting us to her wedding party.

   3 I am proud of having gotten first prize.

   4 They were ashamed of having been late for the meeting.

   5 She is sure of getting an A on the final exam.

   6 He admits to having stolen the necklace.

Lesson 7-7 동명사의 관용 표현

p. 217

A **1** On hearing the news

   2 much money buying

   3 cannot help loving

   4 is looking forward to meeting

   5 had trouble finding

   6 from going hiking

   7 needs repairing (needs to be repaired)

   8 without opening

   9 There's no knowing

   10 is used to writing

   11 were busy preparing

   12 like going

   13 is worth recommending

   14 There's no use crying

   15 were at the point of leaving

Practice More Ⅱ

p. 218~220

A **1** her telling

   2 your winning

   3 my(me) opening

   4 this being

   5 my sister's graduating

   6 his(him) doing

   7 John's coming

   8 the woman's entering

   9 Minji's being

   10 your (you) talking

B **1** lived → living

   2 being → having

   3 having → being

   4 found → finding

   5 to be → being

   6 praised → being praised

   7 to go → going

   8 to prepare → preparing

   9 caused → to cause

   10 to know → knowing

C **1** We are sorry that we are late.

   2 She was worried that she would miss her train.

3 They are afraid that they will fail the exam.

4 I am sorry that I didn't answer your questions quickly.

5 I am sure that Paul will be able to break the world record.

6 Mina was proud that she entered the university.

7 The girl denied that she had seen the accident.

8 I was nervous that I had forgotten his birthday.

9 She remembered that he called her that day.

10 We are proud that she is succeeding in this field.

D 1 I'm looking forward to going to my daughter's graduation ceremony.

2 Cindy was busy making new friends at school.

3 They had difficulty in releasing the movie this Thursday.

4 Sara spent a lot of money buying the dress.

5 He forgot lending his car to me.

6 She has trouble sleeping at night.

7 I don't feel like wearing such a strange hat.

8 Volunteering is worth doing on weekends.

9 He doesn't forget to call his parents every morning.

10 Father prevented me from having my hair cut short.

중간 기말고사 **예상문제**

p. 221

01 ④   02 ③   03 ②   04 ⑤   05 ④
06 ⑤

해설

01 문맥상 '추운 기후에 사는 데 익숙하다'가 되게 하려면, 'be used to+동명사'를 사용한다.

02 keep은 동명사를, pretend는 to부정사를 목적어로 취한다.

03 ② 현재분사, 〈보기, ①,③,④,⑤〉 동명사

04 〈보기, ⑤〉 현재분사, ①,②,③,④ 동명사

05 writing → write

06 '따돌림을 당하는 것'은 수동의 의미를 가졌으므로 'be left out' 의 수동형을 만든다. 전치사 뒤의 목적어는 동명사가 오기 때문에 'being left out'이라고 표현한다.

---

p. 222~228

01 ③	02 ⑤	03 ②	04 ④	05 ②
06 ④	07 ③	08 ⑤	09 ②	10 ③
11 ⑤	12 ①	13 ②	14 ④	15 ③
16 ④,⑤	17 ④	18 ①	19 ③	20 ②
21 ②	22 ④	23 ③	24 ⑤	25 ②,④
26 ②	27 ⑤	28 ③	29 ②	30 ⑤

〈서술형 평가〉

31 be changed

32 worthwhile to see

33 from

34 visit → visiting

35 to smoke → smoking

36 borrowing her new dress

37 to joining the band

38 (1) to win, (2) exchange

39 Making good friends is important.

40 She was sure of my writing a book well.

41 remember seeing my shoes

42 denies not working

해설

01 'give up+동명사' ~하는 것을 포기하다

02 'look forward to+동명사' ~하는 것을 학수고대 하다

03 'be fond of+동명사' ~하는 것을 좋아하다, 'be capable of+동명사'~할 능력이 있다

04 'cannot help+동명사' ~하지 않을 수 없다

05 'want'는 to부정사를 목적어로 취한다.

06 ④ 현재분사, ①,②,③,⑤ 동명사

07 ③ 현재분사, ①,②,④,⑤ 동명사

08 to step → stepping

09 to buy → buying

10 'cannot help+ing' = 'cannot but+동사원형' ~하지 않을 수 없다

11 'be busy+ing' ~하느라 바쁘다

12 helped → helping(또는 help)

13 to be → being

14 ① eat → eating, ② to meet → meeting, ③ argue → arguing ⑤ to taking → taking

15 ① learn → learning, ② to live → living ④ taking → to take, ⑤ make → making

16 ① worried of → worried about, ② of breaking → for breaking, ③ like cry → like crying

17 ④ 동명사가 문장의 주어로 온 경우이다.

18 'decided to+동사원형' ~하기로 결심하다

19 '불을 끄는 것'은 미래의 일이므로 'forget+to부정사'를 써야한다.

20 'imagine'은 동명사를 목적어로 취한다. 문장의 주어와 동명사
의 주어가 다르기 때문에 동명사의 의미상의 주어 'I'의 소유격
'my'를 넣어준다.

21 'there is no+동명사' ~하는 것은 불가능하다

22 'like, continue, start, begin'은 동명사와 to부정사 모두 목적
어로 취할 수 있으며 의미도 같다.
'remember'는 동명사와 to부정사가 올 때 뜻이 달라진다.
'remember to부정사' ~하는 것을 기억하다(미래),
'remember+동명사' ~했던 것을 기억하다(과거)

23 'plan to부정사' ~할 계획이다, 전치사 'of' 뒤에는 명사 또는
동명사가 온다.
'look forward to+ing' ~하기를 학수고대하다

24 ① to meet → meeting, ② to move → moving,
③ to see → seeing, ④ to be → being

25 ② booking → to book, ④ turn → turning

26 〈보기, ②〉 동명사, ①,③,④,⑤ 현재분사

27 〈보기, ⑤〉 현재분사, ①,②,③,④ 동명사

28 'be willing to' ~을 흔쾌히 하다='don't mind~ 동명사'
~하는 것을 개의치 않다.

29 'remember+동명사' (과거에) ~했던 것을 기억하다

30 'postpone'='put off' 연기하다, 미루다

〈서술형 평가〉

31 'need+동명사'='need to be+과거분사'
~되어야 할 필요가 있다

32 'be worth+동명사'='be worthwhile+to부정사'
~할 가치가 있다

33 'prevent.. from+동명사' ...가 ~하는 것을 막다

34 'remember+동명사' ~했던 것을 기억하다

35 'stop+동명사' ~하는 것을 그만두다

36 드레스를 빌려간 것은 과거의 일이므로 'forget+동명사' ~했던
것을 잊다의 형태를 쓰는 것이 알맞다.

37 'look forward to+동명사' ~하기를 학수고대하다

38 (1) 'try to+동사원형' ~하려고 노력하다,
(2) 'give up+동명사' ~하는 것을 포기하다

39 동명사 'making'이 주어 자리에 와서 문장을 시작한다.

40 'be sure of+동명사' ~할 것을 확신하다. 'of'와 동명사 사이에
동명사의 의미상의 주어로 소유격 'my'가 온다.

41 과거의 일이므로 'remember+동명사'가 알맞다.

42 'deny+동명사' ~한 것을 부정하다.
동명사의 부정을 만들 때는 동명사 앞에 'not'을 붙여준다.

Chapter 08 분사

Lesson 8-1 분사의 종류

p. 231

A
1 broken
2 moving
3 excited
4 performing
5 sleeping
6 fallen
7 stolen
8 broken
9 working
10 used

Lesson 8-2 한정적 용법과 서술적 용법

p. 233

A
1 running
2 damaged
3 listening
4 crying
5 mixed
6 standing
7 called
8 terrifying
9 burning
10 tied

B
1 Look at the tower built by the workers.
2 Do you know the girl picking up some fallen leaves?
3 Students having lunch came here to do their homework.
4 The man preparing for the lesson in his office is my English teacher.
5 There are some houses covered with snow.
6 I see a small bird standing on the branch.

Lesson 8-3 현재분사와 동명사

p. 234

A
1 [B]
2 [A]
3 [A]
4 [B]
5 [A]
6 [B]
7 [B]
8 [A]
9 [B]
10 [A]

Lesson 8-4 감정을 나타내는 분사

p. 235~236

A
1 satisfied
2 disappointing
3 surprised
4 depressed
5 excited
6 shocking
7 amazed
8 moved
9 frightening
10 confused
11 interesting
12 bored
13 fascinating
14 tired
15 barking

Practice More I

p. 237~239

A
1 fixing → fixed
2 danced → dancing
3 interesting → interested
4 ran → running
5 catching → caught
6 jumped → jumping
7 stood → standing
8 fascinating → fascinated
9 played → playing
10 wounding → wounded

B
1 is embarrassing / are embarrassed
2 is exhausting / are exhausted
3 is annoying / is annoyed
4 is disgusting / are disgusted
5 is fascinating / are fascinated

C
1 Can you see the girl holding some books over there?
2 Look at the cat lying on the sofa.
3 There is a woman crying in the rain.
4 There is a car parked next to the park.
5 Do you know about the book written by Mr. Han?
6 They found a box covered with black paper.
7 I saw Peter painting the wall.
8 Who is the handsome boy eating lunch on the grass?
9 Linda saw some workers moving heavy bricks.
10 I heard my name calling in the crowd.

D 1 The girl making a speech on the stage is Amy.
2 They were depressed about going back to school.
3 She sat cross-legged on the floor.
4 I love pictures painted in dark colors.
5 My friends and I are disappointed with the result.
6 We could see a big bird flying above us.
7 I know the family living in the house.
8 Jane saw a film made in India.
9 Kelly had her stuff wrapped in paper.
10 He got his leg broken during the game.

Lesson 8-5 분사구문

Check up!
p. 242~243

A 1 Being on vacation
2 I was studying English
3 Feeling hungry
4 Taking a taxi
5 Not having enough time
6 Doing her best
7 Opening the box
8 Not knowing what to do
9 Hearing that the rumor was wrong
10 Watching the drama

B 1 Because she was so tired
2 If you turn to the right
3 and gave her a big hand.
4 Although he was not tall enough
5 while he was talking with his girlfriend on the phone.
6 Because I had nothing to drink
7 If you turn to the right
8 Though she was innocent
9 When she opened her eyes
10 When I watched the movie

Lesson 8-6 분사구문의 쓰임

Check up!
p. 245

A 1 [조건]   2 [양보]
3 [시간]   4 [동시동작]
5 [이유]   6 [양보]
7 [동시동작]   8 [조건]

B 1 Having a fever, I took some medicine.
2 Studying harder, you will get good grades.
3 Not knowing what to do, ask your parents.
4 Turning to the left, you'll find the elementary school.
5 Closing your eyes, you'll feel the wind.

Lesson 8-7 분사구문의 시제

Check up!
p. 246~247

A 1 Having finished preparing for the party
2 Having taken Tim's advice
3 Although he failed to reach the final round
4 Being praised for his project
5 Because I had lost my camera
6 Being left alone at home
7 Not having read the book
8 Although he was invited to my birthday party
9 Having written the letter
10 Because it was built seventy years ago
11 Being seen from the plane
12 Hearing the truth

Lesson 8-8 'with' 분사구문

Check up!
p. 248~249

A 1 I was reading the book with mom sewing beside me.
2 Mary studied English with Linda using my laptop.
3 The girl looked at me with her leg shaking.
4 John was sleeping with his arms(being) stretched.
5 Max kept on running with his face(being) all sweaty.
6 All students got out of the classroom with the light on.
7 The woman was sitting on the sofa with her arms crossed.
8 Harry was walking home with his daughter following him.
9 Kate went to sleep with her dog sleeping beside her.
10 Sue was watching TV with her daughter lying

on the sofa.

B 1 bandage → bandaged   2 writes → writing
  3 broke → broken   4 turn → turned
  5 followed → following

Practice More Ⅱ

p. 250~252

A 1 Having → Being
  2 Repairing → Repaired
  3 Being read → Reading
  4 They → It
  5 tapped → tapping
  6 Having → Being
  7 Felt → Feeling
  8 Knowing not → Not knowing
  9 fulled → full
  10 Leaving → Being left

B 1 crossed   2 Having
  3 Having finished   4 pointed
  5 Turning in   6 Surprised
  7 Being on vacation   8 Having found
  9 Not having seen   10 Having been

C 1 Hearing the news
  2 Exercising regularly
  3 Not liking noodles
  4 Having been sick for three days
  5 with one of my eyes closed.
  6 Having walked her cat
  7 Being written in Chinese
  8 Being sick in bed
  9 After he had been treated by Mrs. White
  10 Because I had been nervous

D 1 Hearing the strange sound, I stood up and looked outside.
  2 Jack was excited, getting first prize in the contest.
  3 The dog looked at sky sadly with its mouth tied.
  4 Having lost his car, he couldn't go anywhere.
  5 Not deciding where to go, they had trouble planning their summer trip.
  6 Having been caught cheating on the English test, they were embarrassed.

7 John was watching the news with the lights turned off.
8 Doing my best, I failed to be elected class president.
9 Being young, he became a great scientist.
10 Having done his homework, he has nothing else to do.

중간 기말고사 예상문제

내신 최다 출제 유형

p. 253

01 ③   02 ⑤   03 ①   04 ②   05 ②,⑤

해설

01 'be interested in' ~에 관심을 갖다
02 감정을 느끼는 주체가 사람(us)이므로 '과거분사'가 와야 한다.
03 moving → moved
04 '접속사+주어+동사'의 부사절은 분사구문으로 바꿔 쓸 수 있다. 접속사와 주어를 생략하고 '동사+ing'의 형태를 만들어 준다.
05 ② While → If, ⑤ As → Although

p. 254~261

01 ④   02 ③   03 ②   04 ④   05 ⑤
06 ③,④   07 ①,②   08 ②   09 ④   10 ②
11 ③   12 ④   13 ②   14 ①   15 ①
16 ⑤   17 ④   18 ⑤   19 ②   20 ④
21 ③   22 ④   23 ②   24 ①   25 ③
26 ④   27 ⑤   28 ④   29 ②   30 ②
31 ③,④   32 ⑤   33 ①

〈서술형 평가〉
34 running
35 standing / with
36 food left
37 Surprised at the news
38 Not knowing where to go
39 Having finished her report
40 When(After) I arrived home
41 Though(Although) he didn't spend much money on himself
42 ⓐ talking, ⓑ named, ⓒ spoken
43 (1)watering, (2)built, (3)taken
44 (1)smiling, (2)broken
45 Considering her situation
46 It being six o'clock, she left the office.

47 Not having met her before, we didn't know whether she was kind or not.

48 Having no time, they had to hurry up.

해설

01 진행의 의미를 가졌기 때문에 '현재분사'를 써야 한다.

02 '광부들을 위해 만들어진'의 수동의 의미를 가졌으므로 과거분사형이 오는 것이 알맞다.

03 수동의 의미를 가진 과거분사형이 오는 것이 알맞다.

04 첫 번째 문장: 'imagine+동명사' ~하는 것을 상상하다
두 번째 문장: 동시동작을 나타내는 구문

05 첫 번째 문장: 'with+명사+분사'에서 명사와 분사의 관계가 수동일 경우 과거분사를 사용한다.
두 번째 문장: '~하고 있는'의 의미를 가지고 있으므로 현재분사형인 'passing'이 와야 한다.

06 ① naming → named, ② played → playing,
⑤ using → used

07 ③ danced → dancing, ④ helped → helping,
⑤ played → playing

08 moving → moved

09 이유를 나타내는 분사구문으로 부사절의 접속사는 'Because'가 오는 것이 알맞다.

10 첫 번째 문장: 동시동작을 나타내는 구문
두 번째 문장: 감정을 느끼는 주체가 사람이므로 과거분사를 사용한다.

11 ③ 현재분사, ①,②,④,⑤ 동명사

12 ④ 동시동작, ①,②,③,⑤ 양보

13 ② 'written in Japanese characters' 일본어로 쓰인

14 ① 감정의 주체가 사람이기 때문에 과거분사를 사용한다.

15 감정의 주체가 사람이기 때문에 과거분사를 사용한다.

16 ① excited → exciting, ② moved → moving,
③ surprising → surprised,
④ disappointing → disappointed

17 annoyed → annoying

18 disappointing → disappointed

19 분사구문에서 '~ing'로 시작되는 것은 주절과 접속사절의 시제가 일치하므로 접속사절로 바꿀 때 과거형이 되어야 한다.

20 문맥상 '숙제를 끝낸 후 쇼핑을 갔다'의 의미가 되기 때문에 'after ~후에'가 나오는 것이 알맞다.

21 〈보기, ③〉 현재분사, ①,②,④,⑤ 동명사

22 〈보기, ④〉 동명사, ①,②,③,⑤ 현재분사

23 'painted by' ~에 의해 그려진, 전치사 'for' 뒤의 목적어는 동명사의 형태를 취한다.

24 감정을 느끼게 하는 주체가 모두 사물이므로 현재분사를 사용한다.

25 첫 번째 문장: 'with+명사+분사'에서 명사와 분사의 관계가 수동이면 과거분사를 사용한다. → with her eyes closed

두 번째 문장: 앞의 'listening'과 일치시켜준다. → watching

26 crossing → crossed

27 〈보기, ⑤〉 시간, ①,② 동시동작, ③,④ 양보

28 〈보기, ④〉 동시동작, ①,⑤ 이유 ②,③ 조건

29 'Tony가 일찍 잤으나 오후에 일어났다'는 문맥상 양보를 의미하는 분사구문이 와야 한다.

30 문맥상 '양보'를 의미하는 '피자를 먹었어도'가 알맞다.

31 ① Open the window → Opening the window
② Feeling not well → Not feeling well,
⑤ Living → Having lived

32 동시동작을 나타내는 'with+명사+분사' 구문이며, 명사와 분사의 관계가 수동이기 때문에 과거 분사를 써야 한다.
turning → turned

33 문맥상 '소리를 지르는 사람들'이라는 능동의 의미를 가졌기 때문에 현재분사를 사용한다. shouted → shouting

〈서술형 평가〉

34 '~하고 있는'은 진행을 나타내는 능동의 의미를 가지기 때문에 현재분사를 써 준다.

35 'with+명사+분사'에서 명사와 분사의 관계가 능동이면 현재분사를 사용한다.

36 목적어 'no food'와 'left'가 수동의 관계이므로 과거분사형을 써 주었다.

37 수동형의 분사구문에서는 'being'을 생략할 수 있기 때문에 과거분사 'Surprised'가 나왔다.

38 'not', 'never'의 부정어는 분사구문의 맨 앞에 위치한다.

39 부사절의 시제가 주절의 시제보다 앞설 때는 'Having+과거분사'를 써서 분사구문을 만든다.

40 문맥상 '집에 도착했을 때(또는 도착한 후) 가방을 가져오지 않았다'는 것을 의미하므로 시간을 나타내는 접속사 'when(또는 after)'이 와야 한다.

41 '비록 그 자신을 위한 돈은 쓰지 않았지만'의 '양보'를 나타내므로 접속사 'though(또는 although)'를 사용한다.

42 ⓐ '말하는 새'의 의미로 명사와의 관계가 능동이므로 현재분사를 사용한다. ⓑ '이름 붙여진'의 의미로 수동의 의미인 과거분사를 사용한다. ⓒ '말해진 언어', 즉 내뱉어진 언어라는 뜻을 가지므로 수동의 과거분사를 사용한다.

43 (1) 현재분사 – watering 물을 주고 있는,
(2) 과거분사 – built 지어진, (3) 과거분사 – 찍히도록 taken

44 (1) 'smiling' 미소 짓는, (2) 'broken' 망가진

45 주어 'she'와 'consider'가 능동의 관계이다. 현재분사를 쓰는 것이 알맞다.

46 주절의 주어와 다를 경우 분사구문 맨 앞에(원래 접속사절의) 주어를 놓는다.

47 주절보다 시제가 앞서 있으므로 'having+과거분사'를 사용했다.
'whether ~ or not' ~인지 아닌지

48 이유를 나타내는 분사구문이다.

Chapter 09 형용사와 부사

Lesson 9-1 형용사의 역할과 쓰임

☆Check up!
p. 265~266

A
1	strange	2	only
3	alike	4	taller
5	afraid	6	asleep
7	meaningful	8	great
9	main	10	former

B
1 She prepared well to avoid making the same mistake.

2 Helen was the only person we met at last night's party.

3 We put all the interesting books on the table.

4 There is no one who could move the heavy statue.

5 How can I buy a cute dog?

6 Thomas will recommend somewhere great for you to go.

7 Everyone was surprised when they heard about Harry's sudden accident.

Lesson 9-2 형용사의 어순

☆Check up!
p. 267~268

A
1 Tim's favorite American
2 famous young bassist
3 this small new black
4 all these dirty green
5 Three pretty girls
6 those three pairs of blue
7 Both of the tall Japanese
8 three small white
9 four nice old green wooden
10 the first four
11 Both of the big Korean
12 the second tallest new green
13 a big black silk
14 the beautiful large green
15 a small old blue

B
1 a smart young English girl.
2 made a big green kite.
3 a beautiful big diamond ring for her.

Lesson 9-3 형용사의 형태

☆Check up!
p. 270

A
1	impressive	2	believable
3	cultural	4	careless
5	friendly	6	dangerous
7	The blind	8	flexible
9	shocking	10	hopeless

B
1 me some friendly advice.
2 careless drivers, traffic accidents happen.
3 was emotional.
4 has a passive attitude
5 sometimes makes useless

Lesson 9-4 수량 형용사

☆Check up!
p. 271~272

A
1 a great number of restaurants
2 Few students
3 so many times
4 Several students
5 little water
6 The number of people
7 very few people
8 More than a few people

B
1 a little
2 amount
3 much
4 amount
5 few

정답 및 해설 **35**

Lesson 9-5 숫자 읽기 (1)

p. 274

A 1 thirty / thirtieth
　2 seventy−nine / seventy−ninth
　3 ten thousand fifty−four / ten thousand
　　 fifty−fourth
　4 four hundred eighty −seven / four hundred
　　 eighty−seventh
　5 two hundred thirty / two hundred thirtieth
　6 seven hundred sixteen
　　 / seven hundred sixteenth
　7 nine thousand eight hundred two / nine
　　 thousand eight hundred second
　8 one hundred fourteen / one hundred fourteenth
　9 ninety−one / ninety−first
　10 sixty−three / sixty−third

B 1 eighty−six thousand, two hundred forty
　2 three sixths
　3 five million, nine hundred eighty−seven
　　 thousand, one hundred forty−five
　4 four sevenths
　5 ten point one five
　6 three million, seven hundred seventy−four
　　 thousand, eight hundred fifty−four
　7 sixty thousand, three hundred fifteen
　8 sixty three point one nine eight
　9 two hundred eighty thousand, two hundred
　　 sixty−eight
　10 two ninths

Lesson 9-6 숫자 읽기 (2)

p. 276

A 1 nineteen eighty−nine
　2 three thirteen
　3 August sixth, two thousand fifteen
　4 one twenty−three
　5 november twenty fifth
　6 seventeen eighty nine
　7 five forty eight
　8 seven twenty
　9 July eighteenth, two thousand thirty−five
　10 February twenty fifth

　11 nineteen ninety
　12 eleven twenty−five
　13 four o(h) three
　14 eighteen eighty−four
　15 January second, nineteen ninety−four

B 1 three times　　　2 half
　3 five times　　　4 quarters
　5 seven times

Practice More I

p. 277~279

A 1 healthy　　　　2 interesting
　3 useful　　　　4 surprised
　5 natural　　　　6 strong
　7 passive　　　　8 foolish
　9 famous　　　　10 curious

B 1 number → deal
　2 a few → a little
　3 many → much
　4 white small → small white
　5 a time → once
　6 little → few
　7 special something → something special
　8 time → times
　9 many → much
　10 disappointing → disappointed

C 1 little　　　　2 few
　3 much　　　　4 few(many)
　5 amount　　　6 few
　7 little(much)　8 number
　9 many　　　　10 Few

D 1 a small metal plate
　2 both of these horrible movies
　3 these fifteen plastic
　4 a large lovely old pink American chair
　5 A large number of people came to the festival
　　 every year.
　6 A great deal of time is needed to fix the car.
　7 She read a few more books to do her
　　 homework.
　8 A few students will go rafting tomorrow.
　9 There was little happiness in people's face.
　10 He used to wear these three big black skirts.

Lesson 9-7 부사의 쓰임

p. 282

A 1 The child nodded his head bravely.
2 Fortunately, all of us passed the graduation exam.
3 My little sister talked with her friend quietly.
4 She was very pleased that she could buy the house.
5 They are looking for the ring carefully.
6 It's certainly not true.
7 Luckily, the gallery was not damaged by the storm.
8 He does his best to speak English fluently.
9 The stone was too slippery to pick up.
10 I think James is having dinner too quickly.

B 1 greatly   2 simply
3 specially   4 possibly
5 happily   6 busily
7 widely

Lesson 9-8 부사 파악하기

p. 284

A 1 a.예쁜 모자 b.아주 더운
2 a.열심히 연습하다 b.아주 단단한
3 a.아주 잘 b.건강한
4 a.옳은 b.우회전하다
5 a.대부분의 b.가장

B 1 Lately   2 close
3 nearly   4 highly
5 late   6 hardly
7 mostly   8 high
9 closely

Lesson 9-9 빈도부사

p. 285~286

A 1 is too sad.
2 sometimes feel
3 often got lost

4 will never win
5 is sometimes easy
6 usually shakes hands
7 are often able to
8 seldom drinks
9 is usually used
10 will never forget

B 1 sometimes watches movies
2 am always nervous
3 Jessy hardly(rarely) practices,
4 usually plays basketball
5 often used to debate

Lesson 9-10 여러 부사의 용법

p. 288

A 1 already   2 either
3 yet   4 still
5 too   6 even
7 ago   8 very
9 else   10 ago
11 neither   12 ago
13 else   14 too
15 neither

Lesson 9-11 이어동사

p. 289~290

A 1 give it up   2 put it on
3 out the wrinkles 4 it off
5 in the paper   6 out the weather
7 with him   8 up her car
9 it away   10 for the books

B 1 try on   2 call you back.
3 put off   4 gave up
5 switched(turned)/off 6 turn off
7 turn/down

Practice More II

p. 291~293

A
1	soon	2	Lately
3	closely	4	is always
5	hardly	6	high
7	often take	8	turn it off
9	nearly	10	most

B
1	do often → often do	2	happily → happy
3	hard → hardly	4	nearly → near
5	seriously → serious	6	Mostly → Most
7	be always → always be	8	easy → easily
9	high → highly		
10	beautiful → beautifully		

C
1	still	2	so
3	pretty	4	yet
5	else	6	before
7	turn the TV off	8	for our turn
9	up my water bottle	10	still

D
1 We often go to the movies together.
2 Jane and I hope to study abroad next month.
3 Jina's not going to hand in her report and, neither am I.
4 Do you still need to wait for your husband?
5 She has already finished making a dress for her daughter.
6 I am still upset about John's mistake.
7 Mary dislikes spicy food, but she often eats kimchi.
8 I think your room is much bigger than mine.
9 I could hardly believe my eyes.
10 My sister is old enough to enter middle school.

중간 기말고사 예상문제

내신 최다 출제 유형
p. 294

01 ④　　02 ②　　03 ⑤
04 She read us a few interesting stories
05 Neither can I. 06 (1) lately – late, (2) hardly – hard

해설

01 ④ 부사–열심히, 형용사 –, ① 어려운, ②,③ 힘든, ⑤ 딱딱한
02 긍정문과 권유의 의문문에는 '약간, 조금'의 의미인 'some'을 사용한다.
03 a little → a few
04 '몇몇 이야기'와 'a few'는 복수형이기 때문에 story를 'stories'로 고쳐야 한다.
05 앞 문장에 대한 부정의 동의는 'neither＋동사＋주어'를 사용한다.
06 (1) be동사＋형용사
(2) 일반동사＋부사: 'hard'의 부사는 그대로 'hard'이다. 'hardly'는 빈도부사로 '거의 ~않는'의 뜻을 가지고 있다.

p. 295~300

01 ⑤	02 ②	03 ③	04 ②	05 ⑤
06 ②	07 ①	08 ①	09 ⑤	10 ③
11 ②	12 ④	13 ②	14 ⑤	15 ④
16 ③	17 ②,④	18 ①	19 ③	20 ④
21 ②	22 ⑤	23 ②	24 ⑤	25 ③
26 ①	27 ③			

〈서술형 평가〉

28 good ~ well
29 longest – long
30 on – up
31 usually do my homework
32 It rarely rains.
33 same room several times
34 His band has twice more fans than mine.
35 It's thirty (half) past eleven.

해설

01 'yet' – '아직'이란 의미로 부정문에 사용한다.
02 '–thing'으로 끝나는 단어는 형용사가 뒤에서 꾸며준다.
03 ③ 명사–형용사, ①,②,④,⑤ 형용사–부사
04 left your hand → your left hand
05 Things bad → Bad things
06 이어동사구에서 목적어가 대명사일 경우 '타동사＋대명사＋부사'의 형태가 된다.
07 'not ~ either' ~도 또한 ...않는
08 ① 명사를 수식하는 수식어구이다. ②,③,④,⑤, 'the＋형용사' ~한 사람들
09 ①,②,③,④ 명사를 수식하는 형용사, ⑤ 비교급을 강조한다. '훨씬'
10 ③ 움직이지 않고서, ①,②,④,⑤ 여전히

11 'much+셀수 없는 명사', 'enough+to부정사' ～하기에 충분한

12 'nothing' 아무것도, 'something' 무엇

13 'ever' – 경험을 물어 볼 때 사용, 'once' 한때

14 '기수-국적'순으로 쓴다. Chinese three → three Chinese

15 '자동사+전치사' 형태의 동사는 두 단어가 합쳐져
하나의 타동사로 쓰이며, 이 두 단어는 분리될 수 없다.
– Larry didn't agree with us.

16 ① very → much, ② happy → happier,
④ has bought → bought, ⑤ much → very

17 'afraid, asleep, pleased'는 한정적 용법에 쓸 수 없다.

18 'two and three fourths'는 '$2\frac{3}{4}$'을 표현할 때 사용한다.

19 25.19: twenty-five point one nine

20 it feels usually → it usually feels

21 hardly → hard

22 'glad'는 서술적 용법으로만 쓸 수 있다.

23 'worth' ～의 가치가 있는

24 권유의 의문문이나, 긍정문에서는 'some'을 사용한다.

25 still → already(yet)

26 ①열심히, ②,③,④,⑤ 어려운

27 ③ neither → either

〈서술형 평가〉

28 일반동사 뒤에는 부사가 온다.

29 'too+형용사'

30 'show up' 나타나다, 도착하다

31 빈도부사는 일반동사 앞에 위치한다. usually 보통

32 빈도부사는 일반동사 앞에 위치한다. rarely 거의 ～않는

33 'several times' 여러 번

34 '배수사+as+원급+as' = '배수사+비교급+than'

35 '30분'은 'half'를 사용하기도 한다.

Chapter 10 비교구문

Lesson 10-1 비교급과 최상급 만들기

p. 303~304

A
1 cheaper – cheapest
2 better – best
3 further – furthest / farther – farthest
4 smaller – smallest
5 later – latest
6 larger – largest
7 wider – widest
8 narrower – narrowest
9 less – least
10 nicer – nicest
11 more famous – most famous
12 luckier – luckiest
13 stranger – strangest
14 worse – worst
15 prettier – prettiest
16 sadder – saddest
17 safer – safest
18 nearer – nearest
19 more kindly – most kindly
20 more happily – most happily

B
1 better
2 worst
3 less
4 more practiced
5 most boring
6 more interesting
7 further
8 eldest

Lesson 10-2 원급비교(동등비교)

p. 305~306

A
1 not as heavy as
2 three times as many goals as
3 as many bananas as
4 as smart as
5 as many new bags as
6 not as fast as
7 as many notebooks as
8 as early as
9 as expensive as
10 as much water as

B
1 as much food as
2 not as dangerous as
3 half as tall as
4 twice as high as
5 four times as large as

Lesson 10-3 원급의 여러 가지 표현

p. 308

A
1 As long as
2 as fast as possible
3 as good as new
4 As far as we know
5 as soon as possible.
6 pretty(very / so)
7 as good as useless
8 As long as it rains outside
9 as she could buy
10 as good as broken

Lesson 10-4 비교급 비교

p. 310

A
1 taller
2 slower
3 smarter
4 silly
5 thinner
6 smart
7 diligent
8 faster
9 less
10 better

B
1 far better
2 The higher / the colder
3 a little longer
4 better and better
5 a little more comfortable

Lesson 10-5 최상급 비교

p. 311~312

A
1 the most exactly
2 the best restaurant
3 the tallest tower

4 The happiest news

5 the most diligent worker

6 the thickest book

7 the biggest tree

8 the brightest star

9 the most moving story

10 the best album

B **1** one of the best movies

2 the second most popular city

3 the most expensive pen

4 the third most popular sport

5 the least difficult

6 one of the most popular actors

7 the least interesting

8 one of the oldest books

9 the least dirty hat

10 the third most popular student

Lesson 10-6 최상급의 다른 표현

Check up!

p. 313~314

A **1** There is nothing more important than a challenge in my life.

2 There is nothing she worries about more than her kids living in China.

3 There is nothing more helpful than regular exercise and a good diet for losing weight.

4 There is nothing more boring than waiting for someone.

5 There is nothing he wants more than a new laptop as his graduation gift.

6 There is nothing more difficult than to be what your mother wants you to be.

B **1** → No(other) shirt in my room was as expensive as this shirt.

→ No(other) shirt in my room was more expensive than this shirt.

→ This shirt was more expensive than any other shirt in my room.

→ This shirt was more expensive than all the other shirts in my room.

2 → No(other) mountain is as high as Mt. Everest.

→ No(other) mountain is higher than Mt. Everest.

→ Mt. Everest is higher than any other mountain.

→ Mt. Everest is higher than all the other mountains.

3 → No(other) fossil is as old as this.

→ No(other) fossil is older than this.

→ This fossil is older than any other fossil.

→ This fossil is older than all the other fossils.

4 → No(other) person in Korea is as rich as Mr. Kim.

→ No(other) person in Korea is richer than Mr. Kim.

→ Mr. Kim is richer than any other person in Korea.

→ Mr. Kim is richer than all the other people in Korea.

5 → No(other) student in our class is as smart as Kate.

→ No(other) student in our class is smarter than Kate.

→ Kate is smarter than any other student in our class.

→ Kate is smarter than all the other students in our class.

Practice More I

p. 315~317

A **1** more funny → funnier

2 higher → high

3 more hard → harder

4 little and little → less and less

5 person → people

6 books → book

7 the most early → the earliest

8 as not → not as (so)

9 two times → twice

10 possible (you) → can (X)

B **1** better   **2** the longest

3 more important   **4** the less

5 the loudest   **6** larger

7 taller   **8** politely

9 the saddest   **10** more useful

C **1** less pleasant   **2** more bravely

3 more honest   **4** more difficult

5 more delicious   **6** short as

7 a little (slightly/somewhat) taller

8 more precious

9 one of the most popular

10 more generous

D **1** Lina began to walk faster and faster

     2 the lower the product's quality becomes.

     3 The air in this village was less polluted than the air in the city.

     4 The damage of the storm is more serious than people thought.

     5 This is the scariest novel I've ever read.

     6 Jack is one of the kindest people we've met

     7 He got the most votes in the school election.

     8 The harder she tries to forget the thing, the more clearly she remembers it.

     9 he became more and more generous.

     10 Jina took better care of the baby than her aunt did.

중간 기말고사 예상문제

내신 최다 출제 유형   p. 318

01 ②   **02** ⑤   **03** ④   **04** ③   **05** ②

해설

01 longer → longest

02 'A not as(so)~ as B' = 'B 비교급+than A'

03 'as~ as'는 동등비교 이고, 'less than'은 열등비교로 서로 같지 않다.

04 ⓐ the+최상급, ⓑ as~as 사이에는 원급, ⓒ 일반동사 앞에 빈도부사 위치 – 'hardly' 거의~않는

05 ⓐ와 ⓑ는 뒤의 'than'이 있으므로 비교급이 와야 하며, ⓒ는 최상급이 와야 한다.

01 ④	**02** ②	**03** ③	**04** ⑤	**05** ②
06 ①	**07** ①	**08** ⑤	**09** ③	**10** ④
11 ②,③	**12** ①	**13** ①	**14** ④	**15** ③
16 ⑤	**17** ④	**18** ②	**19** ③	**20** ⑤
21 ④	**22** ③	**23** ②	**24** ④	**25** ③
26 ①	**27** ④			

〈서술형 평가〉

28 The more thrilling

29 Every time/more and more

30 three times as big as

31 more expensive/all the other dresses

32 no food/more(better) than

33 less easy than

34 I spent no more than ten dollars to buy five books.

35 Rachel is more overweight than the average weight.

36 The more you draw pictures, the better you'll draw pictures.

37 (1) No(other) mountain is as high as Mt. Everest in the world.

     (2) Mt. Everest is higher than all the other mountains in the world.

     (3) Mt. Everest is higher than any other mountain in the world.

해설

01 exciting – more exciting – most exciting.

02 nice – nicer – nicest

03 curious – more curious – most curious

04 셀 수 있는 명사와 함께 쓰이는 'few'의 비교급을 사용한다.

05 'as 원급 as' ~만큼 ...한

06 뒤에 'than'이 있으므로 비교급이 나와야 한다.

07 ② 훨씬, ①,③,④,⑤, 많이

08 ① singer → singers, ② to play → to playing, ③ smartest → the smartest ④ good and good → better and better

09 ①,②,④,⑤는 모두 최상급을 나타내는 표현이다.

10 to better → to be better

11 '비교급 than any other+단수명사', 'Nothing~ 비교급 than' 모두 최상급의 의미를 나타낸다.

12 'very'는 원급 형용사 또는 부사와 쓰인다.

13 'as+원급+as+주어+can' = 'as+원급+as possible'

14 'too~ to...' = 'so that+주어+can't'

15 'A 비교급 than B' = 'B not as(so) 원급 as A'

42 Grammar Master Level 3

16 'the+최상급' = '비교급+than+any other+단수명사'

17 'much'와 'than'은 비교급과 쓸 수 있는 표현이다.

18 'a lot'은 비교급을 수식하여 '훨씬'이라는 의미로 사용된다.

19 'get+비교급' 더 ~해지다

20 'No~ as+원급+as'는 최상급의 의미를 표현한다.

21 'the+비교급, the+비교급' 점점 더 ~해지는

22 'as 형용사/부사 원급 as possible' 가능한 한 ~한

23 the most → the more

24 〈보기, ④〉 ~만큼 잘, ①,②,③,⑤ 상관접속사 'A as well as B' B뿐만 아니라 A도

25 'the+비교급+주어+동사, the+비교급+주어+동사' ~하면 할수록 더~한

26 'the+서수+최상급'의 형태이다.

27 'A~ 비교급+than+all the other+복수명사'로 최상급을 나타내는 표현이다.

〈서술형 평가〉

28 'the+비교급, the+비교급' ~할수록 더~한

29 '비교급+and+비교급' 점점 더 ~한

30 '숫자+times' ~배

31 '비교급+than all the other+복수명사'는 최상급의 다른 표현이다.

32 'There is no~ 비교급+than'은 최상급의 표현이다.

33 'not as(so)~as'='less+형용사/부사+than'

34 'no more than' 단지, 겨우

35 'more 형용사+than' ~보다 ...한

36 'the+비교급, the+비교급' ~할수록, 더~한

37 (1) 'No(other)~ as(so)+원급+as+A'
A만큼 ~한(다른) 것은 없다
(2) 'A~비교급+than all the other+복수명사'
A는 다른 어떤(복수명사) 보다 ~하다
(3) 'A~비교급+than any other+단수명사'
A는 다른 어떤(단수명사) 보다 ~하다

Chapter

11 가정법

Lesson 11-1 가정법 과거

Check up!

p. 328

A 1 If she were not tired, she could study all night.

2 If I were not sick, I could participate in the contest.

3 If he liked Italian food, he would join us for lunch.

4 If it didn't snow heavily, the baseball game would be held.

5 If they knew her address, they could visit her.

6 If harry missed the bus, he would take a taxi.

7 If we had not more time, we couldn't play with our daughter.

8 If Mary spoke Korean, she would talk to people.

9 If I had a sister, I could play dolls with her.

10 If we didn't go to the party, we couldn't enjoy the holiday.

Lesson 11-2 가정법 과거완료

Check up!

p. 330~331

A 1 If I had moved to Seoul last month, I could have met her.

2 If he had been careful, he wouldn't have made a big mistake.

3 If it hadn't rained, Tim could have gone hiking.

4 If she hadn't seen a horror movie alone that night, she could have slept well.

5 If I had had a serious problem, I would have called her for help.

6 If we had played the piano well, the orchestra would have accepted us.

7 If Mina had written the letter in English, I couldn't have read it.

8 If he had tried to keep promise, people would have liked him.

9 If I had made a different choice, the situation would have changed.

10 If she had been sleepy, she wouldn't have started to read a book.

B 1 If she hadn't spent all her money, she could buy a wallet.

2 If John had studied hard, he could pass the exam.

3 If Alice hadn't lost my key, I could enter the room.

4 If the girl had brought her book, the teacher wouldn't be angry.

5 If Tim hadn't left, we wouldn't feel so lonely.

6 If I hadn't broken my brother's laptop, he could play games.

7 If Cindy had read the book, she could complete the report.

8 If Nick hadn't called her this morning, she might be late for the meeting.

9 If he had exercised regularly, he would be healthy now.

10 If he had registered for the course, he could take the exam.

Lesson 11-3 I wish 가정법

Check up!

p. 332~333

A 1 you were not feeling lonely today.

2 they were here with us.

3 I had money to buy that luxurious bag.

4 he had gone to the wine festival with us.

5 I hadn't laughed at one of our classmates.

6 my sister hadn't eaten too much salad for breakfast.

7 the teacher had given us information related to the test.

8 we lived in a world free from the disease.

9 Jane had taken a taxi.

10 I had started preparing for the party earlier.

11 I could have made your dress early.

12 I had traveled around the country when I was young.

13 I had paid attention to the people around me.

14 there were enough restrooms in the park.

15 I had called him last night.

Lesson 11-4 as if 가정법

Check up!

p. 335

A **1** as if he had been a very famous actor in America.

 2 as if they liked to play soccer.

 3 as if she studied English literature in college.

 4 as if he were a scientist.

 5 as if she went to church.

 6 as if she witnessed the car accident.

 7 as if they had made much effort to find the lost dog.

 8 as if he were a professional photographer.

 9 as if he didn't like her very much

 10 as if we hadn't made the same mistake again

B **1** (should) go   **2** (should) destroy

 3 (should) turn   **4** (should) take

 5 (should) finish

Lesson 11-5 'if' 이외의 가정법 표현

Check up!

p. 336

A **1** If it were not for her advice

 2 if it had not been for this device?

 3 If it were not for this map

 4 If it had not been for the book

 5 If it were not for the dictionary

Practice More I

p. 337~339

A **1** I were a professional model.

 2 she were / she couldn't live

 3 had taken the medicine / wouldn't have

 4 he didn't earn / couldn't buy

 5 I had paid attention to the dangerous situation

 6 as if he had had much money to buy a car.

 7 hadn't finished / couldn't have taken

8 hadn't stayed up / wouldn't be

9 had owned / would have driven

10 If it were not for this guide (But for this guide)

B **1** is → were   **2** speak → spoke

 3 be → have been   **4** is → were

 5 knows → knew

 6 listened → would listen

 7 is → (should) be

 8 have → had

 9 pass → have passed

C **1** I wish she would stop eating too much.

 2 If he had not broken his leg, he could go skating with us.

 3 If she hadn't been the only child, she wouldn't have felt lonely.

 4 I wish their best album sold well.

 5 as if she could have afforded to buy the newest car.

 6 If I didn't have the device (If it were not for the device)

 7 If it had not been for the Internet (Without the Internet)

 8 I wish I had taken the graduation exam last semester.

 9 I wish I had accepted his proposal last week.

 10 If it had not been for the rope (Without the rope)

D **1** She pretended as if she had a good relationship with her sister.

 2 If Kate hadn't loved Italian food, she wouldn't have decided to buy the cooking book.

 3 She pretends as if she wrote the novel by herself.

 4 I feel as if I were a real English teacher.

 5 If we had won the lottery, we would have given 1,000 dollars to each one of you.

 6 It is important that the leader change the rules of the game.

 7 If I hadn't met a good teacher, I could not have become a great professor.

 8 I wish the weather would not be freezing cold.

중간 기말고사 **예상문제**

p. 340

01 ③   02 ⑤   03 ②   04 ①   05 ⑤

06 as if I were a princess in the movie

해설

01 과거에 이루지 못한 소망을 말하기 때문에 'I wish+가정법 과거완료'를 사용한다.

02 과거의 사실과 반대를 가정해야 하므로 가정법 과거완료로 바꿔야 한다.

03 'without+가정법 과거'는 'but for, if it were not for, were it not for'로 바꿔 쓸 수 있다.

04 가정법 과거완료 문장은 직설법 과거로 바꿀 수 있다. 가정법을 직설법으로 전환할 때 긍정은 부정으로, 부정은 긍정으로 바꾼다.

05 가정법 과거완료이므로 asked를 had asked로 써야 한다.

06 as if 마치~처럼
   → 주절의 동사(felt)와 'as if'절의 동사가 '동시발생'일 경우 과거동사를 써준다.

p. 341~345

01 ②   02 ⑤   03 ②   04 ③   05 ①
06 ③   07 ①   08 ⑤   09 ④   10 ②
11 ③   12 ②   13 ⑤   14 ④   15 ①
16 ⑤   17 ②   18 ②   19 ④   20 ②
21 ⑤   22 ②

〈서술형 평가〉

23 as if she had cooked food by herself
24 Kelly had come to my party
25 I had taken your advice then / would be
26 hadn't snowed / could climb
27 talks as if she had seen
28 were okay / would go
29 I wish I were
30 She acts as if she were

해설

01 follows → follow
   → '주장'을 의미하는 동사(insisted)의 목적어로 that절이 올 경우, 동사는 'should + 동사원형'의 형태가 되며, should는 생략이 가능하다.

02 혼합가정문 : didn't support → hadn't supported

03 ② '~인지 아닌지'-간접의문문을 이끈다. ①,③,④,⑤ 조건을 나타내는 if

04 과거 사실과 반대되는 일을 가정할 때, 가정법 과거완료로 바꾸어 쓸 수 있다.

05 시점이 과거이므로 과거 사실과 반대되는 가정법 과거완료를 사용한다.

06 주절이 '주어+조동사 과거+동사원형'의 형태로 쓰였기 때문에 if절은 가정법 과거 '주어+동사과거형'으로 쓴다.

07 ② will come → comes, ③ keeps → keep,
   ④ am → were, ⑤ helps → will help

08 가정법 과거에 쓰인 'without'은 'if it were not for'와 바꿔 쓸 수 있다.

09 had been → were

10 'as if' 뒤에 나오는 문장이 가정법 과거완료로 주절의 시제보다 앞에 있기 때문에 직설법으로 바꿀 때는 과거형을 사용한다.

11 'as if' 뒤에 나오는 문장이 가정법 과거로 주절의 시제보다 앞에 있기 때문에 직설법으로 바꿀 때는 현재형을 사용한다.

12 '만약~했다면, ...했을 텐데'의 가정법 과거완료의 의미다.
   'if+주어+과거완료, 주어+조동사 과거+현재완료'

13 '가정법 과거' – 만약~한다면, ...일 텐데.
   'if+주어+과거동사, 주어+조동사 과거+동사원형'

14 is → were

15 looked → (should) look
   → ⑤'~해야 한다'의 의미가 포함되지 않고, 사실을 언급할 경우에는 주절과 that절의 동사는 시제 일치 시킨다.

16 'as if+가정법 과거' is → were

17 'studied → had studied' 혼합가정법은 과거의 일이 현재까지 영향을 미칠 때 사용하며, if절의 동사는 과거완료(had+p.p)를 쓰고, 주절의 동사는 '조동사과거+동사원형'을 쓴다.

18 'I wish+가정법 과거' 현재의 사실에 반대되는 것을 소망하고 있기 때문에 가정법 과거를 사용한다.

19 현재의 반대 사실을 가정법으로 표현하였으므로 '그는 나의 남자친구가 아니다'가 알맞다.

20 'without' ~이 없었다면

21 과거 사실에 대한 유감을 표현한 것으로 가정법 과거완료를 썼기 때문에 직설법 문장은 한 시제 앞인 과거형을 쓰는 것이 알맞다.

22 'would': 가정법 과거형, 'bring': to+동사원형,
   'were': 'I wish 가정법 과거' 사용

〈서술형 평가〉

23 'as if+가정법 과거완료'

24 'I wish+가정법 과거완료'

25 'if'의 혼합 가정법이다. if절에는 가정법 과거완료, 주절에는 가정법 과거를 사용한다.

26 혼합 가정법으로, if절은 가정법 과거완료, 주절은 가정법 과거로 표현한다.

27 'as if+가정법 과거완료'

28 가정법 과거 문장으로 주절은 '조동사 과거+동사원형'을 사용한다.

29 현재의 사실과 반대되는 불가능한 것을 소망할 때 'I wish 가정법 과거'를 사용한다.

30 'as if+가정법 과거형'

Chapter 12 관계사

Lesson 12-1 관계대명사

Check up!

p. 349~350

A
1 who
2 whose
3 whom
4 which
5 who
6 which
7 who
8 whom
9 whose
10 which

B
1 whom I met in the park yesterday.
2 that I've ever had
3 who called me
4 What matters to us
5 which is the most expensive

Lesson 12-2 관계대명사 which, who

Check up!

p. 351~352

A
1 who is interested in traditional dance
2 whose electronic dictionary was stolen yesterday
3 who go to this concert should bring a ticket
4 which was completed in 2014
5 whom we met yesterday was very rude (was very rude whom we met yesterday)
6 which he broke was one of the most expensive ones in the shop
7 who helped the poor woman was my classmate
8 whose song made people happy won first prize in the contest
9 which requires more detailed information
10 whom my sister likes

Lesson 12-3 관계대명사 that, what

Check up!

p. 354

A
1 that work in the animal hospital.
2 What matters to me is the result of the final exam.
3 that was shining under the water.
4 that fell into the sea
5 that is directed by my brother.
6 that people voted for
7 what you bought
8 that helps the poor and the disabled
9 that we could stay in during the day

B
1 who
2 whose
3 that
4 What
5 whose
6 that
7 what

Lesson 12-4 복합관계대명사

Check up!

p. 356

A
1 Whoever / Anyone who
2 whatever / anything that
3 Whoever / Anyone who
4 whatever she wants / anything that she wants.
5 whoever / no matter who
6 Whoever / No matter whom
7 Whatever / No matter what
8 Whichever / No matter which
9 whichever / no matter which
10 Whatever / No matter what

Lesson 12-5 관계대명사의 용법

Check up!

p. 358

A
1 The man had two books, which were written by Harry.
2 There are three more people, who are waiting for John.
3 We met Jane, who seemed to need help.
4 I lied to him again, which made him angry.
5 I like the paintings, which were painted by father.
6 He missed the bus, which meant we might be late.

7 We will fly to London, which means we won't have to worry about the plan.

8 An old woman, who lives next door, gave me some apples.

9 The game was shown on TV, which attracted many people.

10 A nurse, who didn't wear a uniform, was taking care of a sick child.

Lesson 12-6 관계대명사의 생략

Check up!

p. 359

A
1	whom	2	which
3	that	4	whom
5	that	6	that
7	whom	8	who was

Lesson 12-7 전치사+관계대명사

Check up!

p. 360

A

1 → Do you know the girl whom Jane is talking to with a smile?
→ Do you know the girl to whom Jane is talking to with a smile?

2 → This is the house which James was born in.
→ This is the house in which James was born.

3 → The woman is a candidate whom many people work for.
→ The woman is a candidate for whom many people work.

4 → This is a nice guidebook that I found food information in.
→ This is a nice guidebook in which I found good information.

Practice More I

p. 361~363

A
1	who	2	who(m)
3	that	4	who(m)
5	what	6	who
7	what	8	whose
9	which	10	who(m)

B
1 whose → who
2 which → what
3 that → which
4 what → that
5 which → who
6 that → which
7 them → whom
8 that → which
9 tries he → he tries
10 anything → anyone

C
1 The student who didn't do homework was scolded.

2 What is the title of the novel that (which) John told me about last night?

3 Look at those dogs which (that) are lying on the ground peacefully.

4 We couldn't go to the beach party that we weren't invited to.

5 I've never seen Minhyuk who(m) Jane went to the theater with two days ago.

6 My mother gave me this letter, which has influenced me a lot.

7 The bag which he's looking at is expensive.

8 The writer who(m) I met last year in Mexico was very friendly. (He was a very friendly writer who(m) I met last year in Mexico.)

9 The woman who(m) I see every morning in the park bought the coat.

10 Andy can't trust some people who(m) he worked with.

D
1 No matter what I asked, he didn't say anything.

2 I know the boy who ate all the food on the table.

3 Last week, I saw Alice, whom I hadn't seen for two years.

4 Do you remember the girl who ran down the street?

5 Whoever solves the riddle will be the winner of the game.

6 Basketball is a sport that my friends and I like.

7 Whichever you choose, you won't regret it.

8 What matters to me is the result of the test.

9 Please let me know what you want.

10 I will follow whatever you decide.

Lesson 12-8 관계부사

Check up!

p. 366

A 1 on which Helen and he first met./when Helen and he first met.

2 at which many people stayed?/where many people stayed?

3 on which we visited her house today. /when we visited her house today.

4 for which he couldn't attend the meeting. /why he couldn't attend the meeting.

5 in which the teacher deals with his students. /how the teacher deals with his students.

6 in which I have ever visited./where I have ever visited.

7 on which his big brother went to the army /when his big brother went to the army.

8 in which they speak Japanese well./how they speak Japanese well.

Lesson 12-9 관계부사로 쓰이는 that

Check up!

p. 367

A 1 when/that   2 where
3 where   4 why/that
5 when/that   6 that
7 that   8 how/the way

Lesson 12-10 복합관계부사

Check up!

p. 369

A 1 whenever/at any time
2 However/No matter how
3 wherever/no matter where
4 wherever/at any place
5 However/No matter how

B 1 whenever   2 wherever
3 However   4 whenever
5 wherever   6 whenever

Lesson 12-11 관계부사의 생략과 계속적 용법

Check up!

p. 371

A 1 May 15th is the day when we thank our teachers.

2 Let's go to the store where you bought the bike.

3 This is the place where I used to work with my boyfriend.

4 2002 was the year when Korea hosted the World Cup.

5 The bakery where I bought the bread is next to the flower shop.

6 That is the reason why she left us without any explanation.

7 Busan is the city where you can see famous movie stars.

8 She needs to know how she can get along with strangers.

9 Please return the dictionary that you borrowed from the library.

B 1 You met Jim last night, when it began to snow.

2 My brother was running down the street, when he saw Kate.

3 We went to the museum, where I saw famous statues.

4 Jerry moved here in 2003, when his daughter was born.

5 The professor entered the classroom, where he started to give us a lecture.

Practice More Ⅱ

p. 372~374

A 1 when   2 how(the way)
3 where   4 when
5 where   6 when
7 how   8 where
9 when   10 when

B 1 want you → you want
2 what → that(which/where)
3 the way → X

4 came I → I came

5 who → whose

6 when → why

7 where → when

8 what → when

9 which → how (the way)

10 eat you → you eat

C **1** why   **2** in which

3 that   **4** in which

5 came to   **6** the reason

7 tired he   **8** why

9 wherever **10** however

D **1** You may leave whenever you want.

2 My parents scold me whenever I make a mistake.

3 I don't know why they didn't come to the party.

4 Do you know the day when our baby was born?

5 Brian didn't reveal the way he saved money.

6 Let's go to the shop where you bought the cookie.

7 This is the way we can solve the problem.

8 The boys went to the store, where they bought the soccer ball.

9 Whenever I call her, she answers my phone call.

10 The stadium where they played soccer was very small.

중간 기말고사 예상문제

내신 **최다 출제** 유형   p. 375

01 ④ 02 ② 03 ⑤ 04 ④ 05 ③

06 ②

해설

01 ④ 관계대명사, ①,②,③,⑤ 의문사

02 선행사가 사물이고, 각각 주어, 목적어로 쓰였기 때문에 관계대 명사 'that(which)'을 사용한다.

03 ①,②,③,④ 관계대명사 that, ⑤ 관계대명사 what

04 ④ 목적격 관계대명사는 생략이 가능하다. 생략 불가능 – ①,② 주격 관계대명사, ③ 전치사+목적격 관계대명사, ⑤ 소유격 관계대명사

05 관계대명사 that 앞에는 전치사를 사용할 수 없다.

06 'the way'와 'how'는 함께 사용할 수 없다.

               p. 376~380

01 ② 02 ④ 03 ① 04 ③ 05 ③

06 ② 07 ⑤ 08 ① 09 ④ 10 ②

11 ④ 12 ② 13 ① 14 ⑤ 15 ④

16 ② 7 ① 18 ③ 19 ④ 20 ②

21 ③ 22 ②

〈서술형 평가〉

23 on which

24 where

25 These are her plants for which she was looking.

26 Do you know the woman to whom Jerry is talking.

27 She is reading a book whenever

28 why he refused my suggestion.

29 Whoever wanted the bag could have it.

30 I bought a novel which is written in Japanese

해설

01 동사 'love'의 목적어가 되어야 하고, 사람을 나타내므로 'whomever'가 알맞다

02 'wherever' 어디에 있더라도

03 for which → with which

04 이유를 나타내는 선행사 'the reason' 다음에는 관계부사 'why'가 와야 한다.

05 ① 'how', ② 'whose', ④ 'which', ⑤ 'which'

06 선행사가 'the same'의 수식을 받으므로 'that'을 사용할 수 있다.

07 앞에 선행사가 있으므로 'which'가 들어가야 한다.

08 관계대명사 'what'은 그 안에 선행사를 포함하고 있다.

09 'however+형용사+주어+동사' 아무리 ~하더라도

10 'whatever+주어+동사' ~가 무엇을 …하든

11 where–which

12 'the way'와 'how'는 함께 사용할 수 없다.

13 〈보기, ①〉 관계부사, ②,③,④,⑤ 의문부사

14 첫 번째 문장: 선행사가 차의 트렁크, 두 번째 문장: 사막 → 장소를 의미하는 관계부사 'where'가 알맞다.

15 빈 칸 앞의 선행사와 뒤의 명사가 소유의 관계이기 때문에 소유 격관계대명사 'whose'가 온다.

16 관계대명사 'that'은 앞에 '콤마'를 쓰는 계속적 용법으로 사용할 수 없다.

17 주격관계대명사는 생략할 수 없다.

18 what → whatever

19 복합관계대명사는 선행사를 포함한다.

20 ① which → when (on which), ③ who → whose
④ '전치사+관계대명사 that'은 쓸 수 없다.
⑤ which → where

21 선행사에 형용사의 최상급이 포함되어 있으므로 관계대명사 'that'을 사용한다.

22 〈보기, ②〉 관계부사, ①,③ 의문부사, ④,⑤ 접속사

〈서술형 평가〉

23 선행사가 하루를 나타내는 'the day'이므로 전치사 'on'을 써준다.

24 선행사가 장소이므로 'in which'를 'where'로 바꿔 쓸 수 있다.

25 사물을 나타내는 관계대명사 'which'와 'for'를 함께 써주어 'for which'가 된다.

26 사람을 나타내는 관계대명사의 목적격이 나와야 한다. 'to+whom'

27 복합관계대명사 'whenever' ∼할 때마다

28 이유에 대한 관계부사 'the reason why'

29 'whoever' 누구든지

30 선행사 'novel'을 수식하는 주격관계대명사 'which'

Chapter
13 접속사

Lesson 13-1 and / but / or

★Check up! p. 384

A
1 and   2 and
3 or   4 and
5 or   6 but
7 or   8 but
9 and   10 but

B
1 and   2 and
3 or   4 and
5 or

Lesson 13-2 both A and B

★Check up! p. 386

A
1 both   2 but also
3 either   4 but
5 nor   6 is
7 both/and   8 are
9 not   10 Neither

B
1 Not only/but also
2 not/but
3 Either/or
4 not only/but also
5 either/or
6 as well as

Lesson 13-3 that / whether (if)

★Check up! p. 388

A
1 that   2 whether
3 that   4 that
5 whether (if)   6 That
7 Whether   8 that
9 whether   10 that

B
1 It is certain that she will come back next week.
2 She remembered that she had left her wallet on the table.
3 It is doubtful whether she really wants to quit her job.
4 I couldn't know whether(if) Sam was satisfied with the result or not.
5 We think that students should follow the school rules.

Lesson 13-4 when / while

★Check up! p. 390

A
1 before   2 as
3 while   4 after
5 Once   6 since
7 As soon as   8 after
9 before   10 Since

B
1 while you talked with mother.
2 as soon as she left the room
3 since he was a university student
4 until it got too dark to play.
5 when you hear the news.

Lesson 13-5 because / so~that... / so that

★Check up! p. 392

A
1 because   2 so
3 so that   4 so / that
5 because of
6 so that (in order that)
7 As (Because/Since)
8 Because (As/Since)
9 so/that
10 Because of

B
1 as she broke her leg.
2 so spicy that she couldn't enjoy it.
3 Because he has traveled in many countries
4 in order that I could complete my report
5 so that she could buy the luxurious bag.

Lesson 13-6 if / though

A
1 snows
2 Unless
3 Although (Though / Even though)
4 if
5 While
6 although (though / even though)
7 whether (even if)
8 if
9 comes

B
1 Although she tried hard, Jane could not solve the problem.
2 If he can't open the door, he can't find us.
3 Although Thomas was elected as class president, he was very depressed.
4 Unless you are careful with it, you might get into trouble.
5 Even though the students are still young, they know lots of things.

Lesson 13-7 접속부사

A
1 In the end
2 for example
3 however
4 By the way
5 First of all
6 For instance
7 However
8 in a word
9 In other words
10 Therefore
11 On the contrary
12 On the other hand
13 Otherwise

Practice More I

A
1 As
2 and
3 that
4 since (because)
5 If
6 and
7 After
8 but
9 nor
10 or

B
1 Neither → Either
2 but → or
3 It → Whether
4 and → but
5 that → until
6 after → since
7 although → once
8 or → but
9 nor → but
10 Because of → Because

C
1 The girls are not only kind but also positive.
2 He is good at both playing chess and playing soccer.
3 I have a great interest in the concert, however, Jane doesn't like it.
4 We are certain that the rumor is wrong.
5 Jim can't decide if he should go or stay.
6 I haven't made a flight reservation, besides, I have to extend my visa.
7 Her personality has changed a lot since she met John.
8 As soon as they heard the news, they began to call their family.
9 Throw the ball softly so that she can hit it easily.
10 It is true that Mary will get married to him.

D
1 They are sure that it will snow heavily next week.
2 The accident was so terrible that she had to stay in the hospital for a few weeks.
3 I don't know whether I will pass the exam or not.
4 It is natural that people want to enjoy the environment.
5 Not only he but also I like to eat sweets.
6 Until I tell him to stop, he should keep running. (He should keep running untill I tell him to stop.)
7 It is surprising that Helen figured out the magician's trick.
8 I'm sure they'll be excited once they try this game.
9 The boy doesn't know that she is my sister.
10 Either my brother or I can attend the meeting.

정답 및 해설 **53**

중간 기말고사 **예상문제**

p. 400

01 ③ 02 ⑤ 03 ② 04 ③ 05 ④

06 I bought some flowers before I met him.
(After I bought some flowers, I met him.)

07 I could neither laugh nor cry.

해설

01 ③ 명사절 접속사 '~인지 아닌지', ①,②,④,⑤ ~한다면

02 ① can I → I can,
② Do you think who → Who do you think,
③ What do you know → Do you know what,
④ was I → I was

03 〈보기, ②〉 종속접속사 '~처럼', ① 원급 비교 '~만큼',
③ 시간 접속사, '~할 때',
④ 이유 접속사 '~ 때문에', ⑤ 자격을 의미 '~로서'

04 뒤의 절이 완전한 문장이므로 명사절 접속사 'that'이 들어간다.

05 '나는 할 말이 없었기 때문에 조용했다'의 뜻을 가진 문장으로
'because'가 들어가야 한다.

06 꽃을 산 행동이 먼저이기 때문에 'before'는 'and' 자리에 온다.
하지만 'after'는 문장의 맨 앞에 와야 한다.

07 'neither A nor B' A도 B도 아니다

p. 401~405

01 ⑤ 02 ① 03 ⑤ 04 ③ 05 ④
06 ⑤ 07 ② 08 ② 09 ④ 10 ③
11 ② 12 ⑤ 13 ⑤ 14 ① 15 ②
16 ③ 17 ④ 18 ① 19 ②,③ 20 ④

〈서술형 평가〉

21 not only/but also

22 Once you visit my country

23 On the other hand/you are rude

24 As soon as

25 unless it rains

26 so that

27 As Tom got up late

28 Either father or mother goes

29 I like both history and English.

30 Therefore, I went home early.

해설

01 'and' ~와, 그리고

02 'therefore' 그러므로

03 'for example' 예를 들면

04 'in addition' 게다가

05 'not A but B' A가 아니라 B

06 조건을 나타내는 부사절에서는 현재형이 미래형을 대신한다.

07 'neither A nor B' A도 B도 아니다

08 Though → Because(Since, As)

09 so → such

10 ③ 관계대명사, ①,②,④,⑤ 명사절을 이끄는 접속사

11 〈보기, ②〉 ~대로, ① ~만큼, ③ ~때문에, ④ ~함에 따라,
⑤ ~하면서

12 ①,②,③,④ Jane, Sam 둘 모두 나의 학생이다.
⑤ Jane 또는 Sam 중 하나만 나의 학생이다

13 '미술 수업이 시작을 안 했으므로 조금 더 기다려야 한다'는
내용이 문맥상 자연스럽다.

14 'neither A nor B' A도 B도 아니다

15 likes → like

16 'if = whether' ~인지 아닌지

17 ① is → are, ② as well → as well as, ③ or → nor,
⑤ have → has

18 ① ~이후로 (시간), ②,③,④,⑤~이므로(이유)

19 〈보기, ②,③〉 ~인지 아닌지, ① 만약~할지라도, ④,⑤ 만약

20 ⓐ Although, ⓑ Since, ⓒ while, ⓓ that

〈서술형 평가〉

21 'not only A but also B' A뿐 아니라 B도 역시

22 'once' 일단 ~하면

23 'on the other hand' 반면에

24 'on 동사-ing' ~하자마자=as soon as

25 'if not'='unless' ~하지 않는다면

26 'so that' ~하기 위하여

27 원인이나 이유를 의미하는 접속사 문장
'as(because, since)+주어+동사'

28 'either A or B' A 또는 B 중 하나는~

29 'both A and B' A와 B 둘 다

30 'therefore' 그러므로

Chapter 14 전치사

Lesson 14-1 시간의 전치사 (1)

Check up! p. 410

A
1	at	2	at
3	on	4	at
5	In	6	on
7	at	8	at
9	on	10	on
11	on	12	in
13	in	14	at
15	in		

Lesson 14-2 시간의 전치사 (2)

Check up! p. 411~412

A
1	before	2	since
3	for	4	by
5	during	6	within
7	in	8	after
9	until	10	from

B
1	before	2	during
3	for	4	in
5	from	6	since
7	in	8	during
9	before	10	from

Lesson 14-3 장소의 전치사

Check up! p. 414

A
1	at	2	on
3	in	4	in
5	at	6	on
7	at	8	on
9	in	10	at
11	on	12	at
13	in	14	on
15	in		

Lesson 14-4 방향의 전치사

Check up! p. 416

A
1	up	2	onto
3	out of	4	off
5	around	6	through
7	down	8	toward
9	from	10	for

Lesson 14-5 위치의 전치사

Check up! p. 418

A
1	over	2	between
3	next	4	above
5	among	6	near
7	in front of	8	behind
9	under	10	around
11	in	12	near
13	between	14	next
15	around		

Practice More I

p. 419~421

A
1	at	2	in
3	up	4	above
5	in	6	under
7	at	8	until
9	in	10	before

B
1	from	2	until
3	at	4	during
5	into	6	during
7	in	8	since
9	below	10	under (on)

C
1	on → at	2	into → on
3	for → since	4	after → before
5	in → on	6	on → at
7	on → in	8	at → in
9	during → for	10	on → in

D
1 The explorer moved into the cave.
2 Many relics were stolen during the war.
3 There are two small lamps and a book on the table.

4　There was an old lighthouse on the hill.

5　The writer was born on March 13, 1989.

6　They began to do volunteer work from July.

7　We should return to Korea within thirteen hours.

8　Jane found a diary among the books.

9　The girl and her dog were running along the river.

10　Cars are running through the forest to go to the sea.

Lesson 14-6 여러 의미의 전치사 (1)

Check up! p. 424

A　1　by　　　　2　with
　　3　by　　　　4　with
　　5　in　　　　6　by
　　7　with　　　8　by
　　9　with　　　10　by

B　1　with　　　2　in
　　3　on　　　　4　in
　　5　in

Lesson 14-7. 여러 의미의 전치사 (2)

Check up! p. 426

A　1　as　　　　2　by
　　3　in　　　　4　like
　　5　as　　　　6　except
　　7　like　　　8　with
　　9　by　　　　10　Instead of
　　11　except　12　as
　　13　due to　14　according to
　　15　as

Lesson 14-8 형용사와 함께 쓰는 전치사

Check up! p. 427

A　1　at　　　　2　in
　　3　at　　　　4　of
　　5　for　　　　6　with
　　7　for　　　　8　to

9　of　　　　　　　10　about

Lesson 14-9 동사와 함께 쓰는 전치사

Check up! p. 429

A　1　with　　　2　on
　　3　about　　4　for
　　5　for　　　　6　on
　　7　on　　　　8　for
　　9　at　　　　10　to

B　1　came up with
　　2　ran out of energy
　　3　died of (from) a heart attack
　　4　suffered from
　　5　go out with him.

Practice More II p. 430~432

A　1　for　　　　2　on
　　3　except　　4　in
　　5　like　　　　6　for
　　7　with　　　8　to
　　9　Due to　　10　of

B　1　about　　　2　without
　　3　instead of　4　at
　　5　about　　　6　at
　　7　According to　8　for
　　9　like　　　　10　on

C　1　of → in　　　　2　by → with
　　3　with → on　　　4　to → for
　　5　for → about　　6　to → of
　　7　with → by　　　8　he → him
　　9　with → to　　　10　to → for

D　1　All the streets were crowded with people during the festival.

　　2　Mom was holding the basket full of vegetables.

　　3　According to today's news, the monsoon will start next week.

4 Emma was frightened at the accident that happened yesterday.

5 I'm looking forward to seeing them again in America.

6 They believed the rumor about his death.

7 She was busy with work, so she couldn't prepare dinner.

8 I was capable of doing the project all by myself.

9 Sam is looking for books related to global warming.

중간 기말고사 예상문제

내신 최다 출제 유형

p. 433

01 ④   02 ③   03 ②   04 ①   05 ⑤

06 ④   07 among − between

해설

01 'because of+명사(구)'

02 〈보기, ①,②,④,⑤〉 전치사: ~처럼, ③ 동사: 좋아하다

03 at → in

04 ② in foot → on foot, ③ in TV → on TV,
   ④ at the subway → on the subway,
   ⑤ at land → on land

05 첫 번째 문장: 'by+교통수단',
   두 번째 문장: 'by+-ing' ~함으로써

06 'from A to B' A에서 B까지

07 두 개(명) 사이를 말할 때는 'between'을 사용한다.

p. 434~437

01 ③   02 ④   03 ②   04 ⑤   05 ①

06 ③,⑤   07 ③   08 ②   09 ⑤   10 ④

11 ③   12 ①   13 ①   14 ③   15 ②

16 ③   17 ②,③   18 ⑤   19 ②   20 ④

〈서술형 평가〉

21 to − into   22 off − of

23 until − by   24 in the yellow raincoat?

25 stepped on the land with

26 is afraid of / in front of

27 Jay has been interested in music and dance.
   (Jay has been interested in dance and music.)

28 They couldn't concentrate on what the teacher was saying.

해설

01 at+시간

02 비교적 긴 시간을 말할 때 in을 사용한다.

03 'on the weekends' 주말마다

04 'name~ after...' ~의 이름을 따라서 ....이름을 짓다

05 'except' ~을 제외하고

06 ③ in this year → this year,
   ⑤ In last Monday → Last Monday

07 'from' ~로부터

08 첫 번째 문장: 'with' ~을 가지고 있는,
   두 번째 문장: 'be pleased with' ~에 기뻐하다

09 'since' ~이후로

10 'in+장소, 계절'

11 'around' 주위를, 'prepare for' ~을 준비하다

12 ① 'head for' ~으로 향하다,
   'between A and B' A와 B 사이에

13 'be filled with' ~로 가득하다, 'be famous for' ~로 유명하다

14 'be crazy about' ~ 에 열광하다,
   'be covered with' ~로 뒤덮이다.

15 'on+요일', 'in(도구)' ~로

16 with → on

17 ① in least → at least, ④ believe on → believe in,
   ⑤ please → pleased

18 'be good at' ~에 능숙하다, 잘하다

19 'depend on' ~에 의지하다, 의존하다

20 'sting on' ~을 쏘다

〈서술형 평가〉

21 'into pieces' 조각들로

22 'out of' ~밖으로

23 동작이나 상태가 어느 한 시점에 완료되는 것을 나타낼 때는 'by'를 사용한다.

24 'in' ~을 입고 있는

25 'with' ~와 함께, ~을 가지고

26 'in front of' ~의 앞에서

27 'be interested in' ~에 흥미를 가지다

28 'concentrate on' ~에 집중하다

Chapter

15 일치와 화법

Lesson 15-1 수의 일치

★Check up! p. 441

A 1 has 2 is
3 gather 4 are
5 buy 6 was
7 has

Lesson 15-2 시제의 일치

★Check up! p. 443

A 1 needs 2 would
3 will come 4 wasn't
5 was 6 could
7 was 8 had made
9 was 10 bought

B 1 Max said that his sister was busy then.
2 I thought that Alex was not ready to resign.
3 The woman said that she had been waiting for the bus.
4 We understood that the girl hadn't done anything for us.
5 John said that he had never tasted such a delicious pizza.

Lesson 15-3 평서문의 화법 전환

★Check up! p. 445

A 1 He said that he was going to leave there.
2 Mina says that her teacher helps her finish her homework.
3 Nick tells me that he loves me so much.
4 They said that he had practiced playing the piano for a month.
5 She says that she jogs two miles every evening.

6 Helen usually tells us that we have to study hard.
7 John told me that he wanted to eat something delicious.
8 The girls told me that they had seen the movie the previous week.
9 Kate says that her parents are going to visit her school that day.

B 1 Lily says to us, "I want to buy the house to live in with my family."
2 Tom said, "I will not participate in the contest."
3 My father said to me, "I bought something for you."
4 She said to her mother, "I can pass the final exam."
5 They said to Joe, "We don't like to go hiking with you."

Lesson 15-4 의문문의 화법전환

★Check up! p. 447

A 1 asked 2 could buy
3 had been 4 why
5 how 6 when
7 had seen 8 she could
9 could attend 10 we knew

B 1 asked if they wanted to buy that dress.
2 asked me what kind of scarf I liked most.
3 asked Jane if (whether) she was going to go abroad to study.
4 asked me what time I had finished my homework.
5 her if (whether) she would like to have something to drink.

Lesson 15-5 명령문의 화법전환

★Check up! p. 448

A 1 advised her to exercise regularly and eat healthy.
2 told her not to run there.
3 advised the prince to help the poor.
4 told his son not to study all night.
5 ordered us not to be late for the meeting.

Practice More I

p. 449~451

A
1 has
2 is
3 is
4 have
5 were
6 dislikes
7 had seen
8 was
9 invaded
10 was

B
1 he had to finish the project by six.
2 he wanted to go to the amusement park.
3 the economy would improve.
4 the sun rises in the east.
5 he had already bought the shoes.
6 their team would be able to win the game.
7 he had to help his father to repair the roof.
8 she had hidden the box somewhere in the house.
9 we could solve the problem without any hints.
10 she would come back soon.

C
1 she always eats breakfast every morning.
2 if she could pick him up when he came back to Korea.
3 not to forget to bring my homework the following week.
4 what we had seen in the museum.
5 how she had made the stew.
6 he enjoyed watching movies every weekend.
7 if I wanted to go to the party.
8 she didn't think she could pass the exam.
9 why he had repaired his old car.
10 she would always be with me.

D
1 said to me, "You have to buy this shirt for the party."
2 said, "Where can I find the nearest subway station?"
3 told her to stop studying and take a rest.
4 said to me, "Do not eat too many sweets."
5 said, "I have forgotten the location of today's meeting."
6 told us that she had never allowed us to use her kitchen.
7 asked the guide when the long bridge had been built.
8 said, "Do I have to wait for Helen?"

9 told me to drink lots of water and exercise regularly.
10 said to us, "There will be an economic crisis in a year."

중간 기말고사 예상문제

내신 최다 출제 유형

p. 452

01 ②　02 ②　03 ⑤　04 ③　05 ④
06 ②　07 ③

해설

01 ① is → are, ③ seems → seem, ④ was → were, ⑤ has → have

02 ① are → am, ③ doesn't → don't, ④ have → has, ⑤ looks → look

03 주절의 시제가 과거이므로 종속절의 'will' 역시 과거형인 'would'가 알맞다.

04 상관접속사 'neither A nor B' 에서 B에 동사의 수를 일치시킨다.

05 'will → would' 주절의 시제가 과거일 때 종속절의 시제는 과거, 과거완료가 와야 한다.

06 주절의 시제가 과거일 때 종속절의 시제는 과거, 과거완료가 와야 한다. 누군가 반지를 가져간 시점이 그 사실을 발견한 시점보다 앞서기 때문에 과거완료가 알맞다.

07 간접의문문의 주어와 직접의문문의 주어가 일치하지 않는다.

p. 453~458

01 ①　02 ③　03 ③　04 ②　05 ④
06 ⑤　07 ⑤　08 ②　09 ④　10 ③
11 ①　12 ①　13 ②,③　14 ④,⑤　15 ④
16 ③　17 ②　18 ⑤　19 ③　20 ④
21 ②　22 ③　23 ①　24 ⑤

〈서술형 평가〉
25 told/that/would
26 asked if(whether)/could
27 asked/if(whether)/could
28 told/that/would finish/that night.
29 asked/if(whether) I was free/following (next)
30 told/to close
31 He said that he could fix the bike that day.
32 The professor told the students to turn in their reports.

33 Steven asked her where she had put the books.

34 Could you tell me if she took a trip?

35 Who do you think made her sad?

해설

01 주절의 시제가 과거이므로 종속절의 시제도 과거로 바꿔준다.

02 주절의 시제가 과거이므로 종속절의 시제도 과거로 바꿔주고, 'tomorrow'는 'the following day' 또는 'the next day'로 바꾼다.

03 의문사가 없는 의문문의 화법을 전환할 때는 두 문장의 연결어로 'if(whether)'을 사용한다.

04 are → is

05 are → is
→ '② B as well as A', ④ not A but B'는 동사의 수를 'B'에 맞추어야 한다.

06 주절의 시제가 과거이므로, 종속절의 시제 역시 과거형으로 바꿔준다.

07 주절의 시제가 과거이므로, 종속절의 시제 역시 과거형으로 바꿔준다. 의문사가 있는 의문문의 간접화법은 '의문사+주어+동사'의 형태로 써준다.

08 의문사가 없는 의문문을 간접화법으로 바꿀 때 'if(whether)'를 써서 두 문장을 연결한다.

09 명령문의 간접화법은 'to'를 이용하여 두 문장을 연결하고, 동사 원형을 써 준다.

10 명령문의 간접화법 부정은 'not to+동사원형'의 형태를 사용한다.

11 간접화법을 직접화법으로 전환할 때 'that'절의 주어와 목적어는 전달하는 사람의 입장으로 바꿔준다.

12 간접화법을 직접화법으로 전환할 때 'not to부정사'는 주절의 동사와 일치시켜서 부정 명령문 으로 바꿔준다.

13 ① books → book, ④ were → was, ⑤ was → were

14 ④ visits → visit, ⑤ am → are

15 의문사가 없는 의문문의 화법 전환은 두 문장을 연결할 때 'if(whether)'를 사용하며, '주어+동사'의 형태를 취하고, 주절의 동사가 과거형이기 때문에 종속절 역시 과거형으로 한다.

16 명령문의 간접화법 전환 시 두 문장을 연결하는 것은 'to'이며, 부정형은 'not to'로 한다.
→ Mr. Smith told Mark not to make a noise.

17 '적어도 두 번은 운동을 하라'는 간접화법을 이용한 명령문으로 'to+동사원형'이 문장 사이에 온다.

18 상관접속사 'both A and B'가 주어로 사용될 때, 동사는 복수 취급을 한다.

19 첫 번째 문장: 'a number of+복수명사'는 복수 동사를 사용한다.
두 번째 문장: 'half of the+단수 명사'는 단수 취급을 한다.

20 의문사가 없는 간접 의문문은 'if(whether)'로 두 문장을 연결하여 사용한다.

21 'a number of+복수명사'

22 'know → knew' 주절의 시제가 과거형이면 종속절의 시제도 과거형이어야 한다.

23 ② the next day → tomorrow, ③ Did → Do,
④ No park here. → Don't park here. ⑤ was → am

24 간접의문문으로 전환 할 때 '주어와 동사'의 위치를 바꿔 준다.
→ Do you think he will get first prize?

〈서술형 평가〉

25 주절의 시제가 과거이므로 종속절의 시제 역시 과거형으로 바꿔준다.

26 의문사가 없는 의문문은 'if(whether)'로 두 문장을 연결해 준다. 주절의 시제가 과거이므로 종속절의 시제도 과거형으로 바꿔준다.

27 의문사가 없는 의문문의 간접화법으로, 두 문장을 연결할 때 'if(whether)'를 사용한다. 'said to'를 'asked'로 바꿔 준다.

28 평서문의 전환은 'that'을 사용하며, 주절의 시제와 맞춰서 종속절도 과거로 표현한다.
→ She said to her boss, "I will finish this report tonight."

29 He said to me, "Are you free tomorrow?"
간접화법에서 '내일'은 'the following day' 또는 'the next day'라고 표현한다.

30 → She said to me, "Close the window."
명령문의 간접화법은 'to'를 사용하여 연결하며, 뒤에는 동사원형이 온다.

31 'today → that day' 간접화법으로 전환할 때 시제의 일치와 부사의 변화에 주의해서 쓴다.

32 명령문의 간접화법은 'to'를 사용한다.

33 책을 놓아 둔 것이 이전의 일이므로 과거완료를 사용해 준다.

34 의문사가 없는 간접의문문으로 'if(whether)+주어+동사'의 형태를 가진다.

35 간접의문문에서 주절의 동사가 생각이나 추측을 나타내는 경우 의문사가 문장의 맨 앞에 위치한다.

Chapter 16 특수구문

Lesson 16-1 It...that 강조구문

Check up!

A
1. It is the pasta you made that tastes really delicious.
2. It was a piece of cake that Lily found in the box.
3. It was her that I called three times last night.
4. It was in the shop that we met the professor.
5. Who is it that wants to go to the grocery store to buy some carrots?
6. It was John that sent me the letter on August 15th.
7. It was the beautiful dress that my mom made me for the party.
8. What was it that the man showed to the policeman?

Lesson 16-2 강조어구

Check up!

p. 463

A
1. My little brother does like playing soccer.
2. I do love eating something sweet.
3. People did insist that they should be protected by us.
4. I did go apple picking at Billy's house last month.
5. It is much hotter today than last week.
6. We did finish all our summer vacation homework.
7. John didn't show up at all for the meeting.
8. This is the very place where they bought the ring.
9. The phone did ring, but I couldn't answer it.
10. That's the very movie I've been looking for.

B
1. Your summer plan does sound boring.
2. Things are even better than before.
3. We have never been this far away from our base camp.

4. Did she find out anything at all?
5. We did meet our favorite actor at the airport.

Lesson 16-3 도치

Check up!

p. 465

A
1. are
2. were
3. does
4. stood
5. had he
6. turned
7. could I
8. he comes
9. did I
10. did we

B
1. Came down the storm
2. has she read such a horrible story.
3. had Helen entered the meeting room than the light was turned on
4. stood a pine tree
5. had Minhyuk woken up when the phone rang.

Lesson 16-4 생략

Check up!

p. 467

A
1. He played the violin and he danced to the music.
2. Catch me if you can catch me.
3. You can try the contest if you would like to try it.
4. She ate seven pieces of pizza, so one piece is left.
5. My cat is bigger than your cat.
6. I'll go and meet her if it is necessary.
7. The woman welcomed us kindly, though she was sick.

B
1. I don't think that he turned in his report.
2. I believe that the boys will come to the party.
3. I'm afraid that he won't come back to our town.
4. They don't believe that the rumor is true.
5. I don't think they did the wrong thing.

정답 및 해설 **61**

Lesson 16-5 동격

p. 469

A 1 Let me introduce my daughter, Linda.

2 Everyone knows the fact that the boy stole the bike.

3 His dream of becoming a famous actor will come true.

4 They gave up the idea of selling some snacks at the festival.

5 My plan to make a new dress for Sally is possible.

B 1 them from enjoying

2 What

3 to finish

4 prevents / sleeping

5 from leaving

Practice More I

p. 470~472

A 1 that Amy turned in this afternoon.

2 was the old woman

3 that I lost my bag.

4 that hid his car key in the basket.

5 was it that made you sad over the weekend?

6 that the boy wanted.

7 is it that you want to invite to your wedding?

8 stood two girls

9 himself

10 do we have

B 1 like **2** did

3 far **4** is

5 did **6** So was

7 comes the bus **8** had

9 could **10** herself

C 1 started to discuss the issue.

2 if we want to.

3 if true

4 the car bought

5 Though big

6 The novel she wrote

7 When a little girl

8 than last month

9 Though fat

10 The girl Jungmin loves

D 1 from enjoying

2 makes / happy

3 enables / to find

4 of building a big house to live in with his family.

5 to go abroad to study English

6 made her stay up late

7 that the bus fell off the cliff

8 that she was not a thief.

9 from answering

10 enables / to live

중간 기말고사 **예상문제**

내신 최다 출제 유형

p. 473

01 ④   02 ③   03 ④   04 ③   05 ⑤

06 ③

해설

01 It~that 강조구문을 만들 때 강조하려고 하는 것을 It과 that 사이에 넣는다. 위 문장에서 강조하고자 하는 의미는 'on the bus' 이므로 'It was on the bus that she met him last night.' 이라고 해야 옳다.

02 'Never I have → Never have I' 강조를 위해 부정어가 앞에 올 경우 '부정어+동사+주어'의 어순이 된다.

03 ④ 'it~ that' 강조 구문, ①,②,③,⑤ 가주어 it, 진주어 that절

04 ③ 일반동사 do의 과거형 ~했다. 〈보기, ①,②,④,⑤〉 강조의 조동사 do

05 앞에 나온 부정문에 대한 동의를 나타낼 때는 'Nor(neither)+조동사+주어'의 어순이다. 앞의 동사가 'can' 이므로 'Nor can I.'가 알맞다.

06 ① I said → did I say, ② she came → did she come, ④ Never he has → Never has he, ⑤ a lot of flowers stood → stood a lot of flowers

p. 474~478

01 ④	02 ③	03 ②	04 ⑤	05 ③
06 ②	07 ②	08 ②	09 ④	10 ②
11 ③	12 ②	13 ⑤	14 ④	15 ①
16 ⑤	17 ②	18 ③	19 ②	20 ⑤

〈서술형 평가〉

21 they are

22 it was

23 he was

24 did I tell

25 which (that) is

26 I could express the very essence of nature

27 Jane didn't exercise at all

28 None of them have been

29 I did hope that he would come back safe.

30 did I visit Canada after I had returned to my hometown.

해설

01 접속사가 이끄는 부사절의 '주어+be동사'는 생략이 가능하다.

02 비교급의 강조 어구는 'much, far, still, a lot, even' 등이 있다.

03 'Neither+동사+주어'를 사용하여 앞에 나온 부정문의 내용에 동의한다.

04 did taught → did teach

05 ③ 가주어, 진주어, ①,②,④,⑤ 강조구문

06 Amy has → has Amy

07 의문사를 강조할 때: '의문사+be동사+it~ that' 구문으로 바꾼다.

08 ② 훨씬, ①,③,④,⑤ 많이

09 동사를 강조할 때는 조동사 'do'를 사용한다.

10 '관계대명사+be동사' 뒤에 분사가 나올 경우 '관계대명사+be동사'는 생략할 수 있다.

11 'do one's homework' ~의 숙제를 하다
→ 일반동사 'do'의 과거형으로 쓰였다.

12 명사와 형용사를 강조할 때는 'very'를 사용한다.

13 'none of us' 우리 중 아무도 ~하지 않다

14 '부정어+조동사+주어+동사'의 어순을 따라 문장을 완성한다. 문장의 시제가 현재완료형이기 때문에 동사는 과거분사형을 사용한다.

15 ① 'yesterday'를 강조하는 강조구문의 it이다. ②,③,④,⑤ 가주어 it과 진주어 that절이다.

16 접속사로 연결된 절에서 앞 문장의 동사가 뒤 문장에서 반복될 경우 조동사만 쓰고 나머지는 생략할 수 있다.

17 ② 'here'가 문장 맨 앞에 쓰이면 '동사+주어'의 어순이 된다.
note : not in the least 전혀, 조금도 (=not at all)

18 부정어가 문장 맨 앞에 위치하므로, '부정어+조동사+주어+동사'의 형태를 따른다.

19 'not~ always 항상 ~인 것은 아닌' 의 부분 부정의 의미이다.

20 A: 'It ~ that'의 강조구문이다.
B: 'there+대명사+동사'의 형태이다.

〈서술형 평가〉

21 접속사가 이끄는 부사절의 '주어+be동사'는 생략이 가능하다.

22 접속사가 이끄는 부사절의 '주어+be동사'는 생략이 가능하다.

23 문장에서 반복되는 어구가 있을 경우 생략이 가능하다.

24 부정어가 문장의 맨 앞에 나올 때 '부정어+조동사+주어+동사'의 형태를 사용한다.

25 '관계대명사+be동사'는 뒤에 분사가 올 경우 생략이 가능하다.

26 'the very'를 써서 명사를 강조한 문장이다.

27 'at all'을 써서 부정어를 강조한 문장이다.

28 'none of them' 그들 중에 아무도 ~않다

29 동사가 과거형이므로 조동사 do를 did로 고치고 동사는 원형을 써 준다.

30 부정어 'hardly'가 문장의 맨 앞으로 나올 경우 '부정어+조동사+주어+동사'의 형태로 문장을 완성한다.

GRAMMAR
MASTER

| Level 1 | Level 2 | **Level 3** |

http://www.wcbooks.co.kr